COLD WAR *Holidays*

THE NEW COLD WAR HISTORY

John Lewis Gaddis, editor

AMERICAN TOURISM IN FRANCE

COLD WAR *Holidays*

CHRISTOPHER ENDY

The University of North Carolina Press

CHAPEL HILL AND LONDON

Library of Congress Cataloging-in-Publication Data
Endy, Christopher.
Cold War holidays : American tourism in France /
Christopher Endy.
    p. cm. — (The new Cold War history)
Includes bibliographical references and index.
ISBN 0-8078-2871-8 (alk. paper) —
ISBN 0-8078-5548-0 (pbk. : alk. paper)
1. Tourism—France—History—20th century. 2. Americans—
Travel—France—History—20th century. I. Title. II. Series.
G155.F8E48   2004
338.4′791440483—dc22   2003024661

cloth   08 07 06 05 04   5 4 3 2 1
paper   08 07 06 05 04   5 4 3 2 1

A version of Chapter 7 appeared earlier, in somewhat different form,
in Christopher Endy, "Rudeness and Modernity: The Reception of
American Tourists in Early Fifth-Republic France," *French Politics,
Culture, and Society* 21 (Spring 2003): 55–86.

The excerpt of the Art Buchwald poem in Chapter 4 is reprinted with
permission of the author.

To CORA GRANATA

and in memory of CLARK DAVIS,

who loved any excuse to visit France

Contents

Illustrations

Acknowledgments

Journeys of any kind are rarely solo endeavors. Writing this history of tourism has been no exception, and I am eager to recognize many colleagues, friends, and institutions for sustenance and guidance along the way. I thank the history department and graduate school at the University of North Carolina at Chapel Hill for generous research and writing funding, the U.S. Department of Education and the UNC Center for European Studies for a year-long Foreign Language and Area Studies fellowship, and the Society for Historians of American Foreign Relations for their Holt Memorial Fellowship. The Office of Research and Sponsored Programs at California State University, Los Angeles, provided funds for research assistance, which Joaquin Nabarrete skillfully performed. My research trips around the United States were made more affordable and a lot more fun thanks to the sofas and hospitality of Drew Endy, Kurt Reisenberg, Zak Smith, and Bill, Priit, and Rima Vesilind. Peter M. Pozzy aided my research by sharing his memories of France and the Marshall Plan era and by very generously lending me family scrapbooks. In Paris, Anne Quinney and Paul Cohen provided a sounding board for ideas and added greatly to my time abroad with discussions of literature, language, and French soccer tactics. Ellen Furlough, Nancy Green, Odile Gaultier-Voituriez, Wendy Perry, and Marie-Jeanne Rossignol also made my research in France more profitable by guiding me to the right archives and libraries and inviting me to seminars and conferences.

Many other outstanding historians have contributed to this project. For helping me develop my interests in cultural history and foreign relations while I was in North Carolina, I thank professors Peter Coclanis, Calvin Davis, Ole Holsti, Alison Isenberg, John Kasson, Lloyd Kramer, Don Mathews, Sydney Nathans, Louis Pérez, and Don Reid. Will Jones and Dave Anderson had the courage and stamina to read the entire manuscript at an early stage. Our long conversations, fueled by massive volumes of sweet tea and Diet Coke, helped me discover what I wanted to say. I am especially thankful for my graduate adviser, Michael Hunt, whose expert guidance, good humor, and steadfast support sustained this project. His passion for writing and teaching now provides me with a model early in my own career. Having left the South, I am fortunate to have found a new community of writers and teachers in the history department at California State University, Los Angeles. I have also benefited from insightful suggestions on drafts and conference presentations.

For this help I thank Choi Chatterjee, James Clifford, Matthew Connelly, Clark Davis, Andrew Frank, Ellen Furlough, John Gaddis, Cora Granata, Matthew Jacobs, Philip Katz, Cheryl Koos, Richard Kuisel, Alan McPherson, Richard Pells, Charles Rearick, Kirstin Ringelberg, Charles Romney, Christine Skwiot, and Geoffrey Smith. At the University of North Carolina Press, Chuck Grench and Amanda McMillan offered sage advice on how to bring the project to publication and Mary Caviness provided extremely careful and thoughtful copyediting.

This book's completion also owes much to my family. My brothers Drew and Stephen have provided examples for me by consistently following their own creative paths. My parents, David Endy and Elizabeth Vesilind, maintained my motivation by offering unwavering encouragement. To them, and to Pat and Aarne, I owe a happily profound debt. Lastly, Cora Granata has helped this project along since it began as a seminar paper. As a talented historian, she offered incisive readings of the manuscript. Most important, she has been my best friend. As I end this project, I look forward to the new travels we will share together.

Abbreviations

ASTA	American Society of Travel Agents
CAB	Civil Aeronautics Board
CFTC	Confédération française des travailleurs chrétiens
CGC	Confédération générale des cadres
CGP	Commissariat général du plan
CGT	Confédération générale du travail
CMT	Commission de modernisation du tourisme
CNPF	Conseil national du patronat français
COFBA	Comité français de bienvenue aux armées alliées
DDB	Doyle Dane Bernbach
ECA	Economic Cooperation Administration
ETC	European Travel Commission
FNIH	Fédération nationale de l'industrie hôtelière
FO	Force ouvrière
IATA	International Air Transport Association
NATO	North Atlantic Treaty Organization
PCF	Parti communiste français
TDS	Travel Development Section
TWA	Trans World Airlines
USIA	U.S. Information Agency
UWF	United World Federalists

COLD WAR *Holidays*

Introduction

The lobby of the Hôtel George V in Paris has been a good place to observe the rise and fall of great powers in the twentieth century. Founded in 1928 just several blocks south of the Champs-Élysées, the hotel began as a fashionable destination for wealthy Americans and other foreigners. Then, in the summer of 1940, the season when Americans normally descended upon the George V, first the French and then the German military laid claim to the ornate hotel. Four years later, American officers requisitioned the hotel and slept in beds that German officers had abandoned just days earlier. When the U.S. Army finally checked out in 1946, the hotel's managers were eager to revive the glamour the hotel had earlier won among civilians. Yet rather than retreat from the political role the war had given the hotel, the George V's staff newsletter encouraged the waiters, chambermaids, porters, and other workers to see themselves once more as part of the drama of international relations. With the nation's status as a world power in question after the war, good service toward elite foreign guests could win France much-needed supporters, especially among Americans. "In a hotel of this class," noted the newsletter, "we are all, each for his part and at his post, like 'Ambassadors' for our country."[1]

On the other side of the Atlantic, as Cold War tensions mounted, American travel writers also presented tourism in the language of foreign policy. One travel article, appearing first in *Travel* magazine and then in *Reader's Digest* in 1949, offered instruction on how to be an American abroad. Readers learned that Americans vacationing in Europe would likely encounter "the anti-American venom distilled first by Hitler and now by Stalin." At a time when U.S. policymakers declared friendly ties with Western Europeans to be essential for the survival of the "free world," each American abroad needed to speak humbly but confidently about the virtues of U.S. foreign policy and in the process become "truly an ambassador of good will."[2]

Americans' trips to France were Cold War holidays in that leisure culture in both nations fell under the shadow of postwar international pressures. Calls by travel writers and hotel managers for ordinary citizens to act as unofficial ambassadors reflected a broader ideal in which tourists, business owners, and service workers would advance their nation's foreign affairs while pursuing their own pleasure or work. Both the U.S. and French governments at times shared these hopes and created new policies to help ensure that Americans' leisure travel served larger policy goals. For U.S. policymakers, American travel abroad represented an economic and cultural tool that could help win the Cold War, a view also promoted by patriotic travel writers and by American business leaders in the international travel industry. For French politicians and members of France's own travel industry, hosting Americans became part of larger projects designed to promote French power and cultural influence in an era when French prestige seemed threatened by superpower rivalry and colonial rebellion.

Yet these trips were also holidays from the Cold War. After all, appeals to act as "ambassadors" implied concern that at least some tourists and employees needed encouragement to identify with the political roles assigned to them. American tourists frequently sought in Europe a chance to escape the tensions and constraints of life in the atomic age, a goal promoted by the international travel industry's colorful publicity. "Freedom was what the trip was all about," recalled one former traveler, referring not to political freedoms but to a more personal sense of individual realization.[3] French hoteliers and service workers, for their part, remained focused on concerns such as wages and labor conditions that often had little to do with French diplomats' agenda for navigating the Cold War world. In all, tourists, the travel industry, and government officials engaged in a complex give-and-take in which mass tourism became both an extension of and a challenge to traditional foreign policy concerns. This combination of tension and cooperation between leisure culture and foreign policy represented one of the central aspects of both nations' experiences with Americans' postwar travels.

This book tells the story of American tourism in France during the quarter century after World War II. It narrates this history by bringing together perspectives from both nations, expressed in guidebooks, popular movies, hotel and airline industry documents, French service workers' union records, and the writings and memories of tourists themselves. More traditional foreign policy perspectives appear as well, drawn from government archives on cultural diplomacy and propaganda, economic planning, and travel promotion. By integrating the worlds of politics, business, and leisure, this book reveals consumeristic dimensions to U.S.-French relations previously neglected by historians.[4] This approach also shows connections between consumerism, the Cold War, and globalization, three developments crucial to the post-1945 era but rarely considered in relation to each other.

The first of these three developments, consumerism, played a central role in shaping both France and the United States in the twentieth century. As social and cultural historians have shown, both nations increasingly became consumer societies where citizens relied on commodified goods and services to fashion personal identities and where growing numbers of workers and entrepreneurs found employment in hotels and other branches of the service sector. In another hallmark of life in a consumer society, government and business elites in both nations turned more and more to the expansion of consumption as the economy's basic function and as proof of their own political legitimacy.[5] As demonstrated by a lively historical scholarship, leisure travel emerged in the twentieth century as a major element of consumer society, one that reflected and even transformed the ways people have thought about their nation, their class status, their gender and sexuality, their relationship to nature and art, and other important social, political, and cultural concerns.[6] Although much scholarship on tourism focuses on national or local narratives, leisure travel has also been a profoundly international activity, and the history of Americans in France allows us to appreciate how global pressures and interactions have shaped the evolution of consumerism within each nation.[7]

Scholars of the Cold War, and of foreign affairs in general, also have much to learn from this consumer past. Historians of international relations have increasingly recognized the value of situating government policies in their broader cultural and economic contexts. In this view, traditional models of international relations that limit themselves to state policy and state-to-state interactions leave out the rich and expanding web of private interactions that connect national communities.[8] Tourism formed one such connection linking France and the United States. During the Cold War, major issues in U.S.-French relations included France's postwar reconstruction, the building of an anti-Communist "Atlantic Community," and often acrimonious negotiations, on political, cultural, and economic levels, over the United States' powerful influence in Western Europe. Tourism, this study shows, affected all these Cold War issues.

At the same time, Americans' travels in France represented a prime example of the growing economic and cultural exchanges now associated with globalization. The study of tourism shows that there were other major forces besides just the Cold War shaping post-1945 U.S.-French relations. Several of the signature features of globalization lay behind this travel: multinational companies, interdependent economies, and increased border crossings for both people and cultural practices. Tourism's reliance on transportation technology and its close ties to the ballooning service economy further underline its status as a quintessential feature of the twentieth century's globalizing world.[9] All this is not to say that the Cold War did not matter. Instead, the history of tourism suggests that we can best understand postwar U.S.-French relations by looking at the Cold War and globalization in tandem, viewing them as two broad forces that influenced each other.[10]

Taken together, French and American experiences with international tourism shed light on some of the central issues of global history in the second half of the twentieth century. In particular, I argue that tourism can help us understand a seeming paradox: how an era notable for the rise of interdependence and informal exchanges among nations has also been a time of entrenched national identity and persistent and even expanding state power.[11] This broad argument emerges through four supporting themes. First, the rise of tourism in U.S.-French relations was not simply the product of middle-class American prosperity or improved transatlantic transportation. Tourism's growth also depended on a transnational travel constituency, or a loose alliance of business groups, media elites, and government officials operating within and across national borders. In the United States, the core members of this alliance included airlines, hotel chains, travel agents, travel writers, and a group of supportive journalists and editors in the general media. During the late 1940s and 1950s, the alliance also included the U.S. government, eager to use Americans' private travels as a complement to official foreign aid. In France, the main promoters of American tourism were luxury hotel, resort, and restaurant managers and owners and, especially beginning in the 1960s, the French government. Service workers in France represented lesser members in this transnational travel constituency, in part because of their marginal position in government-industry advisory groups and because French working-class identity and interests after the war at times conflicted with efforts to attract wealthy foreign vacationers.

State support, it is worth emphasizing, was indispensable in tourism's rise. U.S. and French government officials subsidized transatlantic air and shipping lines, funded hotel construction and maintenance, negotiated airport landing rights, organized publicity campaigns, controlled passport and visa requirements, and, in the first years after the war, provided tourists and the travel industry in France with special access to scarce food and gasoline. This reliance on government support made industry leaders especially eager to present their businesses as servants of their country's national interests. Pan American World Airways president, Juan Trippe, a pioneering advocate of this strategy, spoke for the hopes of many American and French industry leaders when he referred to his company as a "chosen instrument" of his government.[12]

The importance of collaboration between public and private actors in tourism's expansion points to a second theme. Rather than simply overwhelm the

power of national governments, globalization often allowed state
advance their foreign policy agendas. When U.S. and French offi
to exploit leisure travel on behalf of broader economic policy go
propaganda efforts, they developed a consumer-oriented version
diplomacy" pursued by the United States in the early twentieth
dollar diplomacy's cooperation between the government and powerful financial
cial institutions, what might be called consumer diplomacy represented an
attempt to harness private consumer activity for state goals. Although these
government promotion activities at times brought unintended consequences
for policymakers, they nonetheless illustrate how states have been facilitators
of globalization, not mere victims.[13]

Historians of economic and cultural affairs have long understood how government officials conducted foreign policy not merely through formal diplomatic channels but also by cooperating with corporations, civic groups, and, to
a lesser degree, labor organizations.[14] The concept of consumer diplomacy
reveals that this list of actors has been even larger and needs to include the
small businesses, service workers, travel writers, and, above all, the consumers who took part in international tourism. In the early postwar years, when
both governments desperately sought to channel more dollars to France, diplomats turned to American consumer desires to help solve the problem. Government and corporate travel promoters also exerted a major influence on
transatlantic cultural relations, shaping how Americans and the French have
perceived each other. Tourism publicity, whether distributed by private companies or the French government's tourism office, spread images of France
around the United States more widely than any official cultural diplomacy
campaign ever did. Yet this dynamic remains obscured when scholars focus
only on the government bureaucracies traditionally responsible for cultural
diplomacy, such as the U.S. Information Agency and State Department or the
French Ministries of Foreign Affairs and Cultural Affairs.[15]

Given the many groups involved in leisure travel, efforts to fuse mass tourism
with official economic and cultural diplomacy goals did not always succeed.
Tourists, for instance, were not inanimate displays of American abundance like
those established by the U.S. Information Agency to impress foreigners with the
American way of life. Conducting foreign affairs via tourism required policymakers to tolerate a more diverse cast of actors on the international stage. On
the whole, however, U.S. and French government officials viewed tourism's rise
as an opportunity rather than as a threat. This dynamic suggests that globalization in the post-1945 era encouraged states to adapt and decentralize the ways
they conducted economic and cultural diplomacy.

A third theme in this book explores how Americans' travels did not necssarily yield new transnational identities but more often reinforced distinctly national identities. American vacationers commonly sought a France that seemed different from the world back home. The act of travel outside one's country also prompted many to reflect on what it meant to be an American and to ask what kinds of citizens ought to represent the nation abroad. For the French, hosting foreigners meant articulating visions of the nation to present to guests, choosing which aspects of the nation to publicize and which elements to leave unadvertised. This process could create tension within each national community. Americans often fretted over their compatriots' behavior abroad, while many French observers worried that their fellow citizens acted as ill-mannered hosts. Often the greatest animosities arose not between Americans and the French but within each community. Yet even these internal debates invited Americans and the French to define and police their sense of what it meant to belong to their respective nations.[16]

A fourth, closely related theme underscores the complex process of Americanization and transatlantic cultural exchange. Impressed with Americans' consumer power, French government officials and hoteliers scrutinized American hotel methods and middle-class leisure tastes. Scholars of Americanization have highlighted the adaptability of other societies in the face of American cultural or economic models. Local peoples, they stress, do not passively submit to American cultural imperialism but instead selectively adapt American practices according to their own traditions and needs.[17] The French reception of American tourists reinforces this emphasis on adaptability. As a tourist environment, France did not become Americanized but instead evolved in its own ways, drawing mainly on changing domestic leisure patterns. While American influences mattered in this process, so too did other international influences, especially from emerging competitors elsewhere in Europe.[18]

The question of Americanization might even distract us from other important aspects of U.S.-French cultural relations. Although almost all histories of post-1945 transatlantic cultural exchange focus on Americanization, travel boosters in France generally presented U.S. tourists not as Americanizers but instead as carriers of the "radiance" (*rayonnement*) of French civilization.[19] In the United States, travel writers frequently celebrated the ability of Americans to pay for long transatlantic trips, interpreting this tourism as proof of America's national greatness and wealth. French commentators, on the other hand, often found it more significant that Americans went to the trouble of crossing an ocean to pay homage to their nation and civilization. In other words, the same activity could appear to confirm either nation's grandeur. When it came to national self-confidence and cultural influence, tourism was not a zero-sum game.

Americans' leisure in France offers one of the best pairings of tourist and host for understanding the rise of international travel. Of all nationalities, American consumers held perhaps the greatest influence in shaping the twentieth-century international travel market. Historians often note that the United States produced a remarkable one-half of the world's goods and services in 1945.[20] These historians dwell less often on the international significance of Americans' unparalleled consumer power after the war. American travelers were a critical economic asset for France, at times representing the equivalent of over four-fifths the value of all goods that France exported to the United States in the early postwar years.[21] American airlines and hotel chains, especially Pan Am and Hilton International, also emerged at midcentury as innovators in their fields.[22] Travel industries in France and elsewhere did not always emulate trends created by Americans, but even when they rejected or modified those economic or cultural practices, American models figured in their thinking.

American travel to France is also especially revealing because the small size of immigration from France to the United States has made tourist impressions one of Americans' primary ways of knowing France.[23] In 1951, the Gallup Poll asked Americans for their "first thoughts" on hearing the word "Paris." For men, the most popular responses were such travel icons as the Eiffel Tower, "dancing girls," and "leg shows." Among women, the list began with fashion, perfume, landmarks, and nightlife.[24] Few if any respondents thought to describe Paris as the capital of an empire or the home of international organizations. As this study will show, Americans' collection of touristic themes infiltrated other images of France, including those in movies, political commentary, and news reports. French perceptions of the United States, although to a greater degree tied to other cultural sources such as Hollywood films and French travel writing about the United States, derived in part from French encounters with the millions of American visitors in their own country.[25]

While the United States produced the twentieth century's premier globetrotters, France stood out as the world's leading host. For much of the period under study in this book, France received more foreign tourists than any other nation, a status it also held at the start of the twenty-first century.[26] At the same time, France's cultivation of foreign tourism has been representative of trends in other host nations. Like other states in Western Europe and North America, the French government first engaged in modest tourism promotion in the early twentieth century. Then, in the middle decades of the century, the French state guaranteed paid vacations to its citizens, built and subsidized massive resorts, and encouraged the rise of a corporate travel industry. By the 1960s, even Soviet-bloc countries had opened their borders to Western tourism, and economic development experts were helping Asian, African, and Latin American nations boost their own travel industries. France's history as a host nation, if colored by specifically French contexts, can provide a window into how societies have cultivated and adapted to the growing global market in international tourism.[27]

Although a relatively sophisticated transatlantic travel infrastructure existed in the nineteenth and early twentieth centuries, the end of World War II provides a useful starting point for understanding connections between tourism and foreign affairs.[28] After recovering from the war's disruptions, transatlantic leisure travel experienced a remarkable boom. The 264,000 visits Americans made to France in 1950 grew to 792,000 a decade later, and then to 1.35 million by 1970.[29] Most important, the war also transformed U.S.-French relations, affording the United States unprecedented influence in France. As Chapter 1 shows, leisure travel immediately after the war formed one of the first arenas in which the French and Americans attempted to negotiate this new world together. From recreational tours for American soldiers in liberated France to the first postwar civilian tours in 1946 and 1947, attempts to revive American leisure in the ruins and scarcity of postwar France often proved controversial in both nations. Nevertheless, travel resumed quickly, a revival in which both nations' governments offered crucial material and political support.

By the late 1940s, tourists in France no longer needed ration cards, but government involvement in transatlantic leisure continued in new ways. Chapter 2 describes the rise of cooperative ties between Washington and the transatlantic travel industry during the Marshall Plan years (1948–52). Encouraged by lobbying from American airlines, hotel chains, and travel agents, the U.S. government set aside part of the Marshall Plan for an innovative travel development program. Operating under the notion that every dollar spent by a tourist was one dollar less the government needed to spend in foreign aid, U.S. policymakers promoted and even organized Americans' leisure spending in war-ravaged Europe. This consumer diplomacy strategy, which the conservative Eisenhower administration continued into the 1950s, constituted the high-water mark in the transnational travel constituency's campaign to combine its interests with those of U.S. foreign policymakers.

Travel boosters in France had a more difficult time gaining French government support after the war. As Chapter 3 shows, French travel industry leaders presented American tourism as a means to advance the French policy goals of national economic development and expanded cultural influence abroad. Yet, outside the circle of tourist boosters, American tourism inspired ideologically charged debates over whether the increasing numbers of American visitors represented not a source of French grandeur but instead a metaphorical colonization by the United States. France's powerful economic planners, for their part, favored the development of heavy industry and energy over economy and challenged claims by hoteliers and other boosters that foreigners offered the best path for the nation. On the French left, advo state subsidies to send French workers on vacations of their own within often opposed efforts to have the government spend more scarce resour attract wealthier foreigners. Debates about hosting Americans did not simply emerge from French opinions of U.S. foreign policy or of American society. They also reflected more indigenous concerns with French national identity, social and labor policy, and strategies for postwar economic reconstruction. Given these reservations, the French government took a restrained approach to tourism promotion after the war. Although willing to provide special rations to foreign travelers in the lean years of 1946 and 1947, the government gave scant support to its tourism office and relatively little financial assistance to the country's hotel industry.

Hotels provided one of the main meeting grounds for Americans and the French, and they became sites of special contest during the Marshall Plan years. Chapter 4 examines how U.S. officials in the Marshall Plan attempted to re-form French and other European hotels to make Europe more comfortable for middle-class Americans. This little-studied Marshall Plan program reveals new connections between consumerism and Cold War policy. It also illuminates the complicated process of Americanization. French responses to American-inspired hotel practices, in keeping with French perceptions of American tour-ism in general, reflected complex combinations of nationalism, Cold War ideology, and economic self-interest.

As they sought to align leisure with diplomacy, travel boosters in both nations frequently predicted that American tourists would return home im-bued with a deep commitment to America's new alliance with Western Europe. For U.S. officials and supportive media elites eager to create a Cold War culture, an American public enchanted with Atlantic-oriented leisure would become firmly supportive of the government's new Atlantic-oriented foreign policies. French officials and travel industry leaders held similar hopes and added their own vision of how American visitors would acquire a positive image of France as a modern, forward-looking nation. Chapter 5 traces these public and private cultural diplomacy efforts and their reception among American tourists in the late 1940s and early 1950s. Showing that leisure could often trump foreign policy concerns, the majority of tourists refused to reduce their trips to Cold War–themed vacations. At times their writings, itineraries, and opinions even contradicted specific goals of French and U.S. foreign policy. Nevertheless, the cultural imagery generated by tourism, from travel guides to Hollywood musi-cals, on the whole offered symbols and narratives that could allow Americans to imagine themselves part of a shared Atlantic Community with France. To the extent that American tourists participated in any sort of Cold War culture, they did so mainly on an impressionistic level, not as self-conscious political actors.

The cultural-diplomacy dimension of tourism grew especially controversial in the United States in the late 1950s and 1960s, an era that introduced both transatlantic jet service and the widespread, if often ill-defined, concept of the Ugly American. Chapter 6 analyzes how Cold War–minded Americans perceived their compatriots' overseas travel. On one side, skeptics of mass culture criticized tourists for lacking the expertise and "realism" to serve as effective Cold War ambassadors. Another school of thought, with a more populist and consumer-friendly vision, held that the growing numbers of middle-class Americans able to take trips to Europe presented foreigners with symbols of American freedom and prosperity to which Soviet propaganda experts had no answer. Although neither side succeeded in silencing the other in this debate, the growing attention assigned to tourists' role in the cultural Cold War influenced and reflected broader initiatives taken by Washington on behalf of cultural diplomacy. Dwight Eisenhower's People-to-People program, for instance, borrowed from the populist spirit of travel boosters and aimed to harness private citizens to the Cold War cause. Later, John Kennedy's Peace Corps initiative preserved this ethos of populism yet rejected the consumerism that drove mass tourism.

While U.S. journalists, tourists, and diplomats in the late 1950s and 1960s fretted over Ugly Americans, the French at the same time engaged in a parallel bout of self-criticism concerning their alleged rudeness toward foreigners. Charles de Gaulle's Fifth Republic, established in 1958, even launched friendliness campaigns to improve French manners, with an emphasis on pleasing dollar-laden Americans. The notion of French inhospitality, although grounded in part in actual tourist complaints, also stemmed from the acute diplomatic tensions that strained U.S.-French relations in the 1960s. Most important, the stereotype of inhospitality had deeper roots in France's rapid urbanization and modernization after World War II. As Chapter 7 reveals, both French conservatives and French technocrats endorsed and amplified the negative national image, holding modernization as either the cause of or solution to France's inhospitality. De Gaulle's government itself reinforced the rudeness image to justify its program of modernizing the nation's travel industry. Blaming artisanal hoteliers for poor manners, the French state accelerated the development in France of a more corporate travel industry.

President Lyndon Johnson would have been happier if de Gaulle's government had not been trying so hard to attract and please American travelers. Chapter 8 shows how consumerism conflicted with U.S. Cold War concerns in a new way in the 1960s, when the relative decline of the American economy led U.S. policymakers to try to reduce the flow of dollars out of the country. In the face of a series of crises in the nation's balance of payments, the Kennedy and Johnson administrations' participation in the alliance of overseas travel boosters began to falter. American consumer spending abroad had become an economic liability, at least in regions over which the United States no longer enjoyed economic primacy, such as Western Europe. Yet when the Johnson White House sought restrictions on overseas tourism in 1965 and 1968, a broad spectrum of the American public successfully rallied in defense of Americans' freedom to travel and shop abroad, even if it meant reducing foreign aid or military commitments in Vietnam and Europe. The debates over Johnson's restrictions program offer a unique moment for exploring the political meanings Americans assigned to tourism in the late 1960s. As this episode revealed, consumer privilege, as much as militant anti-Communist containment, had become a core value shaping U.S. behavior in the Cold War world.

Although American tourism in France continued to grow in the following decades, the late 1960s and early 1970s provide a fitting end point for this study. In the United States, the continuing monetary crisis led to the devaluation of the dollar in 1971, in one stroke reducing the overseas consumer power that Americans had enjoyed as a result of their nation's post–World War II economic dominance. In France, the late 1960s and early 1970s brought a wave of high-rise hotels, especially on the outskirts of Paris. These new hotels were in large part the fruits of the French government's dramatically heightened intervention in its travel industry the decade before. In terms of state policy, the tables had turned. The postwar period began with the French government hesitant and the U.S. government eager to promote tourism to France. By the 1970s, their positions had reversed, largely in response to France's postwar recovery and the relative decline of U.S. economic strength.

These changes had important consequences for the tourists, hoteliers, travel writers, and other actors driving mass tourism. France's more traditional hotel industry, typified by the luxurious George V, faced new competition from multinational corporations and even from the French state's own hotel chain. In 1968, the George V found yet another occupier when a British hotel corporation purchased the establishment from the widow of its longtime French owner. Although the hotel continued to receive wealthy Americans, those Americans no longer held the commanding importance for hotels such as the George V that they once did. Through the 1950s and 1960s, Americans had accounted for a steady two-fifths of France's foreign tourism earnings. In just a few years, by the early 1970s, that portion had dropped to one-fifth.[30] Sensing a change in the United States' global position, one American magazine's cover story in 1968 asked of the American tourist, "Does He Still Own the World?"[31] In 1974, *Le Monde* announced that France's reception of foreign tourists was set to enter "the European age," meaning an era when neighboring Europeans mattered more than American vacationers.[32] American travel overseas continued to grow after the 1960s, but by then this consumerism was less exceptional and instead part of a more global travel culture in the late twentieth century.[33]

While American tourists never quite "owned" the world even at their peak influence in the quarter century after World War II, they did occupy a significant place in postwar international relations. Their travels in France became a branch of Cold War foreign policy for both countries. At the same time, the consumer exchanges created by this travel never fully conformed to foreign policy pressures. The chapters that follow examine in more detail this complex process of cooperation, conflict, and negotiation between the worlds of foreign policy and mass tourism.

Chapter 1

RATIONED PLEASURE
LEISURE BEFORE AND AFTER THE WAR

In 1946, with France still recovering from war, the American Legion approached French diplomats in hopes of arranging a postwar pilgrimage for as many as 20,000 Americans. The largest veterans' group in the United States, the legion hoped to continue its prewar tradition of launching massive visits to Europe every ten years, a practice that began in 1927 when thousands of World War I veterans descended on Paris for a pilgrimage that became famous for its raucous drinking and patriotic speeches. The legion's eagerness to sponsor a pilgrimage in 1947 presented a dilemma for French diplomats. With an eye on securing aid from the United States, French officials in 1946 had no desire to appear ungrateful to their former allies. Yet the French diplomats were concerned with the practical challenge of guaranteeing food, lodging, and gasoline for a large tour so soon after the war. They were troubled still more by what the legion, especially its leadership, might do and say once in France. France's ambassador in Washington, Henri Bonnet, pointed to a recent speech by a legion leader in the United States who had declared that the best path to world peace lay in dropping a few atomic bombs on Moscow. After investigating the legion's politics, France's consul in New York described the group's proceedings as racist, anti-Communist, and marked by boisterous public behavior more typical of "collegians on vacation."[1]

French officials feared that extending an official invitation to such rowdy and militantly anti-Communist Americans might make them appear dupes of American extremists. This possibility appeared especially worrisome at a time when the French Fourth Republic rested on a fragile coalition of Christian Democrats, Socialists, and Communists. Even after the ejection of the Communist Party from the coalition in May 1947, any government that rested too close to conservative Americans risked losing legitimacy in France. French diplomats thus debated whether their official invitation should come only on condition that the legion make no foreign policy speeches before the French or international press, an option ultimately rejected as too delicate to raise with the Americans.[2]

French officials, including future president François Mitterrand, then minister for veterans and war victims, thus set out to organize a September 1947 tour "with the greatest care."[3] Given a shortage of cabin space on transatlantic liners and airplanes, the legion could only manage a "token pilgrimage" through France with several hundred legionnaires. To prepare for the trip, legion leaders met with French tourism, diplomatic, and veterans officials, along with the director of the American Express Paris bureau. Together, the group sketched a nine-day itinerary, highlighted by opening receptions in the French Ministry of Foreign Affairs and the U.S. embassy and tours of World War I and II battlefields. As the event neared, the French consulate and tourism office in New York City even pulled a few strings in an attempt to speed through customs a special shipment of twenty cases of whiskey for thirsty pilgrims.[4]

Despite the early French misgivings, both French officials and legion leaders had reason to be satisfied with the pilgrimage. Mitterrand, along with President Vincent Auriol, showered the legionnaires with pomp and circumstance at private receptions, while the major French newspapers did not bother to mention the militant speeches of legion commander Paul Griffith in their coverage of the tour.[5] In his own post-tour report, Griffith himself seemed almost disappointed that the events did not inspire more vehement protest, "even though I included anticommunist allusions many times." In his conclusion, he called for greater U.S. support of the French, even if the French government was not "exactly to our taste."[6] Lastly, although the whiskey shipment still arrived too late for the tour, U.S. ambassador Jefferson Caffery saved the day by making available the Paris embassy's stock, thereby ensuring that the veterans would be able to revive some of the spirited fun from earlier pilgrimages.[7]

Although few tours received the same attention as the legion's, the 1947 pilgrimage symbolized many of the political dimensions to American travel in France in the immediate postwar years. The tour demonstrated the eagerness of Americans to put wartime deprivations behind them and resume prewar leisure patterns. In this case, the legion wanted to reenact established traditions of travel to Europe, using France as a stage for another round of memorialization and boisterous flag-waving. The legionnaires were not alone in hoping to revive their touristic affair with France. As early as 1945, many soldiers and journalists incorporated such longings for old Gallic pleasures into their wartime experiences and representations of France. Yet the years of conflict had also changed travel experiences, especially because the war left the United States in a much more powerful position over France. In a reflection of this growing power, the legionnaires assigned their trips new postwar meanings, declaring the French government friendly enough to merit expanded U.S. aid.

Although not all Americans visiting France came to the same conclusion on foreign aid, the use of travel as a soapbox for issuing foreign policy recommendations became a common feature of postwar American public discourse. The legion's tour also reflected the balancing act that the French government faced with all American visitors. French officials sought dollars and favorable publicity in the American media but remained wary of the domestic costs that came with being too closely associated with the wealthy and fun-seeking Americans, especially in a time of material shortages in France. Ultimately, the French government decided that the foreign policy gains of bringing back American tourists outweighed the potential drawbacks. The years between 1945 and 1947 thus saw American travelers and French hosts struggling to bring a speedy resumption of prewar travel patterns while negotiating the new postwar contexts of French scarcity and unparalleled U.S. power. Despite the tensions created by new postwar circumstances, both groups were frequently able to work around their differences, as well as France's material scarcity, to forge travel experiences that ultimately brought the two nations closer together in Cold War alliance.

Prewar Patterns

Like the legionnaires, most Americans heading to France after the war inherited a powerful set of traditions and expectations, most often oriented around the themes of self-improvement, consumerism, nationalistic self-congratulation, and a search for Old World difference. In the early years of the American republic, hundreds of Americans, generally wealthy white men, sailed across the Atlantic each year for education, business, and diplomacy. Most, like Thomas Jefferson, combined leisure and sightseeing with their trips and then used their experiences to establish a more cosmopolitan outlook and elite identity back home. Young men on versions of the British Grand Tour engaged tutors and often prostitutes as part of their rites of passage. Later in the nineteenth century, women embarked on "finishing" trips, where they cultivated an elite femininity with visits to the Louvre and excursions to Paris dressmakers. For men and women, travel to France offered an opportunity to learn the language of diplomats and artists, to contemplate classical and medieval traditions, or to study the marvels of Paris, whose street lights and sewers made it one of the most modern cities in the world.[8]

By the start of the twentieth century, American travelers to Europe began to number in the hundreds of thousands annually. Improvements in steam-powered ships and rising discretionary income for upper- and middle-class Americans helped boost travel to Europe from 35,000 trips in 1870 to almost

250,000 by 1914. Another push came from the increasing involvement of the United States in international affairs, which made many travel writers consider transatlantic voyages important for the development of their nation as a world power. Before the Great Depression kept many would-be tourists at home, the volume of Americans crossing the ocean each year reached a peak with 359,000 trips in 1930. Most of these tourists made France one stop on tours of several European countries. France's reputation as a haven of both pleasure and refinement, as well as its convenient location between Americans' two other favorite destinations, Britain and Italy, ensured that it remained on the standard tourist itinerary.[9]

Upper- and middle-class Americans also made a habit of viewing their compatriots' behavior in Europe as a symbol of their nation's broader role in the world. In Henry James's popular 1879 novella, *Daisy Miller*, the figure of an innocent American girl catching her death in Europe provided a metaphor for American innocence vis-à-vis the Old World. By the turn of the century, as the United States undertook European-style colonial projects in Cuba and the Philippines, a new generation of travel writers invoked the character of Daisy Miller to demand that American women in Europe shed their innocence and learn to act as equals in European high society. Although these discussions reflected the leisure patterns of only a small segment of American society, they resonated widely among intellectual and cultural elites, who had long defined American national identity by comparing and contrasting their nation to Europe.[10]

American travel in Europe assumed symbolic value again in the 1920s when commentators held the behavior of expatriates and tourists in Paris as expressions of Jazz Age America's reckless energy. As historian Harvey Levenstein has shown, traveling Americans in 1920s France became more comfortable and even emphatic in celebrating their pursuits of pleasure. Certainly this trend held for the many tourists and Lost Generation expatriates who savored their freedom from Prohibition-era America by taking advantage of strong drink and an even stronger dollar in France. This potent combination of alcohol and buying power helped make the American Legion's 1927 pilgrimage, an otherwise somber trip to cemeteries and battlefields, an epic escapade of rowdy, whiskey-soaked good times.[11]

Like the 1927 pilgrims, sober-minded and fun-loving models of travel coexisted for most Americans crossing the Atlantic. In the late nineteenth and early twentieth centuries, business leaders and progressive social reformers increasingly traveled to Europe with hopes of gaining lessons from European experiences with modernity.[12] French universities, looking for cash and international prestige, began to encourage enrollment by American students in the

1920s. Junior-year-abroad programs also began in the 1920s, even if overshadowed in popular memory by the exploits of the Lost Generation and legionnaires. While not all of these academic tourists were dedicated scholars, the spread of such programs illustrates how the rising emphasis on having a good time rivaled but did not displace the pursuit of self-improvement.[13]

In the early twentieth century, the growing numbers of Americans attracted increasing attention from French hotels and businesses. Americans at first had been largely overshadowed by greater numbers of European tourists. In the second half of the nineteenth century, for instance, a string of new luxury hotels opened in Paris and the Riviera to cater to a largely European clientele. Most famously, César Ritz in 1898 created his eponymous institution in Paris's elegant Place Vendôme to dazzle upper-class foreigners, especially British elites.[14] By the 1920s, however, the U.S. dollar rode high over European currencies weakened by World War I. Although still outnumbered by other Europeans, Americans assumed greater importance for the French travel industry. After opening in 1928, the Hôtel George V quickly became popular with Americans and earned fame as a place to spot American celebrities in Paris. Not all this new attention was positive, however, as a handful of Americans discovered in July 1926 when guided tours of "Paris by Night" came under violent attack from a right-wing mob infuriated by the U.S. government's unwillingness to forgive France's war debt.[15]

The Great Depression and then World War II proved even greater challenges to American travelers and their French hosts. Yet even under Nazi occupation, French hoteliers hoped that the postwar era would continue the dynamic growth of American travel from the 1920s. In March 1941, François Dupré, director of the George V and Plaza-Athénée hotels, raised this hope for postwar American tourism when he met with the Third Reich's tourism minister in Berlin. According to Dupré's account, the Nazi minister rebuffed the hotelier. Treating tourism as a metaphor for national strength, the minister insisted that Germans alone would be able to furnish enough peacetime clients for France's hotels.[16]

Just as the George V's director longed for guests from the United States, Americans' touristic fascination with France continued during the war. Popular books such as Elliot Paul's *The Last Time I Saw Paris* and films such as *Casablanca* kept alive memories of friendly shopkeepers and romantic cafés.[17] Americans' habit of viewing France through a touristic lens was so well entrenched that even the carnage of the Normandy invasion could not displace the urge for sightseeing in picturesque France. American media reports of Allied advances included musings on France's sites and pleasures. In August 1944, when the Allies secured the Normandy island of Mont-Saint-Michel, famous for its medieval abbey, *Time* offered readers a picturesque photograph, reproduced a passage from Henry Adams's essay on its beauty and "quiet strength," and claimed that the GIs themselves agreed with Adams's praise.[18] In the spring of 1945, Ben Hibbs, editor of the *Saturday Evening Post*, flew to Europe to report on Nazi atrocities. The editor returned home writing not just of the terrors of war but also of a brighter and more consumeristic future, supplying readers with a "preview" of the comforts of transatlantic air travel that awaited civilians after the war.[19]

Journalists' impatience for the return of touristic France was especially visible in erotic male fantasies of Frenchwomen. Just two weeks after the liberation of Paris in August 1944, *Life*'s correspondents described the "new Paris" for Americans back home. The nightclubs of Montmartre were closed, but, to the thrill of one male correspondent, grateful Frenchwomen, possibly unemployed nightclub dancers themselves, took to the streets to perform an impromptu cancan with "red, white, and blue ostrich feathers." When the magazine reported on "the most noticeable things about Paris today," the first topic was "pretty girls."[20] Publications such as *Life* and the *Saturday Evening Post* repeatedly commented how years of food shortages meant that, in one typical statement, "the latest crop of young girls . . . are more beautiful than French girls ever were before."[21] After almost three years of war, many Americans were ready for fun in Paris.

GIs and an "Internationalism of the People"

Popular anticipation in the United States of a return to prewar leisure patterns grew stronger with the unprecedented level of national confidence and expansiveness that emerged from the U.S. victory in the war. Like earlier generations, Americans held their travels abroad as symbols of the nation's expanding role in the world. In fact, tourism had been one element of the dynamic vision for America's future laid out by Henry Luce, the editor of *Life* magazine, in his influential 1941 essay titled "The American Century." In broadest terms, Luce argued that Americans, blessed by a prosperous society, needed to reject isolationism and accept that the world looked to the United States for political, economic, and cultural leadership. His vision for America's future called for grassroots support of expansive foreign policies, what he described as "an internationalism of the people, by the people and for the people." Luce, an inveterate globe-trotter himself, saw travel abroad as a factor in having made Americans by 1941 "the least provincial people in the world."[22]

The nation's first experiment with Luce's "internationalism of the people" came with the war itself, when millions of American men and women in the military went overseas, with an estimated two million to France.[23] War, of course, was not tourism. Soldiers experienced boredom and fear far more often than tourist pleasures. Nevertheless, many in the military were at times able to see themselves as visitors in an appealing foreign land. One soldier who joined the Normandy campaign in the summer of 1944 recalled later that "my thoughts were not so much of liberating, fighting and helping to chase out the Germans as the thought of stepping foot upon the land of France, of saying one French word to someone French in France." Like many travel writers, he praised his own experience by denigrating others, boasting that despite the dangers, "I was grateful that I had not come as a tourist."[24] Most soldiers did not arrive with the same Francophilia as this one. The cartoons of Bill Mauldin, famous for their "bottom-up" view of life in the U.S. Army, hinted at a more typical combination of attraction and frustration while war raged across a major tourist destination like France. One cartoon satirized the effectiveness of U.S. authorities in posting "off-limits" signs around French towns. In another, Mauldin mocked the snobbish hierarchy of officers who sought to reserve France's natural beauty for themselves.[25]

As the fighting on the front moved east into Germany, U.S. military officials cultivated leisure opportunities in liberated France. GIs received their corner of touristic France in January 1945 when the U.S. Army established a recreation center for enlisted men in the Riviera city of Nice. American officers, who were more likely to come from a higher social class, had their own leisure center in the even posher city of Cannes. In a more democratic gesture, the army allowed both enlisted men and officers to visit liberated Paris, which became the largest U.S. leave center in Europe.[26] Even with the Paris recreation center, not all soldiers had the same opportunities for leisure and consumerism in the wake of the war, a point captured in a story by Mauldin about a GI's wife disappointed that her husband had not brought home any gifts from Paris. In contrast, the wife's friend had received new Parisian clothes and jewelry from her husband, an officer whose desk job behind the front lines in France gave him more free time and spending money.[27]

Although Mauldin reminded Americans that class distinctions still existed, journalists more typically offered celebratory reports of soldiers' leisure that seemed to confirm Luce's ideal of an American society united in its internationalist outlook. *Time*, another Luce publication, dubbed the enlisted men's Nice recreation center "G.I. 'Heaven,'" where common American men put on their best manners as they enjoyed beaches, luxury hotels with "the best French service," nightclubs, alcohol, and, according to the accompanying photograph, strolls with young Frenchwomen. *Time* celebrated Nice as a site of social leveling, where social class and military hierarchy seemed to disappear and

"They must have infiltrated during the night."   *"Beautiful view. Is there one for the enlisted men?"*

Cartoonist Bill Mauldin captures the frustrations of liberating a tourist destination.
On the left, Mauldin satirizes the seeming omnipresence of military police restrictions.
In this case, U.S. Army authorities somehow declare a town off-limits to Allied soldiers
before the Germans have even retreated. On the right, Mauldin suggests that class
distinctions persisted during the war (from Mauldin, Up Front; © *1944 by Bill Mauldin,*
reprinted by permission).

ordinary American men could receive "a millionaire's vacation for peanuts."[28] In the media's feminine variation, members of the Women's Auxiliary Corps bought perfume and other souvenirs along the banks of the Seine River, becoming the "envy of girls all over the world."[29] According to the *Saturday Evening Post* in January 1945, soldiers in Paris knew how to have fun but were better behaved than their predecessors during World War I.[30] At a time when many Americans looked forward to a postwar era of bountiful consumption, conventional media coverage on military leisure in Paris or along the Riviera suggested that the rewards of victory were already being democratically distributed and that everyday Americans were enjoying them with a maturity that matched their nation's expanded power.

As the euphoria of victory receded and U.S. troops remained in France awaiting redeployment or return home, celebrations of egalitarian leisure became overshadowed by new reports of tensions between GIs and the French.

"Her husband spent months shopping for nice things in Europe, Willie. You never did that for me."

Another Mauldin satire caricaturing desires for keeping up with the Joneses after putting down the Nazis (from Mauldin, Back Home; © 1946 by Bill Mauldin, reprinted by permission).

European

G.I.s on the Riviera
No brass hats, no saluting, and gentle MPs.

Time *shows ordinary GIs enjoying "a millionaire's vacation for peanuts" on the Riviera in 1945. While some news reports of U.S. soldiers in France highlighted tensions between Americans and French civilians, Time's touristic view emphasized friendly relations (from Time, 18 June 1945).*

Increasing coverage of aggressive behavior among enlisted men cast doubt on Henry Luce's prediction that ordinary Americans abroad would produce an "internationalism of the people." Soldiers still in France spent most of their time outside the military recreation areas and their enclaves of American abundance. While many enjoyed close or at least cordial bonds with French civilians, public attention in both nations focused on more spectacular cases of tension. With increasing frequency, American and French reporters narrated stories of GIs selling their rations on the black market, quarreling with shopkeepers, brawling in bars, making impolite advances toward Frenchwomen, or committing sexual assault.[31] Part of the problem could be linked to established stereotypes generated from previous decades of travel, with Americans acquiring a sexualized image of France and the French coming to view Americans as exceptionally wealthy. Exacerbating matters, U.S. and French authorities attempted to stabilize the French economy by inflating the value of the franc. As a result, GIs sometimes paid up to five times more for items in France than they might in Germany, a situation that encouraged soldiers to view French merchants with suspicion.[32]

In the United States, complaints over GIS' behavior in France sounded first notes in what would be a long postwar debate over the merits of ordinar, Americans stepping onto the world stage. American press reports frequently blamed drunken and aggressive soldiers and defended the "quiet gratitude" of the French who had to tolerate them. To one *Life* correspondent, his report on America's heroes tarnishing their hard-won status with rowdy behavior in France was "the most difficult story I have ever had to write."[33] "This is not the season for tourists," declared another disillusioned writer in the Catholic magazine *Commonweal* in September 1945, complaining of American servicemen who "looked . . . for playgrounds" in Europe and in so doing added to transatlantic tensions. Declaring that Europe "is our civilization," the writer went on to describe how good Americans must ensure that "the new and savage isolationists do not succeed in dividing America from Europe."[34] For the *Saturday Review*, the arrogance and rowdiness of GIS in Europe, especially in France, risked sending Europe to "extremist elements" on the right or left of the political spectrum. Equally alarming, the soldiers' frustrations with the French, when relayed to friends and relatives back home, would reinforce the "vicious isolationist fallacy" among the American public.[35] To these journalists eager to see their nation play a larger role in postwar affairs, the behavior of everyday Americans abroad was becoming a threat to enlightened leadership. Novelist John Dos Passos, a more nuanced correspondent covering Europe for *Life*, claimed that Europeans were at root frustrated with the U.S. government's lack of any decisive policy on postwar recovery, yet even he did not deny the harmful effects of GIS' "ignorance and rowdyism."[36]

Hosting Tourists in a Time of "Suffering and Sorrows"

For French officials, the increasing tensions surrounding American soldiers presented their own foreign relations difficulties. If U.S. troops returned home with tales of French corruption and hostility, their stories might endanger France's quest for foreign aid and for a greater voice in Allied postwar settlements. Casting an eye toward the postwar travel market, French diplomats also worried that negative publicity from soldiers would discourage American civilians from visiting after the war. In response to such concerns, the provisional French government in May 1945 created the French Committee to Welcome the Allied Armies (Comité français de bienvenue aux armées alliées, COFBA), designed to reduce negative publicity and give American and other allied soldiers fewer reasons to complain about their time in France.[37]

This new military reception program, supervised by the Ministry of Finance, took special interest in what it labeled "the elites" among U.S. soldiers, a escribe any American willing to study French civilization. For

BA teamed with the Tourism Commissariat (Commissariat

ne) to sponsor free five-day tours to the cathedral town of

sites. The U.S. Army supplied the gas, as well as the food and

notels to serve. By the end of 1945, no fewer than 35,000

nad taken the French government's tours. Another 5,000 soldiers used

ine program to enroll in French college courses.[38]

To satisfy soldiers not in the "elite," the French government took a more bread-and-butter approach. "Given the impossibility of making Francophiles of all the Allied soldiers," stated one COFBA report, more soldiers might at least tolerate France if given reduced prices. French officials thus gave Allied military personnel access to less expensive goods and helped create special bars and clubs with controlled prices, all to create "a favorable impression" back in the United States.[39]

Although the program gradually shut down as the soldiers returned home, French officials continued to view the Allied military as a source of publicity that would either encourage or dissuade later civilian travel. One travel brochure for Allied soldiers in 1946 apologized that Paris "is not painted with the brilliant colours that perhaps you might wish" but promised that "all its charms" would eventually return if the soldiers revisited in peacetime.[40] A 1947 COFBA guidebook was even more direct, informing soldiers that "you have not seen the real France." The 200-page book promised to "give you an idea of what France was before the war, and what she will be once more, when you come back on a visit."[41]

This emphasis on converting Americans' presence in France into diplomatic and economic gains continued as the French contemplated a resumption of civilian tourism. Some foreign tourism boosters in France singled out American guests as a means to influence the foreign policy of the world's richest nation. In July 1945, Emile Servan-Schreiber, founder and editor of the business newspaper *Les Échos*, proposed that American civilians be invited to visit France immediately, so long as they brought along their own provisions, as did the U.S. soldiers touring with COFBA. As Servan-Schreiber argued, a quick return of civilian American leisure travelers would provide dollars for France to purchase coal and, just as important, would "bring back to France all these foreigners who consider themselves most sympathetic to our country." If well received, the influential editor calculated, these Americans "will have the greatest influence in our favor on their public opinion. Let us not neglect these imponderables that ultimately translate into ponderables."[42] *L'Ordre*, a daily paper with pro-American leanings, emphasized in early 1947 that tourism was critical for developing Francophiles in the United States. When the American public "loves and admires" France, the paper argued, "one can ask and obtain everything from it."[43] In this view, American visitors offered a way to bind together the United States and Western Europe by promoting grassroots support for American internationalism and foreign aid.

Despite the optimism of these boosters in the French media, the recovery of civilian transatlantic travel came slowly, particularly given transportation shortages across the Atlantic. The war had devastated the North Atlantic fleets equipped for civilian travel. While ninety-one ships carried passengers across the Atlantic in 1937, only fourteen were available for civilian use ten years later.[44] In the aftermath of global war, military and humanitarian refugee organizations received priority on planes and ocean liners. For over a year after the war, the U.S. military reserved westbound traffic on the Atlantic for returning soldiers. Only business executives with approval from the State Department could travel to Europe, and even they had difficulty coming home until most U.S. troops had returned.[45] The U.S. government removed its last restriction on civilian travel to Europe in early 1947, at which point *Business Week* somewhat prematurely declared the start of a "travel boom."[46] The volume of travel to Europe and the Mediterranean did indeed increase from 101,000 trips in 1946 to 147,000 in 1947, with the majority of those Americans visiting France. Still, these numbers fell far short of the prewar peak of 359,000 voyages.[47]

Travel after the war remained a daunting prospect. One tourist, cruising to Europe in 1947 on a French liner, recalled the ominous sight of British voyagers eating "singularly large portions" aboard the ship. Hearty meals, he soon realized, would be more difficult for European residents to acquire once the ship landed in Europe.[48] Pan American World Airways tried to make light of stark conditions in one 1946 press release by joking that food rations allowed the average traveler to reduce "that executive bulge at the waistline."[49]

The scarcity of food and other essentials such as lodging and fuel posed both logistical and political challenges for French tourism organizers. Beyond providing for the comfort of visiting Americans, travel officials needed to balance their quest for tourist dollars with the political imperative of not angering the French public by devoting too many resources to already well-off Americans. Complicating matters further, French officials had to keep Americans comfortable while avoiding any hint that France had no need for foreign aid.[50] When *Life* in 1945 ran an article about France that highlighted Parisians in bathing suits, a journalist for the French paper *XXe siècle* warned that he had been shown the article by five different Americans, one of whom remarked, "Since you live like that, you do not have need for our aid."[51] For the French, hosting tourists became a public relations challenge with potentially hostile audiences on both sides.

For the 1946 tourist season, French officials developed an elaborate system to balance leisure travel with domestic and diplomatic concerns. The Tourism Commissariat created special visa and ration measures to shelter tourists from the instability and scarcity of postwar France. French authorities approved only a small number of tourist visas, approximately 200,000 for all foreigners, to ensure that each tourist received proper attention.[52] For those Americans able to get in, special treatment included tourist-only train cars to meet them at port in Le Havre and transport them to Paris. A tourist card provided visitors with three months of privileged access to food, cigarettes, and coffee. With the help of France's rationing authorities, tourism officials arranged for resort centers to receive extra amounts of fish, powdered milk, and other foods. Thermal spas also gained access to heating fuel on the same basis as hospitals. To help keep visitors safely within their enclaves of relative abundance, the tourist office recommended that most foreigners travel in organized tours.[53]

French officials acknowledged that pampering wealthy foreigners in an impoverished country might raise ethical questions in France. In a March 1946 press conference, Jules Moch, a centrist socialist and the minister who oversaw the Tourism Commissariat, admitted that foreign guests risked "unleashing a current of xenophobia" in France if government incentives to tourists were "too visible." Moch urged the French press to avoid creating a scandal over tourists' special access to gas at a time when French doctors sometimes had difficulty finding their own fuel to make house calls. The minister further defended the government's tourism policy by emphasizing that official travel advertisements focused on France's "suffering and sorrows" and its recon- struction efforts, both of which "are too poorly known abroad."[54]

For its part, the general French media respected the government's early efforts to accommodate foreign tourists. In 1946, the newspaper L'Evènement praised the wisdom of letting a moderate number of foreigners visit and "attest by their presence that she [France] has lost nothing of her radiance in the world."[55] Le Monde endorsed the program of tourist benefits and even called on the government to channel some of its reconstruction efforts into the revival of Parisian charm. Scarce electricity should be set aside, "in spite of the difficult times," to illuminate Parisian monuments at night and satisfy visitors' romantic expectations.[56]

The French government adopted similar supply measures for the 1947 tour- ist season.[57] In fact, two years after the end of the war, food allowances were even more essential to attract foreign tourist spending. Everyday living con- ditions got worse rather than better after the war as France invested large amounts of resources in reconstruction. Bread rations for the French in August

1947, for example, were smaller than at any point during the war itself, and average purchasing power in 1948 had dropped 30 percent since liberation in 1944.[58]

Given such penury, French travel promotion in the United States strove for a delicate balancing act between showing French shortages and enticing Americans to visit. One 1947 advertisement promised that "only in little ways will you find France has changed. . . . Our menus may be slimmer—but our chefs are glorious!"[59] In a publicity tour of the United States in early 1947, France's tourism commissaire, Henri Ingrand, attempted to dispel doubts about his country's readiness to host tourists. Ingrand, paraphrased in one American magazine, stressed that Americans "need have no scruples about coming over to France and gorging themselves next summer. In the pleasantest and most painless manner, they will be saving the Fourth Republic," adding that "no French will go hungry" as a result.[60] A 1947 brochure by Ingrand's tourism office took an even more optimistic tone, stressing the country's revival through statistics on postwar recovery and photographs of some of France's 8,000 rebuilt bridges and viaducts. "France has at last become herself again after six years of oppression," announced the brochure, which also stressed that "the characteristic smiling faces and 'chic' clothes are once more to be seen in the streets" now that "glamorous France again radiates her charm."[61]

Even with the French invitation, the American media debated whether to endorse vacations in Europe. To the dismay of French officials, a group of British food supply experts in April 1947 issued a public statement advising Americans to stay away from Britain that summer. Americans, the report warned, would consume scarce food and generate British ill will, especially since the British had chosen a more austere program for postwar reconstruction than the French had.[62] The French embassy in Washington then watched with concern as the statement circulated through the American press.[63] A *Washington Post* editorial endorsed the warning and suggested that, even though France had called for tourists, Americans would be best off avoiding that country too.[64] The *New York Times*, in a contrasting editorial, declared that Americans should avoid Britain, as well as Italy and Germany. Travel to France, Switzerland, and Scandinavia was possible, even if Europe as a whole "seems a doubtful host." The *New York Times*'s lukewarm endorsement of travel to France in 1947 was something of a mixed blessing. Its explanation for why food shortages were less serious in France than in Britain rested less on the two governments' different reconstruction programs and more on a mythical view of French culinary talents. "Food scarcities hardly trouble them," declared the *Times*, since "the French have ever been able to prepare delicious meals on practically nothing."[65]

By inviting a speedy return to civilian tourism, the French government indirectly encouraged the American media to expand its coverage of France. With the prospect of renewed tourism, magazines and newspapers sent correspondents abroad to test travel conditions and report on daily life. Even if travel to France remained limited in volume, those who could make the trip frequently used the authority that came through firsthand narratives to report on European conditions and issue recommendations on U.S. foreign policy. While French tourism organizers hoped that such contacts would solidify Americans' willingness to give aid, the results proved mixed. American opponents of foreign assistance often drew on travel reports and impressions of European living conditions to argue against U.S. aid. Nevertheless, travel discourse, meaning the images and commentary generated by Americans' voyages in France, could also encourage U.S. aid, especially by articulating impressionistic conceptions of a shared Atlantic civilization.

To a greater extent than French tourism promoters, American travel writers favored optimism in the balancing act between highlighting European suffering and reassuring potential tourists. The 1947 edition of Sydney Clark's popular guidebook on France criticized the allegedly " 'realistic' reporting" of "the tellers of bad tidings" who claimed "with lugubrious tones, that 'Paris isn't what it used to be.' "[66] Testing travel conditions in the summer of 1947, a correspondent for the *Atlantic Monthly* announced that "the French, for whom the press insists on tolling the bell, are, on the contrary, bouncing back with great vigor." An accompanying cartoon showed a well-stocked refrigerator in the heart of France, an image of plenty that came at a time when French bread rations were actually declining.[67] In his 1948 guidebook on France, Horace Sutton, a travel writer for the *Nation* and the *Saturday Review*, emphasized that "conditions for travelers are not nearly so bad as a daily session with the United States press over the past few years may have indicated."[68] Writers such as Sutton were not necessarily opposed to foreign aid; in other writings, Sutton was in fact an advocate of the Marshall Plan.[69] Nevertheless, like many other travel writers, he emphasized a leisure-oriented vision of Europe over a Cold War vision that risked scaring away consumers.

Travel writers' presentation of a picturesque Europe safe for leisure ironically corroborated the rhetoric of opponents of U.S. foreign aid. Although the Truman administration announced the Marshall Plan in June 1947, the aid itself was not guaranteed until Congress approved the plan in March 1948. And while most in Congress agreed that Communism in Europe was a danger, they

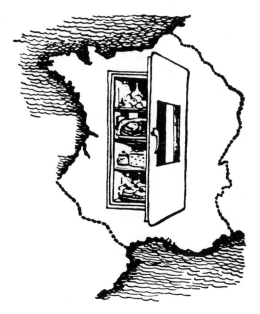

A cartoon from the Atlantic Monthly *shows that the myth of French abundance survived at a time when French bread rations declined below the worst wartime levels (from* Atlantic Monthly, *September 1947).*

disagreed over how much aid the United States should give to contain it.[70] In the often fierce debate over the Marshall Plan, congressional critics of the plan frequently drew on first- and secondhand travel narratives describing European abundance. Congressman Charles Vursell, an Illinois Republican, returned from a trip to France in November 1947 and noted that "the farms of France are teeming with livestock." He argued that Congress should vote against the aid program since France's problem was not scarcity but its "weak and incompetent public officials."[71] In 1947, House Republican George Bender criticized the Truman administration for "hysterically" overreacting with its proposed Marshall Plan. For evidence, he quoted the travel letter of a steel executive who remarked, "Basically, the country looks good. . . . In Paris, there is no outward evidence of distress. The city is well kept and looks the same as before the war."[72] An Ohio congressman in 1947 argued against the plan by referring to European casinos. Blaming Europe's aristocratic leisure class as the cause of Europe's economic troubles, he complained, "The United States of America pays and pays and pays while the royalty of the Old World plays and plays and plays."[73]

Although depictions of French abundance reinforced arguments against the Marshall Plan, American journalists in favor of foreign aid often juxtaposed tourist visions of Europe with accounts of European suffering, dramatizing the disparity between prewar images and postwar reality to urge support for foreign aid. In one example of this rhetorical strategy, the *Saturday Review* in 1946 noted that "a trip to Europe is not as [it was] in the good old days before the war" and that "the most notable thing about Paris is its loss of gaiety. It is not now the great happy vacation city of the world." Contrasting postwar conditions to Americans' touristic ideal of Paris, the magazine argued that "things in Europe will just not take care of themselves . . . we must face our responsibilities in Europe better than we have."[74] "Every traveler to Europe today . . . is shocked by how it differs from the picture in his mind," added Anne Morrow Lindbergh after traveling for two months in Europe on assignment for *Reader's Digest*. The wife of the famous pilot and a writer who only reluctantly supported her husband's prewar isolationism, she described Europe as "one bleak stark picture" and went on to urge public support for foreign aid.[75]

On other occasions, Cold Warriors scrutinized travel narratives to ensure that their imagery reinforced U.S. foreign policies. Writing in the *Nation* in 1947, Stephen Spender, a British intellectual and vocal advocate of an anti-Communist Atlantic alliance, attacked a new travelogue by the American literary critic Edmund Wilson. Spender accused the prominent writer of abusing his role as an intellectual by painting Europe as dark and corrupt and describing Americans as nothing but "an army of Daisy Millers." Deriding Wilson as "the most innocent American traveler who has ever been abroad," he argued that intellectuals and travel writers needed to prepare Americans for greater involvement in European affairs.[76] With Europe in need of assistance, Spender suggested, American travel writers ought no longer delude themselves with nineteenth-century dichotomies between innocent America and a corrupt Old World.

On the other hand, Cold Warriors like Spender would have been happy with the tendency of most travel writers to link the United States to Western Europe by embracing the idea of a noble civilization shared by both European hosts and American guests. Like most Americans, travel writers at the time used the term "civilization" in myriad, imprecise ways, often referring to artistic achievements, Judeo-Christian religion, historical greatness, or a respect for democracy.[77] Given the concept's vagueness, travel experiences and writing played a major role in defining for Americans the nature of civilization and in linking that civilization to France, and to Western Europe more generally. Many travel writers could hardly think of France without invoking the concept. Indeed, the notion of France as civilization was a vital part in Americans' conception of transatlantic travel as a means for self-improvement. Even a distinguished writer such as the *New Yorker*'s Paris correspondent, Janet Flanner, was so taken by the concept that in 1945 she wrote: "Though they have no soap that lathers, both men and women smell civilized when you encounter them in the Métro."[78] Another travel writer, in a 1947 article titled "France

Forever," declared that "France is still the most civilized of all countries."[79] French civilization sometimes revealed itself in common tourist encounters. One writer in France in early 1945 found that "everyone you meet there is nice—warm, friendly, intelligent, and exciting. And that is what civilization should mean."[80]

The touristic vision of France as a pillar of civilization proved a natural complement to the concerns of American Cold Warriors. Although deeply rooted in American culture, the idea of a Western or Atlantic civilization assumed added importance after World War II as a key concept in the formulation of U.S. Cold War policies. Like travel writers, U.S. foreign policy leaders used the term "civilization" in vaguely defined ways, but often in terms that rhetorically tied the United States to Western Europe. Typically, its invocation added an air of timelessness and disinterestedness to the objectives of U.S. policy. When President Harry Truman defended his proposed Marshall Plan before Congress in December 1947, for instance, he declared that "our deepest concern with the European recovery is that it is essential to the maintenance of the civilization in which the American way of life is rooted."[81]

Travel writers' emphasis on a shared Western civilization encouraged Americans to imagine themselves as part of an Atlantic Community and helped justify Cold War projects such as the Marshall Plan.[82] Because many travel writers were also strong advocates of these policies, they at times infused their writings with messages that supported this broader foreign relations agenda. In arguing for foreign aid, Anne Morrow Lindbergh implored Americans to contribute to the civilization they loved to visit. Lindbergh explicitly disassociated herself from economic, political, and military "experts" and emphasized that giving foreign aid to stop Communism would be "the right deed for the wrong reason." Offering a more impressionistic account of Europe on the verge of collapse, she instead warned that "the flame of Western Civilization" would die if Americans did not learn to "think beyond the concept of a nation to the larger concept of a civilization." Lindbergh believed that Americans ought to see foreign aid more positively, as their historic opportunity for "feeding the flame . . . of our civilization."[83]

As a center of civilization, France, and especially Paris, appeared to travel writers as the property of all the world and therefore as something to be defended by Americans. Travel writers repeated as gospel the idea that "every man has two countries—his own and Paris." Horace Sutton's early postwar guidebook described Paris as "the city for whom men cry when she is captive." Expressions of universality led to vows of commitment. A 1947 coffee table souvenir book on Paris closed with the declaration: "Let us be thankful for Paris, our own. Let us never risk its loss, not ever once again."[84]

Conclusion

The revival of American leisure travel after the liberation of France quickly
became part of broader foreign policy concerns in both nations. In a time of
economic scarcity, French officials faced the problem of how far, if at all, they
should subordinate domestic consumption for the sake of luring Americans
and their badly needed dollars. French officials also had to strike a balance
between prewar images of fun-loving, abundant France and new depictions of
postwar French suffering. On both counts, Americans' touristic images of
France had become an extension of French diplomatic efforts to attract aid
from the United States. In the United States, an equally politicized discussion
emerged as journalists and politicians drew on travel writing and travel experiences in arguments both for and against postwar assistance to France and
Western Europe. U.S. foreign policy observers, anxious about their country's
new superpower role, also asked whether ordinary American soldiers and
tourists could represent their nation overseas. Setting the tone for a debate that
would persist through the 1950s and 1960s, these media commentators wondered if leisure travel was compatible with the challenges of exercising informed leadership in an uncertain postwar world. The revival of travel thus
presented both opportunities and challenges for government and media elites
in both countries seeking to promote a U.S.-French alliance. Although never
completely in line with these foreign policy concerns, the politicized images
that emerged from travel after the war more often than not reinforced these
transatlantic political bonds.

Chapter 2

FELLOW TRAVELERS
THE RISE OF TOURISM IN U.S.
FOREIGN POLICY

Saving Europe from Communism and poverty never seemed so easy. Simply by vacationing across the Atlantic and spending lavishly, American citizens could advance the cause of freedom. To help consumers do their part in the Cold War, the U.S. government dedicated a section of the Marshall Plan to arrange group tours, lobby for cheaper ship and air fare, and provide free marketing services to travel companies. This innovative strategy, known in Washington as travel development or travel promotion, appealed to Americans of diverse political stripes. "We might as well soak up a little old world culture for our dollars. It would be almost like eating our cake and having it too," commented the conservative *Indianapolis Star*, which apparently found foreign aid easier to digest when combined with private pleasure. Travel writer Horace Sutton, a regular contributor to liberal journals such as the *Nation* and the *Saturday Review*, seemed to sense a similar unease among the American public over foreign aid and editorialized on behalf of the travel program, calling it a form of "painless intravenous feeding" to Western Europe.[1]

During the Marshall Plan years, tourism assumed new importance in U.S. foreign relations. In the words of one Commerce Department official, the Marshall Plan's tourism program was a "precedent-shattering provision."[2] Before and during World War II, the U.S. government had subsidized airlines and shipping companies, but more to promote commerce, mail delivery, and military operations than to encourage tourism itself. Only after the war did the government dedicate itself overtly to the promotion of overseas tourism. Within the Western Hemisphere, Washington encouraged hoteliers such as Conrad Hilton to expand into Latin America to promote commerce and economic development.[3] Yet the U.S. government's most intensive organizational push behind mass tourism took place in Western Europe with the Marshall Plan. In the process, the government and the American international travel industry heightened cooperative ties that made them fellow travelers in the conduct of U.S. foreign policy. With increased vacations to Paris and elsewhere in Western Europe an official goal of U.S. policymakers, the late 1940s and early

1950s represented a new stage in the practice of consumer diplomacy in the United States.

The Marshall Plan travel program was more than just a response to Europe's severe postwar shortage of dollars or to the specter of Communism. Government officials, travel industry leaders, and media commentators also associated travel promotion with less tangible purposes that reflected elite Americans' outlook toward world affairs in the early Cold War. The idea of harnessing tourism to foreign relations attracted a range of ideologically motivated supporters, from fiscal conservatives fearful of conventional foreign aid to one-world idealists eager to forge a supranational world government. Travel promotion also reflected an expansive American nationalism and optimism in the power of American consumers. To government and industry elites, expanding the number of Americans vacationing in Europe offered a way to create a homogeneous public in which Americans would share the same Atlantic-oriented tastes in both leisure and foreign policy. This strategy also represented an extension of lessons learned during the New Deal to the field of foreign affairs. In the 1930s, liberals advanced the Keynesian argument that the government could promote economic health by intervening to boost consumer spending. The U.S. government's approach to overseas travel after the war applied Keynesianism to the international stage, with American consumers cast as partners in European economic growth. This ambitious agenda faced opposition from the domestic travel industry, which preferred to see Americans vacation at home, and never succeeded in its goal of making tourist trips accessible for all working- or even middle-class Americans. Despite these obstacles, government and travel industry leaders, with support from the mass media, succeeded in assigning Americans' consumer behavior new public purposes after World War II.

The Industry Emerges from the War

The government's program to harness tourism behind its foreign policy came at a time when the American international travel industry was itself turning to Washington. After wartime disruptions to civilian travel, the industry, including air and shipping lines, travel agents, hotel chains, and financial services, looked to the government to speed along its recovery. The industry's attention to Washington reflected some of the travel companies' most basic concerns. For transport carriers, subsidies for their far-flung operations had become a major fact of their existence. Like all national governments, Washington also helped regulate landing rights for planes, controlled passports, visas, and duty-free taxes, and determined when military necessity required the curtailing of civilian travel.[4] Given the U.S. government's financial and administrative power, public policy played a major role in shaping the contours of the travel industry. In fact, state support for the industry reached a scale that suggested the existence of a military-tourism complex without which postwar travel would not have been able to expand as it did.

During the war, the Roosevelt and Truman administrations offered modest support for tourism development in their broader push to reorder the postwar international economy along more liberal lines. Most notably, at the Bretton Woods negotiations of 1944, U.S. policymakers pursued an economic regime emphasizing the principles of free trade. At United Nations–sponsored meetings on tourism, Washington also urged the "immediate simplification" of visa formalities, under the assumption that the free exchange of people facilitated the free exchange of goods. Although encouraging other nations to drop their fees and formalities, U.S. officials never embraced a complete liberalization of travel controls. Given concerns with controlling the nation's borders, U.S. negotiators in 1946 rejected a more radical proposal calling for "the ultimate abolition of visas."[5]

While reduced border formalities represented one concern, industry members' main challenge was recovering from the war's disruptions. Although the government's military mobilization had in many cases tightened the cooperative ties between the industry and Washington, not all in the travel business had been able to adapt to the government's wartime needs. Among the hardest hit was the American Society of Travel Agents (ASTA), formed in 1931 to provide agents with a collective voice and to ensure industry standards. With many agents dependent on transatlantic travel for the bulk of their profits, ASTA considered suspending its operations during the war.[6] The American Express Company, in contrast, found more wartime success. Established in 1850, the company opened its first overseas office in 1895 in Paris, the hub city for American tourism in Europe. There, the company gradually expanded its offerings to include guided tours, a theater box office, and mail service. This tourism division generated no profit but did provide publicity for the company's lucrative business in traveler's checks, a device the company had invented in 1890. After a boom period in the 1920s, American Express continued to prosper during the war by operating overseas banks for U.S. military personnel and for the military itself. These wartime efforts prepared the company for postwar civilian travel. Shortly after the war stopped, the number of American Express overseas offices jumped from 50 to 139.[7]

American-owned passenger shipping lines found the war a mixed blessing. Civilian travel on the Atlantic had long been a big business. During the first half of the twentieth century, most Americans crossed the Atlantic on ocean liners that offered first-, second-, and third-class cabins. Before the 1920s, the smallest and least airy quarters in "steerage" were mainly occupied by working-class Europeans traveling to and from the United States. When U.S. restrictions on immigration in the early 1920s dried up this market, shipping companies renamed their steerage compartments with more leisure-oriented terms such as "tourist third-class" to capitalize on growing demand for modest-budget tourism.[8] Before the war, most American travelers sailed with European companies such as Cunard White Star, easily the largest of the ocean carriers, and French Lines, best known for lavish first-class service. Even though the war gave American shippers military contracts to run supplies and personnel all over the world, United States Lines and other American companies after the war still lagged behind their European competitors.[9]

The U.S. government spent heavily after the war to support the nation's ocean transport industry. To take one example, the USS *United States*, launched in 1952 by United States Lines, revealed both the extent of industry-government collaboration, as well as some of the tensions that occurred when businessmen and military officials attempted to promote national defense and leisure travel at the same time. Already dependent on government subsidies for operating its fleet of forty-six ships, U.S. Lines received government aid that covered more than half of the ship's $78 million construction costs. Although officials in the Truman administration publicly bickered over the exact amount of Washington's contribution, they ultimately supported this friendly arrangement for U.S. Lines.[10] The subsidy was unusually large in this case to compensate for the ship's "special defense features" that would allow the U.S. Navy to transform the 2,000-passenger liner into a state-of-the-art 14,000-troop transport in case of war. Working under the scrutiny of navy security experts, the ship's civilian designer made do without flammable materials such as wood and cotton and sacrificed his plans for windows in the cabin-class lounge. The resulting decor, if suffering somewhat from a lack of natural light, took on a modern feel with plenty of flame-resistant artificial fibers, aluminum, and glass.[11] Such ties between the military and the travel industry, while testifying to the power of the national security state, also reveal how the U.S. military benefited from the consumer-driven networks created by the American travel industry.[12]

Government support also proved instrumental in air transportation. World War II contracts allowed American aircraft makers to improve their designs, and popular postwar civilian models such as the Douglas DC-6 evolved from military transport planes. Even five years after the war, U.S. government orders accounted for close to half of the output of U.S. aircraft manufacturers, allowing the industry to benefit from an economy of scale it would have otherwise lacked.[13] Washington's patronage also helped launch American commercial airlines around the world. In contrast to the European-dominated shipping fleets, the young field of transatlantic air service was more the domain of aggressive American companies. No airline was more assertive than Miami-based Pan American World Airways. Pan Am rose to prominence under Juan Trippe, a Yale-educated entrepreneur well-connected among politicians and media elites such as *Time* and *Life* editor Henry R. Luce. Trippe launched his company in 1927, running mail and passengers to Latin America. A tireless executive, Trippe mastered the art of winning government mail contracts, which proved more profitable than human cargo in aviation's early days. In 1938, the U.S. Post Office offered a generous $2 million subsidy for any commercial operation that could send mail by air to Europe. With this enticement, Pan Am put together a transatlantic fleet and in 1939 proudly offered the world's first passenger flights across the Atlantic. In this fashion, government mail contracts on domestic and international routes underwrote much of the airline industry's early expansion.[14]

Wartime mobilization, along with the Roosevelt administration's campaign for a more liberal international economic system, created new opportunities for expanded international air travel. Before the war, most nations, including the United States, authorized only a single airline to fly international routes. In 1941, Pan Am enjoyed this monopoly. Easily the largest airline in the world, Pan Am had rallied enough members of Congress during the early years of the war to prevent purely domestic companies such as American Airlines and Trans World Airlines (TWA) from winning postwar foreign routes. Defending Pan Am's interests in 1943, Congresswoman Clare Boothe Luce, wife of Henry, boosted her Washington career when she popularized the word "globaloney" to denounce a Roosevelt-inspired "open skies" policy that would deprive Pan Am of its monopoly. Although Washington delivered military contracts to Pan Am during the war, the government also allowed the domestic airlines to expand overseas on behalf of the war effort. In 1944, Pan Am sought to reverse this trend by asking Congress for a permanent monopoly on international air service among American carriers. Juan Trippe's goal was to make his company a "chosen instrument" of the U.S. government. The Roosevelt administration, as part of its free-trade regime, instead pushed forward with its "open skies" approach of greater competition on international air routes. This more liberal system did not seriously undermine Pan Am's status as the largest airline in the world, but it did force Trippe to share international routes with similarly subsidized TWA and American Airlines.[15]

In part to help justify federal support, American air and sea carriers had long indulged in nationalistic imagery. United States Lines was not the only shipping company to give itself a patriotic title. Its competitors included American Export Lines and American President Lines, operating ships with flag-waving names such as *Independence, Constitution*, and *President Wilson*. Pan American, while suggesting hemispheric unity in its name, dubbed many of its planes *Yankee Clippers*. The company also had first ladies from Grace Coolidge to Mamie Eisenhower and presidential daughters such as Margaret Truman "christen" significant new craft. Advertisements for American Airlines featured a bald eagle flying below one of its planes.[16] Such nationalistic associations may have reassured American tourists venturing into unfamiliar foreign countries. Just as important, they reinforced travel companies' more general strategy of associating themselves with the national interest and ensuring government support.

While the U.S. travel industry depended on government backing to expand abroad, it also relied on a synergistic relationship with the mass media at home. Travel narratives, advice columns, and editorials occupied important places in general-interest magazines and metropolitan newspapers. Beginning in the late nineteenth century, magazines devoted to travel emerged to meet readers' interests in foreign places. *Travel* and *National Geographic*, both established around the turn of the century, and *Holiday*, founded in 1946, tempted readers with firsthand accounts of charming Europe and exotic non-Western lands. Special "travel" sections in urban newspapers such as the *New York Times* ballooned with articles and advertisements. For editors and publishers, colorful articles dedicated to foreign places attracted readers and, just as important, advertisers. In promotional material sent to potential travel industry advertisers, the publisher of the *Saturday Evening Post*, the *Ladies' Home Journal*, and *Holiday* promised favorable attention to tourism in its pages.[17] Transportation companies frequently fed the symbiotic relationship by offering "press flights," in which journalists enjoyed all-expenses-paid trips overseas in exchange for the endorsement that often followed in journalists' published travel reports.[18] Together, the mass media and industry members helped portray a world ready for tourist consumption.

With a more explicitly political agenda, another group of Americans eager to praise tourism were members of the one-world movement. The one-world ideal, which called for a strong United Nations or even a unified world government transcending conventional nation-states, reached its peak in the mid- to late 1940s, when organizations such as the United World Federalists (UWF) attracted as many as 50,000 members in the United States.[19] Many one-worlders were also supporters of the travel industry, with the belief that mass tourism could play a part in their larger program of supranational unity. Travel had long shaped the outlook of the world peace movement. That the globe could be crossed so quickly by air in the 1940s particularly impressed many

Lending an air of nationalism to civil aviation, First Daughter Margaret Truman christens a new Pan American plane in March 1949. Pan Am president Juan Trippe watches eagerly from the far left (courtesy Archives and Special Collections, Otto G. Richter Library, University of Miami, Coral Gables, Fla.).

one-world activists. Wendell Willkie, the Republican Party's presidential candidate in 1940, converted to the supranational cause in 1942 after making a rapid voyage around the world, a trip that inspired his best-selling book, *One World*. Willkie introduced the book by conveying a sense of awe in having crossed the world by air in just 160 hours of flying time, and the inside front cover featured a map of the world retracing his itinerary. In similar fashion, Norman Cousins, a leader in the UWF and the editor of the liberal *Saturday Review*, found that a trip to war-damaged Europe in 1948 "raised to a new dimension" his commitment for a change in the international order.[20]

A handful of influential publications that advocated world unity also embraced travel coverage to help advance their campaign. *United Nations World* was one magazine rich in both travel writing and one-world outlooks. Although only lasting from 1946 to 1953, the magazine in its early years attracted 75,000 readers, financial support from Nelson Rockefeller, and a number of well-known writers.[21] In one early issue, contributing editor and Nobel laureate Pearl S. Buck campaigned for a reduction of travel restrictions to combat isolationism and the dangerous "return to localism" among the American public. Expressing hope that open tourist exchanges would contribute to an age of world peace, she also challenged the Soviets to reduce restrictions on travel to and from their nation.[22] Writing for a cosmopolitan middle-class readership, Norman Cousins's *Saturday Review* also connected travel with peace. By giving tourism such lofty purpose, the *Saturday Review* made friends in the travel industry. When ASTA held its first Travel Journalism Awards ceremony in 1949, Cousins gave the keynote speech, calling for public loans to allow more Americans to voyage abroad and prepare themselves for "world leadership and world citizenship."[23]

Members of the U.S. international travel industry often assumed the language and imagery of the one-world idealists in their own advertising and publicity. Pan Am's Juan Trippe spoke during the war of how "this world of ours, in the age of flight, should be one world."[24] Three years after the war, he continued to envision a "world neighborhood . . . in which no one is a foreigner."[25] TWA, owned by aviation pioneer and playboy film producer Howard Hughes, likewise fostered associations between tourism and world unity, as expressed by one 1947 advertisement that invited Americans to fly "where the world is one."[26] As late as 1952, when the anti-Communist McCarran Act regulated the entry of foreigners into the United States, groups such as ASTA took a principled stand against the act and on behalf of the freedom of travel across all national borders.[27]

Although some leaders in the travel industry may have sincerely believed that peace and tourism did go hand in hand, the industry's use of one-world rhetoric was also convenient publicity. The one-world ideal cast the industry as a high-minded servant of humanity and, as did airline advertising, provided a clever way to remind Americans of the global range of their services. Moreover, the travel industry had economic interests at stake as well, since the emerging Cold War threatened to divide the postwar market from one world into two. In an early sign of postwar tensions, the Soviet Union was the only major country to abstain from the 1944 international conference on civil aviation. In October 1946, Pan Am was forced to halt its twice-weekly service to Prague and elsewhere in Eastern Europe.[28]

Whatever their true motives, members of the travel industry proved adept at returning to their traditional flag-waving when one-world idealism declined in popularity. With the intensification of Cold War tensions and domestic anti-Communism, membership in the UWF plummeted by more than half between 1949 and 1951.[29] While the one-world vision never disappeared entirely from their rhetoric, members of the travel industry generally adjusted to the emerg-

Where the World is One

Above all nations, the world around, sky routes are fast and free.
The world up there is everyone's world.
And no one knows it better than your Starliner
pilot and crew—for TWA Starliners
fly more than 5,000,000 miles a
month, up where the world is one.

YOUR TRAVEL AGENT REPRESENTS

TRANS WORLD AIRLINE

A *TWA advertisement that expresses hopes for global unity. As the world map shows,
however, the Soviet bloc already remained off-limits for the airline (from* United Nations
World, *May 1947; courtesy American Airlines).*

ar orthodoxy by relying more on the idea of the United States as the
ıe "free" world. During the Berlin Airlift Crisis of 1948, when U.S.
ıt in Europe seemed to ride on the fragile independence of West
:rican Overseas Airlines and other U.S. lines proudly offered sched-
to the isolated city.[30] In its publicity, Pan American liked to call
itself "the second line of defense" and "virtually an adjunct of the United States
armed forces."[31]

One of the industry's most consistent ideological stances was its embrace of
the "internationalism of the people" articulated by Henry Luce in *Life*. In
speeches and opinion pieces, Juan Trippe echoed Luce's vision of a populist
internationalism to ennoble his business with foreign policy meanings. Often,
Trippe merged vaguely one-world themes with more Cold War–oriented calls
for U.S. leadership of the free world. By making air travel affordable to any
"American who works," he declared in 1944, Pan Am would become "a tool, an
instrument for expanding horizons" and for creating an "informed public
opinion." This informed public, in turn, "is the only way by which, in a
democracy, we can build a strong America, a great foreign trade and ultimately
a stable and peaceful world." "We are a democracy," Trippe pronounced in a
1951 speech. "Our leaders move no faster than the average American voter
believes they should. Thus, foreign travel is no longer a luxury. It is a necessity. . . . Our people must become world minded if our nation is to well
discharge its new responsibilities as the leader of the free world."[32]

Trippe found another outlet for his publicity campaign as chairman of the
Committee on Foreign Travel. The committee was part of the Business Advisory Council, a group of liberal business leaders eager to prevent labor radicalism by ensuring prosperity for American workers. Reflecting this broader
concern, the group called on the government to reduce customs and visa
regulations and cut the cost of passports to help bring "the farmer or the
workman at the lathe" to Europe. The council predicted that, with government
support for working-class travel, "our people would better understand their
new responsibilities as citizens of the most powerful nation on earth." A people
who traveled to Europe would be, in theory, a people who supported Cold War
internationalism.[33]

Washington Turns to Travel Promotion

Travel companies such as Pan Am and American Express saw a new opportunity to receive U.S. government support in postwar Europe's economic
problems. After the war, countries such as France imported heavily from the
United States but were unable to balance these imports because their currency

reserves and overseas investments had been exhausted during the war. These trade and currency deficits threatened Western Europe's recovery and curbed European ability to pay for American exports. Both prospects alarmed the Truman administration, which feared that a depressed Europe would hurt the United States' own economy and leave the region vulnerable to Communist movements. This "dollar gap" crisis would become a major U.S. policy concern during the Marshall Plan years.[34] Turning toward Washington in 1947, American Express circulated a brochure among U.S. government and business leaders promoting tourism as "the quickest way to help foreign countries earn American dollars."[35] Although Europe had few tangible goods to export to the United States, the message went, it could gain dollars by selling its sights and attractions to American tourists.

Proposals to make tourism a part of U.S. foreign economic policy at first found little support from government officials. In August 1947, the Travel Policy Committee, a group of officials from various executive departments mostly concerned with passport and visa questions, considered a proposal that European governments be invited to pay for American goods in the form of paid vacations for the American factory workers who made the goods. The Travel Policy Committee reacted with little enthusiasm. Members commented that the "tourist trade is not what Europe needs" and, with specific reference to France, stressed that country's need for more "basic capital goods production."[36]

By 1948, however, government officials had growing economic and ideological reasons to reconsider the role of consumer spending as an economic policy tool. Part of the reason was the persistence of Western Europe's dollar gap, which worsened even after European industrial production regained prewar levels by the start of 1947.[37] Another key factor in Washington's turn toward consumer diplomacy was, paradoxically enough, antistatist in its values. By late 1947 and 1948, the United States began planning and implementing the European Recovery Program, better known as the Marshall Plan. To implement the plan, Congress created the Economic Cooperation Administration (ECA). As Marshall Plan historians have noted, the ECA resembled a second State Department, with missions in each participating country that guided the use of Marshall Plan funds and rivaled the local embassy in influence.[38] This unprecedented aid program sparked opposition from conservative Republicans. Some feared that excessive foreign aid would contribute to inflation and higher taxes at home or would weaken free enterprise in Western Europe by supporting nationalized European industries. Right-wing critics of the Truman administration, such as influential Republican senator Robert A. Taft, believed that some amount of foreign aid was needed but not on the massive scale suggested by the White House. To help appease the plan's conservative critics, Truman awarded top ECA posts to prominent captains of industry such as Paul G. Hoffman, president of the Studebaker automobile company, who became the ECA's chief supervisor.[39]

Reflecting conservative anxieties that the Marshall Plan challenged free enterprise, the legislative push to make tourism part of the plan came from one of the Senate's more right-wing members, Ralph Owen Brewster from Maine. With an amendment submitted by Brewster, the promotion of American tourism to Europe became a part of the Marshall Plan on 11 March 1948.[40] For an added boost, Congress encouraged freer spending among Americans abroad by raising from $100 to $500 the amount of merchandise that tourists could bring home before paying a duty tax.[41]

The conservative Brewster was a likely candidate to introduce travel promotion to the Marshall Plan. A political ally of Senator Taft, Brewster saw government promotion of American tourism as a way to send dollars to Western Europe through consumers and free enterprise, with only marginal use of direct government aid. Channeling money to Europe through tourists also assuaged conservative beliefs that foreign aid was a form of charity that degraded its recipients. Brewster hammered home this idea by repeatedly arguing that government promotion of tourism would allow Europeans to rebuild their economy "on a thoroughly self-respecting basis."[42]

Brewster also had a record of close ties to the travel industry. As governor of Maine in the 1920s, he created the Maine Development Commission to attract industry and tourism to the state. Entering the U.S. Senate in 1940 with ambitions to reach the White House, Brewster soon positioned himself as an ally of Pan Am, a company whose posh guesthouse in Washington served as a hub of Capitol Hill contacts. In the highly politicized process of setting international air routes and fares, the senator fought for Pan Am through the 1940s. Adolf A. Berle Jr., the State Department official charged with dismantling Pan Am's monopoly on international routes in 1944, was once so frustrated by Brewster's loyalty that he labeled him a "stooge for Pan Am."[43]

Even with a congressional mandate, ECA administrator Paul Hoffman at first appeared uncertain exactly how the U.S. government should promote tourism to Western Europe. When prodded to act by industry leaders such as Pan Am, American Express, and ASTA in early 1948, Hoffman offered only vague assurances of the ECA's favorable attitude toward tourism. In May 1948, several weeks after Congress passed the tourism amendment, he confided to an assistant, "I am not clear as to just how ECA can assist in promoting foreign travel, although it is a project which should obviously have our support."[44]

Reflecting this uncertainty, new tourism bureaucracies emerged in a piecemeal fashion over the summer of 1948. In July 1948, the Department of Commerce, in cooperation with the ECA, devoted part of its Office of International Trade to a new travel branch. The Travel Branch was charged with the task of coordinating contacts between the American travel industry and other branches of the U.S. government. It also set out to collect information and statistical data useful to both the government and travel companies.[45] The Washington-based group originally had just five staff members but soon grew to seventeen in its first few months.[46] In another sign of the growing web of government-industry ties, the Travel Branch received its general directives from a new travel advisory committee, made up of congressional representatives and thirty-one executives from American hotels, transport companies, advertising agencies, and magazines.[47]

One month later, the ECA created its own Travel Development Section (TDS), designed to operate in both the United States and Europe.[48] Like the Commerce Department's Travel Branch, the TDS started small, with a staff of three in Paris. At least one official in the Marshall Plan argued that a staff of one would suffice, since the United States did not need to duplicate the efforts of the European nations' own tourism offices. Hoffman and fellow Marshall Planner W. Averell Harriman, an influential Wall Street lawyer and diplomat, took a more ambitious view of the tourism program. Under their leadership, the TDS grew to a staff of seventeen in Paris, and had a representative in each of the sixteen Marshall Plan countries.[49]

The specialists who joined the Marshall Plan to promote tourism reflected the business and consumer dimensions of the assignment. The chief of the TDS was Théo J. Pozzy, a native of France who immigrated to Maine after World War I. Becoming an American citizen in the 1930s, Pozzy built a successful career in food canning and electrical contracting and served in the U.S. Army during the war coordinating military supplies in Australia and France. His wartime service even included a stint running the luxury Plaza-Athénée hotel in Paris, which, at the time, was reserved for U.S. military officers. After the war, Pozzy returned briefly to his own businesses in Maine but, with the help of family friend Senator Brewster, he joined the Marshall Plan on a volunteer basis. Working for the U.S. government was an occasional source of frustration, as when the military refused to recognize the French spelling of his first name, "Théo," and insisted that for official purposes it should read "Theodore." Whatever the personal annoyances of this dual identity, Pozzy's French background prepared him well for a job that required lobbying both Americans and Europeans. His familiarity with elite culture in France and in Europe more generally allowed him to socialize with his European counterparts in ways that few other diplomats could.[50]

Other officials tied to the TDS had backgrounds in the international travel industry or came from other consumer-oriented careers. The immediate supervisor of the TDS in the ECA's Export Promotions Division was Ralph I. Straus, a former executive with Macy's, whose department store had done much to import Parisian fashions to the United States.[51] Pozzy's deputy assistant, Trevor L. Christie, had been travel editor for the Paris edition of the *New York Herald Tribune*, the primary source of news for American tourists and expatriates in Europe.[52] In 1950, the TDS added a second member from the *Herald Tribune* staff, general manager William Wise.[53] The TDS "information specialist" was another media professional, Julian Street Jr. A 1925 Princeton graduate whose father wrote travel books, Street had experience in journalism, radio scriptwriting, and public relations. A "literary consultant" for the Treasury Department during the war, he had also helped publicize war bond sales. Joining the Marshall Plan, Street continued harnessing American consumer spending to government interests.[54] Other TDS members came with more direct experience in the travel industry. As TDS "programming" assistant, travel agent Yvonne Henderson brought to the Marshall Plan her skill at organizing and promoting tours.[55] In 1950, Clarence Dwinell, with twenty-five years of hotel work experience, joined as the Marshall Plan's "hotel specialist."[56]

As often happened in the Marshall Plan's relationship with preexisting departments, the TDS overlapped somewhat with Commerce's Travel Branch. Both conducted industry and market surveys and communicated with American companies. The TDS differed from the Travel Branch in Washington in that it was more involved in European affairs. Based in Paris, the TDS sought to persuade European governments and businesses to invest in and improve their travel industry and to "create a free travel area" within participating European countries.[57] This mission led the TDS to engage in a campaign to modernize the French hotel industry and to sponsor one of the first examples of European integration, the European Travel Commission.[58] The TDS also received instructions to develop a "travel guarantees program," which offered American investors insurance against failure if they invested in Europe's travel industry. With a hands-on approach to shaping mass travel, the Marshall Plan's TDS represented an unprecedented foray into the travel business by the U.S. government.

Building a Nation of Travelers

Although given an essentially economic task—to bring more dollars to Europe—the government's new tourism promoters also acted on broader desires for unity in postwar American society. Reflecting an era when many elites hoped to build a society free from class antagonism, Marshall Plan officials infused their mission with a populist spirit absent in fiscal conservative justifications of travel promotion.[59] U.S. policymakers sought to transform transatlantic travel from a traditionally elitist pastime into an activity more consistent with postwar ideals of a classless society. As one official in the Commerce Department noted, the U.S. government did not care about the "deluxe tourist" but instead wanted to help "the ordinary man, the shop keeper, the small industrialist, the technician, the school teacher and the housewife." An ECA official in late 1948 complained that American travel in Europe was "still a luxury trade" and needed to come within "the means of the average family."[60] At a time when transportation shortages on the Atlantic limited the potential to increase tourist volume, one might have expected Marshall Planners to focus on ensuring that only those with maximum spending potential made the trip. Instead, U.S. officials often seemed more concerned with the domestic value of getting all classes of Americans to Europe than with their original mission of simply increasing tourist dollar expenditures. In this way, the promotion of Americans' consumerism became both a tool to rebuild Western Europe and a means to pursue a classless society at home.

To be sure, Marshall Planners were correct in assessing the difficulty of working- and even middle-class travel to Europe. Although the trend toward middle-class travel had begun in the second half of the nineteenth century, the transatlantic travel market of the late 1940s and early 1950s still depended on the upper class and the most wealthy of the middle class. According to a French market study in 1952, the wealthiest 33 percent of the United States, those with family incomes over $5,000 a year, accounted for almost two-thirds of France's American guests. In contrast, the one-third of American families with annual earnings under $3,000 represented just 16 percent of American tourists in France.[61] A typical medium-range tour in the early 1950s lasted between four and six weeks and cost an individual about $1,500, one third of which went to the ocean crossing. According to *U.S. News and World Report*, "Americans with moderate means" could enjoy shorter tours for $1,000, yet even this figure remained prohibitively high for the majority of Americans.[62] For working-class Americans, military service in Europe or education on the GI Bill offered the best chance to tour France. Even the GI Bill, however, had its limits. While approximately 8,000 veterans used the bill to study in France, the shoestring budgets provided by the federal government underlined the difficulty of visiting France on the bill alone. One veteran, profiled by the *Saturday Evening Post* in 1949, claimed to get by modestly on his $75 a month from the government. Although he could not afford Paris's nightclubs, he managed to live comfortably in a working-class neighborhood.[63]

Like many business executives, market researchers, and social scientists at

J.S. travel promoters viewed existing class differences not so much as us divide but, in the words of historian Olivier Zunz, as "a mere atum." By identifying the tastes of different social classes, elites could ase those groups and ultimately lead the United States toward a more eous middle-class society.[64] Marshall Plan tourism officials sought to create a uniform consumer society in which all Americans would want to travel to Europe. At the same time, they recognized the need to accommodate income-level differences in order to appeal to all Americans. In their internal correspondence, they avoided the term "class" and preferred labels such as "middle-income groups," which suggested that Americans differed only by degrees of wealth rather than by insurmountable social divisions.[65] Talking with government, advertising, and travel industry leaders in 1949, Pozzy revealed this emphasis on building a more uniform society when he described a European trip as "the dream of every American," quickly adding, "or at least of a large part of the Americans."[66]

ECA tourism officials hoped to create homogeneity not just in consumer desires but also in foreign policy opinion. According to one TDS report, "If the United States is to assume its rightful place as a world power, it must bring up a new generation of leaders with a global outlook as Great Britain did at her peak." Tourism to Europe would help Americans "rub off all traces of provincialism and emerge with a world viewpoint dedicated to American interests."[67] In essence, the Marshall Planners endorsed Juan Trippe and his Business Advisory Council, which had the same vision of a populist internationalism.

To pursue this classless Cold War–oriented society, Marshall Plan officials embraced another elite assumption of the time with their faith in the rapidly expanding field of public relations. As one ECA official noted, the pool of Americans eager to travel to Europe was "tremendous" and its expansion was "entirely up to a clever publicity."[68] U.S. officials' emphasis on public relations rested on a belief that consumers could be easily swayed. When faced with the challenge of drawing more Americans to European health spas, Pozzy suggested that Europeans simply send a few doctors over to the United States, since "the American clientele follows faithfully" the medical advice they receive.[69] Public relations was also central to the TDS "programming" services, in which Marshall Planners organized group tours of Europe designed to generate publicity in mass-market periodicals. The TDS became, in effect, a well-connected travel agency for groups such as readers of *House Beautiful* magazine on a garden tour of Europe. Group tours enjoyed TDS support no matter how far removed in their specific content from Cold War foreign policy, so long as they generated travel-friendly publicity in the United States.[70] Although this was not the first time Washington exploited advertising and public relations, earlier programs such as World War II's bond drives emphasized sacrifice as the path to patriotic duty.[71] In contrast, the Marshall Plan's travel promotion came couched in a language of consumer pleasure, thus embracing not just the tools but also the message of consumer marketers.

To persuade American consumers, the Marshall Planners believed that tourism needed to be presented like other forms of popular culture, especially movies and theater. When arguing for more Marshall Plan–funded travel ads, Pozzy told the ECA's information chief that "tourism is a form of showbusiness; one of the prime ingredients of show business is illusion and illusion must be constantly projected across the footlights to keep the customers lining up at the box office."[72] The TDS helped cultivate illusions by encouraging the creation of the European Travel Commission (ETC), a union of national travel offices from the Marshall Plan countries. The main purpose of the ETC was to place advertisements funded by the Marshall Plan in American magazines and newspapers.[73] The TDS also worked closely with the American media, particularly with figures likely to appeal to middle-class Americans. Pozzy met with humorist Art Buchwald and representatives for the *New Yorker* and the *New York Times* to develop increased press coverage of tourism. He arranged for Hollywood actors such as Douglas Fairbanks Jr. to record public service announcements and even consulted with *Li'l Abner* cartoonist Al Capp to discuss how Capp's own 1950 voyage would appear in his widely read comic strip.[74]

The Marshall Planners, however, limited their promotion activities to mass-circulation media. The ECA expressed no interest in targeting African Americans and gave little attention to the immigrant market, perhaps because immigrants already had an interest in going overseas but also because returning immigrants generally had less money than native-born tourists, and by staying with family and friends, they did not spend as much while abroad.[75] While aiming for a society free of class division, Marshall Planners did so within the limits of an idealized America of native-born whites.

As the supply-side complement to their publicity work targeting consumers, the Marshall Planners also lobbied American travel carriers to prepare for and promote a new age of middle- and working-class tourism to Europe. Since the majority of Americans lacked the money and extended vacation time to travel to Europe, the TDS viewed cheaper transatlantic transportation as a precondition to any demographic revolution in the travel market. For this reason, Marshall Plan officials pushed the travel industry to introduce new tourist-class airfares that would be more affordable to middle-class consumers. In a similar vein, Pozzy even proposed that American ocean liners replace some of their ornate dining rooms with simple cafeterias. If the ocean carriers would serve hotdogs on the North Atlantic, Pozzy estimated, the basic $155 fare could be cut nearly in half.[76]

In trying to promote low-cost travel, Pozzy and the Marshall Planners ran into resistance from the majority of transport companies. In private meetings with government officials, most air and shipping lines showed less concern with the ideological dimensions of tourism than with the ability of higher fares to increase their profit margins. U.S. Lines, for instance, quickly rejected Pozzy's hotdog proposal, arguing that no-frills dining was unlikely to bring the desired reduction in fares.[77] The ocean carrier company might have added that, with tourist-class cabins already booked to capacity on nearly every crossing after the war, the carriers had little incentive to cut tourist-class prices. The government's regulatory commissions, staffed with industry advisers, also frustrated the ECA with their hesitancy to restructure transatlantic fares. With little success, ECA administrator Paul Hoffman lobbied the Maritime Commission (under the Commerce Department) and the Civil Aeronautics Board (congressionally appointed) to reserve more space for "low-cost" fares, particularly for students and other "special groups."[78]

The one transport company that shared the Marshall Planners' enthusiasm for reduced fares was Pan Am. The airline's dominant position in the international air travel market bred confidence that it could prosper more than others with reduced fares. Beginning in 1948, Pan Am lobbied for approval of discounted tourist-class airfare from the International Air Transport Association (IATA), a self-enforcing organization of international airlines formed in 1944 to control prices and routes. The world's other airlines, as well as Howard Hughes's TWA, all significantly smaller than Pan Am, blocked the proposal in the IATA.[79] Even worse, the Civil Aeronautics Board (CAB) in Washington refused to support Pan Am's proposal for fear of upsetting foreign airlines. Juan Trippe turned to top Marshall Plan officials to help make his case. Paul Hoffman and Averell Harriman, both businessmen-turned-diplomats, supported Trippe's position but were unable to convince airline regulators to go against the majority of airlines. Only in 1952 did Pan Am succeed in winning over enough airlines to initiate the reduced-price tourist-class ticket.[80]

U.S. officials also had little success with proposals intended specifically to bring working-class Americans to Europe. An "Industry Travel Plan," endorsed by the TDS as a way to reduce travel costs for factory workers and farmers, aroused only skepticism with the ECA's labor representatives, who responded that "we do not share the confidence that any great number of American workers are either interested in spending vacations in Europe or are willing and able to spend $800 to $1000 per person on such vacations."[81] Another proposal to award workers a "bonus week" of paid or unpaid vacation if they visited a Marshall Plan country did not even advance outside the government's tourism agencies.[82]

While most industry leaders hesitated over Marshall Planners' desire to cut travel fares, industry and government elites shared disappointment over their collective inability to widen substantially the travel market through consumer credit. In 1949, travel agents in New York City launched an installment program in an attempt to lure potential clients who lacked ready cash.[83] The same year, future U.S. diplomat George Ball, then a well-connected lawyer in Paris, tried to convince the French government to create its own installment program for American tourists. Under Ball's scheme, the French would pay the interest charges for "lesser-income Americans" who bought their trips to France on credit. Ball hoped "to make travel as available as automobiles, radios, television sets, furniture, refrigerators, vacuum cleaners and, in fact, all the mechanized amenities which characterize normal American life."[84]

These campaigns for tourism on credit proved just slightly more successful than those targeting industrial workers. The 1949 credit program in New York failed to attract customers, to the dismay of the industry and government leaders in Washington's Travel Advisory Committee who followed the case.[85] For its part, the French Ministry of Finance rejected Ball's proposal as too costly.[86] Airlines had some success in the 1950s inviting consumers to fly on credit, but the travel industry as a whole enjoyed little success with credit plans. Even American Express moved cautiously into the realm of travel now, pay later. The company hesitated to offer travel credit even for business clients in the late 1940s and did not move heavily into credit until 1958, when it introduced the American Express card. Even in the mid-1960s, well into the explosion of consumer credit spending, only around 3 percent of tourists took advantage of installment plans offered by travel agents.[87]

Consumers as a whole treated leisure travel differently from domestic purchases like televisions, appliances, or automobiles. In contrast to cars and other material purchases, the status accrued through European travel did not show itself in tangible form but only in more personalized forums such as conversation and amateur slide shows. On the other hand, this lack of credit use might have also reinforced the status significance of tourism. Direct payment with cash meant that transatlantic travel remained the domain of those whose wealth was already established and not of those counting on future success to pay for their current status trappings.

In the end, these ill-fated programs to bring "lesser-income" Americans to Europe were most significant for what they revealed of elite U.S. foreign policy thinking after the war. George Ball's and the Marshall Planners' anticipation of a trend toward increased use of consumer credit assumed that most Americans were willing to go into debt to share a cultural experience in which mostly an international-minded, cosmopolitan elite participated. To Cold War elites, working- and middle-class tourism held such promise because it would confirm the ideal of a classless society and promote an Atlantic-minded international outlook among all Americans. Nonetheless, supporters of this vision were frustrated by the hesitancy of many travel businesses and modest-income consumers to sacrifice either profits or savings on trips to Europe.

The various American elites who supported government travel promotion faced their most serious challenge from the domestic travel industry, which never fully accepted Marshall Planners' efforts to have Americans spend their vacation money elsewhere. Shortly after the creation of the TDS, one of the first voices to criticize its formation before a congressional hearing was the travel and resort editor of the *Chicago Daily Tribune*, which was not surprisingly the leading American paper with isolationist views. Resistance also came from the East Coast, particularly from states such as New Jersey whose economies relied heavily on vacationers from nearby cities and suburbs in other states.[88]

Although Charles Sawyer, Truman's secretary of commerce, countered that a tourist to Europe "added to the market" for later domestic vacations, government officials engaged in overseas travel promotion did indeed act in other contexts as if they were competing with proponents of domestic travel.[89] In one instance, Paul Hoffman opposed congressional attempts to set up a national travel office in imitation of most other nations, characterizing such proposals as "inconsistent" with the aims of the Marshall Plan. Away from the domestic industry audience, ECA officials called on European nations to increase their advertising to combat the growing publicity budgets of Florida, California, Hawaii, and Bermuda.[90]

Tensions between European travel promotion and domestic travel interests grew sharpest over the question of Marshall Plan funding for advertisements in the American market by the European Travel Commission. By early 1949, the American media reported that European tourist offices were using Marshall Plan money to advertise in the United States. Responding to such stories, members of the Maine Development Commission complained to their senator, Ralph Owen Brewster. In an ironic twist, Brewster found his Marshall Plan tourism program under assault from the same Maine tourism committee he had launched as governor in the 1920s. Western travel groups such as the Montana-based Dude Ranchers' Association also protested against the Marshall Plan's tourism program. Brewster, perhaps to avoid further attacks on the program, pushed through a new amendment in April 1949 banning the direct use of ECA funds for European tourism advertisements in the United States.[91] Given these domestic challenges to Washington's consumer diplomacy, Marshall Plan officials turned down a 1950 invitation by the Advertising Council to throw its resources behind public-service tourism ads, for fear of the reactions from the domestic travel interests.[92]

The ban on subsidies for European ads, however, did not stop the Marshall Plan's tourism promotion. The episode instead brought renewed determination from Marshall Plan officials to continue mass publicity in the American tourism market. In the wake of the ban, Hoffman instructed the ECA to mark tourism funds "not for use in advertising" and then detailed how those funds could be used to create other forms of promotional material such as brochures and posters.[93] For its part, the TDS continued its public relations program and turned out new material such as a series of radio interviews with American tourists in Europe hosted by Dick Driscoll, which the TDS then offered for free use by European tourism organizations.[94] As the Marshall Plan entered 1950, the travel program enjoyed more, not less, support. Influential Senate Democrat J. William Fulbright, for instance, publicly requested the ECA to increase its efforts to promote tourism. In April 1950, given the French economy's persistent dollar gap, the ECA mission in France elevated tourism promotion to one of its top concerns.[95]

Conclusion

From early doubts about whether tourism deserved government participation travel promotion emerged by 1950 with new status as a policy concern. This change toward the use of tourism as a tool of foreign policy reflected a convergence of visions that connected government and private travel boosters. Among these beliefs, the most important and widely shared was confidence that Americans' overseas vacations could help restore Western Europe's economy, prepare Americans for their new superpower status, and cultivate a homogeneous leisure culture back home. Other boosters added to this central vision an emphasis on leisure as a way to add free-market enterprise to the Marshall Plan or, from a more radical ideological view, as a means toward supranational world government. Tourism and the travel industry did not always live up to all these lofty expectations. Nevertheless, that different groups of Americans assigned tourism so much importance in the first place reveals how trips to Europe had become a significant part of U.S. foreign relations.

Despite some frustrations, U.S. policymakers and travel promoters had indeed latched onto a powerful force by harnessing the American consumer to European reconstruction. The average American traveler in 1950 spent $742 in Europe and the Mediterranean, a figure that did not include the ocean crossing, whose costs often went to European carriers. According to one poll, three-quarters of American tourists brought home over $100 each in souvenirs from their trips, suggesting that Congress's removal of the $100 duty-free limit encouraged at least some freer spending.[96] Such liberal policies fueled the popular image of Europe as a consumer's paradise, a stereotype enshrined a few years later in the film *Gentlemen Prefer Blondes*, starring Marilyn Monroe and Jane Russell. After flirting with men on a French ocean liner, the two women arrive in Paris, at which point the film treated audiences to a frenzied montage of luxury boutiques. At the end of their shopping spree, Jane Russell's character proclaimed with satisfaction: "I never spent so much money so fast." As far removed from the Cold War as this scene might have seemed, the mentality it reflected was exactly the one U.S. foreign policymakers set out to encourage at the start of the Marshall Plan.

Tourist spending, taken in aggregate, proved vital to West European recovery. According to figures for 1949, American travel in Europe and on European planes and ships generated $272 million for Marshall Plan countries, more than twice the value of the largest category of European goods (fibers and textiles) sold to the United States.[97] By another estimate, American tourists in 1949 provided approximately one-fourth of all dollars earned by Western Europe.[98] In the case of France, American tourism earnings in 1949 equaled 81.7 percent of the total value of French merchandise exports to the United States.[99] During the four years of the Marshall Plan, Americans spent at the very least $214 million in France, the equivalent of roughly 9 percent of France's $2.4 billion share of Marshall Plan aid.[100] As recent studies of European economic recovery have shown, the plan's major contribution was not so much in rebuilding European production, which had largely recovered to prewar standards by 1948, as in helping stabilize European currencies and balances of payments.[101] Americans' consumer expenditures aided Western European recovery in precisely this critical monetary arena. Although it is impossible to calculate how much of this tourist revenue resulted from U.S. government promotion, Washington actively encouraged this spending by slashing duty-free taxes, lobbying travel companies, and celebrating tourism through the tools of public relations. In the process, U.S. international relations took another step into the consumer age.

Chapter 3

RADIANCE OR COLONIZATION?
FRENCH DIVISIONS OVER AMERICAN
TOURISM

"Let us serve the cause of tourism, source of riches . . . and harmonious agent of French propaganda, influence, and thought throughout the world." With this statement, delivered in a luxury Paris hotel at a 1950 conference on tourism, business leader and former politician Alfred Jules-Julien summarized the basic program of France's foreign tourism boosters. These themes, which travel promoters had first formulated early in the twentieth century, took on new importance in the aftermath of France's defeat in World War II.[1] Bringing more foreigners to France, boosters argued, was essential to restoring the nation's economic and cultural position in the world. Mirroring developments in the United States, a network of French business, government, and media elites hoped that the expansion of American tourism could advance their nation's broader domestic and international interests. Luxury hoteliers, the hotel trade press, and government tourism officials were the leading members of this informal alliance that called for increased state support of France's foreign travel industry. Like its counterpart in the United States, this core travel constituency found support from a number of journalists and political elites such as Jules-Julien. Together, they argued for France's own brand of consumer diplomacy, in which the nation could use American and other foreign tourists to rebuild its economy, secure U.S. foreign aid, and promote the international prestige or "radiance" of France.

To a greater degree than travel boosters in the United States, France's advocates of expanded American tourism faced substantial domestic obstacles in the late 1940s and early 1950s. Although successful in securing food and fuel in the immediate postwar years, foreign tourism boosters in France faced greater frustrations in trying to secure a prominent place for foreign tourism in the nation's long-term economic planning. France's influential planning authorities, eager to create an industrial power, preferred the development of heavy industry, energy, and transportation. The postwar emphasis on industrialization, while offering some indirect benefits for tourism, nevertheless limited the level of government support for hotels and other leisure enterprises. Outside the realm of state policy, Communists and defenders of high culture at times doubted the willingness or ability of American tourists to absorb French culture. Many on the French Left emphasized the need to promote French workers' vacations before subsidizing the leisure of wealthy Americans. Further complicating booster efforts was the fact that hosting tourists was not just a foreign policy question but also a labor issue. While part of an industry dependent on accommodating wealthy foreigners, many of France's luxury hotel and restaurant employees also gave priority to favorable work conditions and embraced the French Left's call for more working-class French leisure. Although these critics were a diverse and disunited cast, they all voiced skepticism on the ability of American tourism to advance French economic independence, social justice, or national grandeur.

These critiques of American tourism challenged both French and U.S. travel boosters. In response, U.S. Marshall Plan officials, eager to expand the volume of American travel in France, increasingly directed their propaganda to improving the French image of American tourists. These efforts, however, ultimately did little to address the sources of French opposition. After all, French views on American tourism emerged not simply from their images of Americans but also from more specifically French concerns over social policy, economic reconstruction, and national identity. Although French foreign tourism boosters and their Marshall Plan allies were successful in warding off most demands for greater state funding for working-class leisure, they never overcame the state's technocratic emphasis on heavy industry and enjoyed only mixed success in their cultural campaign to equate American tourists with French national radiance.

Serving the Cause of Tourism

Business leaders such as Jules-Julien accurately underlined foreign tourism's importance to postwar France. Although industrial production had rapidly recovered to prewar levels by the end of 1946, chronic trade and currency imbalances threatened to halt that economic progress. At a time when France had little ability to export goods and services to the United States, foreigners and especially Americans helped sustain the French economy by bringing in badly needed dollars.[2] Tourism also put bread on a large number of French tables. The size of the travel industry was and remains difficult to measure as a sector of the economy, particularly because it involved so many activities. By one estimate, only 40 percent of tourist expenditures went to hotels and restaurants, with the rest going to transportation services, retailers, entertainers, and other economic actors. Labor statistics also rarely described who counted as a tourism worker. One of the larger estimates, offered in 1946, placed 1.2 million workers in hotels, restaurants, travel agencies, and other fields, making tourism the second largest field of work in France.[3] More reliable figures show that in the early 1950s, between 500,000 and 700,000 people worked in hotels and restaurants, making them one of France's most important sources of employment.[4]

The heart of France's constituency in favor of American tourists was the hotel industry, particularly the hoteliers (owners and managers) of large establishments that catered to foreign guests. Although most hotels in France were small, generally family-run operations that served modest-budget French travelers, the tourist-class hotels were larger and employed roughly as many total personnel as the smaller hotels.[5] As a general rule, the more luxurious the hotel, the more predominant foreign tourists were as guests. Foreigners represented 83 percent of the clientele at top-rank four-star hotels, 64 percent at three stars, 37 percent at two stars, 8 percent at one star, and even less at the smaller establishments and pensions without a ranking. In the four-star Hôtel George V, American guests outnumbered all other nationalities, and in the summer months, they made up over 60 percent of its clientele.[6]

Like American travel companies, French hoteliers were particularly eager to receive financial support from their government to recover from the war. In fact, the French hotel industry had been troubled since the start of the Great Depression. After the George V's arrival in 1928, demand for luxury hotels declined, and no major hotel opened in Paris until Conrad Hilton imported his chain in 1965. World War II proved even more burdensome than the Depression. Many establishments, especially in Paris, endured requisitions by French, German, and then U.S. authorities. While military occupation gave hotel employees work during the war, the buildings themselves often suffered material damages in the process. All told, approximately one-fifth of the 750,000 hotel rooms in France before the war were either destroyed or damaged by 1945.[7] To make matters worse, a 6 January 1945 law placed some German wartime requisitions in the category of illicit profits from the enemy. As a result, some hotels had to forfeit money received from the German military, even if the sums were inferior to the costs and damages incurred during the occupation.[8]

To advance their collective interests, French hoteliers formed a new national association after the war. Replacing an earlier hotel organization that dissolved in 1940, the Fédération nationale de l'industrie hôtelière (FNIH) soon became the industry leader, with 200,000 members representing hotels, restaurants, and cafés.[9] Luxury hotels, by weight of tradition and prominence, dominated the association. The FNIH's longtime president, Marcel Bourseau, administered tourist-class hotels in Paris, Biarritz, and Cannes and a small chain in the French protectorate of Morocco. The same emphasis on elite establishments shaped the travel industry's trade press. *L'Hôtellerie*, the industry-leading weekly, maintained its offices on the Champs-Élysées and helped hotel, restaurant, and café operators keep abreast of the latest equipment and taxes and voiced proposals for making the state more supportive of its hotel industry.

French hoteliers generally positioned themselves as bearers of a distinctly national heritage, even though the industry itself held a strong transnational character. Assuming a patriotic stance, Bourseau wrote frequently of "our country's traditions of hospitality" when describing the industry.[10] Although a common theme, this emphasis on a national style of hospitality obscured the fact that hoteliers and high-ranking hotel employees routinely trained and worked outside France. Consider one of France's most famous prewar hoteliers, César Ritz. A Swiss native, Ritz built his reputation with hotel work in London before drawing on English investors to open his own hotel in Paris in 1898. Charles Auzello, the Ritz's director through the mid-twentieth century, may have been French, but, like many other top employees, he first built his credentials by working in the United States for several years.[11] By de-emphasizing such transnational currents, leaders in the hotel industry, whether consciously or not, developed a nationalistic posture that also complemented their persistent quest to align themselves with French foreign policy.

The hotel industry's quest for state support suffered from the French government's weak tradition of official tourism promotion. At the turn of the century, the promotion of tourism remained the affair of hotels, local booster organizations (*syndicats d'initiative*), and the Touring Club de France, an organization founded in 1890 by wealthy French urbanites eager to see their nation by bicycle and automobile. At a time when the government played almost no role in regulating hotels, the Touring Club pressured rural and small-town hotels to meet the urban middle class's desires for more bathrooms and cleaner bedrooms.[12] The creation of a small national tourism office in Paris in 1910 marked the French government's first explicit foray into tourism promotion, but a tiny budget limited its role to modest efforts such as brochure printing. After World War I, a new national agency increased government publicity efforts and established offices in foreign countries, including the United States. Despite such advances, by the end of the 1920s, French tourism promotion expenses in the United States were still far below those of other European countries such as Germany, Italy, or Czechoslovakia.[13] In the 1930s, that gap widened, especially as fascist Italy and Germany conducted aggressive promotion abroad. At the same time, the French National Tourism Office collapsed in the wake of a 1935 scandal implicating its leadership in illegal profits from investments in a Champs-Élysées hotel.[14] A new Tourism Commissariat emerged in 1936, but a combination of low funding, economic depression, and then war stifled its activities.

Although an enthusiastic ally of hoteliers, the Tourism Commissariat had relatively limited power after World War II. While the state nationalized and poured resources into France's automobile and steel industries, the tourism industry struggled for public funds to support investments. The commissariat, a small section of the Ministry of Public Works and Transports, enjoyed only modest expansion during a period of rapid state growth. In 1946, it moved from its cramped space in a private building on the Quai d'Orsay to a more grandiose building on the bustling Avenue de l'Opéra in the heart of the touristic Paris. There, just a few blocks north of the Louvre, newly appointed Commissaire Henri Ingrand oversaw a staff of twenty-three. Ingrand was a thirty-eight-year-old medical doctor with little experience in the travel industry. His entry into politics came through leadership in the Resistance in his native Auvergne and then in the postwar provisional government. He remained France's top tourism official until 1952, when he joined the Ministry of Foreign Affairs for a more conventional diplomatic career. Ingrand recruited as his assistant a young Georges Pompidou, also from Auvergne. The future French president spent several of his first years of public service in the commissariat before moving on to positions with more upward mobility.[15] From Paris, this staff coordinated activities with its satellite offices in the major cities of Europe and North America. Recognizing the importance of the American market, the commissariat placed the largest such office on New York's Fifth Avenue. The overseas service, known in English as the French Government Tourist Office, employed both French and local staffs to distribute materials, operate public relations campaigns, and collaborate with local advertising firms for the creation of magazine, newspaper, and radio advertisements.[16] While growing, the government's role in tourism remained relatively modest, and efforts by the hotel industry to elevate the commissariat to a more powerful ministry-level status failed to find support higher in the government.[17]

If limited in resources, France's tourism office still managed to channel promotional efforts into one of the first examples of European integration, the European Travel Commission. Formed in June 1948 by the tourism offices of Marshall Plan countries, the ETC's major activity, and the object of all its expenses, was creating collective travel advertisements in the American media. Although the Marshall Plan provided the funds for the initial campaign, protests from the American domestic travel industry meant that the Europeans covered most of the costs for the advertising beginning in 1949. Member nations contributed to the ETC's advertising fund according to the percentage of American tourist dollars they had received the previous year. In 1950, at a time when European countries were desperately short on American dollars for importing goods, the member countries contributed $350,000 to the ETC's fund, a sum large enough to conduct a public relations campaign and run advertisements in the *New York Times* and other publications.[18]

The Tourism Commissariat was perhaps the most enthusiastic member of the ETC, reflecting French confidence that cultural prestige and geography guaranteed their nation the lion's share of any general increase in American tourism to Europe. France even voluntarily increased its share of financial support for the ETC—to around 26 percent of the total in 1949 and 1950—to help appease member countries such as Britain that felt less connected to the Continent's tourist paths.[19] Established two years before the landmark European Coal and Steel Community, the ETC was one of the earliest European organizations pooling resources and coordinating policies to improve an industry critical to the region's economies. In contrast to its larger coal and steel successor, the consumer-oriented ETC pursued European integration not in the industrial Ruhr Valley but on Madison Avenue.[20]

The Ministry of Foreign Affairs also contributed to tourism promotion in the United States. The French embassy's selection of documentary films screened for Americans favored the picturesque over the political. Films such as *Forever Paris*, *Next Time We See Paris*, and *Along the French Riviera* played more often than films with less touristic titles such as *Men of the Maquis* (underground resistance), *Charles de Gaulle*, and *Reconstruction of the Ruins*.[21] French consular officials in the United States reported back to Paris on problem areas in the French tourism industry, notably complaints over high prices in Paris, and they urged French authorities to regulate prices in hotels and tourist shops. France's consul general in Boston enthusiastically converted his consulate in 1950 into "a sort of Tourist Service" with travel brochures in the waiting room and a staff trained to help Americans plan Gallic itineraries.[22]

France's travel industry also found support from a handful of public intellectuals and business experts. Most often at the center or the right of France's political spectrum, these elites presented tourism, or sometimes the entire service sector, as the best path for France's postwar greatness. André Siegfried, an intellectual known for his snobbish disdain for mass tourism and American culture, was also a surprisingly vocal advocate of foreign tourism as a legitimate path for France's future. A member of the *Academie française* and a regular contributor to the conservative newspaper *Le Figaro*, Siegfried penned widely read essays lamenting how the "heroic age of tourism" had given way to a banal age of "administrative tourism." Yet he also cast his eye on the global economy in search of what economists have termed "comparative advantage."

Since other continents were producing and exporting more materia[l], Europe must turn to "services" to succeed in global trade. The service in[dustry] that Siegfried saw as Europe's calling was tourism. While America and Af[rica] both suffered from "uniformity," he asserted, Europe offered "individuality, diversity, and therefore for the foreigner, entertainment." As he put it in 1948, using a favorite metaphor, the foreign tourist brings in money like "the traditional floods of the Nile fertilize the Delta."[23]

Joining the network of boosters, a handful of business experts agreed with Siegfried's analysis that France's comparative advantage lay in foreign tourism. The business journal *Professions* in 1946 defined France as a "country of luxury" whose "incontestable superiority" in art and craftsmanship would allow it to "play her part again in the world concert."[24] Foreign trade counselor Georges Villette took a negative path to the same conclusion, arguing that France's smaller size meant that it could not compete on industrial terms with the United States or the Soviet Union and therefore must cultivate foreign tourism.[25]

This collection of travel industry, government, and media elites waged a campaign to increase public awareness and government support of France's foreign tourism. In this effort, one of their conceptual pillars became the idea that tourism ought to be thought of as an "industry." When the government's economic planning group on tourism, a committee dominated by travel industry leaders, developed a list of its "fundamental ideas" in 1950, it began by stating that "tourism is an ensemble of industries" and that "it is advisable to 'think' of it at each instant as *industrial*."[26]

Defining tourism and its services as an industry, far from mere semantics, carried substantial economic stakes. The chief means by which the French state allocated resources for economic development was through a series of central economic plans. The more tourism appeared "industrial," boosters hoped, the more likely it would appear worthy of state support. In like fashion, hoteliers campaigned to define tourism as an "exporting industry" in order to enjoy the same tax breaks that the French government gave to more traditional exporting sectors like the steel and automobile industries.

In arguing for government support, boosters portrayed leisure and travel as part of an industrial future rather than of an aristocratic past. "Tourism suffers in France from an unfavorable prejudice," complained one sympathetic French newspaper in 1945. All of France lost, the paper claimed, when a vital element of its economy was dismissed as "an anachronistic activity" associated with "the idea of idleness." *L'Hôtellerie* argued similarly that "to think touristically" would be "very Twentieth Century." The hotel trade paper guarded against even potential supporters who downplayed tourism's industrial elements. André Billy, a colleague of André Siegfried at *Le Figaro*, suggested that

ıissariat would be better off leaving the Ministry of Public
rts since the engineers and technocrats in that ministry
ist people" to be "like artists, that is to say like jokers."
d the suggestion as if it were heresy and then detailed
ical aspects that demanded serious practical attention,
nce and renovation.[27]

ıect and government support, France's foreign tourism
.ɔu embraced the concept of national "radiance" (*rayonnement*).
Used in nineteenth-century celebrations of the French empire, the term described the spreading of French language, high culture, and democratic spirit
to the rest of the world. After France's divisive defeat and occupation in World
War II, the term became one of the key words among nationalists eager to
see France maintain its international influence.[28] Moreover, the challenges to
French grandeur only grew in the late 1940s, particularly as the nation faced
ongoing colonial rebellion in Indochina and growing U.S. influence in Cold
War Europe. Whereas 64 percent of French respondents to one poll in September 1944 thought of France as a "great power," only 37 percent thought so in
1948.[29] In this context, French tourism promoters harnessed nationalism behind their efforts and drew attention to how tourism, in one industry leader's
words, could "return to France its place on the psychological level as a great
world nation."[30] Repeatedly invoking the concept of radiance, foreign tourism
boosters argued that the display of France's cultural patrimony was one of the
most effective ways to preserve and extend the influence of French culture in
the world. In one typical usage, the Tourism Commissariat's 1948 report spoke
of foreign visitors as "one of the most authentic elements . . . of French
radiance."[31] Couching tourism in a powerful nationalistic discourse, the travel
boosters' rhetoric of radiance proved popular with mainstream French political figures. Speaking at the sixtieth anniversary of the Touring Club de France,
French president Vincent Auriol, a moderate socialist, praised the group's
efforts to secure for the nation "a new radiance in the world."[32]

Contemplating France—a country ravaged by war and collaboration—as a
tourist destination offered an opportunity to inventory national elements un-
tainted by defeat or internal divisions. In January 1946, *La Tribune économique*
noted the ruined state of the French economy but stressed that the nation "still
has natural riches against which the rage of human destruction had no effect:
the fertility of its soil, the beauty of its sites, the virtue of its thermal [spa]
sources."[33] To one resort town mayor, the French landscape represented an
element of the French nation that survived the occupation and collaboration:
"These riches were fortunately not spoiled by the invader, who destroyed our
factories, pillaged our equipment and our movable property, but could not

capture our springs, our rivers, our climates."[34] Considering that the collabora-
tionist government ruled from the spa town of Vichy, these postwar references
appear somewhat escapist. They nevertheless do show how an emphasis on
continuity in French tourist attractions provided a way for some French observers to minimize the occupation's effect on French identity and avoid thinking about collaboration.[35]

For some politicians from touristic regions, hosting foreigners likewise represented a referendum on France's moral integrity after the occupation. Calling for more government support of tourism, one Parisian deputy in the
National Assembly claimed that the continued appeal of France as a travel
destination after the war testified to the "spiritual radiance" of France's "heroic
resistance."[36] Jean Médecin, the mayor of Nice, agreed, arguing that the stream
of visitors to Paris offered proof that France was still "the country of liberty in
the eyes of the world. . . . Whoever in the world has a passion for public good
takes an interest in the fate of our country. Let us maintain this radiance."[37]

As during 1946 and 1947, French tourism boosters continued to argue that
the ideology of radiance had particular foreign policy value when it attracted
American visitors. Indeed, for some, the cultivation of Francophilia among
Americans had become a sort of national defense strategy. Paul Métadier, a
tourism booster in the Loire Valley, a châteaux region popular with Americans,
argued that tourism was an important defense against American isolationism.
For U.S. visitors, "this old western civilization," of which France "has always
been the model, takes on a concrete character for the foreigners who visit our
country and attaches them more to the defense of this ideal. This is without
doubt especially true for Americans so often tempted by isolationism."[38] Similar thoughts motivated one resort-town mayor to note in 1948 that "many
sentimental ties, whose manifestations are revealed in critical hours, are born
from the visits and impressions of our tourists and curists."[39] In 1950, tourism
commissaire Ingrand described France's 9.5 million postwar visitors as "our
propagandists" who were "all the more precious at the present hour" when
"France has need of all sympathies."[40]

France's travel boosters also described the act of hosting tourists as important for the French themselves. The domestic complement to the ideology of
radiance was the nostalgic idea that hosting foreigners could restore to France
virtues lost during the war. Tourism boosters associated good hospitality with
a healthy social fabric. "Let's try to become ourselves again. . . . Let's try a return
to the good old times," urged France's federation of local tourist promoters in
1949. The French needed to leave behind the "too hard life" of the war, suggested the federation, which imagined an idealized prewar France where people smiled to strangers and offered directions in the street.[41]

As this form of nostalgia might suggest, the ideology of national radiance often lent itself to a culturally conservative vision of France's future. L'Hôtellerie editorialized in 1948 against the trend of French novels, especially those that sold well outside France, to celebrate adultery by married women and thus impugn French family life. French writers "in all genres" needed to present a better image of their nation in case the outside world peeked inside. In other cases, the paper emphasized the importance of presenting a coherent national image for foreigners. Too many French restaurants had "exoticized themselves" by adopting foreign styles. The paper then singled out the presence of English puddings on French dessert menus. This "dangerous game," it warned, would weaken France's ability to project a distinct national image.[42]

L'Hôtellerie revealed the same emphasis on national purity with its attitude on language. The paper held to a positive, if somewhat idealized, image of France's foreign guests, in which foreigners treated the visit as the culmination of years of study in French language and culture.[43] The paper complained that foreign tourists, who were often inspired by a love for the cultivated French language, were disappointed to find that French children and even "the bourgeois rich" no longer spoke proper French, a trend traceable to "a general relaxing in social and individual discipline." In a variation on the rhetoric of national radiance, the editorial warned hoteliers against adopting an "anglomania" that often bothered "the Anglo-Saxons themselves." American and British guests, L'Hôtellerie suggested, were more annoyed than pleased when the French attempted to speak English.[44]

L'Hôtellerie's brand of nostalgia appealed to those in the general media eager to promote conservative values in postwar France. In a 1949 editorial titled "The Eyes of the Foreigner," Le Figaro stressed that, to extract foreign tourism's full economic value, French citizens needed to be on their best behavior. "In the face of foreigners," warned the daily, "each of us must feel responsible for France. The smallest discourteous gesture does wrong to France." Le Figaro then listed a broad set of concerns that had as much to do with a conservative domestic social and political agenda as with the impressions of foreign tourists:

In the presence of these hundreds of thousands of foreigners, witnesses and judges, we perhaps do not consider enough that we are not alone, that the cleanliness of our streets, the methods of our administration, the tone of our newspapers or of our political posters, the honesty of our merchants, our way of dressing, of behaving at the restaurant table, of acting with neighbors on the bus at rush hour are *watched* every day, and become the object of commentaries that implicate all of France, in a favorable or unfavorable way.

The editorial closed with metaphorical flourish, claiming that "all of France is in the situation of those families that lodge with them a guest."[45] The familial metaphor also appealed to Robert Krier, the editor of a conservative-leaning hotel trade paper. Reacting most likely to a wave of strikes in 1951, Krier spoke on behalf of "the house 'FRANCE'" and remarked that tourism can only succeed "in a very clean house where everyone is properly in their place."[46]

Like Krier, travel promoters often feared that labor activism and disruptive strikes would weaken France's ability to play the host. Georges Villette, the foreign trade counselor who believed that France could only prosper in the international economy by catering to service industries, emphasized that older and more generous labor practices would have to take a backseat to more consumer-oriented norms, such as longer, more irregular work hours. Banks that closed Sundays and holidays, for instance, might give employees their day of rest but annoyed tourists who needed to exchange dollars for francs. The "untimely" strikes by transport and civil service workers also came under criticism for their costs to tourism.[47] For its part, L'Hôtellerie proclaimed neutrality on hotel labor disputes that threatened to produce a strike but generally criticized workers when negotiations failed and unions struck.[48] While hardly traditionalist in envisioning a consumer-driven economy, boosters tended toward a conservative emphasis on disciplining the tourist industry labor force.

Although they did not possess an entirely uniform ideology, France's advocates of foreign tourism shared a common language that emphasized hosting foreigners as a path toward national radiance and as a true industry in need of greater support from the state. Indeed, the two concepts complemented each other, since the rhetoric of radiance elevated the specific interests of the travel industry to a national concern. With their focus on improving France's economic and cultural place in the world, travel boosters presented a vision of how foreign tourism could serve the interests of French foreign policy. Much like their counterparts in the United States, the advocates of bringing more Americans to France also acted for domestic reasons, in this case with the idea that hosting Americans and other foreigners offered a way to encourage the French to maintain conservative values and promote national radiance.

Alternative Agendas

Although travel boosters enjoyed success reviving their industry in the immediate postwar years, they still faced significant frustrations in the postwar era. On nearly each point of their overarching ideology, the advocates of linking Americans and other foreign visitors to French national interests met with opposition from diverse sources, including economic planners, Communists, and even hotel workers themselves. As a result, their program to create a society more oriented around foreign tourism suffered, especially in regard to longer-term development funding and integrating American tourism with the ideal of national radiance.

The vision of a national economy fueled by tourism fared poorly among France's influential economic planners, who tended to equate national grandeur with steel and electricity plants. The Commissariat général du plan (CGP), which largely determined funding priorities, was not entirely opposed to the promotion of tourism. One top official, Etienne Hirsch, believed the relatively small sum of 4.3 billion francs earmarked for tourism in December 1948 to be insufficient if the French wanted to maintain monetary stability by the end of the Marshall Plan in 1952.[49] Such beliefs, however, had little reflection in actual policy. In 1950, Minister of Finance Maurice Petsche and his Committee on Investments turned down a request to increase state aid to tourism on the grounds that it "would gravely compromise the realization of certain other programs of vital importance for the national economy."[50]

French technocrats gave conventional industries the center stage for reasons as much charged with national identity and security as with economic efficacy. At a time when many French blamed their recent defeat on superior German factories and foundries, an economy based on production seemed to serve France better than one based on leisure and service. A 1946 planning outline by influential French technocrat Robert Marjolin noted tourism's role in the balance of payments but suggested nothing on government activity to increase it. Citing the examples of the United States, Germany, and the Soviet Union, Marjolin instead emphasized that, to be like "all the great modern countries," France would have to produce all its own steel. Jean Monnet, France's leading planner, remarked that if France failed to invest in the CGP's First Plan (1948–52), "we shall inevitably become like Spain," a once-powerful nation now with weak industry and, he might have added, with few options besides tourism for earning foreign currency.[51]

Part of the problem was that, despite foreign tourism's significance to the postwar French economy, tourism fit awkwardly in economic categories. The Ministry of Economic Affairs saw no place for travel or hotels under the theme of "industrial programs," and the Ministry of Finance was not sure how to categorize the activity. For a time it carried two separate "rubrics," one for "industrial and commercial enterprises" and one for "touristic equipment." Only after some discussion in 1952 did the Ministry of Finance create a new category called "communications," which included tourism, as well as air and ocean transportation.[52] One elected official advocating more investment in tourism hesitated to embrace the "industry" label, placing the word in quotation marks. His gesture suggested that even the faithful were not sure where tourism belonged in government planning.[53]

In a related problem, the travel industry also suffered from a marginal position within French politics. Of the 156 business and labor leaders who advised the government on the Conseil économique in 1946, not one represented the travel industry.[54] The travel industry fell outside national power circles, in part because of mass tourism's relatively new status, and perhaps also because France's largest tourism center, Paris, was also the nation's political, business, and high-culture capital. Only on a regional level, as along the Riviera, did the travel industry possess a strong voice in politics. Mayor Jean Médecin, who was also a deputy in the National Assembly, for instance, was a tireless promoter of France's travel industry.[55]

With a limited voice in French politics, travel boosters frequently resented the decisions handed down by the central economic planners in the CGP. In the initial 1947 version of the CGP's First Plan, tourism appeared only as a source of foreign currency, with no references to receiving government aid. The omission created "bitterness and stupefaction" in travel industry circles.[56] One tourism-friendly journalist criticized the Ministry of Finance for privileging factories and steel-rolling mills over race tracks and hotels, even though the leisure centers were better dollar earners.[57] In 1950, a hotel trade paper declared that the First Plan's emphasis on energy and steel had "cruelly deceived" France, which now needed to turn to tourism as the best way to balance its trade deficit.[58]

Marcel Bourseau, the hotelier and FNIH president, adopted an almost conspiratorial tone to explain French economic planning. For Bourseau, the worst moment came in 1949 when the government took away more than half the credits targeted for tourism to help fund other industries. Proud of how the travel industry provided France with foreign currency, he lamented that "we have not had, alas!, the means to confirm [this fact] by opulent campaigns in the general press, all geared today around steel for example." For whatever reason, France could only suffer when "our distinguished economists, born in the country of Descartes, preferred . . . in lieu of our banal kitchens, prestigious plans of large furnaces and rolling mills, which nobody can seriously say will ever export their products."[59]

Marginalized by powerful economic planners, advocates of foreign tourism in France also faced opposition from some French Communists and socialists who held a rival vision of tourism's future in postwar France, one that emphasized leisure for the French working class. Working-class, or "social," tourism had been a political issue since 1936, when the Popular Front government guaranteed fifteen-day paid vacations to all French workers. Despite the political victory, few French workers experienced the benefits of "social tourism" before the war, given the high cost of train travel and hotels and a lack of government resources to help workers take vacations. The promise of a new age of mass working-class leisure travel remained an unfulfilled legacy of the Left's electoral triumph in 1936. For many of the millions of voters who made the French Communist Party (Parti communiste français, PCF) the nation's largest party after the war, working-class leisure became a goal for the postwar era. Although luxury tourism interests after the war received most of the French government's tourism resources, the push for domestic working-class tourism meant that even this limited government support attracted opposition.[60]

While not always distinct categories, the two types of tourism generally involved different projects that often competed for the same pool of public tourism funds. *Tourisme à devises*, literally "foreign currency tourism," required investment in tourist-class hotels with modern comforts such as private baths for wealthy guests. *Tourisme social*, in contrast, had different needs. At a time when few French workers vacationed at all, let alone in hotels, leisure opportunities for the French masses required the creation of large campgrounds or vacation villages.[61] Within the travel industry, members did not always take sides, and some experts stressed how the improvement of rail service, for instance, benefited both tourism categories. Generally supportive of foreign tourism, *Le Monde*'s Olivier Merlin endorsed special measures in 1946 to attract foreigners, but only if "we too have some facilities this summer" to enjoy the mountains or ocean. Even *Le Figaro* did not like to see only foreigners traveling and suggested that a percentage of foreign tourism earnings be set aside so that French citizens of "modest condition" might have the opportunity to travel abroad themselves.[62]

Tensions between the two priorities, however, emerged within the government's planning authority. The CGP's Commission de modernisation du tourisme (CMT), formed in September 1947, was a critical institution in allocating the government resources that were not diverted to heavy industry.[63] Although it could not appropriate funds on its own, the CMT published lengthy studies and produced policy recommendations that guided the use of government credits in the tourism industry. While the commission contained government tourism officials and planning bureaucrats, the majority of its members were leaders in tourism industry management. Most came from luxury establishments that by power of tradition dominated the hotel and restaurant organizations, while only a few members represented the industry's labor federations.[64]

The government's First Plan gave advocates of social tourism for French workers little to celebrate. In this sense, French planners accepted the tenets of the foreign travel boosters when it came to distributing the state's tourism resources.[65] As one of its "fundamental ideas," the technocrats and luxury hotel leaders dominant within the CMT stressed that French economic policy needed to let "the foreign-currency tourist pass before the beneficiary of 'paid vacations.' " The commission recommended that established tourist areas in France be dedicated to foreigners and suggested that less expensive options for French vacationers could be found by developing rural areas or inexpensive hotels in North Africa. Reflecting its composition, the CMT did not share the Left's vision of popular vacations as a political entitlement for the working class. It instead referred to social tourism only as a way to improve workers' productivity during the rest of the year.[66] In a lengthy 1950 speech before the government's tourist advisory board, the French banker in charge of public aid for French hotels made not a single reference to the French as tourists in their own country.[67]

With the development of the Second Plan in 1952 and 1953, as the French currency crisis softened, competition between foreign and domestic tourism interests on the planning commission intensified. At one meeting, Marcel Bourseau and Jean Médecin walked out of the room when another member raised the topic of social tourism. The two, each leading proponents of luxury foreign tourism, continued their protest by boycotting subsequent meetings.[68] Interviewed later by Le Monde, Bourseau stressed the need to distinguish sharply between social tourism and "tourism of economic importance." Claiming no opposition to working-class tourism in itself, he warned that whereas the First Plan was "ours," the Second Plan risked to "take up again" the Popular Front's prewar emphasis on social tourism.[69] This persistent debate over wealthy foreign and French working-class tourism, like the economic planners' emphasis on heavy industry, limited the ability of France's foreign tourism promoters to build widespread public support for their agenda.

The rivalry between luxury and social tourism further weakened foreign travel boosterism by heightening class tensions within the hotel industry itself. The workers in France's luxury hotels, restaurants, and cafés, although largely dependent on foreign tourists for their livelihood, only partially shared the goals of their bosses. The debate over social tourism placed workers in France's luxury travel industry in an awkward position that pitted working-class solidarity against their dependence on wealthy tourists. Some workers also warned that efforts to attract foreigners threatened work conditions in hotels, restaurants, and other service establishments.

While not the centers of French labor radicalism, luxury hotels nevertheless employed members of militant labor unions. In the Plaza-Athénée and the George V, for example, over 80 percent of the workforce in 1946 belonged to a union.[70] Workers in French hotels and restaurants generally joined specific trade federations aligned with the larger, more ideological confederations. One of the most active trade federations, the Fédération nationale des travailleurs de l'alimentation, des hôtels, cafés, et restaurants, operated under France's largest and most powerful union, the Communist-led Confédération générale du travail (CGT). Other workers joined a less radical Christian union, the Confédération française des travailleurs chrétiens (CFTC), or Force ouvrière (FO), a moderate group that split from the CGT in 1947. Lastly, the Confédération générale des cadres (CGC) represented middle managers. In the George V in 1949, non-Communist activists just slightly outnumbered the CGT members.[71]

To a degree, labor in the travel industry shared some of the same concerns as management. Workers in hotels and other tourist establishments used the "industry" label to claim the same benefits as those enjoyed by industrial workers. In 1946, a shortage of electricity shut down nightclubs, and the French state did not award their 8,000 employees the same compensation as factory workers whose plants had been similarly idled.[72] In this regard, nightclub workers echoed their bosses, who themselves wanted but did not receive the tax breaks that came with official status as an export industry.[73]

In other regards, however, social class played a central and at times divisive role in the hotel industry. The gulf in income levels that separated hotel workers from guests could inspire among workers not only hopes of upward mobility but also a sense of class antagonism. One of the common points of entry for employment in tourist-class hotels was the position of groom (errand-boy), usually filled by working-class boys.[74] About one-third of grooms stayed with hotel work as adults and comprised the majority of workers in more skilled positions such as hotel porter, a figure who played a key role running hotel lobbies and advising guests on their travels. The ideal employee, according to one successful Paris hotel porter, was one who at a young age acquired "the general culture" necessary for interacting with traveling elites.[75] The employee might learn a second language, preferably English, or at the very least honor hotel managers' exhortations to speak proper French. To this end, some hotel employee newsletters offered grammatical advice columns.[76] Staff newsletters accentuated this sense of upward mobility by stressing that some of travel's charms rubbed off on workers. "What a magnificent field of observation, what a school!" exclaimed one, which compared working in a hotel to "voyaging in place." A hotel career, according to another, was "one of the most picturesque in the world."[77]

Not all hotel employees shared this rosy view. Strenuous work and low or unsteady pay made identifying with wealthy clients difficult for many workers. Long and irregular hours, often at night or evening, also demanded sacrifices from hotel employees. A typical day in a hotel or hotel restaurant could run up to fourteen hours, broken by an afternoon rest. Often employees stayed at work for dinner, which was generally provided by employers to compensate for hours that made eating with one's family impossible. These long hours at the workplace might explain why, when the management of the George V offered its employees free English language classes, few workers jumped at the opportunity to spend more time at the hotel.[78]

Hotel workers organized in labor federations to protect wages and improve the often rigorous work conditions. While business experts such as Georges Villette called for French service establishments to keep longer hours, French hotel, restaurant, and café unions occasionally struck to receive a five-day week.[79] Workers and politicians friendly to their cause also lobbied for the government to crack down on employers who failed to provide free meals to employees working long shifts.[80] A burning issue in the hotel and restaurant industries since the 1930s had been protecting the income by tips of waiters and other employees in contact with clients. As the unions charged and as academic tourism experts verified, a minority of employers who adopted a "service included" policy on their bills abused the system by withholding tips from the workers. Although the issue was in theory resolved with a 1933 law that guaranteed workers their service percentages, debates about how well the law protected workers continued into the postwar era and gave rise to tension in the industry.[81]

The combination of luxury tourism and labor militancy made the hotel industry both a contentious environment and, for many workers, the site of ideological compromise. The federations' professional interests lay largely in the promotion of elite leisure, while its ideological inclinations looked toward a more democratic culture. These contradictions were most pronounced in the Communist-affiliated CGT hotel federation newsletter. Articles adopting the general confederation's view on international events such as the Marshall Plan derided the French government as "valets" to the United States, a strident critique perhaps more appropriate for CGT militants in steel factories than for an audience of hotel valets and porters.[82]

At times, Communist hotel workers criticized any emphasis on foreign and American tourism. One such editorial in a hotel labor paper, written several months after the start of the Marshall Plan's tourism program, warned that "the race for dollars" hurt popular tourism for the French working class. The best way to improve the French tourist industry was not to cater to Americans but to raise the average French standard of living and leisure spending. At other times, the union criticized the Tourism Commissariat and the French economic planners for favoring exclusively luxury hotel interests.[83]

More often, the Communist hotel federations staked out a compromise position. They asserted the eventual priority of social tourism but also endorsed the short-term promotion of luxury foreign tourism as a means to secure national independence. In an article for one CGT-affiliated hotel labor newsletter, Virgile Barel, a Communist politician from the Riviera, argued for a hearty reception of Americans and their dollars. In an uncanny echo of conservative Republicans in the U.S. Congress, Barel considered it better for France to earn money from American tourists than to rely on aid from the U.S. government, since the tourists would not meddle in France's internal affairs.[84] "We do not complain," declared another CGT leader, "if, provisionally, the riches of our country are only the property of a handful of swindlers and reserved for parasites," since "one day very soon, the people of France, master of their destinies, will enjoy them fully." In this view, rich foreigners deserved toleration as a source of national revenue, even if their dollars would only serve as a means toward more working-class leisure later.[85]

A similar ambivalence prevailed in other labor federations. The two labor representatives on the government's tourism planning commission, neither of them Communists, consistently placed the issue of social tourism on the CMT's agenda. A rail engineer in the CFTC criticized the commission's decision to award government loans only to hotels that would use the money to elevate their ranking (and therefore their prices too) by adding features such as private baths. Such a policy, he feared, would make hotels even less affordable for the French working class. He also endorsed social tourism as means toward social peace, which if "not profitable in the short term, will be later." The other labor representative, a member of the CGC and head of reception in the luxury Hôtel Royal-Monceau, declared himself "partisan" to the development of social tourism.[86] Even the hotel workers most dependent on foreign tourists hesitated to embrace hotel industry leaders' militant insistence that government tourism funding go to projects aimed at foreign guests.

Unable to achieve unanimity within hotels themselves, France's foreign tourism promoters also failed to convince many French that foreign tourists, especially Americans, were an effective means to secure the radiance of French civilization. The boosters' association of foreign tourism with French radiance contradicted a major theme in the history of tourism and travel writing that viewed tourists as invaders who turned the "natives" into a demeaning spectacle. This negative image of hosting travelers stemmed in part from the legacy of colonial exploration and conquest, as well as from the fact that rich societies generally sent more tourists abroad than poor ones did.[87] In the postwar era, French observers, especially Communists and strong nationalists of any political stripe, were wary of colonization at the hands of the United States. Such concerns were particularly acute given the twin challenges to French grandeur presented by rebellion in its own colonies and by the unprecedented military, economic, cultural, and political influence of the United States in Western Europe.[88] The connection of foreign tourism with French national identity, a linkage at the heart of travel boosters' rhetoric, suggested to many critics not radiance but a metaphorical colonization.

One moment when nationalism worked against rather than for travel boosters came with the French government's decision to waive tourist visas for Americans. To make travel to Europe more convenient, U.S. policymakers after the war began pressuring Western European countries to abolish their visa requirements for American tourists. Some French diplomats supported strict travel controls, worrying that easier access would encourage Mormon missionaries or African American anticolonial activists to enter France, study the language, and then possibly cause trouble in France's overseas colonies.[89] While keeping its visa requirement for American travel in French West Africa, the French government nevertheless eliminated its basic tourist visa for Americans in early 1949.[90] At the same time, Washington's fear of Communists entering the United States meant that, in a break with tradition, France's visa waiver would not be reciprocated. The U.S. government agreed only to waive its fee for French citizens seeking a tourist visa to enter the United States.[91] For some in France, the lack of full reciprocity raised questions about the cost to national prestige entailed by the cultivation of American tourism. The visa waiver was particularly bothersome to *L'Humanité*, the daily paper of the French Communist Party, which denounced the deal as an "open door" that allowed Americans to enter "exactly as if France was an American colony."[92] By the mid-1950s, French diplomats themselves, in internal discussions, began to regret how the 1949 accord had "so frustratingly" violated "the rule of reciprocity."[93]

France's travel promoters' attempts to link American vacationers with national radiance faced an even greater obstacle in the French public's widely held unflattering images of Americans. Given their positions on both the Cold War and French social tourism, French Communists not surprisingly drew especially uncharitable images of American visitors. In its editorial on the visa decision, *L'Humanité* criticized not only how Americans entered France but also how they traveled once they were in France. The paper depicted Americans as uncultured cowboys, "young lords from Oklahoma" who in their search for "old European civilization" turned France into "a sort of Luna Park." The "foreign nobles" indulged themselves in bars and expensive restaurants as they tried to "forget the mediocrity of their American existence." The reference to Luna Park, a Coney Island amusement park that shared its name with an old Parisian nightclub, implied that the cowboy-tourists were more attuned to cheap pleasures than to the radiance of French civilization.[94] Even French defenders of the United States expressed doubt as to whether Americans were willing and able to absorb France's cultural radiance. The business newspaper *Information* in 1952 warned that Americans on speedy tours of Europe did not have "the time to become Francophile." The perceived incompatibility of mass tourism with French radiance meant that, when it came to French foreign affairs, the American tourist was not likely to become a "supplementary defender" of French interests.[95]

In another pessimistic assessment, France's consul in Los Angeles offered a scathing review of American tourists when the embassy in Washington requested in 1952 that he gather any complaints from Americans returning from France. In his reply, the consul dismissed the validity of tourists' complaints and instead singled out Americans as the cause of any problems. Although referring once to "millionaire" tourists who complained that French water was unsafe to drink, he saved his strongest bile for Americans with "modest resources," who "the most often make a bad impression on the French population." Like many French discussions of foreign tourism, the argument at root involved the idea of French national radiance. Some middle-class tourists, according to the consul, did indeed return home "filled with wonder for our cultural riches," but others treated the French "with the same spirit with which they visit Mexico." In search of pleasure, these tourists broke laws and flouted morality in France in ways that would get them jailed back home. Part of the problem, the consul concluded, was the lack of a visa requirement for Americans entering France. With language similar to *L'Humanité*'s "open door" critique, the French diplomat felt that the free entry gave Americans "the feeling of entering a poor country that needs their dollars at all cost." His solution was to reinstate the visa and allow entrance only for Americans with higher incomes, thereby ensuring the most economic gain per tourist while minimizing the "unjustified critiques" that he associated with middle-class tourists.[96]

The Marshall Plan's Defense of the American Tourist

French criticism of American visitors proved especially worrisome to U.S. Marshall Plan officials in the midst of their own campaign to send more middle-class Americans to France. To improve French images of American tourists, and of the United States more generally, U.S. officials in the Economic Cooperation Administration overseeing the Marshall Plan made tourism an increasingly prominent feature of their propaganda efforts in France. The Marshall Planners realized that their effort to keep French public opinion favorable to the United States was in many ways a struggle to reconcile the United States' expanded influence in France with French concerns over national radiance. In 1949, for instance, the French press buzzed with controversy over wide-reaching U.S. influence, from the creation of the North Atlantic Treaty Organization (NATO) to the spread of Coca-Cola.[97] In this context, the ECA's Information Division seized upon the image of American tourists absorbing French culture as a way to build a sense of reciprocity in U.S.-French relations. Highlighting French influence on Americans also was a way to reinforce France's foreign travel boosters by stressing the connection between American guests and national radiance.

The Marshall Plan's principal tool in this campaign to deflate the specter of Americanization was the ECA's widely circulated monthly magazine for French readers. The evolution of this magazine revealed the shifting strategy of the Marshall Plan's propaganda division toward greater coverage of cultural questions and American tourists. Originally called *L'Aide américaine à la France* (American aid to France), the magazine began as a modest production with few images and many dense tables of economic data detailing U.S. aid to France. Distributed free of charge, the magazine claimed a circulation of 110,000 in June 1949.[98] In keeping with the magazine's focus on economic issues, one of its early features on American visitors stressed only their commercial importance. The article even included a drawing of tourists as commodities standing next to sacks of coffee and cotton on a scale.[99]

By early 1950, the magazine gave more attention to tourism, especially as a cultural rather than purely economic topic. The shift was part of a larger change in the magazine toward more human-interest stories and a larger French audience. Renamed *Rapports France–États Unis* (France–United States Relations), the revamped magazine set out to show "the more active participation of France" in the Marshall Plan.[100] The ECA's new emphasis on reciprocity rather than on just U.S. aid reflected concern in the U.S. government that French public opinion had grown more wary of American influence in France. As the ECA pushed its magazine's circulation to over one million, it turned more often to stories of culture-seeking American travelers who could represent the United States in a more human guise than could news reports of a cement factory or a dam reconstruction project.[101]

In contrast to early articles that painted Americans with dollar signs, new stories portrayed them as a means to promote the radiance of French culture. One profile featured a U.S. diplomat who fell in love with Burgundy and its wine after his parents bought a vacation home in the region. Another piece, titled "When American Youth Comes to Breath the Air of Paris," stressed that American students shunned Coca-Cola and instead savored French soft drinks

L'apport du tourisme compense largement le déficit commercial.

Tourists appear as economic commodities in one of the Marshall Plan propaganda magazine's first attempts to present American tourists to French readers (from L'Aide américaine à la France, *special supplement, 1 May 1949).*

such as "*picon-citron.*"[102] One year after France's removal of the tourist visa for Americans, the magazine profiled a former Mormon missionary in France who returned as a visiting professor in 1950. For French readers wary of American missionaries infiltrating France without visas, the article's subheading described the Francophile professor as "a Mormon converted by France."[103]

The ECA's magazine also invoked American visitors to build French support for broader U.S. foreign policy goals. In 1950, while both Communists and Gaullists challenged France's military ties to the United States in the newly formed NATO, the June issue of *Rapports France–États Unis* seemed to skirt the controversial issue by featuring on its cover an image of Basque folk dancers. An editorial comment about the cover picture, however, intervened in the larger policy debate. The editors told French readers that Americans were "particularly fond" of such displays of regional color. Shifting to broader concerns, the editorial explained that French regional culture and Americans' love for it helped both nations "pass beyond the narrow frame of the nation, as it was understood in the 19th century." Touristic displays thus helped cultivate "the primary prerequisite for a larger society—western or Atlantic." With this emphasis on a shared community to go along with an Atlantic-oriented defense policy, the ECA Information Division treated American tourism as a symbol for defining the larger relationship between France and the United States.[104]

For many of its articles, *Rapports France–États Unis* drew on French journalists, often using pro-American writers from *Le Figaro*. French authors helped fulfill the ECA's mission of reducing French fears, whether Communist or right-wing nationalist, that their nation was being "Americanized." *Le Figaro* journalist Georges Ravon, best known to French readers for commentary on the Tour de France bicycle race, wrote in *Rapports* that the French "can be assured that [the visiting American] will not buy our old châteaux, ghosts included," a reference to a popular 1935 film by René Clair in which a wealthy American buys a haunted Scottish château and has it shipped back home to the States.[105] As the magazine stressed in all these articles, the French had little need to worry about Americans taking over France's national heritage.

The ECA's propaganda tool enjoyed some popularity in France, perhaps because of the magazine's light touch and availability at no cost. French newspapers at times reproduced stories and illustrations from the magazine in their own pages, a practice encouraged by the ECA.[106] The ECA was also able to convince Radio Diffusion Française to broadcast a weekly fifteen-minute program on tourism in France, consisting of interviews with American tourists and traveling celebrities, whose comments were dubbed into French.[107]

The ECA's campaign to improve the image of the American tourist, and, by extension, of the United States as a whole, nevertheless suffered in the face of persistent French notions of American tourists as uncultured. French readers of *Rapports France–États Unis*, presumably predisposed to look favorably on the United States, launched critiques of the tourists they saw in the ECA's magazine. One letter by a reader complained of the July 1951 cover, which featured a close-up shot of four American men standing in a street and examining a map of Paris. Despite the men's dapper attire, the Parisian reader deemed the tourists unattractive. "It is not with [their] mugs," the letter-writer advised, "that you can conquer our soul."[108]

Even the French contributors to *Rapports France–États Unis* at times presented American tourists as unattractive or uncultured. The fact that the ECA allowed these negative images to appear suggests that the Marshall Plan propaganda experts were aware that their French readers would not take seriously a flawless portrayal of Americans. One French writer praised the studiousness of Americans, but an accompanying cartoon at the bottom of the page, drawn by a French artist, undermined this claim with an image of tourists speeding through a museum in limousines as a tour guide shouts commentary through a megaphone.[109] Another essay by a French writer mocked Americans for their ignorance of French history, their revulsion for escargot, and their "frenetic visits to museums," which Americans endured only because they felt the need to do something uplifting between rounds of shopping. The article's portrait of Americans was critical enough for the ECA editors to include an opening note distancing the magazine from the French writer's views and returning to their

Another Marshall Plan image attempting to present U.S. tourists in a favorable light. A French reader criticized the effort with the comment: "It is not with [their] mugs that you can conquer our soul" (from Rapports France–États Unis, *October 1951).*

A French cartoon, sanctioned by Marshall Plan information experts, lampooning Americans for a superficial approach to high culture (from Rapports France–États Unis, *August 1950).*

earlier emphasis on tourists' economic value.[110] When Marshall Plan officials felt unsure defending American tourism on cultural grounds, they could always fall back on the economic justifications.

As the ECA's Information Division grew more sophisticated in its cultural propaganda, it at times even turned negative French images of American tourists to its own purposes. A 1950 cartoon pamphlet titled "The Man with the Cigar between his Teeth" used parody and popular culture to defend American guests. Drawn by a French artist and printed by the ECA, it playfully fused the anti-Communist caricature of Bolsheviks with knives clenched in their teeth and the equally common caricature—popular in French Communist publications—of Americans' fondness for cigars and cowboy hats.[111] In the Marshall Plan pamphlet, a swarm of cigar-chomping Americans, men toting cam-

American tourists "invade" France in this Marshall Plan satire of French Communist discourse. If Marshall Plan information specialists could not win respect for U.S. tourists, they could at least mock Communist criticism of U.S. tourism (drawings by "Curry" from Rapports France–États Unis, *1950).*

in loud shirts and cowboy hats, represented a "new Attila" whose
ss manifests itself particularly in July, August, and September."
itriotic calls to resistance, the pamphlet called attention to the
in" of Americans "crossing our countryside in motorized col-
lly Cook Agency tour buses), machine gunning without pity our
vith Kodak shots." Unable to convince the French to see American tourists in wholly positive terms, the ECA's use of parody allowed the U.S.
government to at least exploit negative images in a way that made French
Communists seem ridiculous as well.[112]

Conclusion

The increasing prominence of American tourists in the Marshall Plan's
propaganda reflected U.S. officials' concerns that the French did not solidly
support the U.S. government's program to send more middle-class Americans
to France. The French in fact remained divided over whether American tourists
offered a path toward continued national radiance or toward some sort of
colonization. French images and stereotypes of Americans, while powerful, can
only explain part of this mixed French response. The best way to understand
these internal divisions is to see the subject of American tourism in France as a
point of contest for larger visions of France's future. Travel boosters from both
countries envisioned a France geared toward the service sector rather than
heavy industry and driven more by middle- and upper-class consumers than by
producers or working-class consumers. This elite-led consumer push explains
how André Siegfried, a conservative intellectual well-known for penetrating
critiques of American society and mass tourism, emerged as one of the most
vocal supporters of increasing French efforts to attract American tourists.
Other advocates of greater American tourism expressed confidence that French
culture could survive mass-marketing and packaging with its grandeur and
radiance intact. These boosters also emphasized tourism as a complement to
closer diplomatic relations between France and the United States. Although
promoters of American tourism claimed that all of France benefited from
American visitors, this broad agenda was not universally accepted in postwar
France. While some of the skeptics held negative stereotypes of Americans as
uncultured, much of the criticism had little to do with Americans per se.
Instead, the question of hosting Americans became entangled with concerns
over social policy, national radiance, and industrial development. As a result,
the promoters of American tourism in France faced substantial obstacles in the
late 1940s and early 1950s in their efforts to organize French society around
wealthy American visitors.

Chapter 4

MAKING FRANCE SAFE FOR
MIDDLE-CLASS AMERICANS
THE MARSHALL PLAN AND THE
FRENCH HOTEL INDUSTRY

When a panel of French hoteliers and government technocrats reported in 1948 on how the nation's hotels should evolve, it summarized its views with a grandiose statement: "The hotel, like the ocean liner, must be a permanent exposition of national genius."[1] This ideal, that hotels represented France's face to the world, was popular among members of the French travel industry. But what exactly was "national genius" and how did it manifest itself in hotels? On this question, French government tourism officials, hoteliers, and service employees never reached consensus. For some it meant cultivating older traditions of labor-intensive service, while for others it required cutting labor costs and investing more in new technologies. Among workers, national genius could mean higher wages for hotel employees, which one labor leader argued was the best way to show foreigners the true meaning of "French radiance."[2] Members of the French hotel industry might have shared a common ideology arguing for greater state support and for equating their industry with national radiance, but they took different approaches to the practical matters of how hotels should operate.

What would have been a divisive question in its own right became even more complicated in 1948 when U.S. diplomats began lobbying the French hotel industry to reform in ways that would better serve middle-class American consumers. This program, which the Marshall Planners labeled "hotel modernization," complemented the U.S. government's campaign back in the United States to lure more Americans across the Atlantic. The American push for hotel modernization also reflected the ambitious goals of the Marshall Plan. Rather than simply supplying Europe with foreign aid, Marshall Plan officials pressured Europeans to imitate Americans' managerial and industrial practices. Only by increasing productivity, U.S. leaders argued, could Europe's economy expand and ward off Communism.[3] Yet if productivity was relatively easy to calculate in the case of steel or automobile manufacturing, it was harder to define when the product was something as subjective as a satisfied tourist. In the absence of universal standards for productivity in commercial hospitality, U.S. officials defined hotel modernization according to vacationing habits in the United States. This approach meant encouraging French hoteliers to increase material conveniences and reduce personal service, as more and more American hotels and motels frequented by middle-class Americans were doing. Even if a few reforms called for innovations unknown in the United States, such as a campaign against tipping in hotels and restaurants, the overall tenor of this Marshall Plan agenda was to Americanize French hotels.

The U.S. government's new campaign to reform France's travel industry found a mixed reception in the French hotel world and, consequently, produced only limited results. To understand the varied French reactions requires taking into account the multiple forces at play in the French hotel industry. Widely held conceptions of the hotel as a display of Frenchness to the outside world ensured that the managers and workers in French hotels perceived their own interests not simply through economic calculations but also through the equally powerful lenses of national identity and Cold War politics. Even among hoteliers most dependent on an American clientele, responses to the U.S. agenda most often revolved around the question of whether catering to American leisure habits was compatible with the hotelier's definition of French national radiance.

From Diplomats into Hotel Critics

Convinced of the consumer power of middle-class Americans, the Marshall Plan officials in the Travel Development Section sought to transform the French and European travel industry. Like most U.S. diplomats, members of the TDS approached this task with an air of superiority toward Europeans' business sense. Marshall Plan tourism officials were most frustrated by what they saw as Europeans' inability to grasp consumer marketing. After an inspection of Paris's two airports, TDS chief Théo J. Pozzy remarked to a colleague, "I have been amazed to note the lack of ingenuity" on the part of the French. In this instance, Pozzy was disappointed by the airports' "inadequate and poorly displayed merchandise for American tourists."[4] When European officials proved slow to help plan a series of tours co-sponsored by the TDS and *House Beautiful* magazine, an American travel agent employed by the TDS complained that "in Europe the wheels turn slowly when new ideas revolutionize established procedures."[5]

Since the Marshall Plan agreements gave European nations considerable control over how to use the aid, the U.S. government's main levers of influence were veto power over specific investment allocations and pressure on behalf of favored projects.[6] As a result, U.S. tourism officials were limited to spreading information and lobbying the French government and hoteliers to make changes on their own. U.S. diplomats overseeing the Marshall Plan in the Economic Cooperation Administration made many suggestions to European authorities based on their own travel experiences. For instance, one diplomat complained to the TDS of high taxes on automobiles ferried across the English Channel. Pozzy forwarded the complaint to European officials, along with the deputy's belief that higher levies on large cars discriminated against Americans abroad.[7]

In their quest for a more consumer-friendly Europe, Pozzy and the other Marshall Planners made hotels their central concern. Hotels were particularly important to American experiences in France. The vast majority of Americans visiting France, 94 percent according to one 1950 ECA poll, stayed in a hotel.[8] Each "tourist-class" hotel in France bore a classification set by the Tourism Commissariat, ranging from four stars to one star. Below the tourist-class ranks, a large number of unrated, often residential, hotels served a mainly working-class clientele. American consumers' importance was especially evident in establishments at the upper end of the French hotel world. Foreigners comprised strong majorities of the clientele in France's four- and three-star hotels, with Americans the largest foreign nationality, especially in top Parisian hotels.[9]

Pozzy himself stayed mindful of his Marshall Plan mission during his frequent travels through France and Europe on business and pleasure. As his son and frequent traveling companion later recalled, Pozzy regularly offered advice to owners or managers of the hotels and restaurants he visited.[10] After an unsatisfactory stay in one provincial hotel, Pozzy wrote French tourism commissaire Henri Ingrand to complain about the lack of a bellhop, scarce bathtubs, and, on the third floor, a dirty toilet seat cover. "This hotel certainly was first-class—in 1900," he chided.[11] Pozzy also forwarded to Ingrand complaints from individual Americans, including one irate letter that suggested that certain French and Italian service workers "be reeducated as to the absolute necessity of customer good-will" or else "be eliminated from contacts with tourists."[12]

Pozzy could write or pass on such brusque language to French and European tourism leaders in part because of the attention he gave to befriending those Europeans. Pozzy's son remembers how his family would socialize with the families of such leaders as France's Ingrand. Drawing on his status as a naturalized U.S. citizen from a wealthy French family, Pozzy purchased a hunting lodge outside Paris with an old high school friend. From this social base, he invited French and European tourism officials and industry leaders to weekend bird hunts. Personal relations thus provided one avenue for the Marshall Plan's push for reform.[13]

The Marshall Planners' emphasis on reforming French hotels rather than building new ones reflected both the rapid recovery of French hotels from the war and the limited funds made available for tourism by the French government. Although many French hotels during the war suffered from damage and lack of maintenance, the industry as a whole rebounded quickly. By the end of 1948, just as the TDS began operation, France offered 95 percent as many tourist-class hotel rooms as it did before the war.[14] Marshall Planners in France urged the French government in early 1950 to invest more in tourism, but French planning authorities continued to favor heavy industry.[15] ECA tourism experts nevertheless took the limited resources in stride, stressing that hotel modernization was as much about changing service norms as it was increasing capital investment.[16]

The French government's lack of new hotel construction funds and the ECA's focus on reform hampered plans by American hotel chains to use Marshall Plan funds to subsidize expansion into Europe. As early as 1948, American companies such as the Inter-Continental Hotel Corporation, a subsidiary of Pan American World Airways, and Hilton International lobbied Marshall Plan officials and the French government to make funds available for new hotels in France. In one meeting, Pan Am president Juan Trippe urged ECA administrator Paul Hoffman to circumvent European governments' influence over the use of Marshall Plan funds.[17] Yet U.S. officials proved unwilling to battle European governments over scarce investment funds just for the sake of American hotel chains.[18] In the end, only the Turkish government invited a U.S. hotel chain to break ground with Marshall Plan money, a decision that resulted in the opening of the Istanbul Hilton in 1955.[19]

Rather than impose U.S.-owned hotel chains on the French, Marshall Plan officials took a more subtle but ultimately more expansive approach. In an effort to Americanize all French hotels, they focused on persuading French hoteliers to imitate the practices of the American hotel industry and "reach the as yet largely untapped middle-income travel market in the United States."[20] As the Marshall Planners stressed, to appeal to those Americans, French hoteliers needed to modernize and increase their productivity by learning from American hotels. The Marshall Plan tourism program thus bore the stamp of modernization ideology, with its focus on middle-class consumer power, rationalized labor practices, investment in new technology, and the application of American business techniques.

The U.S. government showed little interest in promoting tourism for the French themselves. Indeed, what distinguished the Marshall Plan's travel promotion from conventional modernization theory was that the middle-class consumer base was to come not from France but from the United States. Given

France's dollar shortage, the TDS emphasized that French leisure in general needed to be discouraged so that French hoteliers and retailers could concentrate on attracting a maximum of dollars from Americans. The TDS calculated, for instance, that a single dress bought by an American tourist had the same value to the French economy as three dresses bought by French consumers.[21] U.S. officials generally treated tourism by the French masses as a problem, especially given the limited supply of leisure accommodations and rail cars. The French thus needed to end their tradition of vacationing in August in order "to make room for visiting Americans."[22] With its faith that American tourist dollars could lift France's economy as a whole, the TDS had little patience for French travel, a view that placed the United States on the side of French conservatives in France's long-running debate about paid vacations and "social tourism" for workers.

U.S. officials repeatedly emphasized to Europeans the need to adapt to the buying power of the American middle class. According to an ECA report, deluxe hotels were important dollar earners, but the "great need" of Western Europe was in "moderately priced hotels" to cater to the new type of American consumer. At the same time, these less expensive hotels also required "a higher standard of sanitary facilities, comfort, and convenience, in order to satisfy American visitors."[23] A Commerce Department official, speaking before a meeting of national tourism organizations in 1949, urged that "special attention" be paid to lodging "the rapidly expanding portion of the American touring army which is what we refer to as the middle-income group."[24]

Marshall Plan officials drew their views on travel trends from an American hospitality industry that was itself in transition. In the nineteenth century, American hoteliers had created some of the largest and most opulent urban and resort hotels in the world. Many, however, struggled through the Great Depression and were past their prime by the late 1940s. The real twentieth-century boom came in motels, whose popularity soared with the automobile. From 1928 to 1948, the number of motels rose from 3,000 to 26,000, outnumbering more traditional hotels. Less expensive than most hotels, motels cut costs by doing away with stately lobbies and dining rooms and by reducing the amount of personal service and attention devoted to guests. For middle-class Americans, who generally had less desire to see and be seen in high-society circles, the increased anonymity of motels could represent an advantage rather than a drawback.[25]

Although still cheaper than hotels, American motels in the postwar era offered increasing levels of material niceties. In the 1930s, the quality of motels had varied so greatly that motorists customarily inspected motel rooms before agreeing to check in. In the 1940s, middle-class consumers, aided by a return to prosperity after years of depression and war, developed a heightened emphasis on physical comfort.[26] By the 1940s, organizations such as the American Motel Association and the American Automobile Association pressured motels to offer features such as private showers, bathtubs, and hot water. Along with increased expectations for air-conditioning, these motel industry standards reflected a trend in American vacationing habits away from the "roughing-it" style of early automobile tourism and toward a new style of leisure, in which Americans came to expect as many if not more comforts and modern conveniences than they had at home.[27]

The need for American motel keepers to update their rooms with the latest technology and comforts favored the emergence of motel chains that began to displace the early mom-and-pop motels. When Holiday Inn, the most successful of the chains, emerged in the early 1950s, it typified the new emphasis on higher standards and modest prices. With attached restaurants and the latest comforts, such as in-room telephones, Holiday Inn also symbolized how the once-clear distinction between motels and hotels had become blurred in the pursuit of middle-class travelers. This shift in the hospitality industry also traveled up the class ladder. Stately hotels increasingly became the property of emerging chains such as Hilton Hotels, which used economies of scale and innovative time-motion studies to help raise material standards while offering rates that, although expensive, attracted some middle-class clients.[28]

Meanwhile, European hotels developed according to different priorities, with greater emphasis on labor-intensive service. As one group of French travel experts reported in 1950, hotel standards were "purely subjective" and depended on national customs. The French placed a higher value on hotel restaurants and on personal service, while "Anglo-Saxons," in the report's words, emphasized "certain material amenities," particularly private bathrooms.[29] Elite hotels such as the George V offered private baths in all or most rooms. Other tourist-class hotels assumed that guests could make do with common facilities, but they still offered valets, porters, and other service personnel in numbers beyond what Americans expected from a hotel of similar price in the United States.

For aficionados of European luxury hotels, detailed personal service could represent one of the voyage's main attractions. On arrival, guests could watch a *baggagiste* whisk their luggage upstairs while a porter escorted them into the hotel. Guests would then meet the concierge, or head porter, who could answer questions on what to do in town. If the traveler was in Paris and hoped for a lively evening, the concierge, or his assistant at the hotel's ticket office, might quickly estimate the guest's tolerance for nudity and pricey champagne and then recommend a suitable nightclub. For dining, the concierge would likely refer the guest to the maître d'hôtel, whom skilled tourists would understand to be not the head of the whole hotel but only that of the hotel restaurant. On reaching their room, guests in some luxury hotels would find a valet carefully unpacking the luggage, yet another step in the flurry of service offered by the hotel. Some clients found thrills and status in navigating this pampered and personalized world. Consider one such tourist, an Austrian man, who recalled receiving a disapproving and "very old-fashioned look" from a valet who unpacked his bags but found no pajamas. "After this setback," he noted, "it took me years to regain my self-confidence and improve my valet-rating, which is to a hotel guest what the Gallup Poll is to a politician."[30]

Despite the wide range of standards for commercial hospitality, the TDS did not so much respond to an existing crisis as envision a future when American middle-class tastes would dominate in Europe. In contrast to the urgent tone of the Marshall Planners, Americans generally displayed satisfaction with existing French and European hotels. According to one 1950 ECA market study, 73 percent of American tourists found French hotels either excellent or good, a figure second in Europe only to Switzerland's 89 percent approval rating. While one-quarter of American tourists found French hotels expensive, half reported the prices "reasonable," and one-fifth considered them inexpensive.[31]

In the absence of a clear and present hotel crisis, the ECA instead looked toward a future of middle-class Americans roaming Europe. The future, Marshall Planners believed, belonged to consumers who would prefer to do without the class-tinged rituals of interacting extensively with hotel porters and valets. Their prototypical American was one who would insist on four-star material comforts at two-star prices. Three years after the ECA's 1950 poll found Americans largely satisfied with their European hotels, a *Saturday Evening Post* article hinted that middle-class Americans were more likely than wealthier tourists to be unhappy with European hotels. According to the *Post*, American travel agents agreed "unanimously" that the lack of private bathrooms in foreign hotels was "the biggest headache in the business." Interviewed in the same article, a French government tourism official in New York hoped for a more stoic attitude among tourists and told the magazine's middle-class readers that "an American must make concessions if he cannot afford de luxe accommodations in Europe."[32]

By criticizing French hotels, Pozzy and the other Marshall Planners were, whether consciously or not, also extending a tradition of French consumer lobbying. Early in the twentieth century, the French urban elites in the Touring Club de France launched their own campaign to improve the nations' hotels. Yet the specific goals of the Marshall Plan differed from the Touring Club's prewar complaints. The club's blueprint of a model "hygienic" inn for well-off travelers in 1907 had just one bathtub for a fourteen-bedroom establishment.[33] Even after the war, French tolerance for communal bathrooms continued. In 1950, the French government declared that a three-star hotel needed private baths in only 10 to 30 percent of its rooms to keep its rating.[34]

In encouraging Europeans to deliver more material comforts with cheaper prices, Marshall Plan officials stressed the very American concepts of productivity and modernization.[35] "A hotel must be considered a production plant," wrote Pozzy to one European official.[36] According to this factory metaphor, hotels needed to reduce the labor required for each unit of production, in this case an occupied room or a satisfied tourist. Hotel and restaurant equipment thus needed to be "ultramodern and extremely efficient."[37] Anticipating that this program might inspire fears of Americanization among Europeans, Pozzy insisted in a speech before European hoteliers that "modernization" did not imply pure imitation of the United States. Nevertheless, the only allowances for European tradition that he mentioned in the speech were for European hoteliers to borrow their decorating schemes and restaurant fare from the surrounding region.[38] In other words, the local color prized by tourists was acceptable, but European traditions of service and business operations needed to cede to newer models.

Few features of the travel experience were too small to escape the attention of Pozzy and the TDS. The Marshall Planners' efforts to influence the everyday elements of travel in France revealed an overarching desire to make Western Europe as nonthreatening as possible for visiting Americans. Marshall Plan travel experts targeted some of the more egregious problems, such as hotels that charged Americans higher prices than they did other tourists.[39] TDS officials also criticized European business practices that they believed disoriented Americans, as in Pozzy's campaign to have hotels list prices in each room and quote rates with tax and service already included.[40] The TDS also opposed the French restaurant cover charge, which many restaurateurs added to guarantee a small profit from clients who lingered at a table and ordered little. Pozzy lobbied the French government to eliminate the charges, which he claimed were "regarded as a racket by Americans" who did not understand why they should pay entry fees "even in small restaurants."[41] Advancing what might be called an open-door policy for French restaurants, Pozzy and the rest of the TDS pursued for middle-class American consumers what U.S. diplomats had sought for decades for U.S. businesses: a commercial environment made safe and accessible for Americans who ventured abroad.

Even though Americans commonly tipped at home, Marshall Plan officials also wanted to eliminate the practice in Europe on grounds that, in a foreign context, knowing when and how much to tip caused Americans too much anxiety. Tipping did indeed occupy a prominent place in American travel guides as a subject for practical instruction, particularly important given that the French tipped some service workers, such as theater ushers, who in the United States went unpaid by customers. In his 1950 guide to Paris, travel writer and humorist Art Buchwald expressed common anxieties over tipping by borrowing from Shakespeare:

> To tip, or not to tip; that is the question:
> Whether 'tis nobler in the mind to suffer
> The barbs and glances of outraged waiters,
> Or to give francs against this sea of faces
> And by placating end them.

His soliloquy ended with the line, "Thus 'ser-veece' does make cowards of us all."[42] In seeking to eliminate tips, the TDS did not hope to impose an American model onto Europe but only to make Europe predictable and worry-free for Americans. To encourage the French to adopt a service-included system, the TDS collected complaints from tourists, such as the one from a traveler who claimed that the entire staff of a French hotel had asked him for tips. So ingrained was the French habit of asking for money, according to this disgruntled American, that even a French guest staying in an adjacent room had solicited him with an open hand.[43]

Perhaps the only aspect of French hospitality that Marshall Plan officials left untouched was the cooking in France's hotel restaurants. At one point, U.S. diplomats considered lending American expertise to French hotel chefs by distributing studies of American restaurants, but they backed down without trying. In the words of one official, the French "are still, to the astonishment of American operators, through apparently no system whatsoever, able to sell amazingly good food at amazingly low prices."[44] After years of training and apprenticeship, French restaurateurs might have been surprised to learn that they lacked any system. But if Marshall Planners were willing to tolerate French tradition in the kitchen, they remained eager to lend their own methods to the rest of the French travel industry to ensure easier navigation for middle-class Americans.

A Mixed Reception

With their emphasis on accommodating middle-class American tastes, Marshall Plan travel promoters heightened divisions that had been latent within France's travel industry. In their trade journals and professional meetings, hoteliers and hotel workers debated how best to serve Americans. Some hoteliers viewed the Marshall Plan's focus on productivity as a way to ensure that French hotels would stay up-to-date and thus continue to serve as displays of French radiance before foreigners. Others viewed the emphasis on productivity as a challenge to the labor-intensive styles of personal service that, to many hoteliers, defined French commercial hospitality. A number of hotel workers also objected to the Marshall Plan's program out of concern with work conditions or over Cold War ideological differences. Whether the French acted for profit, national tradition, or ideological leanings, the Marshall Planners found themselves negotiating contested terrain when they involved themselves with tourism in France.

Even before the Marshall Plan, French hoteliers had begun to discuss how to serve Americans, often in a bemused tone that revealed a discomfort underlying their attempts to cater to American guests. At the George V and its sister hotel, the Plaza-Athénée, the employee newsletter in 1945 attempted to explain that, if Americans seemed "somewhat wasteful," it was less because of personal vice and more the result of the United States' large-scale and abundant natural resources, which had created a people with no time for penny-pinching.[45] Dispensing advice to colleagues in 1950, one Paris hotelier warned that to treat an American like a British client would be a "grave error." He then proceeded to describe American tourists through a host of French stereotypes about U.S. culture. In conversation with guests from the United States, he wrote, it was best to avoid complicated matters such as literature, music, and art and instead to stick with movies. Even better would be to inquire about "his home town, lost in the depths of Arizona," a subject that might prompt the guest to forego the customary American handshake and jump straight to a hug. According to the self-proclaimed expert on Americans, French hotels could also impress American clients by replacing their library with a bar, preferably one with soft music. As the hotelier observed, "boredom is, with lack of hygiene, a great enemy of the American who wants, above all, 'to have fun.'" This hotelier contrasted his portrait of the American as provincial pleasure-seeker with his image of English tourists, who were "more cold, more reserved, more distant" but also more interested in learning and understanding France.[46]

At a time when the vast majority of American visitors to France were white, a small number of French hoteliers went so far in anticipating American norms as to reproduce racial segregation. An investigation in 1950 by French human rights groups singled out seven hotels in Paris that excluded nonwhite clients, mainly those from France's West African colonies, allegedly to please white American and British guests. Framing the issue in terms of national radiance, the human rights newspaper *Le Droit de vivre* (The Right to Life) argued that hotels "must be the first to represent to our visitors the most pure

French traditions" and insisted that Americans "must take us as we are."[47] In the National Assembly, the scandal became entwined with Cold War and colonial politics. Socialist and Communist politicians in the assembly applauded condemnations of "Anglo-Saxon" tourists' racism, and both the left and center banks of the assembly expressed sympathy with African war veterans who were denied hotel service in the country they had fought to defend.[48]

In the end, the combined force of French republicanism and colonialism overpowered the few Parisian practitioners of Jim Crow. Under public pressure, the Tourism Commissariat encouraged Parisian hotel organizations to condemn the practice.[49] The hotel industry as a whole never defended racist practices, but one of the more conservative trade periodicals lashed back at the critics. While not explicitly endorsing racial discrimination, the paper argued that the bigger offense was for French citizens to criticize their own hotel industry in the face of foreign competition. Deploying the domestic metaphor often used by the more right-wing advocates of foreign tourism in France, the paper insisted that the French "wash our dirty laundry within the family in the most strict intimacy."[50] Like the 1949 visa waiver, the episode revealed how associations between tourism and French national identity proved a double-edged sword for hoteliers. Whatever the gains of tying their businesses to national radiance, hoteliers also had to accommodate multiple conceptions of French identity.

Although the application of Jim Crow segregation on the banks of the Seine was something of an anomaly among French hotels, the controversy reflected a more general concern among hoteliers and tourism officials about catering to perceived American preferences while still preserving distinct French features. The philosophy at the George V was not to imitate American hotels but, in the words of the hotel's internal newsletter, to make improvements and innovations "à la française." If the French atmosphere disappeared, managers reasoned, Americans would have no more reason to go abroad.[51] For one Dijon hotelier, this balancing act inspired the installation of a plumbing system that brought white and red wine into each room. If American hotels excelled by offering ample ice water, he reasoned, his hotel could offer Burgundy's wine. Exemplifying the idea of modernization "à la française," the hotelier made sure that the white wine came out properly chilled.[52] Members of the Commission de modernisation du tourisme, the industry-government panel that advised France's economic planners, also set forth a dualistic ideal that would integrate hotel innovation with traditional French features. While calling for the scientific study of employee and consumer behavior, the commission also emphasized that "the qualities of good sense, measure, and distinction in taste, so specifically French, must shine in the projects."[53] French tourism chief Henri

Ingrand went even further in embracing French specificity, expressing his preference for small-sized establishments that, if not the most efficient, still displayed "the artisanal character" of French hotels.[54]

To counter this emphasis on French tradition, the ECA tourism experts adopted the common Marshall Plan strategy of guiding European industry leaders on study missions to the United States. Although largely funded by European employers, these trips were organized and hosted by U.S. officials and business leaders. As with most of the productivity tours, the French hotel delegation came from upper-level management, since French labor unions generally stayed away from the trips to avoid being seen as too friendly with the United States. Between January and May 1950, three groups of European hoteliers took five-week tours. They met with key members of the U.S. international travel industry, including advertising firms, travel magazine editors, and representatives from American Express and the American Society of Travel Agents.[55] They also met with American hoteliers and accounting experts and studied motels, then barely known in France. All the while, the U.S. officials who led the tour emphasized the consumer power of the American middle class. Herbert Wilkinson, the head of the Commerce Department's Travel Branch and a close partner of the Marshall Plan's TDS, greeted the first group in January with a speech that extolled the importance of "the middle-income bracket" in the United States. This "new type of American tourist," Wilkinson told the European hoteliers, "is not a sophisticated traveler, but he is friendly and appreciative."[56]

After the trip, the head of the French delegation, luxury hotel manager Lucien Serre, endorsed the Marshall Plan emphasis on adapting to middle-class Americans. In an interview, Serre warned against "badly placed chauvinism" among French hoteliers who needed to realize that theirs were "no longer the avant-garde" among the world's hotels.[57] The delegation's report, written by Serre, focused on ways to make Americans feel more at home in France. Hotel restaurants, for instance, ought to serve ice water immediately after Americans sit at the table. Coffee was not to be too strong and was best served in the large cups that Americans preferred for all their beverages. Hotel rooms ought to be furnished with modern pieces, since "old furniture amuses Americans, but does not attract them." Hygiene occupied a special place in Serre's report. Cleanliness in the United States was "carried out to a point which would surprise us," and hotel kitchens "have become, in America, spotless laboratories, with sanitary conditions known only in hospital operating rooms." Bathrooms required free soap and hot water at all hours. The report ended with a full-page map depicting a "commonly-used bathroom in America," complete with a caption pointing out that Americans generally did not use bidets.[58]

Reflecting Marshall Plan officials' awareness of French concerns with Americanization, Serre included a caveat that French hotels should still "retain a large part of our traditions," since such "attractions give the voyage its very meaning." Although he did not detail those French features to preserve, he did at least note that hotels could earn extra revenue by adding a gift shop, where tourists would presumably buy souvenirs distinctive to France.[59]

Serre's criticism of his nation's hotels also emphasized vital concerns within the hotel industry, especially its calls for more aid from the French government. Remodeling hotels to please Americans, Serre realized, required money. Since "the traveling American *always wants the best*," the French hotelier feared a "vicious circle" in which modernization would lead to higher prices that would in turn deter middle-class tourists. Serre thus called for more government-subsidized loans, fewer taxes, and the deregulation of hotel room rates as incentives for the industry.[60]

Serre's report represented an unusually complete consensus between French hoteliers and the Marshall Plan reform program. His report pleased the ECA, which distributed 6,000 copies to the French travel industry. The *Christian Science Monitor* praised the hotelier's visit in a way suggestive of how American hopes were not just in restoring France's balance of payments but also in the tempting idea that France and all of Europe could be made less intimidating for Americans. In the *Monitor*'s eager words, "Ice water served with no eyebrow raising in Parisian pensions may be in the offing for American tourists."[61]

In their reform campaign, the Marshall Planners also recruited French hoteliers and writers for its French-language magazine, *Rapports France–États Unis*. The magazine invited sympathetic leaders from the French travel industry to endorse the basic items on the TDS agenda, such as the need for fixed-price menus and hotel employee training centered on the "Anglo-Saxon temperament."[62] The ECA sometimes reprinted these articles in free brochures that it then distributed to the French travel industry. The Marshall Planners also employed popular writers and cartoonists in its campaign. Pierre Daninos, a best-selling humorist and contributor to *Le Figaro*, wrote an essay titled "The Tourist and You," addressed to both hoteliers and hotel workers. Daninos echoed the speeches of U.S. officials in describing the free-spending American traveler of the 1930s as "a prehistoric species." French tourism workers therefore ought not to expect the lavish bills and tips for which Americans had become famous. Modest-budget postwar Americans, Daninos warned, did not appreciate being seen as "the International Monetary Fund personified." To drive home the article's message, *Rapports France–États Unis* added cartoons of French hotel workers yelling at or soliciting tips from Americans. Providing a portrait of Americans considerably more charitable than the sketches offered by *L'Hôtellerie* and the George V newsletter, Daninos instructed the French to avoid treating the postwar American as a cultural neophyte or "child." To Daninos, the United States had found a new maturity during World War II and the early Cold War, and the American touring France might now be a wartime veteran or even one of America's newly respected intellectuals.[63]

Prominent voices in the French hotel industry, however, equated the recommendations of Serre and Daninos as a threat to France's national radiance. Speaking a few months after Serre's hotel study trip, Jean Bertrand, a Riviera hotel owner and influential member of the Fédération nationale de l'industrie hôtelière, worried that French traditions might be lost in "this moment where productivity haunts the spirit of our economists." He admitted that the French could learn how to cater to Americans and praised the ECA for lobbying the French government to reduce its taxes on hotels. Nevertheless, the hotelier insisted that "the constant preoccupation with better productivity" was antithetical to "the French conception of hotelery." He was particularly critical of one French senator who had called for "a rationalization" of luxury hotels through a reduction in the size of their workforce. Bertrand feared that French hotels without labor-intensive personal service and attention for clients would no longer be French.[64]

An editorialist for *L'Hôtellerie*, also writing after Serre's trip, challenged the economic importance and cultural worth of American tourism. Lamenting how every study of the French travel industry seemed to focus on American guests, he demanded more attention to visitors from neighboring European countries. Referring to an ECA study that mentioned housewifery as the most common occupation among visitors from the United States, the hotel journalist questioned "the authority of housewives to appreciate good reception in hotels." This feminized view of American tourism drew on a broader French stereotype of the United States as a society where men were so busy earning money that they irresponsibly abandoned cultural life to the whims of American women. On the subject of hygiene, a central concern for Serre, Americans' high standards of cleanliness appeared to this writer as an American "phobia." And on the question of whether to serve ice water with meals, the editorialist coolly responded: "I will make no comment. It is sad, quite simply."[65]

Criticism of Serre and the Marshall Plan reform agenda reflected many hoteliers' concerns with national radiance and with finding some form of reciprocity in U.S.-French relations. That same editorialist emphasized that, rather than "bending oneself" to Americans, French hotels should "have them appreciate" French norms.[66] When other writers in *L'Hôtellerie* adopted a more positive tone regarding Americans, they too stressed the idea of radiance: "He [the American] will give us the means to make our necessary purchases

French cartoonists and the Marshall Planners teamed up to show French hotel and restaurant employees how not to serve the postwar U.S. tourist (from Rapports France–États Unis, July 1950*).*

and, at the same time, he will take a 'bath' in high culture, of which he increasingly understands the necessity."[67] In other words, conceptualizing American travelers as an economic boon for the nation was not enough to satisfy all French hosts. Positive French views of American tourists were to a large degree dependent on the idea that France had something of cultural value to offer their dollar-laden guests.

Other sources of hotelier opposition to the Marshall Plan revolved around more purely economic issues. In 1951, the ECA and the U.S. embassy in Paris sponsored an exhibit for French hoteliers' annual trade fair in Paris, emphasizing the need to cut prices to appeal to middle-class Americans. According to the embassy's summary of the exhibit's reception, French hoteliers on the whole remained skeptical that they could reduce their room rates and still earn a profit.[68] Another point of contention involved the Marshall Plan campaign against tipping and for "everything-included" billing. On this front, ECA officials did enjoy some victories. In 1950, Pozzy celebrated with leading French restaurateurs when the Union des restaurants français introduced plaques that would identify dining establishments as "Restaurants du tourisme," a status granted only to restaurants that replaced cover charges and tips with an everything-included (*tout compris*) system.[69] Despite this victory, many hotel, restaurant, and café owners preferred the tipping system. With tips, employers paid the bulk of their labor costs under the table and in the process reduced their taxes. To preserve this system, hoteliers managed to block a proposal by French economic planners that would have made everything-included billing a prerequisite for any hotel seeking loans from the state.[70] Resistance from owners to the everything-included format ensured that the question of tipping would continue unresolved through the 1950s.

On the issue of service charges, the Marshall Planners shared a common agenda with French service employees, who had traditionally favored everything-included billing. Nevertheless, neither French workers nor Marshall Plan officials effectively made use of this opportunity to advance their goals. ECA officials themselves had little direct contact with labor organizations in the travel industry and instead preferred to cultivate ties with government officials and hotel and restaurant managers and owners.[71] Among French tourism workers, Cold War concerns led Communist-affiliated hotel labor unions to view skeptically the United States' expanded influence in postwar France, including the hotel modernization program. This lack of cooperation despite a shared agenda highlighted the importance of national identity and Cold War ideology in shaping French responses to the Marshall Plan hotel campaign.

A series of hotel labor protests in 1949 illustrated the shared goals of service workers and Marshall Planners, as well as the limits of their actual cooperation. In luxury establishments such as the Hôtel Crillon in Paris, members of the Communist Confédération générale du travail and the Catholic Confédération française des travailleurs chrétiens staged work stoppages to pressure hotel managers who allegedly abused the everything-included system. Several months later, workers printed cards in English and French that warned "This Hotelier is dishonest" and invited clients to deduct 15 percent from their bills and give the money directly to the staff.[72] When these union tactics came to the attention of Pozzy, the Marshall Plan official urged French hoteliers to address the problem. In Pozzy's words, the workers' visible discontent "has a very bad effect on the American tourist as it confirms his impression that the service charges are not rightly divided among the staff members."[73] Nevertheless, thi. shared agenda produced no greater cooperation between the American diplomats and the hotel workers.

Cold War ideology played an important role in fostering this divide between service workers and U.S. diplomats. For unions in the CGT, the Marshall Plan's injunctions to cater to Americans seemed to presage a loss of national grandeur. The Communist hotel and restaurant labor press greeted with skepticism the Marshall Plan's TDS on its arrival in France. In one 1949 article, Communist deputy Virgile Barel, from the touristic Alpes-Maritimes department, welcomed American tourists for their dollars but remained suspicious of "the American imperialists" working in the TDS. "Just as we do not believe in Father Christmas," Barel declared, "we are suspicious when the Marshall Plan occupies itself with tourism." Barel emphasized the section of the tourism program in which the ECA offered investment protections to American hotel chains, a policy that Barel feared would make Western Europe dependent on the United States.[74]

Relations between the ECA and French hotel labor continued on a sour note. To lodge the numerous American officials and consultants passing through Europe, the ECA and other U.S. agencies occupied entire Paris hotels and at times even became the official employer of the hotel staff. As were all U.S. federal employees at the time, those French hotel workers were then required to sign forms denying Communist ties and promising not to strike against the U.S. government. This policy provoked protests in the French National Assembly, where delegates from the Left bemoaned both the ideological insult and the forfeiture of the right to strike. Communist deputy André Mercier charged that some hotel employees had been fired for their political views. Speaking just after the creation of NATO, Mercier called the affair "a pre-taste of the occupation regime." Defenders of the United States countered that the employees received a 20 percent increase in wages as compensation. This clash between French hotel labor and the anti-Communist climate of postwar America led hotel workers to put up posters declaring, "PARISIANS, you will never allow France to become an American colony."[75]

This conflict over union activism contributed to hotel labor's more general mistrust of American influence in the hotel industry. When the inaugural issue of a new hotel trade magazine featured Pozzy and an American Express manager on its front page, one member of the Communist-affiliated CGT hotel union in Paris reacted with suspicion. Responding to Pozzy's article, which championed everything-included billing, the hotel worker broke with the traditional labor view and suggested that Americans had enough adding machines to figure out the service charges for themselves. In response to American

...im that it was the leading client of French hotels, the hotel unionist
...riotic call for French working-class tourism and reminded readers
clients were still more numerous than Americans. To the U.S.
...uggestion that French hotels replace the single large bed with the
separate beds that Americans preferred, he asked, "How far does
one want to coca-colonize us!"[76] Small differences between American and
French hotel furniture, combined with Cold War ideology and the French
Left's social claims, alienated the ECA from at least this one hotel worker.

Anti-American rhetoric did not suit all French hotel workers. Reflecting
broader divisions in France's labor organizations, dissenters within the CGT-
led hotel unions formed an "independent" anti-Communist Paris hotel union
in 1948.[77] Assigning its own foreign policy meaning to hotel work, the union's
newsletter urged employees to respect U.S. Cold War policies. The new union
challenged the ideological balancing act of the Communist hotel activists, who
wanted to profit from American tourism while condemning U.S. foreign policy. Signs in Paris calling for Americans to return home threatened to drive
away American guests, "the richest contingent of tourists." One member of the
independent union feared that Americans would head to "a more welcoming,
industrious country not at all desirous to kill itself by imbecilic graffiti."[78]
Although their acceptance of American influence in France marked a break
with the CGT hotel unions, these workers continued the CGT's habit of interpreting American tourism through the lenses of both economic interest and
Cold War ideology.

Conclusion

While U.S. officials lobbied for some practices that had no equivalent in the
United States, such as everything-included billing, most elements of the Marshall Plan's self-proclaimed modernization agenda specifically sought to make
French hotels more like those in the United States. The Marshall Plan's hotel
campaign thus offers an opportunity to reflect on the nature of Americanization and modernization. Viewed in a broad historical perspective, the Marshall
Plan's Americanization drive represented one stage in a longer set of negotiations in France between middle-class consumer advocates and the producers of
service. The U.S. government's hotel reformers advanced an agenda that had
been launched earlier by the French consumer advocates in the Touring Club
de France. Nevertheless, the new American nature of this postwar campaign
altered French responses to the modernization debate. As a result, the best way
to understand why some in the French hotel industry supported and others
opposed the postwar reform agenda is to pay attention to both economic

interest and varying conceptions of French nationalism. Many hoteliers financial reasons to resist U.S.-backed reforms such as everything-included billing and the installation of private bathrooms. Just as important were cultural and ideological beliefs, especially the question of whether American tourism was compatible with French national radiance. For some hoteliers, adapting to Americans seemed the best way to improve their economic standing, as well as the nation's, while also spreading French culture to their guests. Yet to hoteliers who considered Americans uncultured colonizers, accommodating Americans' travel preferences was a threat to hotels' traditional status as expressions of national identity. This opposition could make for strange bedfellows. Defenders of elite artisanal hotel practices took the same side against the Marshall Plan as did French Communists, who viewed hotel reform as symbolic of an American ruling class that threatened to enforce repressive labor practices on France.

Much of this disagreement over hotels also revolved around the highly subjective nature of the concepts of productivity and modernization, especially when applied to hospitality. To the Marshall Planners, productivity meant lodging a maximum of tourists in rooms with private baths with a minimum of labor, a standard grounded in the context of American commercial hospitality. Yet many French observers remained skeptical of this standard. After all, what made private baths in every room necessarily more efficient than communal facilities on each hall? And what was especially modern about serving ice water with dinner or providing coffee in large cups? By the same token, most French hoteliers lamented the high cost of hotel labor, but many defended those costs against the productivity experts. From the artisanal hoteliers' point of view, traditions such as labor-intensive reception service were not impediments to productivity but the very product that French hotels offered.

That many French hoteliers and hotel workers resisted this Americanization campaign did not mean that they were opposed to modernization per se. Indeed, French hoteliers were as vehement as the Marshall Planners in insisting that hotels formed an important industry that the French government needed to subsidize as it did steel manufacturers. French hoteliers who declined the advice offered by U.S. officials did not so much oppose modernization as hold to a different vision of modernity. Theirs was a modernization in which hotels, benefiting from greater state support, would be able to welcome middle-class tourists into the rituals of elite culture rather than having to adapt to middle-class American norms. Given these cultural conceptions of hotels, much of the U.S. modernization agenda remained unfulfilled by the time the Marshall Plan tourism program ended in 1951.[79] As we will see, many of the same issues would also resurface a decade later under Charles de Gaulle's Fifth Republic.

Chapter 5

PLEASURE WITH A PURPOSE

THE STRUGGLE TO CREATE AN

ATLANTIC COMMUNITY

In 1949, a group of American farmers arrived in Paris for a study tour of Western European agriculture. Their trip had been organized by Marshall Plan officials, who, along with French diplomats, encouraged such special-interest tours as a way to bolster the American public's support for Marshall Plan aid. The farmers, who paid $1,200 apiece for the month-long tour, made sure that their trips also included the traditional sights. On their first night in Paris, many headed to the famed nightclubs and erotic spectacles of Montmartre. Some men ventured out on their own. Others took in the city night with their wives. A group of married women went out on their own, with one telling a *Chicago Daily Tribune* reporter that "there's no reason we shouldn't have fun on the trip."[1]

The *Tribune*'s coverage of the tour, a seemingly innocent report on the pleasures of visiting Paris, touched a nerve with U.S. and French officials. This was not the first time the American media had transformed an agricultural study tour into an exposé on rural Americans' encounters with Parisian nightlife. *Life* magazine's coverage of an earlier tour by Iowa farmers, for instance, yielded only a few small pictures of French farms overshadowed by a full-page photograph of Iowa men in Paris watching topless female dancers.[2] The Marshall Plan's information director, Alfred Friendly, who would later become editor of the *Washington Post*, worried that the *Tribune*'s frivolous reporting on the farm tours worked "to our very great detriment" and risked undermining congressional support for the Marshall Plan.[3] The *Tribune* travel story also frustrated France's consul general in Chicago, who saw the report as just one more example of Americans' inability to "take us seriously." Writing to his superiors in Paris, the consul complained that the American media was blinded by touristic stereotypes of romantic France and thus tended to "ignore all the difficulties of life that the mass of the French people must face." Searching for a culprit, the French diplomat in Chicago blamed "flashy" tourist publicity, which portrayed France, and especially Paris, as the " 'Playground of America,' where the citizens of the United States can free themselves of all constraint."[4]

Seen from the perspective of cultural history, this episode reveals the power of deeply embedded expectations and scripts in shaping Americans' understanding of what they should do once they arrived in France. Viewed from the perspective of diplomatic history and government archives, this episode also unveils some of the efforts that government officials made trying to rewrite these tourist scripts in ways that would best reinforce their policy goals. Diplomats in both countries in the late 1940s and early 1950s hoped that American travel in France would reinforce the American public's commitment to an emerging Cold War alliance with France. Tours like the one by the farmers would ideally help Americans see themselves as part of an Atlantic Community. For both U.S. and French officials, the development of this kind of transatlantic identity among Americans was essential to building support for continued foreign aid and, beginning in 1949, for the new mutual defense pact created in the North Atlantic Treaty Organization. This ideal of tourism as a transatlantic community-building tool held great appeal for travel industry leaders in both countries who sought material and moral rewards by presenting their businesses as complements to their nations' foreign policy.

While the goal of tourism as a Cold War tool circulated in government and industry circles, the motives and experiences of actual tourists proved far more complex. Like the farmers heading to Paris nightclubs on their first evening in Europe, most Americans visiting France were eager to leave behind everyday worries and routines. In search of Old World pleasure and escape, tourists and travel writers commonly sought a France that was different from the United States. This romanticized and often sexualized conception of France proved a mixed blessing for advocates of an Atlantic Community. The consumeristic quest for French difference could reinforce the notion of an Atlantic Community, especially when Americans interpreted those differences as complements to seemingly "American" traits. Such positive bonds included the common images of France as an Old World haven for relentlessly forward-looking Americans and as a place for respectable heterosexual desire among both American men and women. Ironically, the sexualized imagery that frustrated some diplomats was also one of the popular sources of attachment that many Americans held for France.[5] Yet other common tourist experiences and images threatened to reduce Americans' commitment to France, especially when the romantic and sexual lenses reduced respect for France as a serious political and military ally. Moreover, many American visitors learned that large numbers of French citizens, and not just Communists, opposed the increasingly militant Cold War alliance between the United States and France. Tourists' discovery of strains within the Atlantic neighborhood weakened many travelers' sense of belonging to a shared community with France.

AT A NIGHTCLUB IN PARIS' FAMED PLACE PIGALLE
IOWANS PRESENT 1947 VERSION OF OLD QUESTION:
"HOW YA GONNA KEEP 'EM DOWN ON THE FARM...?"

Life's coverage of Iowa farmers on an agricultural study tour subordinated the ideal of purposeful travel to the more traditional pleasures of visiting France. The magazine avoided any hint of disapproval with the scene in either its caption or accompanying text (from Life, 20 October 1947; courtesy Yale Joel/Time Life Pictures/Getty Images).

These tensions presented a dilemma for travel boosters, especially when foreign policy experts in the American media sharpened their criticism of tourists for not being "realist" enough in their perceptions of Cold War Europe. To help preserve the idea that mass travel served their nations' foreign policies, U.S. and French government officials and U.S. travel industry leaders felt compelled to reduce the gap between Cold War concerns and the largely pleasure-driven motives of tourists. These elites developed new efforts to instruct tourists on how to think about Cold War Europe. Industry leaders and policymakers, especially on the American side, tried to promote the idea that postwar tourists were abandoning earlier patterns of seeing France as a romantic playground in favor of sober-minded tours more appropriate for a Cold War superpower. Yet, as the press coverage of the farmers' first night in Paris suggests, the escapist consumer motives that gave tourism its mass appeal frequently weakened these efforts to connect tourism to Cold War policy. Although historians generally present the late 1940s and early 1950s as a time of deep consensus in the United States in support of U.S. foreign policy, that consensus did not make all Americans into active Cold Warriors when they ventured across the Atlantic.[6] Instead, travel boosters struggled to make American tourists toe the Cold War line.

Escape from the Cold War and the Search for Difference

As European living conditions improved and the U.S. military removed restrictions on ocean crossings, Americans had an easier time renewing earlier transatlantic leisure patterns. While no generalization can capture every tourists' motives, most made the journey for reasons related to personal identity or social status. Voyages in France, and in Western Europe generally, represented less a time to explore political problems and more a chance to leave behind worrisome issues and everyday routines.

Long a central motive behind Americans' travel to Europe, the goal of escaping everyday routines and personal concerns gained added intensity in the anxious years of the early Cold War. Travel writers frequently advised tourists to leave behind thoughts of the Marshall Plan and other Cold War developments. "For your own pleasure, try to forget," advised two *New York Times* writers who felt that most tourists would have a better trip if they did not think about their tax dollars at work on the Marshall Plan.[7] *Time* expressed a therapeutic ideal when it described how, aboard a ship leaving port for Europe, "vacationers' cares fade with Manhattan's towers."[8] When foreign tensions figured in mainstream travel enticements, the point was generally not to study international affairs but to take advantage of "the last chance to see Europe before another war." "It's now or never to see Europe," echoed one American travel agent in *Business Week* in April 1951 in the midst of the Korean War.[9] One young Texas woman who bicycled through France in 1950 with her husband also found escape from the pressures of domesticity that marked American society in the early Cold War. She later described the trip as "a gloriously, magnificently, wondrously, and beautifully crazy senseless thing to do." Reflecting on why she left on the trip, she recalled, "I was determined we would not fall into the same rut as some of our friends."[10]

Among the various destinations in Europe, the escapist appeal was especially strong for France. Beyond Paris's reputation for lively nightlife, France seemed especially foreign because few Americans had relatives to visit there. Given the small scale of French immigration to the United States, family motives mattered much less for France than for Europe's other top destinations, such as Britain, Germany, and Italy. Immigrants and naturalized Americans and their children in the late 1940s accounted for approximately 40 percent of American travel to Western Europe as a whole, but for France that figure represented only 6 percent.[11]

For the vast majority of Americans going to France, the visit was less a trip to maintain or discover family ties than a time to experience cultural difference.[12] Most Americans located that difference in Old World sights, a focus evident in the itineraries Americans followed in France. According to studies by the French government, Americans were more likely than those from most other nations to place France's cultural heritage at the top of their list of interests. In contrast to European travelers, who gravitated to France's beaches, mountains, and spas, Americans, along with other long-distance tourists from Canada, South America, and, later, Asia, more often cited monuments and museums as France's central attractions. Paris, predictably, was the essential stop in quests for Old World culture and difference. Although Americans were not the most numerous foreign tourists in France (visitors from Britain, Belgium, and, beginning in 1955, Germany all outnumbered Americans), U.S. tourists made up the largest nationality visiting the French capital after the war. Leaving Paris, Americans headed disproportionately to the nearby Loire Valley, known for its Renaissance chateaux. The other popular stop for Americans in France was the Riviera, where they joined more numerous European guests for beaches, casinos, and other Mediterranean diversions.[13]

Back in the United States, the mass media reinforced this emphasis on France's difference. Hollywood studios exploited technological advances such as Technicolor to tempt audiences with swirling images of a lively France. Films such as *An American in Paris* presented France as a land of flowers and pastel colors. The film's colors made its spectacular backdrops as important as its conventional romance story. *Time*'s review, drawing on the same pool of adjectives used in travel descriptions of Paris, described the "Technicolorful result" as "smart, dazzling, genuinely gay and romantic."[14]

In their search for difference, tourists and travel writers often treated the European tour as a chance to escape modernity. Postwar Europeans, declared one travel book, "embody the customs and pageantry of the past." Another guide encouraged travelers to "walk with kings and courtesans, with queens and paramours" on trips to Loire châteaux. A well-circulated 1949 essay titled "How to Be an American Abroad" instructed tourists to celebrate difference in foreign places and to "enjoy the leisurely pace of their living."[15]

In their celebrations of France as an unhurried Old World, travel writers at times expressed an antimodern critique of postwar America's emphasis on mass production, efficiency, and consumerism. While the image of an Old World was part of a long tradition in American travel views of Europe, this antimodern vision assumed a tone specific to the postwar era. Some travel discourse suggested that vacations in France provided therapeutic relief from modern America. To the author of a 1948 guidebook, "Paris offers a respite from the fierce and ulcerating race most of us are running." A small town in France appeared to another travel writer as "symbolic of the timeless and enduring in a fretful world."[16] Travel writing even prompted questions about the merits of modern material comforts and corporate discipline. According to a *National Geographic* travel writer in 1952, Parisians enjoyed themselves because they managed to live "in defiance of the hobgoblins of efficiency" and to act as if "the clock was made for man, not man for the clock." That foreigners could be so happy with fewer consumer products moved travel writers toward a humble assessment of their own society. "Perhaps we might come to wonder," mused guidebook author Horace Sutton in 1951, "about the real value of our chrome-trimmed progress, to ponder, for example, if we haven't created a lot of necessities that aren't necessary."[17]

This critique of modernity and consumerism shied away from a full-fledged intellectual censure of postwar America and rarely advanced beyond romanticized images of Europe. Finding homeless Parisians under a bridge, one travel writer remarked that "even the hoboes looked pleased with themselves . . . as though living under a bridge on such a beautiful river was the best life a man could ask for." "We need reassurance," declared another writer in Italy, "that even in the fury of the twentieth century, . . . penniless people still sing to the stars." Travel writer Elliot Paul saw little tragedy in France's recent suffering. "As long as the French can make sweet uses of adversity," he wrote, "the rest of us should, at least, be able to face the future with the courage of some of their convictions."[18] That travel writing could present as picturesque the real poverty or political instability of postwar Europe suggests that these critiques of American consumerism represented less a call for serious social change and more nostalgia for seemingly simpler times. After all, the same travel writers critical of modernity in the United States also contributed to guidebooks that judged European hotels according to the state of their plumbing.[19]

Further defusing its radical potential, antimodernism often acted as an enticement for Americans to buy more consumer goods while abroad.[20] Casting old Europe as a complement to modern America, guidebooks such as the *Shopping Guide to Europe* instructed Americans to take advantage of European skills in traditional crafts and arts. Modern or mass-produced European goods, however, were "no match for the American assembly-line." In its section on "things not to buy" in France, Temple Fielding's popular travel guidebook bluntly listed "anything mechanical." Although the French apparently had not yet mastered the machine age, Fielding enthusiastically detailed the fashions, perfumes, and antiques to be found in France.[21]

Beyond stylish clothes and other luxuries, another product in which the French excelled, according to tourists and travel writers, was the erotic spectacle. As reported by the general manager of the American Express office in Paris, 90 percent of all requests the company received by tourists for concerts and theater performances in Paris were for nightclubs such as the Folies-Bergère and the Lido.[22] The president of Paris's cabaret association confirmed the importance of tourism for the clubs, noting in 1947 that two-thirds of their audiences were foreigners.[23] To veteran observers, the clubs' lavish eroticism, featuring scantily clad female and male performers, offered little that Americans could not see in New York City revues. Humorist Art Buchwald's 1950 nightlife guide warned that "Paris night clubs are not one-quarter as sinful as a tourist's imagination would lead him to believe," suggesting that what mattered most for tourists was the chance to experience firsthand Paris's long-standing reputation as a city of pleasure.[24] Indeed, tourists could easily integrate Parisian eroticism with the standard tourist itinerary, a practice satirized in one *New York Times* cartoon of a kindly old lady who tells another, "I want to take in l'Opera, Notre Dame and something naughty."[25]

Travel writers further confirmed the respectability of Paris by speaking little of prostitution there. Although precise information on tourists and prostitution is scarce, the proximity of Paris's prostitution quarters to its touristic nightclubs suggests at least some overlap in clientele. Prostitution, however, may have played a relatively smaller role in American travel experiences after the war than it did in earlier periods. In part because they offered symbols of collaboration with the Germans, French prostitutes and brothels faced a government crackdown after the war.[26] Although a feature of at least some tourists' trips, prostitution hardly registered as a topic in American travel discourse, except in reports on the closing of brothels.[27]

This tolerant, even yawning, discussion of French erotic revues and sexuality was only a pale reflection of earlier debates over whether Americans, especially the young and female, should travel to Paris, which one anxious American back in 1874 called that "vast moral whirlpool."[28] In contrast to these Victorian concerns, travel discourse beginning in the 1920s encouraged women to enjoy the spectacles, food, and shopping of France without fear of moral downfall. By 1949, middle-class magazines such as the *Ladies' Home Journal* courted travel industry advertisers with the slogan, "Never underestimate the power of a woman!" At a time when women accounted for 40 percent of postwar American travel to Europe, the magazine's motto reflected how female travel had evolved from an issue of morality into one of consumer entitlement.[29] With old Victorian fears safely contained, French eroticism could appear as just another desirable feature of the Atlantic Community rather than as a dangerous element in the neighborhood.

Difference and the Atlantic Community

Like the rhetoric of civilization that preoccupied travel writers in the immediate postwar years, the touristic emphasis on French difference could provide rhetorical reinforcement for closer U.S.-French ties. Devoting an editorial to the meaning of Europe in 1954, *Holiday* magazine argued that Europe's "polite, artistic, mature civilization" and America's "strenuous, self-reliant" version together "correct and supplement each other." Even images of Gallic frivolity could heighten Americans' notion of a common Atlantic Community through the idea that the two nations' differences complemented each other to form a complete whole. In a passage on French fashion, one 1952 guidebook noted that "the mere idea of a man spending his life thinking up new styles and fripperies for women's clothes . . . is . . . foreign to most Americans," but added, "one may indeed permit oneself to wonder, at least briefly, whether prettier women may not be as important as faster airplanes." Although such discourse ultimately placed the United States in the more powerful role of energetic leader, the emphasis on differences as complementary provided a cultural framework that lent a positive meaning to American stereotypes of feminized or frivolous France.[30]

Contemplation of timeless European civilization gave some travel writers greater faith in the strength of America's Atlantic Alliance. One writer roaming through France and Italy for *House and Garden* in 1948 expressed concern with "social, economic and political uneasiness" but remained optimistic: "On the shores of the Mediterranean one feels that Western culture which has gone on for many centuries may not, after all, be poised, in 1948, on the brink of irremediable collapse. From Perpignan to Padua, there still is freedom and happiness; there still is that feeling of reverence for human dimensions."[31]

For some travel writers, escapist portraits of Europe represented a self-conscious tool to bolster the American public's support of the Atlantic Alliance. *New York Herald Tribune* foreign correspondent William Attwood, weary from reporting on sobering events in Europe, found an outlet writing a whimsical 1949 travel book. In the preface he stated, "I wrote this book . . . particularly because I am tired of arguing with my fellow citizens who think that Europe is just a grim shambles where everybody is either a Communist, a black-marketeer, or a starving D.P. [Displaced Person]—and where nobody has any fun." Europe, he stressed, "is not merely the scene of a cold war but also a place where April is all bright green and soft blue and where most people would rather have you taste their good wine and admire their old churches than talk about the threat of war and Communism." Attwood then described some of the fun to be had, as in his ballooning excursion over the French countryside. Amid these flights of fancy, the journalist did not ignore all signs of the Cold War. Yet at a time when U.S. foreign policy officials drew dark pictures of Western Europe on the verge of Communist revolution, Attwood breezily presented French Communists as "lugubrious" figures who struggled in vain to maintain their revolutionary fervor in the face of the infectious pleasures of life in France.[32] As one *New York Times* reviewer noted, Attwood's lighthearted portrait "gives the lie direct to those who aver that Europeans are a beaten and inert people."[33] In other words, pastel-tinted travelogues could offer reassurance in the viability of the Atlantic Alliance.

French tourism promoters and diplomatic officials, themselves eager to tighten bonds with the United States and attract tourist dollars, also exploited the rhetoric of Old World civilization before the American public. One successful example of the French making strategic use of their cultural reputation came in 1951, when city leaders in Paris decided to hold celebrations for the 2,000th birthday of their hometown. As city counselor Jeanine Debray told William Attwood, "we want to reflect Paris's role as the capital of Western Civilization. We want to strike a note that will attract Americans."[34] Given scant archaeological evidence, Paris officials admitted to having no clear idea just when Paris was first settled. The celebration's timing instead owed much to the fact that French tourism promoters were looking for an attraction to rival the feat pulled off the year before by the city of Rome. Teaming with the Vatican, Italian officials had declared 1950 a "Holy Year" and benefited from additional thousands of American and foreign tourists. In France, the Paris anniversary seemed more hype than substance. The city of Paris gave the celebrations so little funding that the committee head, novelist Jules Romain, resigned in protest.[35]

While the Paris celebration committee languished, the anniversary mobilized Francophiles across the United States in a public relations bonanza. Officials in the Ministry of Foreign Affairs and the French Government Travel Office helped establish the high-profile Paris 2,000th Birthday Coordinating Committee, in which American media elites such as the producer of *The March of Time* and the editor of *This Week*, a high-circulation Sunday newspaper magazine, stirred up publicity. Through the spring of 1951, the sixty million readers of the *Lil' Abner* comic strip followed adventures in Paris. National television specials hosted by Frank Sinatra, Faye Emerson, and Milton Berle offered tributes to Paris. For viewers of NBC's *Your Show of Shows*, Sid Cesar and Imogene Coca acted out "typical tourists in Paris." In an early example of Hollywood "synergy" marketing, the Birthday Coordinating Committee began a joint publicity campaign in June 1951 with Hollywood's Metro Goldwyn Mayer in support of the studio's new Gene Kelly release, *An American in Paris*.[36] Even a gesture as simple as the committee's invitation to the mayors of the fourteen American towns named Paris generated waves of free publicity in newspapers, as with the stories of Paris, Maine (population 4,358), where the mayor's office had trouble finding someone who knew French to read the invitation, and of Paris, Maryland (population 60), where residents did not even have a mayor to respond.[37]

After the celebrations, French officials considered the anniversary a success for both its touristic and diplomatic payoffs. In a letter of thanks to the Tourism Commissariat, Ambassador Henri Bonnet in Washington described the events as a boon for the promotion of French tourism and commercial exports and as "one of the most effective forms of French propaganda." Reporting to the Ministry of Foreign Affairs in Paris, Bonnet praised how the event generated a "warm homage to the City of Lights" in the American media. Of particular importance to the ambassador was an editorial on the celebrations in the *New York Times* that noted how the "soul" and "true spirit" of Paris had survived the war and would prove resistant to Moscow.[38]

On a more regular basis, French tourism promoters reinforced the idea of a common Atlantic Community by appealing to the religious interests of many Americans. Government brochures for Americans included titles such as "France: Pilgrimages" and "Cathedrals and Churches of France." This emphasis tapped most easily into Catholic organizations in the United States that organized pilgrimage tours combining standard visits to Paris with excursions to Lourdes cathedral and other religious monuments unavailable at home.[39]

Ignoring France's modern secularization, one government brochure promised that "the Church is eternal and plays its part in men's lives to-day as it did yesterday and in the age when the most impressive religious monuments were erected."[40] To appeal to a wider range of Americans, the French government in 1951 launched a successful series of brochures on Protestant itineraries to follow in France. Although French officials most likely had market demographics on the top of their minds when creating this publicity material, their emphasis on making France seem part of Americans' heritage fully complemented their more general goal of using tourism as a way to secure closer ties with the United States. Referring to France's "large protestant minority" and Calvinist heritage, one brochure promised that travelers from North America "will not find themselves strangers in France."[41]

The French government further exploited the Old World motif with its popular son-et-lumière, or sound-and-light, shows. Introduced in 1951, these nighttime spectacles added colored lights and music onto otherwise static old buildings and monuments, most notably Versailles and the Loire Valley châteaux, both popular among Americans. Some shows completed the historical fantasy by adding narration or live actors and dancers. One part history lesson and one part stage show, the spectacles by the early 1950s attracted hundreds of thousands of visitors and allowed the French government to channel the ticket revenues into monument restoration projects and still more spectacles.[42]

While French tourism promoters successfully marketed their nation's past, French industrialists were less satisfied with Americans' image of an Old World nation. In the nineteenth century, Americans and other foreigners visited slaughterhouses, sewers, and stock exchanges in France, but few Americans in the postwar period saw France on the cutting edge of industry or urbanism.[43] Eager to boost exports to the United States, French industrialists embarked on a new program known as technical or industrial tourism. By one account, technical tourism's origins came in 1949 when *Life* magazine dubbed French industry a "sleeping beauty." Members of the Conseil national du patronat français (CNPF), France's principal employers' organization, responded to the charge by opening factory doors to Americans.[44] Although few industrialists envisioned legions of tourists foregoing trips to the Folies-Bergère in favor of factory tours, the CNPF's new tourism commission hoped that foreign visitors, especially Americans, would increase French exports, attract investment, and, more broadly, show the vitality of the nation.[45] Yet the first year of technical tourism in 1950 brought just several hundred foreigners to factories. In 1952, the CNPF expanded its efforts by subsidizing a new publicity outfit, the Association France actuelle (Current France Association). Drawing on advice from future U.S. diplomat George Ball, then a lawyer in Paris, the group sought to inform American journalists and business leaders that the "old stereotype notion" of France as a land of châteaux had ceded to "a new reality" of factories. By the mid-1950s, the program had developed a modest following, with French factories hosting roughly 10,000 foreigners a year, about half coming from the United States.[46] Nevertheless, the program never developed the broad appeal of France's more consumeristic or Old World attractions. Similarity, it seems, did not sell as well as difference.

Tourists' fascination with Old World difference, while a source of pleasure and sentimental bonding for many Americans, also presented some problems for advocates of a greater Atlantic Community. As a cultural stereotype, the touristic conception of Europe as a haven for Old World leisure could provide fodder for Americans opposed to the tightening alliance with France and other Western European nations. For U.S. officials, one of the danger signs came in a 1949 survey by the Marshall Plan's Travel Development Section. The survey found that, for all the rhetoric of a shared civilization and a superpower accepting its responsibilities, actual travel experiences produced no consensus on U.S. Cold War policies. In fact, the survey yielded more negative than positive comments from tourists about the Marshall Plan. One tourist felt that the Marshall Plan "is making many people lazy" and that Europeans "are doing nothing to help themselves." Others found elite European leisure habits a violation of both moral and fiscal conservative values. One remarked, "We noted luxury spending and gambling at high stakes in Riviera by French and Italian people. Wonder whether Americans do not pay for this." "In France," complained another, "I have seen more diamonds, furs, luxury yachts and expensive cars than I have ever seen at home. To give aid to the poor of France when the wealthy of France are able to do so is a fraud and a betrayal of the U.S. tax payer."[47]

Similar views by travelers made their way into Congress. A group of Midwestern farmers who toured Europe in 1950 reported to their senator that the government should "drastically cut" aid to all countries except Germany. The farmers singled out France and Italy as emblematic of the problem, using language that revealed the power of the Old World preconception of Europe. Making no reference to the ambitious modernization programs in France, the disappointed travelers remarked that these countries "are still worshiping their past history and old buildings. They do not understand the American idea of looking ahead."[48] Contrary to the hopes of consumer diplomacy advocates in the United States and France, traveling to Europe did not necessarily make Americans more willing to adopt the Cold War line and support foreign aid.

Many travelers also had difficulty seeing themselves as part of a Cold War Atlantic Community after encountering "Yankee, go home" graffiti or posters while abroad. These messages reflected how substantial segments of the French populace, including Communists and Gaullists, questioned U.S. influence in France, especially the U.S. troop presence. The hostile messages were widespread in early Cold War France, to the point where, according to one French poll in 1953, over half of the French population had seen such inscriptions.[49] For French officials advocating closer ties with the United States, these increasingly common signs of trouble in the Atlantic Community presented a contradiction in need of resolution. André Morice, France's minister overseeing tourism, gave public speeches in 1952 and 1953 disparaging anti-American protesters as unpatriotic, since their graffiti impeded the nation's economic recovery by driving away American tourists.[50]

These symbols of protest also became a new and often disturbing sight for traveling Americans. Some hoped to make light of the situation. In an attempt to turn protest into publicity, Pan American World Airways boasted that it had hired a man to seek out "Yankees, go home!" graffiti and paint underneath it: "via Pan American."[51] But not all tourists shared Pan Am's insouciance. "My heart is very heavy these days," wrote one Colorado woman to her senator after a trip to France and Italy in which she discovered that "we do not have the warm friendships of nations that we think we have."[52] Another alarming account appeared in the *Chicago Daily News*, where a traveler reported seeing an American soldier scribble underneath an "Americans, go home" graffito the subversive addition, "We agree."[53] Tourists also reported face-to-face encounters with critics of U.S. policy. Following a 1952 tour, a Montana businessman wrote his congressman to complain of a tour guide who candidly admitted that Europeans "take you Americans for a nice, big, luscious juicy orange to be sucked, and that is what we are doing." In the backseat of a taxi he had also heard a French driver blame "American warmongers" for international tensions. These comments led him to conclude that the United States ought to "cut bait" and withdraw troops from Western Europe.[54] While these complaints did not produce a reduction in U.S. troop presence, they did form part of a growing and ultimately successful campaign by fiscal conservatives in Congress to reduce U.S. foreign aid to Europe.[55]

The Push for Sober Travel

The tendency of some travel reports to provide ammunition for opponents of the Atlantic Alliance inspired rebuttals by Cold Warriors in the American media. Journalistic defenders of U.S. foreign aid often combined cultural criticism of mass tourism with the ideology of "realism" that reigned in American academic and diplomatic circles. According to foreign policy realists such as columnist Walter Lippmann and diplomat-turned-public-citizen George F. Kennan, public opinion tended to exert an emotional and volatile influence on foreign policy. Realists like Lippmann and Kennan fortified their negative view of public opinion's role in foreign affairs with a broad distaste for mass culture. A chief architect of U.S. Cold War containment policy, Kennan decried in his memoirs "the thoughtlessness" of "modern urban society" and claimed a "deep skepticism about the absolute value of people-to-people contacts for the improvement of international relations." Kennan's widely read 1951 treatise, *American Diplomacy*, instead argued the need for "the principle of professionalism" in the conduct of foreign policy, in contrast to "diplomacy by dilettantism." Skeptical of how the people could contribute to public affairs, Cold War realists thought foreign relations best left to the sober and rational considerations of trained experts, a view at odds with *Life* editor Henry Luce's 1941 call for "an internationalism of the people, by the people, and for the people."[56]

Some foreign policy observers extended this realist concern for expertise and professionalism into a critique of tourists' role in foreign affairs. Influential diplomatic historian Thomas A. Bailey, although eager to see Americans travel more and become better informed on world affairs, lamented in 1948 how "most of our Mainstreeters" who went abroad failed to have "enlightening" trips.[57] Near the end of the 1949 travel season, a *Saturday Evening Post* editorial warned of the "immense risk to common sense" from returning travelers. Since tourists lacked expertise on political and economic affairs, their exaggerations of European recovery and reports of European ingratitude represented "unintentional sabotage" that could "seriously compromise Europe's future by their effect on public opinion at home." The ideal tourist kept his "fool mouth shut" and let the experts inform the American public. Putting a religious cast on the issue, the *Christian Century* added, "It is outright sin to imperil the recovery of a country by careless conversation."[58]

Even worse for travel promoters, some of this criticism singled out the mass, commercial nature of transatlantic travel. The same writer in the *Christian Century* who feared that tourism imperiled European recovery found one culprit in the travel industry, which kept tourists on a "leash" and steered them from "anything that might dampen spending zeal." An editor with the *Christian Science Monitor*, given an all-expenses-paid tour of Europe courtesy of TWA in 1950, hardly repaid the airline's favor when he criticized travel of the "conducted-tour carefully cushioned kind." Too many Americans took only "an air-conditioned look" at France and failed to understand the economic problems of the French working class and how those problems bred resentment toward U.S. policies aimed at increasing French military expenditures.[59] Tourists, of course, have often been the target of derision. In a near-universal dynamic of mass tourism, self-proclaimed "travelers" have long affirmed the value of their own voyages by maligning the putatively inferior experiences of mere "tourists."[60] In the context of Cold War America, such conventional critiques of mass tourism often served as a point of departure for foreign policy commentary.

While some U.S. foreign policy observers worried about the effects of tourists on American public opinion, others identified tourists as a source of anti-Americanism overseas. One writer for the *Saturday Review* argued that the arrival of hundreds of thousands of Americans in Europe "fills officials in our embassies and consulates with fear and trembling," an image suggesting that foreign relations was best left to the professional Foreign Service. Although only a handful of tourists flaunted American wealth through such gestures as lighting cigarettes with franc notes, that minority offered "Grade-A material for anti-American sentiment."[61] A writer for *Reader's Digest* located a source of France's "u.s. go home" signs in the boorish behavior of Americans who disturbed the tranquil "charm of the little Paris hotel" by speaking "in hog-summoning tones."[62] One retired vice admiral in 1953 blamed the "wave of 'hate America'" sentiment on "a small percentage" of noisy and boastful tourists.[63] The view was shared by U.S. officials who, while preparing for an international conference on travel in 1954, concluded that poor-behaving tourists, even if a minority, could become "a focal point for criticism by foreign nations."[64]

Cold War critiques of tourists as creators of ill will and misinformation challenged travel boosters, who insisted that their business was in the United States' best interest. Because this claim helped attract assistance from Washington, any suggestion that American tourism in France undermined the Atlantic Community represented a threat to the industry. Unable to gain universal support for the idea that tourists aided U.S. Cold War efforts, Marshall Plan tourism officials and industry leaders faced even greater challenges in 1950 with the outbreak of war in Korea. The war, which came several months after red-baiting Senator Joe McCarthy arrived on the national spotlight, inspired fears in the United States that a Soviet invasion of Western Europe might be close at hand. This climate of heightened anxiety made frivolous leisure travel seem especially out of touch with the times.[65] Many industry leaders, along with Marshall Planners and sympathetic travel writers, adjusted to the sense of crisis by arguing that American tourists had undergone a cultural transformation. They argued that postwar Americans, in contrast to hedonistic prewar travelers, had suddenly become sober-minded observers of current international conditions.

Beginning in the late 1940s, boosters developed a new concept, purposeful travel, to describe citizens crossing the Atlantic not to visit nightclubs and cathedrals but instead to study current European politics and everyday life, as in the 1949 trip by farmers to study European agriculture.[66] Although only a minority of actual travelers embraced the "purposeful" ideal, the concept gained appeal among travel promoters at a time when Cold War tensions threatened to curtail the growth of the international travel industry.

Travel promoters' response to the outbreak of the Korean War illustrated their increasing attempts to spread the idea that postwar travelers had become earnest Cold Warriors. As U.S. forces rolled from one defeat to another early in the war, the generally silent editor of the American Society of Travel Agent's internal journal, *ASTA Travel News*, captured the travel industry's pessimistic mood in a striking editorial titled "Profits or Prophets (of Doom)?" Fearing a Soviet invasion of Western Europe and a ban on civilian travel, the editor concluded that "the only intelligent course of action" for the travel agent was "to sell, sell, and keep on selling until he is told pleasure travel is taboo."[67] A few weeks later, the president of the association adapted to the crisis with a more upbeat message. Rather than associating travel to Europe with pleasure, Newell Grinnel characterized tourist motives as more serious and attuned to the Cold War. "America's key role in international affairs," he declared to the press, "has stimulated an unprecedented desire to meet the people of foreign countries."[68] The TDS adopted a similar posture. In an October 1950 press release, it announced itself "especially pleased to find" that the most popular aim of Americans in Europe was to meet the people and that last on their list of objectives was Europe's nightlife.[69]

Of course, most travel agents had no intention of ignoring the more established pleasures of travel in Europe. When ASTA held its annual convention in Paris the next year, the travel agents themselves still enjoyed a private performance at the Folies-Bergère.[70] Nevertheless, this emphasis on sober-minded tourism became a recurring theme for the organization. In an interview with the *Saturday Evening Post* two years later, another ASTA leader described "the trend toward purposeful travel" as "the most important change in the business."[71]

Joining the chorus of travel boosters eager to close the gap between Cold War concerns and tourist motives, the European Travel Commission trumpeted the rise of purposeful travel in its own publicity in the U.S. media. The U.S. State Department's Office of Educational Exchange picked up on the concept when it encouraged students to study abroad on "vacations with a purpose."[72]

To be sure, a portion of American travel to France involved less overtly escapist motives, as with academic tours and study-abroad programs. In the spring of 1948, the University of Vermont announced a twelve-week course geared around the Marshall Plan for schoolteachers seeking advanced degrees. Within a month, over 1,000 teachers had applied for the program.[73] The State and Commerce Departments themselves encouraged this growth in 1947 by helping students cross the Atlantic in the summer on military transport ships. In 1950, the Carnegie Endowment replaced the government's sponsorship and encouraged the new Council on Student Travel to send more students abroad.[74] Nonprofit student travel organizations made such a rapid impact on the market that travel agents quickly complained that educational groups damaged their businesses with unfair competition.[75]

Purposeful travel also appeared in corners of the travel market that catered to Americans with heightened political sensibilities. Enough readers of *United Nations World* took part in its 1949 " 'Marshall Plan' Tours" that the magazine repeated the venture the next year. On the tours, internationally inclined Americans could, for under $1,000, "see the cathedrals, museums, and scenic features" and "meet representatives and dignitaries and discuss matters of international interest."[76] Other smaller organizations offered similar tours, with an emphasis on meeting everyday Europeans outside the travel industry. Friendship Tours International, based in New Haven, Connecticut, sold "an opportunity for YOU to strengthen international brotherhood" by living with European families.[77]

The U.S. government generally encouraged politically inspired trips, although with notable exceptions. Through the 1950s, the State Department withheld passports from some leftist activists with real or suspected Communist ties. After a group of activists traveled to Paris and from there to the Soviet Union, conservative legislators such as Nevada senator Pat McCarran pressured the State Department to tighten its restrictions against travel abroad by "subversives." Such measures in effect barred from foreign travel those whose "purpose" seemed threatening to U.S. Cold War interests.[78] More to U.S. officials' liking were tours that they themselves helped organize. One joint venture between the ECA and a popular midwestern radio program brought thirty-two women to Europe. As one ECA official remarked with satisfaction, "Although not convinced that Marshall Aid was necessary before this trip, the ladies are returning, in the main, with the idea that it is essential." Once back home, the women generated favorable newspaper coverage and hours of radio stories. One former tourist made twenty-three speaking engagements upon her return.[79]

To its advocates inside and outside the government, the rise of purposeful travel symbolized a broader shift in the American national character toward a new age of sobriety and world leadership. Figures such as Marshall Plan tourism chief Théo Pozzy and travel writer Horace Sutton often set up a dichotomy

With a sightseer focused on Marshall Plan–funded machinery, this cartoon illustrated, and gently mocked, the postwar ideal of "purposeful travel" (from U.S. News and World Report, *16 September 1949).*

between travel styles in 1929 and 1949, claiming that postwar Americans shared none of the frivolity that allegedly tainted their prewar counterparts.[80] Endorsing this concept, Marquis Childs, foreign policy columnist for the *Washington Post*, denigrated the prewar era as a time when "thirsty Americans sailed from a prohibition-ridden America." Visitors to Europe after the war, by contrast, were "thoughtful travelers" with "a serious and specific purpose."[81]

Some media commentators added the idea that this new sobriety was the result of middle-class virtues, often ignoring how transatlantic travel in the late 1940s remained inaccessible to most middle-class Americans. "It's we-the-people who've come to Paris this time," announced one veteran studying abroad on the GI Bill in a 1949 profile by the *Saturday Evening Post*. The magazine added that this sober young man had "nothing Bohemian, nothing Flaming Youth about him," unlike travelers in the "giddy invasion" of the 1920s. "His own background is strictly middle-class," stressed the magazine, which approvingly noted how he strolled through the Left Bank in a plaid lumberjack shirt.[82] *U.S. News and World Report* contributed to this trend with a report on how the thrifty "1949 variety" of tourist won respect from French hosts for their newfound seriousness. To illustrate this new sobriety, the magazine included a cartoon of a camera-toting American ignoring a pair of bikini-clad women at a beachside resort. Turning away from sea, sex, and sun, this model postwar tourist focused his camera on a piece of heavy machinery provided by the Marshall Plan.[83] *Le Monde* found the article interesting enough to summarize for its readers, including a reference to the cartoon tourist "coldly turning his back on two seductive bathers." The French paper's summary also bore the somewhat skeptical title, "An American tells . . . ," suggesting that *Le Monde*'s staff was not entirely convinced of any profound change in American touring style.[84]

William Nichols, editor of *This Week*, also doubted the existence of any sea change in postwar tourist motives, but he agreed that the ideal of purposeful travel was noble enough to encourage. After a trip to France in 1951, Nichols returned home disillusioned with how tourist advertising stressed ordinary sightseeing or, even worse, cancan dancers. In order to combat isolationism in the American public, he asserted, Europe should be presented more seriously, in a way that stressed Western Europeans' commitment to reconstruction and Cold War defense. He thus launched a poster campaign in *This Week* to publicize that "Travel is the mark of Liberty" and "Only free men travel freely."[85] Nichols also used his publishing connections to assemble a 1952 guidebook that emphasized travel's Cold War meanings. If each American made one friend in Europe, the guidebook calculated, "then it would not be long before the North Atlantic Community would be as real and as closely knit a community as your own home town."[86]

Pulitzer Prize–winning foreign correspondent Leland Stowe took a similarly constructive tone in his 1952 *Reader's Digest* essay titled "The Knack of Intelligent Travel." Blending Cold War politics into conventional travel concerns, such as status and self-improvement, Stowe presented standard advice on how to avoid parochial blunders as a way to do good "in a Communist-menaced world." For instance, the tourist who loudly insulted foreign coffee was "really telling the world he hasn't been around much." Such unsophisticated Americans, Stowe instructed, were those "to be most pitied."[87] As Stowe showed, Cold War–inspired pleas for better behavior were in some ways a natural fit with the genre of travel advice writing.

In other ways, however, the concept of purposeful travel rested uneasily with consumer-oriented travel promotion. After all, the ideal purposeful traveler, eager to explore everyday life on vacation, had no desire to indulge in class-climbing or erotic fantasy and felt no need to escape Cold War tensions. Few ideologies were more at odds with dominant trends in postwar consumerism. This tension inherent in purposeful travel became clear when U.S. and European officials met with a New York advertising agency to plan publicity for the European Travel Commission. Founded in June 1948 with monetary support from the Marshall Plan, the ETC's main purpose was to create tourism advertisements in the American media on behalf of the sixteen Marshall Plan countries.[88] In their private meetings, members of the ETC drafted advertising slogans such as "Travel builds world peace" and "Marshall Plan countries invite you to Europe," which they then brought to J. M. Mathes, Inc., a Manhattan advertising agency whose tourism experience included work for Bermuda's travel office.[89]

In what became something of an annual ritual, the ad agency urged government officials to temper their political themes with more consumeristic appeals. Théo Pozzy and the Europeans argued that the ETC advertisements should underline tourism's importance in carrying out the Marshall Plan and in forging a closer Atlantic Alliance. To persuade Mathes, Pozzy repeated the idea that postwar tourists were no longer interested in mere pleasure and instead wanted first "to meet, see, and talk to people." At one meeting, however, a Mathes executive "remarked that it had been thought best not to confuse people by mentioning the Marshall Plan."[90] The next year, ETC representatives reconvened at the J. M. Mathes office with sober-minded slogans such as "Understanding through travel is the passport to peace." As before, foreign affairs clashed with Madison Avenue. The ad agency argued that political themes "may not always be useful in advertising" but agreed to use them "whenever possible."[91] In the end, ETC advertisements combined foreign policy concerns with the consumer savvy of Madison Avenue. The ads downplayed the Marshall Plan but did feature the "passport to peace" slogan. Some ads also suggested that travel to Western Europe would reveal for Americans a real Atlantic Community. The text for one February 1950 ad in the *New York Times* described Europeans as "neighbors across the Atlantic" and as "people much like . . . neighbors back home."[92]

Marshall Plan officials also made efforts to ensure that members of Congress visiting Europe on "fact-finding" missions received the right "presentation" of Europe.[93] Congressional tours presented the ECA with many of the same challenges it faced with ordinary tourists, but with higher stakes, given Congress's control of the ECA budget. According to ECA Information Division policy, each country mission was to emphasize only "*visible* recovery projects" and ensure that all projects on the tours bore clear markers attesting to the use of U.S. aid. The latter point presented some difficulty, since French authorities preferred to minimize such publicity, lest their government appear a puppet of the United States.[94] Another part of that presentation meant shielding Washington visitors from evidence of anti-American sentiment—hence the need for each country mission to launch "counter-propaganda" before important visits.[95]

Marshall Plan officials worried as well that members of Congress dining on the Champs-Élysées or in the elegant Hôtel Crillon would leave with an inflated impression of typical French living conditions. ECA Information Division director Alfred Friendly considered staging a series of countermeasures; one proposal was to "line up a number of hardy and picturesque old union members," all non-Communist, who could invite American politicians over for dinner and show their Washington guests "that life for them is extremely difficult." With such measures, Friendly hoped to avoid the kind of press coverage that appeared in the *Chicago Tribune*'s report on the farmers' tour.[96]

For ordinary tourists, Marshall Plan officials created a series of pamphlets designed to make Americans venturing abroad better advocates of U.S. policy both while in Europe and once back home. While the Marshall Plan's magazine for French readers insisted that American tourists symbolized transatlantic friendship and respect, the ECA's pamphlets for tourists encouraged Americans to live up to this lofty standard. One of the earliest efforts to turn tourists into amateur diplomats was a thirty-two-page pocket-sized booklet published in 1948 by the ECA offering "Information for Americans Going Abroad." Judging from its content, Marshall Plan officials were most concerned with putting leisure travelers in a Cold War mind-set. In an introduction signed by ECA administrator Paul Hoffman, the booklet warned readers that "you will be asked" about the Marshall Plan and predicted that "you will want to be able to discuss this topic with the people you meet in Europe." The booklet then sketched a basic outline of the Marshall Plan, dedicated to statistics and summaries of the ECA's various functions, with no reference to Western European Communist opposition to the plan. A revised edition printed later in the summer of 1948 took a slightly more anti-Communist tone than did the first printing, adding a warning that some tourists might hear Communists claiming that the United States wanted to dominate European economies.[97] The booklet left the tourists to devise their own response to such charges.

One year later, with Cold War tensions increasing, the booklet appeared in a much more aggressive version. With subject headings such as "You Will Hear Propaganda" and "This Is the Communist Line," the 1949 edition offered a point-by-point defense of the Marshall Plan. For help with distribution, the ECA turned to *ASTA Travel News* at the start of the 1949 tourist season. In an article titled "How to Help Your Clients Preserve Democracy," the trade journal urged travel agents to ensure that Europe-bound tourists received "this mental armament." So as not to take the fun out of the whole trip, the booklet itself avoided technical jargon in favor of colloquialisms. It explained European criticism of the United States as "Communist gobbledygook" and "just plain lies." In the process, the booklet ignored non-Communist nationalist groups such as the Gaullists who also criticized U.S. influence in France and wanted their nation to take a more neutral position in the Cold War.[98]

Offering Cold War instruction for tourists was a fresh expression of the old tradition of passing along advice to novice travelers. The brochures functioned like travel guides, taking advantage of how travel to Europe could be an unsettling experience, especially for first-time American visitors. Under the heading of advice from "Seasoned American travelers," one ECA brochure, titled "Tips for Your Trip," offered pointers on how to sightsee and what to expect at customs. Between these two routine travel comments, the brochure squeezed in the injunction: "Don't let anyone tell you the Marshall Plan is a charity scheme."[99]

When the Marshall Plan ended in 1952, government efforts to make tourists mouthpieces of U.S. foreign policy goals shifted to the U.S. Information Agency (USIA). In contrast to Marshall Plan brochures, which were both written and funded by the government, the USIA sought private sponsorship for its brochures, a collaboration between private and public sectors typical of U.S. cultural diplomacy efforts in the 1950s.[100] One 1952 brochure, written by the USIA's Office of Private Cooperation, received sponsorship from patriotic groups such as the Common Council for American Unity and the American Heritage Foundation, the latter dedicated to "more active, personal participation in citizenship." Contributions also came from more self-interested businesses such as the Paris edition of the *New York Herald Tribune*, the leading newspaper for Americans traveling in Europe.[101]

As during the Marshall Plan, these brochures integrated travelers' private concerns with foreign policy questions. The 1952 illustrated booklet titled "What Should I Know When I Travel Abroad?" began by trying to bridge the gap between pleasurable travel and the Cold War. It promised tourists that they were "going to have a whale of a good time!" Part of that fun depended on studying the booklet's advice, which would prevent "boners" and "add a lot of pleasure to your trip." Understanding no-smoking signs in foreign languages, for instance, would lead to "more fun," whereas breaking the law was "even less fun . . . abroad than at home." Mixed in with practical advice on how to tip and what to expect at breakfast came more diplomatic suggestions. The booklet warned against the use of demeaning terms like "Frenchies." For fear that some travelers might strike Europeans as colonial conquerors, it also added: "Don't ever use the word 'natives.'" Switching into a first-person narrative, the pamphlet described how an experienced traveler knew that good behavior around the French would be rewarded with friendliness, while rudeness would prompt the French to pretend they do not speak English.[102]

Elements of the 1952 booklet hinted that its USIA authors held a realist-inspired lack of confidence in everyday tourists. The booklet advised Americans to avoid "controversial" topics such as "politics" and, as a second line of defense, provided a "suggested outline of the American point of view" for any tourist caught in a political conversation and in need of dialogue lines. For example, tourists who happened to encounter a European opposed to the U.S. military's presence in Europe or to a U.S.-sponsored rearmament of West

Germany were to respond that "it seems to us that in the fight between what is *right* and what is *wrong* there just isn't room for neutralism."[103]

Tourists, however, did not allow their ideas to be as easily scripted as the USIA wanted. In a follow-up investigation, the USIA found that the booklet received a mixed reception from actual travelers. According to a study of 221 former travelers interviewed at home in 1953, 42 percent had seen the booklet and 70 percent of those who saw it had actually read all of it. Favorable responses praised it for helping to "put on my best behavior." One respondent "would have been at a loss without the booklet." A recurring phrase among those who appreciated the material was that it helped ease the anxiety that came with foreign travel and allowed them "to feel more secure." A few Americans with more self-confidence saw the booklet's main advantage in confirming their superiority over other tourists, as with the one who wrote, "I liked to refer to it every time I saw tourists do the things you tell them not to do."[104]

But in many regards, the USIA survey found troubling results. Almost one in five readers criticized the booklet as either vague or juvenile, perhaps a reference to the numerous cartoons in the booklet or to its emphasis on providing Americans with scripts of ready-made responses to political issues. A few travelers expressed resentment against Europeans, as did the one respondent who said he was "slightly fed up with the constant remonstrances for Americans to behave. It's the Europeans who need to be told that." Another disgruntled tourist asked, "Why must Americans constantly prove to Europeans that they are grown-up?"[105]

To the USIA investigators, the booklet proved especially disappointing on the critical issue of instilling in tourists a rigid Cold War mind-set. The USIA report concluded that tourists were "ill-equipped" to explain something as basic as "America's concern with Communism." Rather than having a firm anti-Communist vision of U.S. foreign policy, tourists more often formed independent opinions on Cold War issues based on their own experiences in Europe. On the issue of European neutrality, the USIA study found that "on the whole," tourists tended to take "a less determined stand" than the U.S. government would like. One-third of the former travelers felt that they understood European desires for neutrality in the Cold War after seeing war-damaged Europe for themselves. When the subject of neutrality arose in conversation with Europeans, one tourist explained, "I couldn't insult them or make them feel bad by hurting their self-respect." Another conceded, "I couldn't say anything. I could only sympathize."[106] In other words, face-to-face encounters with European critics of U.S. policy contributed to a more nuanced view. These tourists sympathetic to European neutralism might have imagined themselves part of a transatlantic community, but, ironically enough, it was not the same vision of a militantly anti-Communist community that U.S. foreign policymakers hoped to instill.

Many French observers found their own confirmation of the difficulty of changing touristic impressions in late 1952 when *Life* ran an editorial comparing Fourth Republic politics to a theatrical sex farce periodically interrupted by cancan numbers. *Life* even imagined Marianne, the symbol of the republic, cast in the role of a promiscuous mistress. The editorial drew widespread criticism from the French press and an official protest by the French embassy in Washington. One French sociologist blamed American tourists' superficial images of France, while *L'Aurore* warned that *Life*'s depiction rendered the French as "white Negroes" (*nègres-blancs*) in the face of American power, a comment that translated *Life*'s gendered and touristic imagery into the language of race and colonial relations.[107] Despite years of efforts by French diplomats and industrialists and U.S. officials, little had changed to alter deep-rooted American images of France. The American media, like tourists, continued to view France through the lens of romantic and often sexualized difference.

Another indication of tensions between consumerism and the United States' increasingly militant approach to the Cold War was the premature decline of the TDS itself. As the Cold War intensified after the outbreak of the Korean War, the Truman White House directed a radical shift in the Marshall Plan, replacing the focus on European business reform and economic growth with a new emphasis on European military rearmament.[108] ECA officials tried to recast their travel program for the new standards set by Washington. Pozzy reasoned that modernized hotels would provide useful lodging for the U.S. military if a new war erupted in Europe.[109] Invoking the concept of purposeful travel, Pozzy also insisted that tourists represented America's most "democratic weapon against Communist propaganda."[110] Such arguments, as well as pleas from European tourism officials and hoteliers and American travel companies, proved insufficient in the face of U.S. foreign policy's militarization. The Truman administration reduced the size of the TDS in December 1950 and shut it down completely several months before the closing of the entire ECA in December 1951.[111] Some members of the TDS continued their travel promotion activities for the U.S. government after the ECA closing and into the Eisenhower years. Nevertheless, the travel boosters in both the United States and France were unable to protect what had been their principal bureaucratic ally in the U.S. government.

Conclusion

Although its demise resulted from a more general turn toward militarism in U.S. foreign policy, the Marshall Plan's travel program had since its inception struggled to reconcile tourism's cultural meanings with Cold War concerns. Throughout the late 1940s and early 1950s, American and French travel promoters in the government, media, and business worlds maneuvered to balance foreign policy concerns with consumers' desire for escape. While their Madison Avenue advertisers pushed boosters toward the consumer side, pressures from U.S. foreign policy observers demanding a "realist" outlook on Europe exerted a countervailing force. Seeking a middle ground, boosters' campaign for purposeful travel attracted some tourists and complemented efforts by French industrialists to show off modern France. Yet this movement never became a dominant force in postwar tourism. While historians of postwar America generally emphasize the pervasive influence of a "Cold War culture" on American life, tourists and travel writers showed that this culture represented more the hopes of a small number of elites than the mind-set of ordinary Americans heading overseas.[112] In a dynamic that helps illuminate the broader workings of Cold War culture, popular indifference to foreign policy only increased the efforts of Cold War–minded Americans to instill a geopolitical consciousness in leisure travelers.

Left largely to its own consumeristic concerns, travel discourse yielded mixed results for American and French advocates of a greater Atlantic Community. Tourists and travel writers generally embraced an Atlantic Community when that community could be conceived in consumeristic terms. Travel promotion that emphasized romantic difference, as with nightclubs, châteaux, and celebrations of Parisian history, proved successful, in contrast to the limited appeal of French factory tours. Yet these expressions of affection between Americans and France remained on a sentimental level often far removed from debates on specific policies. Although travel discourse was a powerful long-term force shaping Americans' commitment to Europe, lofty expressions of a shared transatlantic community were offset by travel reports that more directly challenged U.S. Cold War policies toward France. Moreover, tourists typically sought to ignore the Cold War and, when occupied with foreign affairs, frequently developed unorthodox opinions. Even at the heyday of the Cold War consensus, most Americans were unwilling to sacrifice traditional tourist pleasures for purposeful Cold War holidays.

Chapter 6

THE UGLY AMERICAN
THE TRAVEL BOOM AND THE DEBATE OVER MASS CULTURE

On 1 May 1952, in New York City, eighty-seven men, women, and children boarded a Pan American World Airways Super-6 Clipper dubbed the *Betsy Ross*. They filed into a cabin that had been reconfigured to seat about thirty more passengers than customary for transatlantic flights at the time. During the thirteen-hour voyage, they received simple sandwiches, in contrast to the full meals and free alcohol typically enjoyed by passengers crossing the Atlantic. Despite the cramped cabin and stingy service, the flight appeared to many as an event to celebrate. The voyage of the *Betsy Ross* occurred on the first day of tourist-class flights across the Atlantic, a development that helped bring air travel within the reach of middle-class Americans. Prior to 1952, air service across the Atlantic was strictly a first-class affair, in which clients paid a premium, enjoyed fine meals and drinks in a common lounge, and could even retire to private sleeping chambers. The new tourist-class category on Pan Am and other airlines cut the one-way fare from New York to Paris from $415 to $290 and within three years helped airlines overtake ocean liners as the principal means for crossing the Atlantic.[1]

For some observers, tourist-class airfare inspired optimism for the future of U.S. relations with Western Europe. The year before, as the world's airlines debated whether to allow the reduced rates, the *New York Herald Tribune* lobbied for tourist fares, which "would greatly strengthen" the North Atlantic Treaty Organization by allowing for more face-to-face contact between Americans and their allies. A San Francisco newspaper called the lower rates "good foreign relations" at a time when both airfare and warfare seemed to be on the rise. For the flight of the *Betsy Ross*, Pan Am solicited an endorsement from Henri Ingrand, France's chief tourism official, who announced that the reduced prices "will bring to France a new type of tourist and give the average Frenchman an opportunity to meet middle class Americans." "We feel certain," he added, "that this will result in better Franco-American relations."[2]

The rhetoric surrounding the flight of the *Betsy Ross* represented the latest evolution in Americans' long-running debate over popular participation in

Travelers on the first day of tourist-class flights to Europe. In the center of the first row, a young boy dressed in a cowboy outfit symbolized Pan Am's hopes of presenting air travel as an activity for more than just cosmopolitan elites (courtesy Archives and Special Collections, Otto G. Richter Library, University of Miami, Coral Gables, Fla.).

foreign affairs. Continuing their efforts from the Marshall Plan years, international travel boosters in the United States lobbied vigorously to combat the "realist" critique of tourism and to promote instead the idea that mass travel aided the U.S. Cold War crusade. Although rooted in earlier discussions, this debate took on new characteristics in the 1950s and 1960s. As Americans adjusted to the idea that the Cold War would require a long-term cultural and economic rivalry with the Soviet Union, U.S. foreign policymakers gave increasing attention to foreigners' opinions of the United States. Private citizens venturing overseas thus stepped into a more demanding public spotlight. All the while, developments such as tourist-class airfare were making travel to Europe an increasingly visible fixture of middle-class consumer society. This conjunction of expanding leisure and growing Cold War concerns with world opinion led many observers to ask if mass culture and popular travel were compatible with effective world leadership.

These concerns in many ways paralleled intellectual debates in 1950s and 1960s America over the implications of advertising, television, and other features of mass consumer society on healthy public life. Some intellectuals celebrated this ascendant mass culture as a tool for creating a more harmonious society. With mass culture, social class divisions would disappear as growing numbers joined the middle class and enjoyed rising standards of living. Yet for others, these same trends brought dangers by sapping Americans of their individuality and of their physical, moral, or intellectual vigor.[3] Discussions on tourists' role in the Cold War followed similar lines, and they show how growing middle-class prosperity produced as much anxiety as confidence for postwar Americans. To skeptics in the government and media, the mass character of postwar travel only isolated tourists from the real world and undermined their ability to make good impressions on foreigners. Holding a more optimistic view of mass culture, travel industry leaders and allies in the media countered with the populist idea that roving middle-class Americans made better ambassadors than wealthier travelers when it came to winning friends overseas.

This division over mass tourism, while an important episode in American cultural history in its own right, also created a conceptual framework that helped shape cultural diplomacy campaigns such as academic exchange programs, Eisenhower's People-to-People Foundation, and Kennedy's Peace Corps. Although their cultural diplomacy efforts differed in style, the Eisenhower and Kennedy administrations both attempted to reconcile the contrasting principles of realism and populism in an effort to manage popular participation in the Cold War.

The Travel Boom

Beginning in the early 1950s, travel across the Atlantic soared in volume. What became known as the postwar "travel boom" grew from numerous sources: rising income and credit opportunities for middle-class Americans, cheaper and more abundant air transportation, the mass media's persistent attraction to foreign places, and continued support from the U.S. government after the Marshall Plan.[4] Drawing on this convergence of forces, Americans in 1953 made 376,000 trips across the Atlantic, surpassing the previous record set in 1930. Volume doubled between 1953 and 1959 and doubled again to 1.4 million by 1965. In 1970, Americans made 2.9 million trips to Europe and the Mediterranean.[5] With dramatic rates of growth, the international travel boom attracted increasing portions of middle-class postwar prosperity. Even as Americans' overall consumption ballooned, by 63 percent between 1953 and 1963, Americans' expenditures on foreign travel (to all countries) grew even faster, by 89 percent over the same ten years.[6]

Beginning in 1955, most of these Americans flew rather than sailed across the Atlantic, taking advantage of a combination of technical and marketing innovations in civil aviation. Improvements to piston-engine planes in the early 1950s and the introduction of passenger jet planes in 1958 reduced travel times and costs. On top of these engineering feats came a series of equally critical pricing changes, especially the hard-fought emergence of tourist-class airfare. Since 1948, Pan Am, the world's largest international air carrier, had pressured the International Air Transport Association for the right to offer a tourist-class fare. The IATA, a self-enforcing organization of international airlines formed in 1944, had for four years refused Pan Am's request, since other airlines feared that lower fares would only increase Pan Am's dominance. Resistance to reduced fares from several European carriers finally gave way in 1952 after Pan Am publicly threatened to defy the IATA and create tourist service without the association's approval. According to Pan Am's logic, European countries eager for Americans' tourist dollars would not exercise their right to bar landing permission to airlines that violated the IATA. The U.S. airline's pressure tactics worked, and the IATA soon endorsed what would become a major shift in the social history of transatlantic travel. Indeed, Pan Am president Juan Trippe later described the introduction of tourist-class airfare as the third biggest milestone in aviation history, behind only Charles Lindbergh's 1927 crossing of the Atlantic and the 1958 introduction of jetliners.[7]

The success of tourist-class airfare was matched in 1958 with the introduction of "economy class" service that offered prices 20 percent below tourist-class fares. Travel by air, especially on a budget, was rarely a pleasurable undertaking. Those who flew on a tight budget in the early 1960s recall noisy fifteen-hour flights marred by heavy vibration and stuffy cabins. One young American, whose family insisted that she arrive in Europe in high heels, remembers how she could barely walk off the plane when she finally landed.[8] But speed and price mattered more than comfort. By 1963, around three-quarters of U.S. tourists traveled to Europe by air, and the great majority of those passengers purchased low-fare service.[9]

The rise of consumer credit in the 1950s also helped expand the middle-class travel market. While travel agents and other tourism promoters had difficulty promoting travel-now, pay-later schemes in the late 1940s, such practices spread as Americans made consumer debt a pillar of middle-class life. In 1954, Pan Am continued its pursuit of middle-class travelers by teaming with the Household Finance Corporation to launch a successful airline installment plan. Travel agencies intensified their own efforts with installment programs, offering, for instance, three-week tours of Europe in 1956 for a down payment of $76.[10]

Another contributor to the travel boom was the U.S. government itself. Although the TDS ceased operation in 1951, the Eisenhower administration continued to promote Americans' trips to Western Europe. Dollars from tourists still offered a substitute for foreign aid at a time when foreign countries struggled to import U.S. goods. Also as before, this strategy held particular appeal for advocates of limited government and the free market. In a play on the conservative refrain of "trade, not aid," the Eisenhower administration dubbed its tourism policy "Vacations, not donations." The conservative U.S. News and World Report endorsed the strategy as "foreign aid that's fun" and approvingly noted how the $1.27 billion Americans would spend abroad in 1955 was nearly double the government's foreign aid budget.[11]

In substance, the Eisenhower administration's participation in travel promotion was less extensive than the Marshall Plan program. In 1953, the Department of Commerce sent two "travel technicians" overseas to continue the Marshall Plan's mission of showing foreigners how to host Americans.[12] In an unsuccessful attempt to encourage shopping sprees overseas, Eisenhower, along with travel writers and industry leaders, lobbied Congress in 1954 to raise the amount of purchases that American tourists could bring home without paying duty from $500 to $1,000. The measure, which would have expanded the increase from $100 to $500 that accompanied the Marshall Plan, failed in the face of opposition from U.S. importers and domestic manufacturers, suggesting that travel boosters' ability to gain support diminished as foreign economies began to strengthen. Nevertheless, Eisenhower and his cabinet members still praised overseas travel in speeches as a means to improve the world economy and international understanding.[13] These endorsements by the White House at the very least allowed travel industry leaders to continue to associate their businesses with the national interest.[14]

An even more vital cheerleader for the travel industry was the mass media. With the expansion of the travel market, urban newspapers and middle-class magazines gave more space to tourism, particularly in special travel supplements. For many periodicals, covering travel grew from one journalist's side activity to a full-time activity for one or several writers.[15] Hollywood also caught the travel bug. Between 1951 and 1965, studios produced no fewer than twenty-five films featuring Americans living in France or portraying some other touristic aspect of France such as cancan dancing.[16] "The movie that affected me the most was *Sabrina*," recalled one woman who had grown up eager to escape life in small-town Ohio. Speaking in retrospect, she attributed part of her desire to visit France to the 1954 film in which Audrey Hepburn played an American chauffeur's daughter who "had gone off to Paris and come back, and she was glamorous, wonderful, and sophisticated. . . . When you think of Marion, Ohio, this was the most romantic, the most wonderful thing."[17]

Although movies such as *Sabrina* relied on a Cinderella-style narrative, Hollywood in the 1950s also turned to more realistic, travelogue-style treatments of France and other destinations. In an age when television began to challenge movies for American audiences, films increasingly offered viewers more striking European backdrops, shot on location and in color to give a sense of immediacy unavailable through television. Consider, for example, the contrast between Vincente Minnelli's 1951 *An American in Paris*, shot mostly on a studio set with fanciful painted backdrops, and Alfred Hitchcock's 1955 *To Catch a Thief*, which featured prolonged car chases shot from the air in full color to highlight not the drivers but the Riviera landscape. Hitchcock's cultivation of a vicarious travel experience for viewers even included the unsubtle gesture of running the film's opening credits over a close-up shot of a French Government Tourist Office display window.

As the scale and visibility of travel to Europe increased, tourism promoters helped define for postwar Americans what it meant to belong to the middle class. In its publicity campaign for the flight of the *Betsy Ross*, Pan Am stressed that most of its passengers were "from the middle-income class," a point reproduced in the press the next day.[18] The company's first scheduled jet flight to Europe in 1958 gave fifteen minutes of fame to an Ohio farmer and school bus driver and his family of six, who won a free trip courtesy of Pan Am and Kellogg's Corn Flakes.[19] In 1962, *Ebony*, a magazine aimed at middle-class African Americans, described international tourism as "the new status symbol." Although African Americans accounted for only 1 percent of U.S. air travel across the Atlantic in the mid-1960s, the statement suggested a growing connection between middle-class life and travel abroad.[20]

In the 1950s, airlines found that they could further make international air travel a middle-class norm by catering to women consumers, who represented about half of the Americans flying across the Atlantic. By the late 1950s, most of the major international airlines had created women's marketing departments, which typically focused on advice for first-time travelers. TWA created the character of Mary Gordon, who appeared in advertisements to give hints on topics such as what clothes to pack for Europe. The airline also hired five actresses to play Gordon for in-person events around the nation. Pan Am opted for an actual person, Jane Kilbourne, who in 1958 became the airline's first "women's promotion manager." Air France followed the fictional approach, introducing Americans to Colette d'Orsay. Despite her name, Colette d'Orsay was an American with "that classically American gypsy instinct . . . found even in the soberest, most comfortable U.S. citizens."[21]

Another reflection of European travel's rising importance for middle-class status was the growth of student and youth travel to Europe. Many students stretched their budgets by sailing on discounted "student ships" or by carrying on the tradition of "tramping" through Europe.[22] According to a U.S. Foreign Service officer stationed in Paris in the early 1960s, approximately one young American each day arrived at the U.S. consulate, out of cash and in need of a loan to get home. In almost all cases, the State Department offered enough for a one-way ticket.[23] More responsible but still thrifty young women could find work as au pairs in French households. One woman, just out of college, spent a long summer with a French family eager to teach its children English.[24] As early as 1952, enough hikers and cyclists were tramping through the American Express office in Paris that its director enlarged its public bathroom to provide more room for youthful tourists to clean themselves. Youth travel also received a boost from European rail services, which in 1958 initiated the "Eurail" program allowing students from outside Europe to travel cheaply through Western Europe. A 1965 survey found that 11 percent of all U.S. college students had traveled to Europe before graduation and that 8 percent had been to France and Germany, students' two most popular countries.[25]

The expansion of the market meant that greater numbers and varieties of package tours emerged in the 1950s and 1960s. Women's groups and fashion magazines such as *Charm* and *Mademoiselle* sponsored tours, as did *Playboy*, which launched its own tours of Europe, the Caribbean, and the Mediterranean in 1960 for men and women seeking "a new concept in unregimented travel."[26] Even on more tightly structured tours, visitors still asserted their autonomy. One veteran of a twenty-eight-day, five-country bus tour recalled how she and fellow tour members "managed to slip away many times" to explore streets and eat on their own. Even with the group, some package tourists created spontaneous moments. Once, while riding in the back of the bus, this woman and her friends flirted with a young European on a motorcycle, who then proceeded to crash his bike into the rear of the bus.[27]

Most Americans visiting Europe opted for even more independence, making the package tour a relatively minor feature of transatlantic travel. According to one estimate, the percentage of Americans traveling in package tours to Europe increased only slightly from 1955 to 1963, from 17 to 19 percent.[28] Travel agents, who received their largest profits from package tours, experienced the 1950s and 1960s as a time when their influence over travelers seemed endangered by Americans' preference to forge their own way abroad. The growing confidence of American travelers, argued one trade journal, led even more of them to do without the assistance of travel agents. The journal worried especially about the coming-of-age of "a whole new generation which refuses to be intimidated by Paris." In response to such fears, the American Society of Travel Agents in 1959 began its first general magazine advertising campaign to promote travel agents' services.[29]

Whether arranged independently or through an agent, travel to Europe was becoming so popular in the 1950s that some voices in the media wondered if it still carried the same status. In 1961, the *New York Times* saw fit to run an editorial lamenting the banality of so many tourists returning home to compare stories of where they had been. According to the *Times*, "this status-versus-status game will soon begin to bore all participants." Perhaps; but the *Times*'s claim also underscored the cultural capital Americans acquired by having been to Europe, since the paper assumed that everyone who was anyone vacationed abroad. International travel was becoming less an exotic luxury and more a new necessity.[30] In the words of one businessman surveyed by social scientists in the mid-1950s, "one is expected to know that little street off the Champs-Élysées, and if a man comes from a background where he doesn't he will seize the first free 48 hours to hop over there."[31]

If any single personality was most emblematic of the middle-class travel boom, it was Temple Fielding, author of the best-selling American guidebook on Europe through the 1950s and 1960s. *Fielding's Travel Guide to Europe*, revised annually after its 1948 debut, enjoyed an unparalleled popularity among Americans venturing out on their own in search of fine meals, luxury service, and clean hotels with private baths. By 1958, *Time* anointed Fielding "the U.S. tourist's No. 1 travel guide," a status he enjoyed into the 1970s.[32] Fielding boasted in the late 1960s that Ernest Hemingway had become a devoted reader and that President John F. Kennedy had kept a copy of the guide on Air Force One, a status otherwise reserved only for Kennedy's dictionary, his Bible, and his Congressional Directory. Fielding's popularity led to side projects such as the *Shopping Guide*, overseen by his wife, Nancy, and "Temple Fielding's Epicure Club of Europe," which allowed Americans, for $15.50, to receive prime table seating and "V.I.P." treatment in several dozen well-regarded European restaurants that contracted with Fielding. As John McPhee in the *New Yorker* remarked of the Epicure Club, "Fielding is selling prefabricated prestige, and it works."[33]

The typical "Guidester," which was Fielding's term for his readers, was a comfortably middle-class adult eager to experience Old World charms without Old World inconveniences such as communal hotel bathrooms. Fielding wrote for tourists who sought status and luxury but, as consumers in unfamiliar places, also feared social blunders and con games. In this sense, his Guidester was exactly the tourist targeted by the Marshall Plan's hotel reformers in the late 1940s and early 1950s. Fielding positioned himself in his guidebook as a typical American who came from "Middletown U.S.A."[34] The 1955–56 edition explained that he and his wife conducted research incognito, as "Mr. and Mrs. Joe Smith, routine American tourists (which we are!), who apparently speak nothing but English." Truth be told, despite years of life in Europe, Fielding never learned any foreign language.[35]

If Fielding was a "routine" tourist in some ways, his Middletown persona masked an unusual background. Born in 1914 to a wealthy New York City family, Fielding graduated from Princeton and gained his first experience with travel writing as an army lieutenant during World War II. In 1941, stationed at Fort Bragg, North Carolina, he helped new recruits navigate their way through the base by penning a surprisingly lighthearted "Guide to the Field Artillery Replacement Training Center." Later in the war, the budding writer joined the Office of Strategic Services, precursor to the Central Intelligence Agency, and conducted covert propaganda in Yugoslavia. Looking for work after the war, he found that existing travel books were not "worth a good God damn" and that they only told readers that in Europe "everything is either picturesque or Romanesque."[36]

Fielding's self-proclaimed "new school of travel journalism" proudly gave less attention than earlier guides to Europe's cultural or historic attractions. His book's few paragraphs on each country's museums were generally written by his wife. Where most other travel writers supplemented practical travel information with lengthy essays on history or architecture, Fielding enlivened his guide with brash opinions or, if deemed warranted, gushing praise for European peoples, all written in an energetic style that he called "Fielding-ese."

Indulging in one of many stereotyped national portraits, for instance, Fielding described the French as "volatile, emotional, sentimental, shrewd; confused and depressed by today's bewildering complexities; brave warriors, even in the face of overwhelming odds."[37]

With his aversion to lengthy cultural commentary and his attraction to stereotype, Fielding appeared to some critics as a sign of the unthinking oppressiveness of mass culture. Horace Sutton, the *Saturday Review*'s literary-minded travel writer and a guidebook author himself, denounced Fielding in 1958 as "autocratic" in his advice to readers and alternatingly "savage" or "over-benevolent" in his description of foreign places. Sutton preferred the leading guidebook writers of earlier decades, such as Sydney Clark and Clara Laughlin, who combined practical information with extended essays on the history and customs of foreign places written in a "lazy looping style" that was "not recommended for those looking up something in a hurry."[38]

In fact, Fielding was just the latest in a long line of guidebook writers to be criticized for allegedly diminishing the cultural experience of travel in Europe. As early as the 1840s, popular German writer Karl Baedeker faced charges of destroying cultural appreciation when he employed a star-rating system that ranked the importance of each location's monuments. When Clara Laughlin's books appeared in the 1920s, she herself dismissed "old-fashioned" academic essays on high culture and favored her own first-person reflections on the charms of foreign places.[39]

A man of his time, Fielding found success in the post–World War II travel boom in large part by focusing on the anxiety of travelers, especially first-time travelers. Fielding gave his readers the usual instructions on how to dress, tip, and find good local cuisine, yet he also spent unusual energy detailing how to spot scams and avoid fines at customs. For the sake of his readers and himself, he preferred not to list any restaurant, no matter how fine, whose staff did not speak English. Targeting inexperienced or insecure tourists, Fielding presented Europe and especially France as either a leisure paradise or a swindler's den. On the subject of tipping, Fielding described the French, along with Egyptians and Italians, as "the greediest people on the globe." Long after tobacco lost its black market value for postwar Europeans, he instructed tourists in France to hide or carry their cigarettes with them at all times lest the hotel staff steal them during the day.[40]

The emergence of Fielding, as well as *Playboy* and *Mademoiselle* magazines, as actors on the transatlantic travel scene led some in the industry to ask if roving Americans were still interested in Europe's cultural and historical heritage. In 1956, *ASTA Travel News* reported on a poll of package tourists whose main criticism of the entire trip centered on a talkative guide in Paris who kept them too long in the Louvre.[41] For all the sporadic evidence and criticism of philistine guidebooks, however, most people in the industry believed that appreciation for high culture would increase, not decline, in an age of mass travel. Americans, in fact, exhibited a voracious appetite for French high culture. In November 1964, an estimated thirty million U.S. television viewers took an hour-long tour of the Louvre with NBC and Hollywood narrator Charles Boyer. Two years later, a study by the French government found that 26 percent of American visitors said they most appreciated France's "monuments," a response rate far higher than any other nationality's. David Ogilvy, a leading advertising executive, counseled travel agents in 1966 to continue "selling cultural and status overtones," since the bulk of American tourists, no matter their age, "are status-seekers and culture-vultures." The appeal of social and cultural improvement, Ogilvy argued, was the only way the travel industry could help Americans justify the cost of the trip.[42] What emerged in most travel promotion and literature was a combination of high culture and indulgence. The goal, it seemed, was to have fun while improving oneself. In this broad sense, despite the rapidly expanding travel market, the motives of transatlantic tourists changed little from those of their nineteenth-century predecessors.[43]

Despite the continuity in Americans' transatlantic quest for culture and pleasure, the sheer volume of the travel boom inspired growing cultural criticism. The more Americans traveled in Europe, the more some cultural authorities lamented how the travel industry had made the experience less adventurous. In 1961, *Time* produced its first-ever cover story on foreign tourism. Apart from a section on Greece, the magazine directed readers away from "safe, recognizable places" such as Western Europe to focus on Africa, Asia, and the Caribbean, destinations where one could "rediscover some of the old-fashioned sense of adventure that used to go with traveling—as in the days when Baedeker advised the tourist to carry his revolver, or when Americans never ventured into postwar Europe without their own soap."[44] Just ten years after the U.S. government pleaded with European hoteliers to provide free soap, critics of mass tourism lamented this courtesy as an obstacle to the thrill of travel.

In a telling sign of discontent with mass tourism as marketed by the likes of Temple Fielding, a new guidebook called *Europe on $5 a Day* appeared in 1957, aiming to restore a sense of "adventure" to European travel. Written by Arthur Frommer, the budget-conscious guidebook circulated among students, middle-class adults, and any traveler looking for a more "authentic" experience by staying in cheap pensions and eating at inexpensive restaurants. Lacking Fielding's elite background, Frommer was the son of a Jewish textile worker from Missouri. Like Fielding, however, Frommer got his start in travel writing through the U.S. military. Stationed in Germany with the army in 1954, he used his free time to explore Europe. Shortly thereafter, while working as a Manhattan lawyer, he penned the "GI's Guide to Europe," which he published on his own and distributed through *Stars and Stripes* newsstands. Encouraged by his success, he produced a civilian version three years later. Retitled *Europe on $5 a Day*, it sold 15,000 copies in its first year. By the early 1960s, 150,000 Americans each year bought the $1.95 paperback, and many more tourists borrowed copies from others. The popularity of Frommer's guide allowed him to build a vertically integrated travel empire, with a series of budget-travel books, a "$5-a-Day-Tours" company, a partnership with KLM airlines, and even a handful of midpriced European hotels in which he placed many of his tour subscribers.[45]

While Fielding embodied a postwar middle-class drive for material comfort and sophistication, Frommer coached frugality to such an extent that he almost represented a critic of consumerism. Appearing the same year as Norman Mailer's provocative essay "The White Negro," Frommer's 1957 guide expressed a parallel, if more restrained, critique of middle-class comfort and conformity. Like Mailer's "hipster," Frommer's "$5-a-Day" tourist was an archetypal figure who abandoned stifling materialism on a romantic search for authenticity and spontaneity. While Mailer wrote of affluent white Americans imitating African American culture, Frommer sought vitality among Europe's working class. Frommer pitied luxury package tourists "sitting disconsolately in the lobbies of glacial, commercial hotels, as effectively separated from the real life of Europe as if a bubble had been built around them."[46] He stressed instead the pleasures of genuine contact between people, as in the cramped quarters of European pensions or working-class restaurants. His cardinal rule on hotels was "Never ask for a private bath," a doctrine that ran against Fielding's advice and the hotel reform campaigns conducted earlier by the Marshall Plan. Compared to Mailer, Frommer lacked intellectual pretensions, but his guide accomplished what few highbrow treatises could when it became a dog-eared companion for hundreds of thousands of Americans. Even travelers who did not read Frommer echoed parallel sentiments. One American, touring Europe as a college student in the early 1960s, recalled how he lamented the diminished experiences of those "locked into traveling first-class."[47]

The success of Frommer's guide illustrates one of the central ironies of consumerism: offering an escape from mass culture has often been one of the best mass-marketing strategies.[48] The emergence of the $5-a-day tourist as an alternative model to Fielding's high-living sophisticate also revealed one of the travel industry's persistent dilemmas. The growing volume of travel led to a corresponding rise in cultural criticism. The more Americans became tourists, it seems, the less laudable the figure of the "tourist" became. Even ardent advocates of mass travel such as Juan Trippe at times felt compelled to criticize tourists. In one commencement address in 1956, he urged college graduates, if they wanted to improve global understanding, to "try a complete reversal of the average tourist's thinking" when they ventured abroad. Temple Fielding himself instructed his staff writers to avoid referring to their readers as "tourists," since "nobody likes that."[49] This ambivalence, which might be one of tourism's most universal features, had particular importance for Americans in the midst of their Cold War struggle against Communism.

Tourists and the Battle for World Opinion

Growing numbers of Americans were heading overseas on vacations just as foreign policy experts were paying more attention to the reputation of the United States abroad. With the Korean War quieted to a stalemate by 1953, for many Americans, the Cold War seemed to settle into a long-term economic and cultural rivalry between the United States and the Soviet Union for the allegiance of "world opinion." Although new Cold War hot spots erupted outside Europe, Cold Warriors still feared that negative Western European impressions of their nation could send the region into the arms of Communists or at the very least reduce the ability of the United States to lead a unified "free world" in the global struggle. From the question of whether ambassadorial posts should be filled by amateur political appointees or career diplomats, to the use of state-sponsored tours of jazz musicians as emissaries of goodwill, Americans debated what kinds of Americans best represented the nation abroad.[50] Given these foreign policy concerns, the travel boom became a testing ground to judge whether middle-class citizens, enjoying the fruits of postwar consumerism, could serve their nation in the Cold War.

Edward L. Bernays, a leader in the public relations industry and an adviser for the U.S. Information Agency, articulated a skeptical vision of tourists' role in cultural diplomacy. As part of a 1955 *Saturday Review* forum asking, "What Do We Say to the World?" Bernays presented the influence of consumer culture on U.S. foreign relations as a liability. A voice for Cold War realism, Bernays warned of the "problem" of American tourists, movies, and books going abroad. These "discordant voices," although "the essence of our democracy," also gave Communists the ability to "build up our conflicts and deviations." To counteract "the multiplicity of unofficial channels of communication," Bernays argued for larger government propaganda programs abr

As concern with foreign opinion of the United States in policy observers responded with raised expectations that tour litically aware. In 1957, *Life* ran an article titled "How We Appear to Others," based largely on interviews with Western Europeans. Given that the United States "has risen suddenly to leadership of the West," the magazine warned, "the American traveling abroad to see the sights is now himself a sight." Reflecting the Cold War anxieties of the era, *Life* stressed that "the times require" Americans abroad to "be not just themselves but deliberate, tactful, thoughtful exponents of their nation's role as leader of the free world." Although optimistic that the ordinary American was already a "reasonably effective" agent of goodwill, *Life* also cited tourists as a common reason for " 'anti-Americanism' among friends." According to this demanding vision, tourists needed not just good manners but also the willingness and skill to explain and defend U.S. policies.[52]

For many media commentators concerned with the Cold War, the increasing scale of tourism led to fears that the travel industry itself was stripping American citizens of their ability to fulfill this role. One *New York Times* travel writer in 1959, focusing on the mass nature of transatlantic travel, described tourists as victims of the travel industry's "system," which "manufactures and distributes facts" and "reduces international communication." Concerned that illusions were unavoidable in mass travel, he revealed his emphasis on realist expertise by suggesting that the "ideal thing" would be to restrict travel to those who had studied the language and culture of "one or two" foreign countries. This critique of mass tourism, although not as strongly gender-coded as the widespread Cold War rhetoric of "over-civilized" and emasculated American men, carried the same suggestion that consumerism had made Americans too prosperous for their own good. Indeed, the same article in the *Times* featured a cartoon of an effeminate male tourist drifting through clouds and another of American men and women wearing blinders and being led like horses by their tour guide.[53]

Even the *Saturday Review*, a magazine that had long expressed optimism in the ability of tourists to promote international goodwill, at times turned against the travel industry in the 1950s. A 1957 editorial in the magazine targeted international tourism's "huge industry." The tourist, still a noble global citizen at heart, was "getting lost in the midst of all the expensive machinery of transportation and reception created to serve him." In another editorial, the *Saturday Review* lamented that "some of our great tourist organizations" promised "familiar menus, mores, and plumbing," resulting in "an unconscious bow to . . . the xenophobia that vexes so much of our private thinking and public policy these days."[54] U.S. commitment to international understanding, it seemed, was being hurt by the parochial offerings of the travel industry. *Review* editor Norman Cousins himself maintained his populist belief that

Drawings by Roy Doty.

Misguided tour—The visitors who sign up are helpless: they parade through an imaginary Europe that isn't there any more.

A cartoonist takes aim at mass tourism, emphasizing traveling Americans' loss of independence and their tenuous grasp on reality. At a time when Cold Warriors in the United States were greatly concerned about world opinion, both cartoons included confused or concerned European onlookers (from New York Times Magazine, 2 August 1959; courtesy Roy Doty).

CLOUD 9—The tourist ordinarily moves through Europe in a dream.

tourism had the potential to make "foreign policy ... everybody's business," but he grew skeptical of comfortable European travel. In a 1956 editorial, Cousins contrasted "the plush vacation" on the Riviera with more worthwhile trips "to the trouble zones or to places in the news," such as the Soviet Union, Egypt, or Indonesia.[55]

Adding to the rising tide of Cold War–inspired criticism, American commentators quickly redefined the term "Ugly American" as a reference for tourists abroad. The expression achieved quick notoriety in October 1958 as the title of a pedantic novel by William J. Lederer and Eugene Burdick. In the novel, the Ugly American was a quietly heroic government employee whose earnest and humble desire to help Asian peasants made him a more effective representative of the United States. In contrast, the majority of U.S. officials in the novel, portrayed as urbane but arrogant, won no friends among the Asians. Although the novel itself made no reference to tourists, the expansion of the term's meaning to refer to ill-mannered travelers can be traced in rapid steps. As early as August 1959, *Time* complained that Americans often erroneously assumed that the title character was a villain, suggesting that not everyone who talked about the book had actually read it. Still, *Time*'s critique made no reference to the term being used for tourists. Four months later, *Newsweek* referred to "poorly oriented" study-abroad students in Europe as "the 'ugly' ones." In June of 1960, the mass-circulation *Parade* magazine ran a tourism article titled "Don't Be an Ugly American," complete with a photograph of Americans sitting at a French café. *Parade* thus solidified the transformation of the Ugly American from a hero working politely with Asian peasants to an American tourist acting boorishly among European urbanites.[56]

The new touristic connotation to the Ugly American quickly entered political discussions of mass travel. In fact, the *Parade* article was written by Frances Knight, director of the U.S. Passport Office. Like Lederer and Burdick, Knight expressed the somewhat naive hope that all foreigners were ready to like the United States; Americans needed only first develop expertise by studying the language, history, customs, and "current problems" of the countries they planned to visit. Several weeks later, a South Carolina congressman, citing Lederer and Burdick's novel, proposed that Congress legislate a program that would teach American tourists to say "thank you" in foreign languages before leaving the country.[57] Although Lederer and Burdick intended to critique the U.S. Foreign Service, some Americans chose to respond with instead a critique of tourists.

The barrage of concern with cultural relations had some impact on everyday travelers, but perhaps not enough to satisfy all Cold Warriors. "There was a lot of hype about not being an Ugly American," recalled the woman who toured Europe by bus in the summer of 1961. The chaperones of her college tour "really drilled" the concept before departure.[58] Directors of group tours were among the most enthusiastic in stressing the political dimensions of polite behavior abroad. In this case, chaperones might have found that Cold War discourse emphasizing disciplined behavior dovetailed neatly with their own private interest in maintaining group order. Another woman on a student travel program remembered extensive orientation sessions on how to be "citizens of our country." As she described the sessions, she noted that they "probably caused us to stop and think," but she added that they were not nearly as exciting as the prospect of leaving home and seeing a new place.[59] At the other end of the spectrum, some travelers could have clearly used more reminders on the values of decent behavior. A U.S. consular official in Paris during the late 1950s recalled the story of a U.S. federal judge whose Paris vacation included a rowdy fight in a local nightclub. With the consulate's help, the judge was released by the Paris police after he paid for material damages suffered by the club.[60]

The Cold War reproach of tourism received intellectual reinforcement with the 1961 appearance of the book *The Image,* a critique of mass consumer culture by influential conservative historian Daniel Boorstin. To Boorstin, American affluence had created a society dangerously out of touch with the rest of the world, more attuned to celebrities and other "pseudo-events" than to "reality." With an implicit Cold War message, Boorstin wanted Americans to "clear the fog so we can face the world we share with all humanity." In a chapter titled "From Traveller to Tourist: The Lost Art of Travel," he blamed Americans' clouded vision in part on travel agents, airlines, and other members of the international travel industry. Package tours came under particular disapproval for isolating Americans from real life in the countries they visited. Nostalgic for a time when travel abroad belonged to just "a privileged few," he criticized how the "democratic revolutions" in travel had created an "easy" and therefore meaningless "path to cultural sophistication." Much of his critique rested on the questionable assumption that twentieth-century travelers, unlike their more refined predecessors, sought only pleasure, comfort, and confirmed expectations while abroad. According to Boorstin's pessimistic view of mass culture, the popularization of travel reduced Americans' sense of the real world and, in the process, impeded Americans' efforts in the Cold War.[61]

Pessimism over tourists' participation in international affairs did not sit well with all Americans, even within elite cultural and political circles. Criticism of mass tourism contradicted central tenants of U.S. Cold War ideology, namely that mass consumption and egalitarian spirit were positive forces that would help the United States win the Cold War through democratic means. Given this ideological quandary, other American observers took a more positive view of the popularization of overseas travel. In the same 1955 *Saturday Review* forum where propaganda expert Edward Bernays presented tourists as a Cold War liability, the liberal travel writer Horace Sutton countered with a more populist view. In an essay titled "Leave It to the People," Sutton argued that official information programs like those endorsed by Bernays could only achieve "a stalemate" with similar Soviet propaganda. "The great hope," declared Sutton, were "citizens of the great middle class" using tourist-class airfare to vacation abroad. These "humble" Americans represented a force for the United States against which the Soviets had no defense.[62]

This critique of state-centered cultural diplomacy resonated with broad segments of American society and culture. Echoing the populist spirit of Henry Luce's "internationalism of the people," this theme also surfaced in Hollywood. A year after former diplomat George Kennan exalted the principle of professionalism in foreign affairs, the 1952 Warner Brothers' movie *April in Paris* offered a populist satire of this same professional-versus-dilettante debate. The plot begins when the State Department accidentally invites an unknown working-class New York chorus girl to represent the United States at an International Festival of Art in Paris. The chorus girl, named Ethel Jackson and portrayed by Doris Day, has never traveled abroad before and is thrilled at the chance to visit Paris. The blundering State Department officials panic until they realize that the American public loves the idea of an ordinary working girl representing the United States. But trouble soon sets in for Ethel and the professional diplomats. Sailing on a French liner, the free-spirited Ethel chafes under her stuffy government chaperones obsessed with protocol and upper-class manners. In frustration, Ethel flees to the ship's fun-loving French crew in the ship kitchen. Announcing "Lafayette, I am here," Ethel allies herself with the working-class Frenchmen. One French waiter calls the exuberant Ethel "the true spirit of democracy," reinforcing the film's recurring message that Americans are at their best when they abandon pretension and simply have fun. Although one of the U.S. officials eventually falls for Ethel, the other diplomats decide that "the noble experiment" has failed and that Ethel is unfit to represent the United States abroad. Appearing increasingly as the movie's antagonists, the State Department officials cynically declare that "the American people expect their officials to be appointed from the people but not to act like the people."

In an era of red-baiting, when Hollywood offered few films that lampooned U.S. politics, *April in Paris*'s combination of satire and musical comedy helped voice a sense of unease with the tenets of foreign policy realism.[63] Even with the film's satirical cover, one irate viewer wrote the *New York Times* to denounce the movie as the work of "Hollywood Reds" intent on "pouring poison into the minds of our people."[64] Despite this accusation, the film's critique of elitist diplomats in fact paralleled Senator Joseph McCarthy's attacks on the "lace handkerchief crowd" in the State Department. But this was no red-baiting movie. Instead, the 1952 film shows how McCarthy's attack on Foreign Service experts capitalized on a broader populist concern that ordinary Americans, and not elites, should represent the nation.[65]

Doris Day's working-class character in *April in Paris* had few counterparts in reality, but a small number of working-class Americans did travel to Europe. Although rare, such trips received disproportionate attention in the U.S. media, which turned them into Cold War beacons of American prosperity and equality. A group of around 100 female workers from Fort Wayne, Indiana, became minor celebrities when they left their General Electric factory for a tour of Europe in 1953. In the words of *Fortune* magazine, "the notion that American factory workers might be able to afford a three-week summer vacation in Europe would surely have caused Karl Marx's mind to totter." *Newsweek* described how, when the group met Europeans, even Communist unionists were impressed by the consumer power of American workers. As was often the case with celebrations of mass tourism, praise of the Fort Wayne tourists revolved around references to the sober-minded purpose and cultural training that went into their trips. The factory women were not hedonistic consumers out on a lark but sincere self-improvers who had diligently saved money for several years and studied European etiquette and the French language before leaving. *Fortune*'s enthusiasm was tempered only by its reluctant acknowledgment that working-class travel was far from routine. The workers, who earned around $3,000 a year, spent at least $1,022 for their guided tour, flying tourist-class but staying in luxury hotels.[66] Much like during the Marshall Plan years, working-class travel to Europe remained a tempting but still elusive dream for postwar elites eager to see a classless American society.

Because few American workers were able or willing to make a trip to Europe, media commentators eager to claim a more positive role for tourism had to settle on middle-class travel as a symbol of American prosperity. According to influential *New York Times* columnist James Reston in 1957, American tourists were "symbols of a society that works." "These grandsons of Mark Twain's 'innocents'—these friendly, loose-limbed camera-toting Americans," Reston editorialized, were "the true revolutionaries of the world today." To Reston, these vacationers were teaching Europeans the value of catering to customers, an important lesson in forging a healthy consumer society. His triumphant example of this phenomenon was that the opulent Café de la Paix in Paris had begun serving hotdogs.[67] Reston's focus on that most populist of American foods carried the additional suggestion that middle-class American tourists were also helping Europe shed aristocratic pretension for more egalitarian pleasures.

Just as they did during the Marshall Plan years, travel boosters at times valorized middle-class tourism by denigrating travel by the very wealthy before World War II. Reporting in 1955 on the postwar travel boom, *U.S. News and World Report* emphasized that foreigners "are seeing more nearly average Americans." "Quiet, hardworking citizens from towns and villages," these ordinary Americans "demand less luxury" and "behave more quietly" than the "city sophisticates and 'playboys'" of earlier decades.[68] Writing in the *New York Times* in 1957, Abram Chasins, a self-proclaimed "veteran traveler," lauded the "new" tourists, whom he saw as "our average, hard-working citizens and their children." During his own six-week tour of Europe, Chasins encountered only a few ill-behaved Americans, whom he dismissed as "relics of days . . . when travel was a prohibitive luxury and an opportunity for crude show-offs to expose themselves." The next week, the *Times* ran four letters praising Chasins, including one that declared it "high time someone congratulates the United States tourist."[69]

Chasins himself had reason to make European sophistication seem compatible with "average" American cultural life. A New York City radio director and popularizer of classical music, Chasins had several months earlier been called by the House Un-American Activities Committee (HUAC) to testify on the alleged Communist leanings of a New York music academy. In the hearings, Chasins dismissed the idea that certain forms of music were inherently subversive. His subsequent defense of tourism, coming at a time when cosmopolitanism itself seemed on trial, may have offered a way to reduce the perceived gap between Americanness and refined European culture. Whether writing about music or mass tourism, Chasins wanted to redefine populism by making all Americans cosmopolitan in their tastes.[70]

Reconciling Populism and Realism

Realists such as Bernays and populists such as Chasins or Sutton never resolved the question of whether mass tourism aided or hindered U.S. foreign relations. Instead, the debate revealed a contradiction inherent in postwar American political culture. Free expression and middle-class prosperity might offer symbolic Cold War weapons for the United States, yet foreign policy experts were not sure if the nation gained when those traits were put into action in the form of actual Americans heading overseas. Nevertheless, detractors and defenders of mass tourism could agree on at least one issue: the government and civic-minded private organizations had the ability to improve or perfect the behavior of American tourists. Although similar initiatives began during the Truman administration, the Eisenhower White House proved most receptive to these efforts. Its emphasis on small government and public volunteerism favored the integration of tourists into the government's cultural diplomacy efforts. Foreign policymakers who came to power with John F. Kennedy, typical of their "best-and-brightest" approach, took a more skeptical view on tourist exchanges and instead sought less consumeristic forms of grassroots cultural exchange, an approach exemplified in the Peace Corps. Although the two administrations differed in their assessment of consumerism, both attempted to resolve the contradiction between mass participation in politics and realist skepticism by managing how ordinary Americans engaged in world affairs.

On the question of popular participation in foreign affairs, Eisenhower often seemed caught in an ideological bind. The conservative president favored small government, or what historian Robert Griffith has labeled the "corporate commonwealth." In this ideal, civic and corporate groups, not the government, would do most of the work of promoting a pro-business consensus at home. This cooperation would then preserve domestic order and also serve as effective propaganda overseas. Tellingly, the U.S. Information Agency under Eisenhower described American society as "People's Capitalism," an oft-repeated slogan coined by T. S. Repplier, president of the private Advertising Council. Despite this volunteer ethos, Eisenhower privately considered mass participation in politics to be disorderly and wrought with self-interest, a view more consistent with the elitist sentiments typical of foreign policy realism.[71]

Divided between a fear of the masses and a desire for civic participation, Eisenhower turned to the ideal of the corporate commonwealth for a solution. By drawing on business leaders and their public relations skills, the United States could integrate the people into its foreign policy while ensuring that such participation conformed to realist Cold War concerns. Tourism proved to be one arena in which business elites and civic organizations could manage the people's entry into foreign affairs. Eisenhower's ambivalent outlook on popular participation in politics helps explain why his administration placed an unusually high emphasis on improving the behavior of tourists overseas.

Soon after taking office, Eisenhower included references to tourism in his speeches on foreign relations, drawing on patriotism and religiosity to guide tourists toward a sense of civic responsibility while abroad. In one high-profile 1953 speech on foreign trade, Eisenhower called on each traveling American to "portray America as he believes it in his heart to be: a peace-loving nation living in the fear of God but in the fear of God only."[72]

The Eisenhower administration also encouraged civic groups and travel companies to promote good behavior abroad. Francis Colligan, a career diplomat in the State Department's International Educational Exchange Service, diagnosed a problem with tourist behavior in a 1954 policy statement titled "Americans Abroad." His solution followed the Eisenhower tenets of realism and the corporate commonwealth. Colligan contrasted consumer culture with good diplomacy and declared that "the tourist, whose purpose is frequently novelty-seeking or just relaxation, is least apt to want his fun curtailed by an admonition to be 'serious.'" For Colligan, the dilemma was changing tourist behavior "in ways which are appropriate in a free society, marked not by governmental decrees but by private initiative and personal independence." The answer lay in the mass media, which could encourage proper tourist behavior, and in civic organizations, such as women's clubs, that could organize tours around goodwill themes. With a vision of limited government activity and an emphasis on private volunteerism, Colligan stressed that Washington would play only a supporting role in these efforts.[73]

Volunteering their own efforts, members of the travel industry took steps to allay the fears of tourism's critics. In 1955, *ASTA Travel News* admitted that "something is wrong with the approach of many Americans abroad to 'winning friends and influencing people.'" The trade journal ruled out restrictions on "problem travelers" since "who is to say them nay in a democracy?" Instead it proposed that travel agents sneak small lessons on cultural sensitivity and respect for foreign difference into their promotional film screenings and brochures. For its part, American Express presented customers a brochure titled "Ambassadors of Good Will." In the words of company president Ralph Reed in 1956, tourists were America's "most effective" ambassadors because they embodied "the astonishing proportionate growth of our dominant middle class—a growth specifically the result of our free society." Reed emphasized that "the majority" of tourists were already acting as ambassadors; his brochures were only for those few in need of a reminder.[74] For American Express clients willing to read more than a pamphlet, the company also teamed with the Book-of-the Month Club to send package tour customers free books on the countries to be visited.[75] Such crash courses in area studies were another way to make ordinary tourists more like realist foreign policy experts.

To help spread such initiatives, Eisenhower launched the People-to-People Foundation in 1956. A reflection of Eisenhower's volunteerist ideology, the People-to-People program sought to encourage the private sector to organize exchanges between Americans and foreigners. Eisenhower named retired General Electric president Charles Edward Wilson to head the group, which coordinated activities and raised funds for forty-one participating committees, whose membership ranged from American hoteliers to book publishers to banking leaders.[76] Despite its entrepreneurial ethos, the foundation spent its first year operating under the USIA before becoming truly independent in 1957.[77] Minimizing its Washington origins, Eisenhower and Wilson praised how the People-to-People Foundation was free from the taint of propaganda.

Speaking before the New York Women's Press Club in 1958, Wilson justified the group's independence: "Abroad, the communists have so despoiled the temple of government that 'official' statements of any government, however honest, fall upon doubting ears and cynical eyes. Who then, is to bridge the gap?" The answer, which would have frustrated advocates of state propaganda such as Edward L. Bernays, involved everyday Americans initiating personal contacts overseas.[78]

To ensure that private Americans did their part to promote friendlier ties, the People-to-People Foundation drew on the tools of public relations and mass persuasion. At the start of the 1957 tourist season, the foundation placed privately financed posters in airports and ocean liner docks urging departing Americans to act as agents of goodwill.[79] It also brought out a similar instructional booklet distributed to tourists. Drawn by *Lil' Abner* artist Al Capp, who had earlier collaborated with the Marshall Plan's travel program, the booklet fused Cold War concerns for better diplomacy with travelers' common interest in getting off the beaten path, a combination stressed in the booklet's title, "You Don't See These Sights on the Regular Tours."[80] Another People-to-People effort was a program led by Chase Manhattan bank that recirculated a 1920s silver dollar bearing the word "peace" on one side. The coins were then to be distributed abroad by American travelers, apparently as symbols of the beneficence of both U.S. foreign policy and consumer spending. The White House contributed to these efforts by providing in each new passport a brief note signed by the president on the importance of good behavior.[81]

The mainstream media greeted these measures with some skepticism. Although endorsing Eisenhower's message as a useful step, *Life* concluded that "many an American tourist still requires more than a printed note clipped to his passport to make him aware that a single foolish action on his part can damage his country incalculably."[82] In like fashion, the *New York Times* approved of the measure as "a wise and constructive step" but added that the necessity for the president's letter "is an unhappy commentary upon some of our behavior patterns" while we travel.[83] Participating in one People-to-People conference, novelist William Faulkner hardly helped improve the image of the tourist when his list of suggestions for winning the Cold War included a proposal to suspend all American passports for one year.[84]

With at best mixed reviews, the People-to-People Foundation also failed to maintain its institutional momentum. In 1958, *ASTA Travel News* declared the program a disappointment and blamed both the government and the private sector for inadequate funding. Although some of its committees continued to function, the foundation itself drifted into inactivity.[85] The People-to-People program's lackluster fate reflected the general priorities of the State Department and the Eisenhower administration. As historian Walter Hixson has found with respect to U.S. propaganda in Eastern Europe, the "elitists and self-proclaimed realists" conducting U.S. foreign policy in the early Cold War placed military concerns over cultural diplomacy.[86] Without strong government support, Eisenhower's ideal of an enlightened private sector failed to maintain momentum.

The new Kennedy administration brought a different attitude toward tourism and cultural diplomacy. In a 1961 speech, Francis Pickens Miller, a prominent Virginia liberal who joined Kennedy's State Department, echoed the warning of Daniel Boorstin by arguing that Americans abroad had become dangerously lost in consumer luxury. Adopting a manly critique of consumer society that was typical of the Kennedy administration, he argued that travelers needed to reject a "view of life" that was "soft, opulent, flabby, muddleheaded, sentimental, and self-centered." With a realist emphasis on expertise, Miller warned that "a small group of professional Foreign Service officers" could have "their most brilliant achievements . . . undone in an hour by a single citizen who fails in an unexpected situation to advance the true interests of his country."[87] Where travel boosters might have praised consumerism as a sign of their nation's superiority over the Soviet Union, Miller reframed consumer society as a handicap in the Cold War struggle.

This anticonsumer rhetoric matched the Kennedy administration's cultural diplomacy initiatives. Rather than praise tourists and rely on existing consumer travel behavior as Eisenhower had done, the Kennedy administration placed more energy in government-directed forms of travel. At a time when the vast majority of overseas tourists headed to Western Europe, Kennedy sent thousands of specially trained Americans off the beaten track to Asia, Africa, and Latin America as two-year Peace Corps volunteers. In his public rhetoric promoting the Peace Corps, Kennedy emphasized how the volunteers often went "where no American has ever lived or even travelled" and how in all cases the volunteers received expert training before leaving. Kennedy also presented the Peace Corps as travel stripped of consumer culture comforts, where volunteers could have "rich and satisfying" experiences by living with locals.[88] Seen in this light, what separated the Peace Corps from Eisenhower's cultural diplomacy was not a populist spirit, which was already celebrated by Eisenhower and other tourism boosters in the 1950s. Instead the difference lay in how Kennedy tried to minimize the reliance on consumerism and the free market in person-to-person encounters.

Kennedy's focus on expertise and state-led programs also brought a renewed emphasis on formal educational exchanges. In 1961, the Kennedy administration promoted the Fulbright-Hays Act, which increased the number

of scholars traveling to and from the United States. In contras
who had allowed the State Department budget for educati
decline in the 1950s, Kennedy elevated the head of the field of
cultural affairs to the rank of assistant secretary within the State
By shifting the focus from existing consumer behavior to car
scholars and Peace Corps volunteers, the Kennedy solution w
the role of the state to manage how ordinary Americans particip
national affairs.

Conclusion

These debates over mass tourism and the U.S. government's attempts to manage popular participation in foreign affairs ultimately stemmed from deep-rooted tensions between postwar American consumer society and Cold War foreign affairs. As historians have shown, the Cold War era represented in some ways the "age of the expert," a time when Americans trusted authority figures to provide leadership and direction to American society and when dissenters were either McCarthyites or critical leftists such as sociologist C. Wright Mills.[90] To a degree, the history of tourism supports this interpretation. Critics of mass tourism in the media and the government fused foreign policy realism with disdain for mass culture by emphasizing the need for travelers to possess expertise. For these realist critics, mass tourism deprived Americans of their toughness and clear-sightedness just as they were putting themselves on display before the rest of the world.

At the same time, the realist critique of mass tourism revealed two dilemmas in postwar American political culture. Criticizing tourists called into question two qualities that presumably distinguished the United States from its Cold War enemies: consumer abundance and popular participation in public affairs.[91] Given these contradictions, the tenets of realism left unsatisfied a range of elites in the United States, from the makers of *April in Paris*, to travel industry leaders, and, to a degree, to the Eisenhower administration itself. To resolve these tensions between Cold War realism and mass tourism, government officials, travel industry leaders, and foreign policy–minded journalists sprang into action with various publicity measures in hopes of making ordinary tourists think of themselves as Cold War actors. In the battle to contain Communism, Americans' consumerism also had to be contained and reshaped in more disciplined ways.

Chapter 7

THE RUDE FRENCH
MODERNITY AND HOSPITALITY
IN DE GAULLE'S FRANCE

Pierre Dumas had high hopes for the 1965 tourist season. At the very least, the state secretary for tourism under Charles de Gaulle hoped to avoid the frustrations of the previous year, when the American and French press, and even French senators, accused the French of being rude toward foreign guests. When warmer weather returned in April, the Gaullist official traveled to the new Orly Airport outside Paris to launch his response. He greeted foreigners, mostly Americans, as they disembarked for stays in France. Young women dressed in the white gloves and modern pink dresses of official *Hôtesses de France* stood beside him, handing out free roses and bottles of perfume. Dumas himself distributed booklets of "smile checks" (*chèques-sourire*), which the government had printed for its new "National Campaign for Reception and Friendliness." When tourists felt they received particularly good service in a hotel, restaurant, or elsewhere, they were to tear out one of their ten smile checks, inscribe the name and institution of the friendly employee, and then mail it, no postage required, to the government's tourist office. At the end of the season, the government would award the ten most-honored French workers with vacation trips of their own to Tahiti, the Antilles, or New York City.[1]

While stereotypes of the French as unwelcoming existed in earlier periods, none of them equaled the widespread perception of rudeness that emerged on both sides of the Atlantic during de Gaulle's presidency (1958–69).[2] Many French after World War II, especially in the first half of the 1960s, used words such as "crisis," "pity," and "slump" to describe their nation's reception of foreign tourists.[3] Although some spoke of a crisis in terms of hotel conditions and price levels, much of this commentary focused on the more subjective matter of the French people's friendliness, or lack thereof, toward foreigners. Indeed, the smile-check campaign of 1965 itself assumed problems in French hospitality and in the competence of French travel industry workers and their managers. Unfortunately for Dumas, the smile checks did little to improve France's reputation. The publicity surrounding them may have even drawn more attention in the American media to unfavorable stereotypes of the

French. The next spring, Dumas declared the program a success but then quietly decided not to reissue the checks.[4]

While many Americans did complain of French inhospitality, the stereotype of rudeness was in fact more a creation of the French themselves and of long-term developments in French society and culture. French journalists, politicians, and travel industry leaders expressed heightened concern over the nation's apparent rudeness in ways that reflected and in turn influenced a broader debate in France over modernity. In an era of rapid economic and social change, the perceived crisis in French tourism and hospitality provided opportunities for French people of various political and professional stripes to advance their own agendas for the future of France. Those French wary of modernization, such as defenders of artisanal tradition, endorsed the idea of French inhospitality to confirm their belief that modernization and mass culture were harmful to the nation. Technocratic modernizers, in contrast, were eager to condemn their compatriots as unwelcoming because such claims advanced their critique of ostensibly outdated artisanal economic practices. These concerns with rudeness at home grew more acute in the context of growing competition in the international travel market. As neighboring countries, especially Spain, attracted increasing numbers of French and foreign tourists in search of vacation bargains, French observers cast a more demanding eye on their nation's own travel industry.[5] The concept of French rudeness in these ways provided rhetorical ammunition in arguments over how France's travel industry should evolve in an era of rapid modernization and rising international competition.

The Gaullist state responded to this perceived crisis by initiating a series of tourism programs that integrated both the antimodernist and the technocratic explanations for France's tourism problems. While pursuing a nostalgic publicity drive for the recovery of lost manners, the state also promoted modern high-rise hotels and fostered a more extensive tourism infrastructure designed to minimize misunderstandings between tourists and service workers.[6] In other words, the Fifth Republic's tourism program stressed technocracy in political economy and nostalgia in culture or moral values. As much as any other feature of French society, this approach to foreign tourism illuminated the often paradoxical nature of ideology and policy in de Gaulle's France.[7] These Gaullist policies also represented a major intensification in the French state's involvement in the nation's travel industry.[8] The Gaullist state in some ways carried out the program promoted by U.S. Marshall Plan officials years before. As with the Marshall Plan agenda, the goal was not simply Americanization but the creation of a more consumer-oriented France.

This era of friendliness campaigns and hotel reform also represented an important chapter in the history of U.S.-French relations. Gaullist efforts to attract and please American tourists occurred just as the French government increasingly challenged U.S. foreign policymakers on a range of political, military, and economic issues. De Gaulle in the 1960s sought to revise the U.S.-French relationship and increase French independence from American influence. In security matters, his Fifth Republic pursued an independent nuclear arsenal, opposed the U.S. war in Vietnam, withdrew France from NATO's military structure, and called on the U.S. military to vacate its bases in France. On the economic front, de Gaulle rejected the U.S.-backed British application for membership in the new European Economic Community out of concern that the British were too close to the United States. By the mid-1960s, his government also challenged the Bretton Woods gold-dollar link by converting French dollar holdings into gold. To de Gaulle, the Bretton Woods monetary regime aided U.S. corporations in their purchase of French assets and enabled the U.S. government to spend billions of dollars on its destabilizing war in Vietnam. In just the first half of 1965, the French government exchanged $600 million for U.S. gold reserves. De Gaulle even commissioned Air France planes to retrieve the metal, an unusual measure designed to increase the move's public visibility.[9] Such policies made many Americans question the depth of France's commitment as an ally. As will be seen, these Gaullist policies also contributed to American perceptions of French rudeness.

Yet de Gaulle was no simple anti-American. French foreign policy in the 1960s did not aim to shatter the U.S.-French alliance, only to reshape it into a less hierarchical relationship and to create a "third way" between the two Cold War superpowers. Moreover, in areas where closer U.S.-French ties could bolster rather than reduce France's international standing, de Gaulle's Fifth Republic courted Americans. In his first years as president of the Fifth Republic, he encouraged American investment in France as a tool to fuel French economic growth and modernization. Later in the 1960s, when that same investment began to appear to Gaullists as a new form of American domination, he began to criticize the large influx of private American capital.[10] Here again he revealed a broader concern with ensuring that close transatlantic ties promoted rather than reduced French independence. American tourism formed an important part of this Gaullist approach to transatlantic relations. Unlike U.S. military installations or corporate investments, tourist dollars came without the same loss of autonomy for the French military or economy. The French government in the 1960s thus attempted to greet American vacationers with open arms while turning a cold shoulder to other forms of the American presence in France.

In sum, the discourse of national rudeness stemmed from both domestic and international developments. At root, the stereotype of French rudeness emerged from a long-developing cultural contest in France between artisanal and technocratic visions of the nation. This contest, which was integral to the French experience with postwar modernization, in turn helped shape the French state's tourism policies and the evolution of France's travel industry. Yet this French debate did not take place in a vacuum. Increased competition in the international travel market added urgency to this internal discussion, while diplomatic tensions between the United States and France, especially in the mid- to late 1960s, provided a short-term catalyst that furthered the negative stereotype. Taken as a whole, the image of French rudeness proved a central construct shaping both domestic French affairs and U.S.-French relations in the 1960s.

Tourism and the Gaullist Pursuit of Grandeur

A breakthrough in the French state's promotion of tourism came in 1959. Just months after creating the Fifth Republic, de Gaulle appointed diplomat Jean Sainteny to head a revitalized Tourism Commissariat.[11] An international insurance broker and wartime *résistant*, Sainteny had served as France's chief representative in Vietnam in 1945 and again in 1954, emerging as an advocate for ending France's colonial war in Asia. After helping France shed its colonial past in Vietnam, he strove to make tourism a larger part of France's postcolonial future. Given his background, Sainteny's appointment in 1959 won praise from the newspaper *Combat* as a sign of "energetic government action" to help France "regain the favored place that she once knew with American tourists." Other newspapers looked forward to tourism becoming one of the Fifth Republic's major concerns, predicting that Sainteny would bring to tourism a "taste for action."[12]

The former diplomat did indeed begin by taking action. Sainteny ensured that his Tourism Commissariat would have a larger and more independent budget than the organization that preceded it in the Fourth Republic. In addition, he arranged for tourism to receive greater attention in de Gaulle's cabinet and forged ties between his bureaucracy and the newly created Ministry of Cultural Affairs, led by the charismatic writer André Malraux.[13] The new Gaullist government also initiated a dramatic increase in public financial support for French hotels, including new tax breaks and guaranteed low-interest loans. Between 1960 and 1963 state loans to hoteliers jumped from 70 million to 161 million francs.[14] Through the 1960s, the government also invested heavily in Mediterranean resorts designed to keep French vacationers within the country. One hotel industry expert would later recall these years as "the era of easy money."[15]

With increased resources, the commissariat expanded its overseas marketing efforts. In 1960, Sainteny traveled to North and South America to promote French tourism and inspect the French government's newly opened tourism offices in Miami, San Francisco, and Beverly Hills.[16] This promotional work contributed to the broader goal of using France's cultural reputation to bolster the nation's standing in the Cold War world. Sainteny's visit to the United States, for instance, came just after a visit to the Soviet Union in July 1960, where he helped establish an Air France bureau and an official French tourism representative in Moscow. France thus became one of the earliest Western nations to establish tourism offices with both Cold War superpowers, a move that mirrored de Gaulle's search for a "third way" through the Cold War.[17]

The Gaullists' effort to have tourism serve their broader international vision also shaped the Fifth Republic's new approach to advertising aimed at American consumers. Although typically apolitical on the surface, international tourism advertising is best seen as a form of state-sponsored cultural diplomacy. As one tourism official put it, France's travel office was "obliged to take into account factors other than profitability and effectiveness" in designing its publicity.[18] The Gaullist emphasis on modernization posed a difficult balancing act for tourism officials, who recognized that most Americans in France sought Old World pleasures and attractions. How could publicity appeal to typical tourist tastes for the old while also trumpeting Gaullist enthusiasm for the modern and industrial side of postwar France? Moreover, how could advertisements make the French seem friendly without making them seem servile? According to André Alphand, France's chief tourism official in the United States and a former diplomat, the task was to publicize "the paradox of France," a phrase meant to highlight the persistence of tradition amid a modernizing nation.[19]

To solve the challenge of presenting France as old yet modern, refined yet not too intimidating, French tourism officials turned to American advertising agencies. In the first months after de Gaulle's return to power, Alphand's office in New York began pushing its superiors in Paris for permission to fire its current Manhattan firm, Grey Advertising, after a disappointing series of advertisements. One of the ads, panned as unrealistic by *Advertising Age*, depicted a couple from Long Island painting pictures in the Provence countryside while French strangers approached their easels to offer friendly comments.[20] Alphand himself complained of the agency's "overly commercial style" and noted that the advertisements fell short of "a certain artistic level" that representations of France demanded. Particularly damning for any French official with thoughts of national grandeur was the fact that the agency gave more attention to its slightly larger account selling Americans Polident denture cream. "We think," declared Alphand, "that our country's publicity must draw inspiration from a different spirit."[21]

Sainteny agreed and oversaw the search for a Madison Avenue firm that could present an image of France that was both marketable and consistent with Gaullist diplomacy's search for international prestige. Few agencies seemed to fit the bill. One prospective firm suffered from "banality" with a proposed campaign celebrating "the Riveter on the Riviera" and "the Lumberjack in the Louvre." Another, in contrast, appeared "a bit too intellectual" for most Americans. A third lost out for "giving the impression of trying to 'sell' France like soap or toothpaste," a comment suggestive of lingering disappointment over Gray Advertising's greater attention to the Polident account.[22]

The winning agency was Doyle Dane Bernbach (DDB), an innovative firm that was just beginning American advertising's "creative revolution" of the 1960s. The company's fresh approach, labeled "hip consumerism" by writer Thomas Frank, used irony and wit to create a distinctive style in the otherwise staid world of 1950s advertising. In its most famous campaign, launched the same year France hired the firm, DDB remade the image of Volkswagen with advertisements that acknowledged popular malaise with mass-production conformity while cleverly proposing mass-produced Beetles as the remedy.[23] DDB's ironic approach complemented French officials' vision of "the paradox of France." Indeed, the French government stayed with the firm for an unusually long period, from 1959 to 1969, almost the exact years of de Gaulle's presidency.[24]

The resulting advertisements, which appeared in newspapers and popular magazines such as *Life, Time*, and the *New Yorker*, represented what might be called "hip Gaullism." Casting a Janus face worthy of de Gaulle himself, DDB's ironic approach could celebrate French folk culture while simultaneously predicting its demise. One 1961 piece offered a postcard-gorgeous coastline with Breton women in traditional white starched hats. This image of timeless tradition appeared over a caption reading, "Five years from now it won't be the same."[25]

French tourism advertising by DDB in the first years of the Fifth Republic frequently suggested that a more modern and nationalistic France was also a friendlier nation. One 1959 advertisement promised Americans: "There's a big smile on the face of France!" The advertisement's text read like a billboard for Gaullist modernization. It informed Americans of a France "young and strong again" and "boiling with energy" in science, jet technology, automobile pro-

The 1959 advertisement that cost a Madison Avenue agency its account with the French Government Tourist Office. The U.S. press panned it as unrealistic (from New Yorker, 21 March 1959; photograph by William Klein; courtesy French Government Tourist Office).

This 1961 Doyle, Dane, Bernbach ad highlighted both French folk traditions and relentless modernization. The firm used advertising's "creative revolution" and newfound sense of irony to capture the paradoxes of Gaullist France (from New Yorker, 11 March 1961; courtesy French Government Tourist Office).

duction, and cinema. Suggesting that modernization went hand in hand with cheerfulness, the caption trumpeted "the gaiety of a people who are vital again, *leading* again." Another ad from early 1963 offered a close-up photograph of a sun-drenched French flag stretching across two magazine pages, with the simple headline, "Welcome."[26] With the French at last finding their own confidence, these ads implied, they would no longer be so resentful of American visitors.

As part of this Gaullist image makeover, André Malraux's new Ministry of Cultural Affairs launched its own campaign to clean centuries of grime from cathedrals and other national monuments. The ministry's cleaning effort reflected the president's belief that cultural grandeur could both unify the French and bolster the nation's status abroad. Sparked as well by concerns about industrial pollution tarnishing the nation's cultural heritage, the wave of cleanings represented another step in the state's increased commitment to managing France's tourist environment.[27] Malraux's scrubbing of Notre Dame cathedral and other monuments coincided with local government campaigns to clean up popular tourist areas. In 1965, for instance, the Seine Prefecture launched "Operation Cleanliness" for the Paris area. The campaign won the praise of *Le*

There's a big smile on the face of France!

If you haven't been to France in the past few years, you are in for some tremendous surprises. From countryside to city street, France has become young and strong again. Her people happy. Alive. Vigorous. Boiling with energy and accomplishment. You see it in the outpourings of countless industries: jet aircraft, automobiles, electronic devices, silks. In the phenomenal advances of French scientists and technicians. In the dramatic renaissance of the cinema and theater. And in Paris—lighthearted, witty Paris—you find the gaiety of a people who are vital again, *leading* again. Wherever you go in France today, you see happiness on the faces of her people. You feel it in the way they welcome *you*. Now is the time to go. See your travel agent, or for folders and information write, Dept. NY-11, Box 221, N. Y. 10, N. Y. The French Government Tourist Office: New York • Chicago • Los Angeles • San Francisco • Montreal

1. North-Picardy 2. Normandy 3. Ile-de-France 4. Brittany 5. Loire Valley 6. Berry 7. Poitou-Charentes 8. Limousin-Quercy-Périgord 9. Bordeaux-Guienne 10. Toulouse-Languedoc 11. Corsica (not shown) 12. Champagne 13. Lorraine-Vosges-Alsace 14. Burgundy 15. Franche-Comté-Monts-Jura 16. Auvergne 17. Alps-Savoy 18. Dauphiné 19. Lyons-Rhône Valley 20. Provence-Côte d'Azur 21. Riviera-Côte d'Azur 22. Mediterranean-Languedoc-Roussillon 23. Pyrenees-Basque

A 1959 Doyle, Dane, Bernbach advertisement that came on the heels of Jean Sainteny's "smile offensive." The emphasis on French technology and gaiety suggested that a modern France was a friendly France (from New Yorker, *31 October 1959; courtesy French Government Tourist Office).*

Monde, which lauded it for lending truth to the maxim that "a welcoming country is first a clean country."[28]

Constructing French Rudeness

In their efforts to attract and please Americans and other foreigners, Gaullist tourism officials also made the recovery of friendliness toward foreigners a persistent theme in their public appearances. In one typical speech before a French audience in 1960 on the importance of American tourism, Jean Sainteny invoked a lost age of hospitality and challenged his compatriots to "relearn" the "legendary smile of the French."[29] Official expressions on the need for more friendliness reached the point where French newspapers quickly labeled Sainteny "the high commissaire for smiling" and described his work as the "smile offensive."[30] French tourism officials themselves referred to these efforts as "indirect education," meaning that the aim was both better hospitality and increased public awareness in France of tourism's value to the nation.[31] Jean Ravenel, the former mayor of the alpine resort town of Chamonix who succeeded Sainteny in 1963, turned to the mass media to advance this "education" agenda. On a June 1965 television talk show, Ravenel invited journalists from the United States, Britain, and Germany to present foreigners' complaints about France. As a result, ten million French viewers heard a litany of grievances ranging from dishonest taxi drivers to the practice of tipping.[32] For those who missed the television program, Ravenel's colleague, State Secretary Pierre Dumas, created a call-in radio contest in which French listeners pretended to help a foreigner in an imaginary tourist situation. Dumas added posters, celebrity endorsements, and his attention-grabbing smile checks to the campaign.[33]

But did the French travel industry and general population require this kind of lecturing on the need for a warm reception? In contrast to the image of inhospitality, government and market surveys found that American and other foreign tourists generally had a good time in France. According to one French government study conducted just before Sainteny's arrival, four-fifths of foreigners found the French "friendly and helpful," opposed to only 5 percent who responded with negative assessments.[34] French officials took particular interest in Americans, who accounted for 40 percent of France's tourism earnings through the 1960s, despite representing just 10 percent of its foreign visitors.[35] Eight in ten Americans polled declared themselves "very satisfied" with their travels in France, while a mere 4 percent voiced negative opinions.[36] A 1961 survey found only one in ten Americans dissatisfied with French hotels, whereas 83 percent expressed satisfaction.[37] According to another government study during the summer of 1963, only 0.3 percent of tourists registered complaints with French authorities.[38] All the while, France figured in travel itineraries for over half of Americans in Europe, a rate matched by no other European country.[39]

If anything dissatisfied American visitors, it was French methods of billing and tipping. Practices such as the restaurant cover charge, a fee added at the end of a meal, were little known in the United States and appeared to some Americans as a charge added just for them. The voluntary gratuity might have been common in the United States, but American tourists and journalists had long complained of not knowing when or how much to tip in France, or of being expected by French service workers to tip extravagantly. Indeed, the move toward *tout compris* (everything included) prices had been one of the central concerns of the Marshall Plan's tourism program in France a dozen years earlier. In one government survey of foreign tourist opinion, tipping was one of the few clear problem areas, drawing negative feedback from around half of foreign tourists in the survey. The *New York Times* in September 1964 reported on widespread complaints by Americans. "It bites me when these French look at me like I'd beaten a child with a stick when I don't distribute money all over the restaurant when I leave," lamented one Californian interviewed by the *Times*.[40] "There was a fair amount of confusion," noted another visitor years later, whose travels in France in the early 1960s were inconvenienced but by no means spoiled by service employees asking for gratuities.[41] Even with the complaints, however, France's foreign tourism was not in a clear crisis. Earnings from foreign visitors increased on average a healthy 10 percent each year during the supposed slump in French tourism.[42]

Given the persistent appeal of visiting France, the question remains as to why the impression of a tourism crisis emerged and why the French government felt compelled to introduce smile checks and other hospitality measures. In part, the sense of a crisis sprang from transatlantic diplomatic tensions over de Gaulle's attempts to revise the U.S.-French alliance. At times, American political commentators employed the same concept of rudeness to describe both French diplomacy and French manners, a fusion that furthered the stereotype of the innate disposition of the French to dislike Americans. Summarizing the outlook for French policy in 1965, influential columnist Stewart Alsop predicted that "de Gaulle will no doubt go on being rude to us."[43] To some Americans, de Gaulle himself seemed responsible for the French people's rudeness toward Americans. After a trip to France in 1965, Senator Stephen Young, an Ohio Democrat, announced that he had "witnessed for myself" how "the French people, in a crude imitation of their leader, have come to despise Americans."[44] The *Saturday Evening Post*, attempting to explain the rudeness of

Parisians, similarly concluded in 1965 that de Gaulle "gives a sort of official stamp of approval to all acts by private citizens which are hostile and selfish."[45]

Tourism also offered a way for Americans to express frustration over French diplomacy. Upset by Gaullist policies, some Americans retaliated by calling for consumer boycotts on travel to France. Even an American as committed to international travel as Senator J. William Fulbright, whose Fulbright Program sent hundreds of American scholars to France each year, advised Americans in 1965 to "spare themselves the sophisticated debauchery and artistic pocket picking of Paris." To protest de Gaulle's challenges to U.S. monetary policy, Americans ought to vacation at home "without insults or shakedowns."[46]

Close attention paid by the media of each country to opinion across the Atlantic reinforced rather than assuaged critical views. In a cycle of negative imagery, references to French inhospitality in one nation's media often attracted attention across the Atlantic. In one early incidence of this cross-reporting, French senator Edouard Bonnefous in September 1964 complained of his compatriots' inhospitality. *Newsweek* then used his comments to reinforce the idea that the French indeed offered "poor service and incomparable insolence from servants." Quoting a Paris barman, the same *Newsweek* article summed up the French attitude for American readers: "We're just naturally inhospitable to foreigners."[47] When, in 1965, one American frustrated by de Gaulle printed cards urging traveling Americans to "avoid France and other USA enemies," *Le Monde* reproduced the card, along with a reference to Senator Fulbright's earlier remarks. The *New York Times* found *Le Monde*'s editorial decision newsworthy enough to run its own story the next day with the headline: "French Reprint Card Urging Americans to Shun France."[48]

One episode that highlighted the French media's role in the construction of a hospitality crisis came with the so-called Fielding Affair, sparked by the popular weekly *Paris Match*. Concerned with rising competition from Spain, *Paris Match* in 1964 profiled best-selling American guidebook writer Temple Fielding to gain insight on what Americans thought of the French. Describing Fielding as "a sort of supreme court judge with unlimited power," *Paris Match* ignored how Fielding's guide praised France as a friendly destination. Instead the magazine quoted two unrepresentative passages in which Fielding warned of France's relatively high prices and automobile fatality rate. Claiming falsely that American tourists were only spending thirty-six hours in France, *Paris Match* faulted high prices and an outdated hotel industry and wondered if the French people might be the "grouches of Europe." The article struck a nerve with readers. *Paris Match* published an unusually large number of reader responses, divided evenly between defenders and critics of France's travel industry. Debate over Fielding's alleged attacks soon reached the French Senate, where Secretary Dumas felt it necessary to defend de Gaulle's administration by quoting more representative, approving passages from Fielding's guidebook.[49]

Although diplomatic tensions and sensational media cross-reporting furthered the sense of a tourism crisis in France, the debates of the mid-1960s also represented the culmination of several longer-term trends shaping postwar France. One crucial reason for the perceived crisis was the fact that the French were increasingly traveling themselves. This social context altered the nation's so-called tourist balance, an economic concept that referred to France's foreign tourism earnings minus French travelers' expenses abroad.[50] The nation's worsening tourism balance stemmed, ironically enough, from French prosperity. With rising wages and benefits such as politically guaranteed paid vacations, the French increasingly headed to Spain or Italy, where their strong franc notes went further and where local governments, especially Franco's in Spain, aggressively promoted their own hotel industries. In 1965, for the first time ever, French people leaving on vacation outnumbered and outspent France's foreign visitors.[51]

More than a simple economic issue, concerns over the tourism balance also sprang from self-perceptions of France as a center of civilization. The belief that tourism ought to add to rather than detract from France's currency holdings appeared a truism for nationalists accustomed to seeing their nation as the world's leading travel destination. Senator Bonnefous, for instance, described the possibility of a tourist deficit in 1964 as "the paradox of paradoxes" and joined a chorus of voices calling for improvements in France's reception of foreign tourists. To L'Aurore, the stories of rude service and fleeing French vacationers made the 1964 season "a Waterloo for French tourism." Another journalist that same year saw a negative tourist balance as a challenge to France's status as the "country of tourism par excellence" and asked, "Will what has always been taught us prove false?"[52]

As France's tourist balance approached a deficit, many French responded with increased expectations that foreign tourists would make up the difference. Unfortunately, the same high prices that encouraged the French to leave home also encouraged foreigners to consume less in France than they did in other parts of Europe. In the early 1950s, Americans spent more money in France than in any other European country. By the late 1950s, however, Americans still visited France more than any other European country but spent fewer dollars there than in either Italy or the United Kingdom.[53] Moreover, some American observers connected French inhospitality with rising prices. According to Time in 1965, "the early tourists didn't care too much if the garçon sneered at what they knew was a very generous tip. . . . They care now."[54]

Many French journalists were willing to endorse and amplify this negative image of French service workers. Indeed, the rising perception of French rudeness toward foreigners owed much to the internal trend of growing numbers of French people leaving home for vacations or restaurant meals in the 1960s. Complaints by Americans gave added ammunition to French consumer advocates speaking in the name of France's own middle class. In 1964, under the headline "An American in Paris," one such consumer-oriented newspaper, *Paris-Presse*, printed a letter by a Parisian describing a Champs-Élysées café waiter chasing after an English-speaking tourist who left without paying a tip. Unable to speak a common language with the tourist, the waiter could not explain that service was not included. According to the Parisian eyewitness, the tourist paid but left "convinced that Paris is a city of gangsters."[55] *Paris-Presse* most likely would not have printed the story about the American tourist if the incident had not occurred in the midst of the newspaper's own campaign calling for "an end to tips." Each day for over two months, *Paris-Presse* ran front-page stories detailing how both foreign and French consumers resented leaving tips for service employees. Although the newspaper claimed no hostility against French service employees, its articles and cartoons depicted them, especially hotel workers, as concerned less with quality service than with the pursuit of tips. *Paris-Presse* encouraged its readers to challenge overzealous solicitations. By detailing the normal tasks of each type of hotel employee, the newspaper informed unskilled French consumers that most services did not require an extra tip. An errand boy, or groom, who ran out to buy cigarettes or a newspaper, for instance, was just doing his standard job for which he received a basic salary. If asked for a tip, he was displaying only the spirit of greed that had given the French a reputation for being inhospitable.[56]

Despite some confusion and resentment over tipping, market surveys, as we have seen, showed overwhelming satisfaction among tourists who came to France. A combination of diplomatic tensions, sensationalistic journalism, and shifting leisure patterns in French society and in the international travel market, however, masked the reality of largely satisfied Americans coming to France in ever-increasing numbers. Although some French travel market observers saw this relative decline in French tourism in these terms, French politicians and media commentators just as often seized on and even exaggerated the nation's tourism problems to point to flaws in France's own national character and in the service traditions of the nation's hotel industry. Both cultural conservatives and technocratic modernizers had their own reasons to portray their compatriots as rude and unwelcoming. While Americans at times did speak of the French as rude hosts, the image of French rudeness was as much a product of internal French debates.

Some French observers, positioning themselves as guardians of traditional

exemple de pourboire abusif

French culture, explained the inhospitality of their compatriots in terms of broader critiques of social change and mass culture in postwar France. Rapidly growing industrial production and consumer power raised fears about the effects of modernization on virtually every aspect of a nation that until recently had been mostly rural. Growing numbers of teenagers wore blue jeans, danced to rock music, and, despite the best advice of conservative elders, drank Coca-Cola. Startling representations of France's changing youth and consumer cultures, as in Jean-Luc Godard's *A bout de souffle* (1959), portrayed aimless French youth infatuated with violence, cars, Hollywood, and Americans. At the same time, decolonization created deep national divisions and vitriolic debate. The loss of colonies in North Africa and Southeast Asia prompted a search for new ways in which the French could envision their nation's cultural

CABU

"... *paumes vers le ciel, tendez les doigts!...*"

In the midst of a perceived crisis in French hospitality, these cartoons were part of Paris-Presse's campaign on behalf of U.S. and French consumers and against greedy French hotel employees. The captions read (left) "example of an abusive tip" and (right) "palms toward the sky, hold out the fingers!" (from Paris-Presse, 20, 21, 22 September 1964; courtesy Cabu).

grandeur and radiance.[57] The perceived crisis in France's foreign tourism grew from and in turn fueled this conservative reaction to postwar social, cultural, and international changes.

In December 1964, debate on foreign tourism erupted in the Paris Municipal Council, propelled in part by a councillor who had received a *New York Times* news clipping from a friend on the subject of poor Parisian hotel service. The councillor blamed his city's reputation for rudeness on declining moral education and "failing families." Even "in families highest on the social scale," he lamented, "the most elementary politeness seems like a vestige of a disappeared age." If the French could not be polite within their families, the message went, how could they be polite to foreigners in public?[58] In 1967, a government tourism official likewise faulted families and schools, as well as cinema and television, for encouraging "the spread of 'relaxed' behavior." Mass culture, it seemed, ruined the "respect for others . . . and oneself" that the French used to display.[59] In this view, mass culture's promotion of individual gratification and informality threatened the selfless manners required of hotel workers and all good French hosts.

Cultural conservatives singled out the stress of life in Paris as another key source of France's bad reputation among tourists. The same municipal councillor argued that the "unhappiness" of life in noisy and dense Paris led its denizens to take out their frustration on innocent foreigners.[60] In a similar vein, when Paris city planners offered an anthology of essays in 1964, one contributor, Georges Dupont, attributed the city's poor reception of tourists to "the hell of its modern rhythm." Calling for "a civilization of leisures," he envisioned a gentrified city in which streets would be turned into pedestrian zones surrounded by "a world of privileged habitation" for people willing to pay more for charming apartments with "character." With industry and lower-income housing relegated to the city's "peripheral zones," Paris "could become again a city good for both living and visiting."[61] Dupont was hardly alone with this vision of a leisure-oriented Paris designed for foreign tourists and the wealthy French. One 1958 government study's concern with creating a tourist-friendly environment led it to detail the very few complaints it found from tourists. The study took pains to itemize each type of grievance. Of the 10 percent of foreign respondents who reported any unpleasant encounter with the French, 2 percent expressed unhappiness with French beggars, 1.5 percent were critical of prostitutes, and 0.3 percent complained about "Arabs."[62] In 1959, Jean-Marie Le Pen, the Parisian parliamentarian and future far-right leader, wrote in a tourism trade newspaper that Paris needed to be remade for visitors, and he issued a vague call "to recreate a sort of unity" in his own neighborhood of the city, the Left Bank's Fifth Arrondissement.[63]

These calls to make urban centers more pleasing for tourists helped justify profound social changes in and around Paris. Conservative attempts to recover a golden age of polite and stress-free urban life occurred at a time when city elites were conducting a program of "sanitizing" Paris, demolishing working-class neighborhoods and transforming the city into a more middle- and upper-class center. Between 1954 and 1974, for instance, Paris's population declined by 19 percent and its working-class population declined by 44 percent, moving mostly to dense "new cities" in the suburbs.[64] The perceived crisis in French tourism added legitimacy to dystopic visions of urban France and thus reinforced the trend among Paris officials toward the gentrification of the city.

Showing that the perception of a hospitality crisis could span the political spectrum, even L'Humanité, the Communist daily paper, joined in the criticism of France's reception of American tourists. In a July 1965 report declaring, "The hunting season for dollars is open," L'Humanité criticized greedy taxi drivers who went on "tourist-safari" by overcharging American passengers.

Unlike the nostalgic conservative critics, the paper posited no golden age of French morality. Highlighting the image of French rudeness for its own purposes, the paper instead implied that such unseemly behavior was the natural result of both American naïveté and the corrupting influence of the profit motive.[65]

Put on the defensive, some French hoteliers and hotel and restaurant workers acknowledged hospitality problems but blamed the reputation for rudeness on another feature of modernity: rising middle-class consumption. To these critics within the industry, the rise of middle-class travel to France, as well as the increased consumer power of the French people, produced unsophisticated clients unready to participate in refined leisure culture and therefore more likely to voice complaints. As early as 1954, *L'Hôtellerie*, the leading hotelier trade journal, argued that the client, whether French or foreign, was "himself responsible for this state of things because he does not know how or does not dare to have himself respected." According to the journal, unskilled clients encouraged hotel and restaurant workers to let their standards drop, reflecting "a certain modernism" and a "desire for easiness in life, all without respect for the reputation of our country."[66]

Hotel workers themselves more often focused solely on their increasingly novice clientele to explain troubles in French tourism. In another early comment, one hotel labor leader lamented the difficulty of serving clients whose inadequate "education" gave them an arrogant attitude toward hotel servants.[67] Jacques Retel, a sociologist who worked several years in a luxury hotel, argued in 1965 that hotel work was easier when clients "knew how to order." According to Retel, "real aristocrats" and working-class regulars were easier to serve than uninformed middle-class consumers who did not understand how luxury hotels functioned and who presumably came from the largely American middle class that predominated in Parisian luxury hotels. Another hotel employee explicitly framed the issue of skilled versus unskilled customers in terms of nationality. This *équipier*, whose tasks included cleaning the hotel lobby, posited that certain nationalities of clients, such as the French or Swiss, knew how to avoid interfering with hotel work. "The Americans," on the other hand, "never understood." They would occupy sofas and place their feet on the table just at the moment when they were to be cleaned.[68]

Exasperated by growing public criticism at home and abroad, *L'Hôtellerie*'s principal columnist in 1964 proposed that clients undergo an apprenticeship training program before participating in travel culture. Too many tourists, "ignorant of the life of the city," did not know, for example, how to choose a restaurant they could afford. In another, even more sarcastic column, the same writer suggested that the government issue each tourist a "classification card" in the same fashion that the government ranked hotels. That way, hoteliers and service employees would know in advance how silly or difficult a client's requests might be.[69]

The explanation for the hospitality crisis that proved most consequential came from the technocrats and politicians who molded France's political economy in the postwar era. To them, the roots of France's alleged inhospitality lay in the artisanal and therefore backward nature of French hotels. Center-right political leaders, particularly under de Gaulle's Fifth Republic, placed great faith in large-scale industrial mergers, high-technology firms, and state-directed technocratic leadership. Only by modernizing in this fashion could France maintain its grandeur and prosperity in a postcolonial, Cold War world.[70] On the whole, French hotels in the 1960s featured everything that this Gaullist ideal disdained: small size, artisanal or even familial management, and low-technology labor practices.[71] Gaullist minister of finance and future French president Valéry Giscard d'Estaing, frustrated with the hotel industry's unwillingness to submit to price controls in 1964, described the hotel business as "the most disagreeable, quarrelsome, and *poujadiste*" industry in France, an unflattering but partially valid reference to Pierre Poujade's short-lived right-wing movement centered around shop owners and artisans in the mid-1950s.[72] The *poujadistes*, with their emphasis on reducing taxes and defending French traditions, had indeed won supporters among hoteliers.[73] When Giscard's Ministry of Finance conducted special investigations into the hotel industry in 1964, its inspectors found an industry "very isolated from the movement of ideas and affairs" and "a profession sometimes more concerned with complaining than progressing."[74]

The Gaullist state's image of a backward, inhospitable hotel industry had important consequences for the development of tourism in France. Speaking before tourism officials and journalists in 1963, for instance, Gaullist prime minister Georges Pompidou publicly condemned French hotels as "often badly managed and rarely welcoming." Pompidou, who had served in the government's tourism office in the late 1940s, accused French hoteliers of acting as if they "were doing the client a great honor to agree to receive him." Significantly, when Pompidou criticized the haughtiness of hoteliers, he also proposed that the government aid new hotel construction, under the theory that increased competition would make hoteliers more likely to please clients.[75]

In the French media, advocates of economic modernization joined Gaullist politicians in criticizing French hotels. At a time when technocrats lauded nuclear power plants and jet planes as the new symbols of national radiance, like-minded journalists treated the Old World business practices of hotels as hopelessly behind the times.[76] In February 1964, the magazine *Perspectives* declared tourism the "sick man of the French economy." Especially at fault was a "hotel trade of papa" that "resembled more an artisanal sector jealous of its liberty and privileges than the dynamic sector that it must be." The business magazine *Entreprise* similarly described France's hotel industry as "a trade too often dedicated to artisanship." In its story on Temple Fielding, *Paris Match* repeated the sentiment, faulting an outmoded "hotel trade of 'granddad'" as one reason why Americans were supposedly shunning France.[77]

By focusing on snobbish or grouchy hoteliers, advocates of modernization offered a highly selective interpretation of the problems facing the French hotel industry. A more dispassionate explanation might have focused on hotels' financial woes in the 1950s and early 1960s. During a time of rising wages and rapid growth in the overall economy, French hotels attracted few investors willing to pay the relatively high costs for building construction and service labor. In some cases, owners or investors even converted existing hotels into more profitable office buildings or residential apartments.[78] In the midst of a postwar international travel boom, French hotel capacity increased only 20 percent between 1953 and 1965 and even declined slightly between 1963 and 1965. This stagnation was most evident in the service-intensive three-star, four-star, and deluxe four-star hotels that represented the lifeblood for foreign tourism.[79] In other words, France's hotel problems had little to do with existing French establishments, which still pleased their guests, and more to do with a lack of capital for renovations and new hotels. Yet by focusing on rude hoteliers, advocates of modernization delegitimized artisanal practices and suggested that any solution to the crisis would require a shift away from artisanal hotels.

Reshaping France's Travel Industry

Drawing force from a range of domestic and international factors, the rudeness image in turn influenced the elaboration of France's infrastructure for receiving tourists. In the early years of the Fifth Republic, both public and private initiatives expanded and reshaped the French travel industry. Government programs in particular aimed to alter the everyday experiences of tourists in France. For French hoteliers and other industry elites, the state's growing attention proved a mixed blessing. Although industry leaders had long called for more state assistance, the newly empowered Tourism Commissariat also came with added regulations, heightened competition, and what many hoteliers and restaurateurs saw as an assault on their traditions of service.

One area of cooperation between the travel industry and the government involved the perceived need to provide foreigners with a more structured reception. Indeed, to a certain extent, French officials shared one of the assumptions of artisanal hoteliers and skilled hotel workers: that ill-informed, middle-class, and often American tourists were responsible for part of France's reputation for rudeness. A French government investigation of tourist opinion in 1966, for example, attributed hospitality problems to "inexperienced" visitors unfamiliar with the French language or "our customs." These tourists, whom the study found to be disproportionately American, "felt very vulnerable" and were therefore "particularly suspicious" when abroad. The study emphasized that these insecure tourists required "particular protection," especially from potentially confusing situations.[80] One such innovation was a telephonic hotel finding system begun in 1958 to ensure that tourists arriving in Paris without accommodations could, without knowing a word of French, find a hotel that matched their expectations for comfort and price. By 1961, the system spread to other French cities, and in Paris, approximately 500 hotels participated.[81] If the smile offensive proved inadequate, French tourism promoters hoped that a more extensive reception system could compensate. As the editor of *L'Hôtellerie* approvingly noted in 1960, "a good organization is a permanent smile."[82]

Government and industry concerns with hospitality also fueled the growing employment of young women as professional "hostesses" by the state and by local tourism offices. The position of the hostess had originally taken hold in the 1930s with the advent of airline stewardesses, known in French as *hôtesses de l'air*. Within France, the use of tourism hostesses assumed heightened importance in the 1950s and 1960s. Tourism hostesses spoke English, stood behind information booths, patrolled airports, provided directions, and offered a smiling face. In other words, their job was to act according to the ideal of courtesy that France's tourism promoters hoped to instill in all French citizens. Hostesses became particularly popular with local boosters at hotel dispatch and welcoming centers, where over three-quarters of the employees were female.[83]

For many French industry experts, hostesses represented a twofold solution to the crisis in French hospitality. The young women provided the labor for the nation's expanded tourism infrastructure, and they represented widespread hopes that the French could overcome their reputation for rudeness by feminizing the business of hospitality. Indeed, the proliferation of hostesses in the context of the perceived French hospitality crisis reflected commonly held assumptions about women as naturally benevolent toward strangers. One French tourism official in 1965 found it "natural that the delicate missions . . . of welcoming are more and more conferred to women." *L'Hôtellerie* praised the hostess as "this kindhearted girl, issued from one of our gracious provinces" who offers "a smile that is not ordered."[84] Hostesses, embodying the virtues of feminine and rural France, offered a way to show foreigners an innocence seemingly lost in urban France.

The same emphasis on a premodern and feminized France infused the Tourism Commissariat's campaigns to have the French beautify their nation with flowers. Like the hostess profession, flower contests had existed earlier but grew in both size and nationalistic rhetoric under de Gaulle. After modest efforts in the mid-1950s, tourism officials under de Gaulle initiated a more ambitious *Fleurir la France* campaign.[85] In a nostalgic vein, the campaigns envisioned a more livable nation for both the French and foreigners alike. One publicity poster from 1966 showed a young woman standing by a window that was overflowing with flowers, thus combining the premodern floral vision with the feminized ideal of the hostess.[86] By 1965, one French town in every ten, along with thousands of individuals, participated in *Fleurir la France*. French hotels, especially in rural areas, also joined in the flower movement and competed in special government contests for the best decorated hotel.[87]

In other cases, however, the government's initiatives created tensions within the travel industry. One of the most controversial elements of the government's efforts to improve tourist-host relations was the campaign to promote the *tout compris* system of billing customers. Long a divisive issue in the French hotel and restaurant industries, the way customers paid their bills affected vital industry interests, namely how employers reported taxes and how employees received their income. As early as 1936, workers in many grand hotels, starting in Paris, went on strike to gain fixed salaries and greater social security benefits so they would not have to rely on customer tips as their primary source of income.[88]

Some within the industry opposed tipping on nationalistic grounds, viewing the practice as an insult to the dignity of French employees that had no place in a modern nation. One hotel industry expert in 1955, for example, regretted that "certain men, in the twentieth century, can still hold out their hand and submit to the humiliating consequences of their gesture."[89] *L'Écho touristique* in late 1961 found it "humiliating" that "a proud people like us tolerates in the interior of its territory this constant begging."[90]

Although the worker-friendly *tout compris* system had been gaining popularity in France, it still met with resistance in the 1960s, mostly from restaurant and café managers who feared paying higher taxes once their full labor costs became reportable income.[91] In 1964, for instance, thirty waiters in a Champs-Élysées café launched a one-day strike when their owner moved off the *tout compris* system. The owner, aided by the willingness of some but not all clients to carry food and drinks to their own tables, managed to fend off the waiters' demand for a formal *tout compris* system. Waiters did at least earn the right to add by pencil an unofficial 15 percent service charge to the bills. Although only a partial success, the strike brought leaders of France's five hotel-café-restaurant labor unions to meet with the minister of labor in a push for the *tout compris* system.[92]

This service labor controversy, along with complaints from tourists in opinion polls, helps explain why Gaullist prime minister Georges Pompidou attempted to resolve the matter the next year by government decree. At the peak of France's perceived tourism crisis in 1965, Pompidou attempted to overrule industry opposition to the *tout compris* practice. His goal was a more homogeneous consumer environment less likely to create employee-tourist disputes, especially involving foreigners who did not speak French. Members of the hotel and restaurant industry, unhappy to see the state dictate the terms of its operations, delayed and ultimately defeated the reform's enforcement.[93] As a result, the state was left to indirect means to achieve its goals. It maneuvered, for instance, to require that institutions adhere to everything-included practices in order to be included in government promotional material. Although less effective than a government decree, this state pressure helped solidify the industry's voluntary transition toward the reform.

French authorities had an easier time asserting increased power over tourism establishments by freezing prices in a campaign called *Opération vacances* (Operation vacations). This government initiative set out to counter France's reputation as an expensive destination among French and foreign consumers. Launched by Finance Minister Giscard in 1964, the operation allowed the local administration in each French department to use coercive or persuasive measures to limit prices in all aspects of French tourism, from hotels and restaurants to boat rides. By 1966, eighty-two of France's ninety-five departmental prefects had stepped in to cap restaurant prices.[94] To publicize the campaign, Giscard himself traveled to tourist towns and invited the press to watch him eat inexpensive meals in restaurants using the *tout compris* system.[95]

This period of widespread concern over French tourism also yielded more concrete results in an expanded and transformed hotel industry. Although public funding for hotels increased dramatically under de Gaulle, funding policies often disappointed established hoteliers. The state administered its new assistance in ways that promoted large, often chain-operated, hotels designed to deemphasize the small-scale, labor-intensive character of the French hotel industry. The new state support thus responded not just to the long-standing financial woes of French hotels but also to the technocratic assumption that artisanal hotels offered poor hospitality.

For instance, while the government increased credit for hotels, it also set new standards of service and material comfort that hotels were required to adopt to maintain their rankings and receive that credit. The state issued these so-called new norms in December 1964, at the peak of public concern over French rudeness. With criteria that became increasingly strict as hotels ascended from the one-star to four-star categories, the detailed code gave hoteliers seven years to install comforts such as more bathrooms and phone lines. The Gaullist state even insisted that two-star hotels employ reception staff fluent in at least one foreign language. Three-star hotels, to keep their rankings, needed to provide reception personnel fluent in English and one other language, a reform that subordinated linguistic nationalism to consumer demands.[96] Despite expanded financial support, the Gaullist agenda also presented challenges for established hoteliers. Even with the grace period, many smaller hotels could not undertake the extensive renovations required to equip themselves with private baths and other material features. Between 1967 and 1972, eighty Parisian hotels closed, mostly small establishments unable to keep up with the government's new standards.[97]

De Gaulle's Fifth Republic also encouraged the trend toward higher material standards and larger hotels by reaching an agreement in 1961 with Conrad Hilton, who had long expressed interest in expanding his Houston-based hotel chain to France.[98] Five years later, the Hilton International chain opened a hotel at Orly Airport outside Paris and another just blocks from the Eiffel Tower. In an interview with *Le Monde*, Hilton derided French hoteliers for their "Middle Ages mentality" and proposed instead a high-technology formula: cut down on expensive personnel and invest instead in time-motion studies and in devices such as direct telephone lines that reduced the need for service employees. *Entreprise*, critical of France's artisanal hotel tradition, praised the arrival of Hilton and his emphasis on reduced personnel and assembly-line food service, two features that separated Hilton's hotels from luxury French establishments.[99]

Elsewhere in Paris, foreign companies, mostly American or British, bought existing French hotels, renovated their interiors, and added more or newer bathrooms. Significantly, they also reduced their service personnel, under the philosophy that new middle-class tourists were not interested in having too much personal contact with employees, however friendly or rude they might be. When Pan American World Airways bought the stately Continental Hotel, where Americans comprised 65 percent of the clientele, the new manager retained only three-fifths of the personnel typical for a hotel its size. Although guaranteed their old jobs by French law, less than a third of the hotel's old employees stayed under Pan Am's self-described "factory" regime. Many of the old workers, admitted the new manager, had "difficulty with the rhythm" of the refashioned hotel workplace.[100]

This influx of foreign hotel investment in the 1960s sparked concern among nationalists that France was losing its ability to present its own nation to foreign guests. Worries that French businesses were letting the nation slip into the hands of foreign, and especially American, companies were by no means specific to hotels. Such concerns also formed the crux of Jean-Jacques Servan-Schreiber's argument in his best-selling 1967 clarion call, *The American Challenge*.[101] Disapproval of outside investment in hotels took on a special intensity given hotels' prominent role in representing the nation to foreigners. For this symbolic reason, the business daily *Les Échos* responded to Hilton's arrival by urging the French to build and finance their own hotels.[102] Frustrations mounted in 1965 with the failure of proposals to convert the ornate but obsolete Gare d'Orsay train station into a luxury riverfront hotel. Saddled with aesthetic restrictions on a building that would eventually become an art museum, no hotel company could present an acceptable proposal. "Is it then impossible," asked *Le Monde* during the Orsay debacle, "to build a luxury hotel in Paris without turning to foreign companies?"[103]

These nationalistic frustrations intensified efforts already under way by the French state and private companies to create new French-owned hotels that de-emphasized traditional service norms.[104] In 1962, the Banque de Paris et des Pays-Bas, with added capital from other banks and Air France, launched the successful Sofitel hotel chain. That same year, the government announced a public-private venture to build two- and three-star hotels in a new Frantel chain, a decision that made established hoteliers nervous over new competition from the state. Sensing a dangerous shift in the political economy of hotels, *L'Hôtellerie* ran an unusually large headline asking, "State Hotels in France?"[105] By the late 1960s, the first hotel with majority state financing opened its 200 rooms on the outskirts of Paris. In the early 1970s, as small Left Bank hotels closed, three new French-owned high-rise hotels were built on the edge of Paris. Some held over 800 rooms in twenty-three-story constructions, and all followed the Hilton emphasis on comfort and technology over personal service. In the 812-room PLM–St. Jacques hotel, for instance, electronic cards and mechanical drink dispensers reduced the need for guests to interact with service workers, thereby reducing the possibility for interpersonal misunderstandings.[106]

The state's measures drew protests from the established hotel industry. Denouncing the government and media's "campaign of denigration" against his industry, one prominent hotelier defended labor-intensive service standards on grounds that American hoteliers were in fact the real poor hosts. After all, American hotels treated guests "anonymously," as if they were entering a mere commercial transaction.[107] When Pierre Dumas traveled to the Alpine region of Savoy for a September 1964 hotel convention, hoteliers refused to meet with the Gaullist official. Instead, they took their message to the streets, calling for better treatment from the government with signs bearing the slogan, "No hotels, no tourism."[108] One trade journal editor responded to the price freezes by arguing that hoteliers and restaurateurs "are not diplomats, but merchants" and therefore ought to be left "to work in peace."[109]

Defenders of artisanal hotel service also emerged among workers in the elite hotels. When British investors sought to buy the George V and Plaza-Athénée in Paris, workers demonstrated in the streets for job security and traditional work practices rather than suffer the fate of employees at the Continental. In one March 1968 protest, the service workers connected their job security to a defense of artisanal traditions and the nation's "hotel patrimony." All of France suffered, they argued, if the hotel became a "sleep-factory" (*usine à dormir*). Although the George V's new British owners eventually laid off some personnel, the employees maintained control of workplace operations and had one of their own ranks promoted to hotel director.[110] Hotels such as the George V, whose top-flight prices gave them a share in the smaller but persistent upper-class travel market, were exceptions, however.

These challenges to established luxury hotels provoked worries in the broader public, especially among cultural conservatives. In large part, these concerns reflected the hotel's position as a symbol of national identity through which the nation presented itself to foreigners. Much of the intellectual framework for this conservative critique had been established in 1955, when André Siegfried included a chapter on tourism and hotels in his *Aspects of the Twentieth Century*. Warning that rising labor costs and growing middle-class travel would encourage the spread of "the American-type hotel," Siegfried concluded his chapter by asserting that "it is in the very interest of the highest civilization that a beautiful European hotel tradition does not disappear."[111] As hotel traditions came under assault in the 1960s, other conservative commentators also spoke out on behalf of traditional luxury hotels. Edouard Frédéric-Dupont, a Paris city councillor and a former leader in the *poujadiste* movement, patriotically defended the superiority of French hotels. Establishments in the United States and elsewhere might be cheaper, he noted, but they often did away with services such as porters to carry one's bags.[112]

Defenses of artisanal traditions at times carried suggestions that elite forms of leisure, including labor-intensive service, were necessary for France to preserve its prestige in a postcolonial era. Paris fashion industry leader Jacques

Heim, for instance, took to the pages of *Le Monde* in 1965 to protest the technocratic spirit of the times. Speaking on behalf of couture, art, and "tourism of quality" (as opposed to "industries of quantity"), Heim argued that artisanal practices helped foreigners "remain faithful to the 'french [*sic*] way of life.'" This Francophilia among the world's elites would create for France "a veritable world empire, woven with sympathy." If French leaders continued to rely on technocracy, Heim cautioned, even nations such as the United States would no longer remain a "cultural colony." Heim's reference to empire and colonies hinted how, in the aftermath of decolonization, French nationalists sought new ways to prove to themselves and the world that France remained a great nation. As Kristin Ross has argued, this search for a postcolonial national identity, among other factors, added force to the technocratic and modernizing ideal in 1950s and 1960s France. Yet for those French outside the technocratic consensus, including couturiers such as Heim, France's path to renewed grandeur lay not in new technology but in elite forms of tourism and the export of artisanal products.[113]

In the end, the wave of new hotel construction helped drown out concerns over the manners of French service workers that had contributed to the 1960s hotel boom. By the late 1960s, the French no longer debated with such vehemence the question of their compatriots' friendliness toward foreigners. Instead, new debates emerged over whether these high-rise hotels contained any elements that were distinctly French. *Le Monde* derided Air France's new Parisian hotel, Le Méridien, as "France without genius." Features such as Le Méridien's automatic doors symbolized the defaults of a hotel where hurried guests came and went anonymously. "Where in this palace, the result of long market studies, is the stamp of the capital?" lamented the paper.[114] In the 1967 film *Playtime*, director Jacques Tati depicted an American tour group wandering through a sterile glass-and-steel Paris. Offering only quick glimpses of the city's traditional charms, the film seemed to ask if visitors to modern Paris had any real contact with Parisians at all.[115]

Doubts about cultivating leisure on an industrial scale surfaced again with the student revolt and general strike that shook France in May 1968. Students and workers nearly toppled de Gaulle's government that spring, in the process sending American and other foreign tourists fleeing to neighboring countries.[116] On the Nanterre campus near Paris, where the student movement began, some protesters criticized France's growing travel industry. Contrasting the alleged sterility of commercial tourism with the vitality of rebellion, one example of the May 1968 student graffiti read: "See Nanterre and live. Go to Naples and die with Club Méditerranée."[117] The social and cultural upheaval of May 1968 also led some French travel boosters to question the nation's consumeristic push. The May revolt stimulated new thinking for J.-F. Simon, *Le Monde*'s tourism journalist. Throughout the 1960s, Simon had frequently criticized his compatriots for treating tourism as "a purely folkloric activity" rather than as a "'serious' industry" in need of state support. In a 3 June 1968 article, written just as the French establishment was reasserting authority, Simon abandoned his role as an advocate of France's travel industry. He instead cited vacations mass-produced "like automobiles" in "a 'tourism industry' dominated by producers [and] controlled in part by the state" as a cause of France's social discontent.[118]

Yet these critiques of mass culture and state intervention failed to alter the consumerist trajectory charted by the French government earlier in the 1960s. Albin Chalandon, the Gaullist minister who oversaw tourism in the late 1960s, moved in the opposite direction as Simon and the Nanterre graffitist. Speaking before an international hotel equipment conference in Paris in October 1968, Chalandon stressed that "we must be able to sell tourism . . . like one sells an automobile or a refrigerator." Emphasizing the need to attract more foreigners, Chalandon called for "a finished, homogeneous and competitive product, fabricated in large scale." To encourage this technocratic vision, he announced a 20 percent increase in state funding to the hotel industry. In an interview several months later, Chalandon emphasized the need for "a radical change in the state of mind of tourism professionals" to match the state's increased support. In other words, the state's technocratic campaign against artisanal hotels continued with little change despite the turmoil of May 1968.[119]

American Responses: Francophiles and Francophobes

Throughout the 1960s, the French government dedicated substantial funds and political initiative to making France a more welcoming destination for Americans. Although these promotion efforts also targeted French and European vacationers, Americans, with their high purchasing power, remained a central concern of French officials. Unfortunately for the French government, these measures, especially the friendliness campaigns, did not necessarily improve American images of the French. Moreover, some Americans rejected the Gaullist strategy of welcoming American consumers but not other forms of American influence. These grassroots American critics of de Gaulle in the late 1960s instead intensified campaigns to boycott travel in France.

In the American media, France's friendliness efforts yielded largely negative results. Guidebook writer Temple Fielding, whom some French had accused of undue hostility, was one of the few travel writers to respond positively to the amicability program. Although the 1966 edition of his guidebook declared the smile checks a failure, it also stressed that the French had long welcomed Americans and enjoined readers: "Don't Miss the New France."[120] More commonly, press reports on the smile offensive included other statements implying the existence of serious flaws in French hospitality. " 'Offensive' French Are Now on the Defensive," announced the New York Times, which discounted the government's efforts as an "undoubtedly transient mood of self-castigation." One Los Angeles businessman, after shaking hands with Secretary Dumas at Orly Airport, told a Times reporter that he remained skeptical of the campaign's potential to change the French, adding, "but it's nice to know they know they've been rude." Another report quoted French waiters and taxi drivers who "sniffed indignantly" as they described how Americans were arrogant customers. The article concluded that government efforts were "little and late."[121] The French state's pressure for everything-included billing also presented a no-win situation. In one Newsweek account, the image of the supercilious Parisian waiter aggressively seeking tips ceded to the image of a surly Parisian waiter aggressively offering bad service. Explained the magazine, "His 15 per cent tip, of course, is already added to the bill."[122] A 1967 French government investigation found that, if anything, opinion of the French as hosts had worsened since the early 1960s. The survey found 18 percent of American tourists unhappy with French people, a rate of dissatisfaction shared by non-American guests and a threefold increase over earlier surveys.[123]

Efforts to bribe the French into cheerfulness proved particularly alarming to America's Francophiles, who feared that "pasteurized good will" and consumer reforms would ruin the France they loved. "The day may come," predicted one such travel writer, "when perfectly housed, flawlessly served tourists will nostalgically prowl this country in search of an old-fashioned curmudgeonly French concierge or a surly Paris waiter to sneer them on their way."[124] Laurence Wylie at Harvard University also observed Francophiles' concern that easy friendliness might signal an alarming French embrace of modernity. In a landmark book by American scholars "in search" of modern France, Wylie reported that "the [American] visitor complains that there is not even the thrill of being scolded by hotel owners."[125] As these writings suggest, Francophile tourists considered French rudeness, and the challenge of winning friendship, an integral part of their trips. And just like many French commentators, they used the rhetoric of rudeness to express their own concerns over broader social and cultural changes in postwar France.

The greater challenge confronting France's tourism campaign to woo Americans came not from Francophiles but from Americans opposed to Gaullist foreign policy. The French government's strategy of welcoming American tourists while attempting to limit other forms of U.S. influence provoked frustration among some Americans. As New York senator Jacob Javits remarked in March 1968, quips circulated through the U.S. media "to the effect that Americans were only welcome in France when they occupied military cemeteries or expensive hotels."[126] Some critics of de Gaulle suggested using American consumer spending as a foreign policy tool to discipline an erstwhile ally. Calls to boycott travel to France, along with French wine and other imports, peaked in 1967 and early 1968, a particularly tense period in U.S.-French relations.[127] Members of the American Legion urged Americans to pursue a wholesale boycott of travel to France, a proposal identical to one launched by a group of California politicians.[128] In late 1967, Senator George Smathers, a Florida Democrat and loyal supporter of President Lyndon Johnson's foreign policies, proposed a special $250 tax levied on Americans who entered France.[129] Much like the media's contributions to the rudeness stereotype, press coverage of this anti-Gaullist movement at times intensified the drama. Relying on anecdotal evidence, American press accounts in 1967, with headlines such as "Gaullism Empties Bistros," reported major declines in American tourism in France.[130]

In France, the alarming reports of hostile sentiments in the United States sparked renewed efforts at tourism promotion. A French hotelier traveling through the United States on a promotional tour warned *L'Hôtellerie* of the intensity of "anti-French" opinion he encountered. Visiting Disneyland, he was disturbed to see its "French café" empty while other theme eateries buzzed with customers. As he cautioned his colleagues, France needed a massive publicity effort to regain the American public's favor.[131] The French Government Tourist Office did try to repair damage from the boycotts with a publicity campaign in early 1968 targeting American travel agents and writers. In the words of its public relations director, the New York–based office hoped to persuade these American tourism professionals that "they could, in good conscience, continue to promote French tourism."[132] France's tourism advertising in the U.S. market also showed a marked shift away from the early 1960s campaigns that had trumpeted Gaullist self-confidence, nationalism, and modernization. As diplomatic tensions flared through the mid- and late 1960s, French ads, still done by Doyle Dane Bernbach, now highlighted France as "a time machine" for those who have "had it with 20th-century push." Although not an explicit rebuttal to the anti–de Gaulle backlash, these new ads reversed earlier efforts to associate vacations in France with Gaullist ideology.[133]

Americans in the international travel industry, along with Francophiles, also joined in the counterattack. *ASTA Travel News* endorsed the French government's efforts and promised American travel agents that their customers would receive a "*sincerely* hospitable" welcome from the French people.[134] Supporters of France also deployed the long-established rhetoric identifying

France as a home of civilization. In January 1968, an editor for *Life* offered an essay titled "How to Hurt a Frenchman." Declaring France home to "perhaps the most satisfying sights of civilization," the editor, a self-identified Francophile, coolly observed that Americans who boycotted France with "crude" protests hurt themselves more than they hurt de Gaulle.[135] After a letter to the *New York Times* called for a boycott on French leisure travel in December 1967, another reader responded in defense of visiting "this cradle of European civilization." Deriding the boycotts as an "example of isolationism," this defender of France emphasized that the trips allowed Americans an "opportunity to learn and improve ourselves."[136]

In the end, grassroots attempts to discipline French foreign policy using consumer boycotts cost France some tourist income but hardly brought a dramatic shift in Americans' leisure patterns. On one level, the boycotts succeeded in calling greater public attention to the rifts in U.S.-French relations. Moreover, the growth rate of American tourist arrivals and expenditures in France for 1967 reached only 2 or 3 percent, a rate of increase smaller than in previous years. Nevertheless, the boycotts did not reverse the trend of overall expansion, and Americans in 1967 still made more visits and spent more dollars on travel in France than they had in any year before. The number of American visits and amount of tourist spending in France did fall 30 percent in 1968, although the role of the boycotts in this decline is difficult to separate from the impact of France's month-long general strike that year. As relations between the French and U.S. governments improved late in 1968, calls for boycotts diminished. This rapprochement, along with France's recovery from the strikes, helped American tourism in France return by 1969 to the record levels set in 1967. From there, American travel to France resumed it steady growth into the 1970s.[137]

Conclusion

In the short run, the Fifth Republic's attempts to attract American consumers and convince them of French friendliness brought little success. The more Gaullist officials tried to show that the French were friendly, the more American and French observers assumed that the French lacked hospitality in the first place. Moreover, the French government's attempts to please American tourists while simultaneously challenging U.S. foreign policy brought added complications. American frustrations with Gaullist diplomacy contributed to the rudeness stereotype and even led some Americans to employ their leisure as a form of political protest.

Cast in a longer-term perspective, however, Gaullist tourism policy appears more successful. The diplomatic tensions of the 1960s should not distract us from the most enduring legacy of Gaullism for French tourism, namely the state's increased attention to travel promotion. The late 1950s and 1960s represented a period of dramatic development in France's tourism infrastructure. The Gaullist state's more active policies toward tourism and hotels left France better prepared for the continued growth of international travel in later decades and helped make France the most visited nation in the world at the end of the twentieth century.[138]

The modernization drive that transformed France's travel industry during the early Fifth Republic resulted from multiple factors, including growing competition in the international travel market, social and cultural conflicts within France, and strains in transatlantic relations.[139] Particularly important was the image of the backward and inhospitable French, which gained such notoriety due to a confluence of U.S.-French foreign policy tensions and more profound domestic changes in French society. The image of French inhospitality became especially powerful within France because it could confirm competing domestic ideologies. For cultural conservatives or defenders of artisanal tradition, the idea of French inhospitality offered proof of the decadence of a France where modernization threatened artisanal pride or even refined civilization itself. For modernizers, who exerted influence through the state, French inhospitality confirmed the inadequacy of labor-intensive artisanal practices for a France that needed to modernize to compete in the international economy. The end result was a wave of hotel construction and a more extensive foreign tourism infrastructure designed to reduce the likelihood of cross-cultural misunderstandings.

Even if efforts such as the smile checks failed to eliminate all negative stereotypes, the Fifth Republic's aggressive approach to tourism demonstrated the importance of state intervention to the rise of mass travel. This strategy also suggests that de Gaulle, often viewed as profoundly critical of American consumer society, was willing to accommodate American consumers as a means to pursue French economic and cultural diplomacy.[140] International tourism did not overwhelm traditional French policy concerns but instead offered a new tool for Gaullist policymakers in search of economic independence and national grandeur.

Chapter 8

THE DOLLAR CHALLENGE
THE PERSISTENCE OF CONSUMERISM
IN THE 1960S

"I just sat and stared at the television, not believing what I heard." The new year of 1968 did not begin well for one American travel agent whose business depended on tourism to Europe.[1] President Lyndon Johnson had chosen New Year's Day to deliver a televised speech highlighting the vulnerable state of the national economy. On a day known for setting resolutions, Johnson asked Americans to postpone "all nonessential travel outside the Western Hemisphere" for the next two years. The president's call to consumer sacrifice, accompanied by new regulations on overseas investment, echoed a similar campaign he had attempted three years earlier. Both times, in 1965 and 1968, Johnson acted in the midst of an acute balance-of-payments crisis. If Americans could not keep more dollars from leaving the country, he warned, monetary outflow would threaten the stability of the dollar and endanger the nation's leading position in the international economy. On each occasion, Johnson reinforced his pleas to Americans to stay in the United States with legislative proposals for higher duties on travel purchases. In his 1968 effort, the Johnson administration went a step further and raised the possibility of head taxes levied on Americans leaving the country and of per diem taxes for time spent outside the United States.[2] Compared to the 1965 episode, public debate in 1968 was more intense, reflecting the growing urgency of the balance-of-payments situation, the stronger measures proposed by the Johnson administration, and the domestic tensions fostered by the increasingly unpopular war in Vietnam. Yet both the 1965 and 1968 campaigns met the same fate. Although the White House found some domestic support, its tourism agenda ultimately failed in Congress and among American consumers. In the words of one administration official in 1968, Johnson's call for travel restrictions represented "probably his most thoroughly unpopular legislative proposal in the Congress."[3] As the White House's chief economic adviser noted in the days after the speech, "Somehow, the tourism part of the program seems to be the lightning rod."[4]

Johnson's attempts to limit overseas tourist spending shed light on key changes in the relationship between transatlantic tourism and Cold War history in the late 1960s. The balance-of-payments crises of the 1960s, although overshadowed in popular memory by the domestic turmoil of that decade, had profound Cold War consequences, constraining the U.S. government's ability to fund military bases in Western Europe and to wage war in Vietnam.[5] To help meet the monetary challenge, the Johnson administration withdrew government support from the loose alliance of travel boosters that had been forged in the late 1940s, an era when U.S. policymakers had eagerly sought ways to distribute American dollars around the world.

While Johnson's program called on Americans to subordinate their own leisure desires to government policy concerns, the international travel industry led the way in offering a consumer-oriented alternative. Industry leaders found support from many of the same political and media actors who had earlier helped make tourism part of the Marshall Plan. Once again, the industry's key allies were fiscal conservatives eager to promote travel as an alternative to foreign aid and liberals who emphasized grassroots exchanges as a path toward international understanding. Consumers also voted with their feet and pocketbooks by largely continuing to travel and shop overseas. In all, the international travel constituency's vision of U.S. foreign relations proved more influential than Johnson's, revealing how desires for unfettered consumerism and travel had become a major force shaping U.S. international relations.

More than an economic debate, the discussion generated by Johnson's proposals also compelled Americans to articulate the political values and meanings they assigned to travel abroad. Most notably, the debate revealed two different approaches to anti-Communism. One version, held by the Johnson administration and a small number of supporters, emphasized the disciplining of consumer exchanges to preserve the state's Cold War commitments in Western Europe and Vietnam. In contrast, defenders of tourism used their own anti-Communist rhetoric to argue that consumer interests came ahead of state concerns.[6] Put on the defensive by Johnson's proposals, travel boosters and consumer advocates emphasized overseas vacations and the "freedom to travel" as practices that separated the United States from Communist nations. In the eyes of travel boosters, even consumer privileges such as duty-free exemptions emerged as political rights, not simply economic luxuries. In the process of opposing Johnson's proposals, travel boosters' rhetoric grew more aggressive. While boosters during the late 1940s and 1950s had presented themselves as complements of U.S. policy aims, now they often declared tourism to be more important than Washington's Cold War goals.

Lastly, when viewed alongside the French government's increased interest in attracting American tourist dollars in the 1960s, Johnson's attempts to restrict overseas travel reveal an important shift in the place of tourism in U.S.-French relations. In the Marshall Plan years and through the 1950s, both the U.S. and French governments shared the goal of increasing American leisure in France, with Washington at times acting as the more enthusiastic promoter. During the 1960s, in contrast, the two states pulled in opposite directions, as they did with so many other issues that decade. While the U.S. government reduced its ties to the international travel industry, French policymakers, as we have seen, increased their promotion efforts in the American market. Johnson's chief economic adviser even monitored French tourism policy, notifying the president of the 1965 smile-check campaign and taking some satisfaction in informing Johnson of potential losses suffered by French tourism from the 1967 boycotts.[7] On the other side, French travel industry leaders and journalists worriedly followed news of Johnson's antitravel measures. Nevertheless, the Johnson administration, in trying to limit American travel, had chosen the more difficult task. Promoting consumerism proved easier than restricting it.

The White House Turns against Overseas Travel

Johnson's attempts to limit overseas tourism expenditures stemmed from larger problems facing the American position in the international economy. The Bretton Woods system, established with U.S. leadership at the end of World War II, made the dollar the benchmark currency for international transactions. Under this system, the United States guaranteed that every dollar could be exchanged for gold at the rate of $35 per ounce. This fixed gold-dollar link meant that the central banks of foreign countries could back their own currencies by stockpiling vaults of U.S. dollars, since, according to the Bretton Woods agreements, those dollars were as good as gold. This monetary system underwrote key facets of American expansion in the Cold War. Americans could spend large amounts of dollars in the international arena for military bases, foreign aid, and overseas investment without driving down the international value of the dollar or creating excessive inflation at home. U.S. allies could then use those dollars to provide their own currency with a solid foundation while expanding their economies and trading with the United States. The dollar-gold link thus represented a cornerstone of U.S. Cold War economic policy. This system even aided American tourists' consumer power, since the gold-dollar link boosted the value of the U.S. currency and thus made foreign goods and services cheaper for Americans abroad.

The United States' ability to support this Bretton Woods monetary system began to weaken in the late 1950s. The U.S. government at first managed balance-of-payments deficits by selling off reserves of gold and circulating more dollars. Foreigners, confident in the gold-dollar link, initially accepted the expanded dollar supply as a way to boost their own reserve holdings. However, as the supply of dollars in the world economy increased, the market value of those dollars relative to gold fell. In the private London gold market, for instance, it took $40 in 1960 to buy an ounce of gold. In this context, the U.S. government's Bretton Woods promise to sell gold at only $35 an ounce encouraged private currency traders and foreign governments to exchange their dollars for U.S. gold reserves. As a result, by the late 1950s and early 1960s, the U.S. government's gold reserves were suffering significant losses.[8]

As early signs of this deteriorating monetary situation emerged in the late 1950s, the administration of Dwight Eisenhower did little to alter the established relationship between the U.S. government and the international travel. An advocate of limited government and "vacations, not donations," Eisenhower continued to encourage travel abroad. "One thing we don't want to do," he told reporters in 1960, "is to develop an isolationist practice of staying at home." The president instead ordered a reduction of overseas military dependents in late 1960, a move that pleased travel agents fearful of restrictions on tourism.[9] Eisenhower also took modest steps to promote domestic tourism. A major economic report within the Eisenhower administration in 1958 called for the creation of government tourism offices overseas to help improve the balance of payments.[10] The U.S. government had for so long been concerned only with sending dollars abroad that in the late 1950s it was one of the few industrial nations in the world without a national tourism office to lure foreign vacationers.[11] Still, the proposal failed in the face of Republican Party opposition. Congressional conservatives such as John Rooney and Frances Walter derided proposals for a travel service as a ploy by the "smart boys of Madison Avenue" to have the U.S. government advertise for American businesses. Walter, as chair of the House Un-American Activities Committee, also feared that consumer-friendly measures such as waiving visa requirements for foreign tourists would let "a potential saboteur" enter the United States. Given congressional opposition, the president merely declared 1960 a "visit USA" year and cut 40 percent from the budget of the Commerce Department's Office of International Travel, a bureaucracy formed during the Marshall Plan years to study and promote travel abroad.[12]

Pressures to reduce government support for overseas tourism increased as the nation's monetary problems grew more urgent later in the 1960s. The French government contributed to part of this monetary crisis in the mid-1960s by exchanging its dollars for U.S. gold, a policy that formed part of de Gaulle's larger strategy for challenging the United States' superpower status. The crisis also resulted from Americans' own actions. American investors and corporations contributed to the growing outflow of dollars by acquiring foreign factories and other assets at an accelerating pace. Between 1958 and 1968, the productive capacity of American manufacturers increased 471 percent overseas, in contrast to just a 72 percent growth rate at home.[13] Military commitments in Western Europe and Southeast Asia accounted for another source of the problem. From 1965 to 1968, the years of Johnson's massive escalation of the war in Vietnam, U.S. direct military expenditures abroad leapt from $2.9 billion to $4.5 billion a year. American tourists also contributed to the nation's worsening monetary situation. In 1966, for instance, Americans spent $2.6 billion outside the country, a figure that represented about 7 percent of the U.S. balance-of-payments outflow.[14] As U.S. gold reserves dwindled, members of the Kennedy and Johnson administrations realized that the current state of monetary affairs could not continue indefinitely and thus looked for new ways to reduce the flow of dollars outside the country.

One arena for action was tourism. On entering the White House in 1961, John F. Kennedy and his advisers took a more aggressive approach to promoting domestic travel and discouraging overseas travel. The Kennedy administration sponsored the creation of the U.S. Travel Service to draw more foreign vacationers to the United States and revived the blue-and-white "E" pennants originally awarded to companies during World War II for excellence in wartime production. Hoping to use patriotism to promote monetary policy, the White House now gave "E" pennants to firms that improved the nation's balance of payments by boosting U.S. exports or attracting foreign tourists. For instance, Pan American Airways won a pennant in 1963 for its promotion of foreign travel to the United States.[15]

The Kennedy administration also made shopping abroad more expensive. Acting at Kennedy's request, Congress in 1961 scaled back the duty-free exemption limit for returning travelers. The duty-free exemption determined how much in purchased goods Americans could bring home without paying U.S. taxes. In the late 1940s, when the U.S. government hoped to spread dollars around the world, Congress raised the exemption from $100 to $500. Since other governments, including France, often exempted foreign tourists from local sales taxes, Washington's generous duty-free exemption meant that Americans abroad had long done much of their shopping free from taxation. In comparative terms, Kennedy's new $100 limit was still a relatively mild measure. France and West Germany, for instance, limited their own citizens to under $15 in duty-free exemptions, and Britain, with its beleaguered pound, at times did away with exemptions altogether. Nevertheless, the new duty-free measures had some impact. In the years after the exemption dropped to $100, the average value of goods brought back by tourists fell from $84 to $55.[16] Just as important, the new act represented a significant move away from earlier U.S. policies that had given American tourists status as exalted consumers.

Kennedy's increased taxation on American tourists, along with Europeans' own growing consumerism, caused some travel agents and writers in the early 1960s to worry about Americans' place in the world travel market. In the wake of Kennedy's calls to reduce duty-free spending, *ASTA Travel News* noted how "many were shocked to realize that America's financial position had deteriorated to such a point."[17] "As Americans we tend to think of ourselves as the prime movers," noted the *Travel Agent* in 1964. Complaining that Europeans were now seizing the best hotel rooms in Europe, the trade journal warned that "the truth is that Americans are no longer in first place."[18] Americans in the travel industry thus began discussing the relative limits of the American economy well before most Americans became attuned to the nation's international economic woes in the late 1960s and 1970s.

The rise of the Common Market gave industry observers further reason to take notice of Western Europe as a rival consumer power. Formed in 1957, the market drew Western European economies into a free-trade zone designed in large part to intensify economic ties within the region. Industry reports in the United States commented eagerly on an age of speedier border crossings within Europe but also expressed some reservations about the market's potential to boost European economic power. Evaluating the implications of the Common Market for American travel agents in the 1963, Trevor L. Christie, a veteran travel writer and former official for the Marshall Plan's Travel Development Section, urged agents specializing in U.S. travel to Europe to diversify their businesses. According to Christie, the Common Market would make Europeans the world's new globe-trotters. Some day, he mused, Europeans visiting Florida and California might even dismissively light their cigarettes with dollar bills.[19]

Like members of the travel industry, U.S. policymakers also associated travel and consumer power with the nation's larger standing. For some White House advisers, this connection suggested that the government should not take action against overseas leisure spending. Johnson's economic advisers in December 1964 admitted that travel was a "large and growing deficit item" but argued that any restriction would be "contrary to the larger interests of U.S. foreign policy."[20] Two years later, Undersecretary of State George Ball, who emerged as one of the administration's most vehement critics of tourism restrictions, similarly described travel taxes as "unbecoming to the leading power with responsibilities in the four corners of the world."[21]

More concretely, some officials feared that travel restrictions would undermine core economic policies established by the United States. Ball, along with Secretary of State Dean Rusk, worried that taxes on tourist expenditures abroad would stall efforts to reduce tariffs, a project then under way in the Kennedy Round of the General Agreement on Tariffs and Trade.[22] Others expressed concern that travel restrictions would destabilize Latin American states that were especially dependent on American leisure spending. As one White House memorandum put it, the health of the tourism-fueled Caribbean economy was "directly related to our own security interests."[23]

Given these reservations, why did the Johnson administration advance its travel measures in 1965 and again in 1968? In part, Johnson and his aides hoped that travel restrictions would perform a symbolic function at home. By focusing attention on a mass culture activity such as tourism, administration officials sought to increase the American public's interest in the esoteric world of monetary affairs and the balance of payments. Secretary of Commerce John Connor argued for an additional reduction in the duty-free allowance in 1965 because "it causes people to think and it causes people to be conscious of the fact that their expenditures abroad, whether they pay duty or not, are having an impact . . . on our national accounts."[24] Connor's concern contrasted with skeptical comments from outside observers less willing to view leisure travel in macroeconomic terms. "It is fantastic to think that Aunt Minnie spending a couple thousand dollars to see the sights of Paris and Rome is putting the United States on the path to economic ruin," complained one Illinois newspaper in 1965.[25] Senator Jacob Javits, who strongly opposed any duty-free reduction, likewise asked, "As the richest nation on earth, what is wrong with letting Americans enjoy life a little?"[26]

Johnson's campaign against tourist expenditures held further symbolic value in pressing for other parts of the government's balance-of-payments program. If Johnson could show that private consumers would have to sacrifice to save the national economy, he could then increase his pressure on military officials, industrialists, and financiers to cut back their own overseas expenditures. In the words of one cabinet report in 1965, travel taxes would produce "a favorable psychological effect" with the U.S. military, especially with personnel stationed abroad.[27] The same logic shaped the 1968 restrictions drive, when Johnson approved a decision by his advisers to present Congress with a 30 percent tax on tourist expenditures above $15 a day. In one aide's summary of the strategy, the strict proposal had "virtually no chance" of becoming policy but would be useful "to show that we are moving on all fronts . . . and to show the military that we are moving on the civilian area."[28] In the words of Ernest Goldstein, Johnson's special assistant on balance-of-payments issues, "if everybody else has to bear a share of the balance-of-payments deficit cost," tourists should too, or "at least you go through the motions."[29]

Although some in the White House had doubts, Johnson's proposals also emerged from a genuine belief that the government could use taxes and patriotic appeals to limit tourist expenditures. Defense Secretary Robert McNamara attempted to persuade fellow policymakers in 1965 of the feasibility of effective tourist restrictions.[30] In late 1967, economic adviser Gardner Ackley was so alarmed by the balance-of-payments deficit that he presented the goal of the administration's agenda in stark terms: "to *get through 1968 without an international financial crisis.*" Given the high stakes, Ackley advised Johnson that "a properly designed" travel tax could pass Congress.[31] Treasury Secretary Henry Fowler, more preoccupied than other advisers with monetary issues, was the most adamant in insisting that tourists contribute to any balance-of-payments program. Months after the failure of the 1968 tax proposals, Fowler still defended them as "necessary and desirable" and faulted a Congress that "had no stomach" for imposing a travel tax.[32] Even Goldstein, in the midst of the 1968 crisis, advised the president that a spending limit on tourists overseas could be effective because "the majority of Americans will be patriotic and honest."[33]

A final underlying factor was the administration's concern that the United States needed to reduce its economic commitments in Western Europe. Throughout the 1960s, U.S. officials negotiated with European allies to lessen the American share of NATO defense costs.[34] This desire to adjust the Atlantic Alliance's economic dimensions also shaped the tourism component of Johnson's balance-of-payments program, especially in 1968. While Johnson's 1965 campaign simply encouraged Americans to stay at home, his more ambitious 1968 program, which included proposals for new taxes on travel, targeted travel outside the Western Hemisphere. Since Western Europe received over four-fifths of American tourist expenditures outside the hemisphere, the 1968 campaign, in essence, focused on travel to that region.[35] The logic of the Western Hemisphere exemption rested on the fact that Canada and Latin America relied so heavily on U.S. exports. Most of the American tourist dollars spent in Canada or the Bahamas, for instance, returned to the U.S. economy when those countries purchased U.S. goods and services. In comparison, Western Europe, with its more diversified economies and regional trading patterns, depended less on the American economy. In effect, the Western Hemisphere exemption tacitly suggested that Americans could be allowed to travel and consume freely only in those areas where the United States maintained economic hegemony.

Johnson's campaign to limit overseas travel found some support outside the administration, especially from those who saw ways to tie the program to their own Cold War agendas. Arkansas Democrat J. William Fulbright, the influential chairman of the Senate Foreign Relations Committee, emerged as one such supporter of the 1965 campaign. An internationalist politician committed to foreign aid programs and international scholarly exchange, Fulbright might have been expected to defend overseas travel as a necessary part of the United States' global presence. Instead, he urged reductions in tourism, military expenses, and business investments "as a matter of priority" to protect the foreign aid programs that he supported. Forced by the monetary crisis to choose between forms of internationalism, Fulbright preferred state-directed cultural exchange and foreign aid to market-driven consumer tourism.[36]

Johnson's program also gained some supporters by tapping into patriotic appeals to "See America First." Americans who heeded Johnson's calls often used the occasion to celebrate America's cultural sophistication. Syndicated economic columnist Sylvia Porter in 1965 endorsed Johnson's early agenda and noted that avoiding Europe would not be so bad, since "there are more Rembrandts in New York than in Amsterdam."[37] Sister Mary Thomasita, a Milwaukee college professor, canceled her annual tour of Europe in 1965 to honor Johnson's program. Making the best of the situation, she offered a one-day "Europe in Milwaukee" tour. "As no one thinks of Paris without the Louvre," her brochure observed, "so no one thinks of Milwaukee without the Art Center."[38]

The Johnson administration cultivated this patriotic spirit with a public relations campaign in the American media. In 1965, Johnson contributed an article to *Parade* magazine, in which he praised domestic travel as a means toward "a lively awareness of America's potentialities."[39] The White House also counted on patriotic media elites to promote tourism within the United States. Comic strip artist Ed Dodd, for instance, agreed in 1966 to contribute to the cause. In one strip series, a smiling Secretary of Commerce John Connor recruited Dodd's rugged cartoon hero Mark Trail to guide young Americans through their own nation.[40] William Randolph Hearst Jr., the newspaper and magazine tycoon whose father's xenophobic nationalism fueled the 1930s "Buy American" movement, also promoted domestic travel. Johnson sent a note of thanks to him in January 1968 for his newspapers' series "See the Americas First," which highlighted the attractions of the Western Hemisphere.[41]

The White House's campaign to limit travel spending in Europe received added support from a handful of Americans who saw the efforts as a new way to punish France for its independent foreign policy. With anti-French boycott calls already circulating in late 1967, Johnson's 1968 New Year's Day balance-of-payments speech amplified grassroots desires to withhold consumer dollars from France. Two days after the speech, a woman in Hollywood wired the White House to encourage Johnson to "hold your line on travel restrictions." She explained that "I am 60 years [old] and am giving up my first trip to Europe at your request." Such sacrifice seemed "the least we can do," she wrote, adding that Johnson could do more still with "special restrictions on France if possible please."[42] A San Antonio businessman wrote the president to praise the same speech and to recommend that the U.S. government go a step further by denying passports to any American trying to visit France. "The elimination of tourist trade in France," he predicted, "would quickly bring President de Gaulle back to earth." Johnson's reply, drafted by Goldstein, pointed to "serious constitutional questions" in any ban on travel to France but added, "I very much appreciate the spirit which prompted your letter."[43]

In Defense of Consumerism

Few Americans, however, were willing to sacrifice leisure patterns at the president's request or for the sake of a political statement against Charles de Gaulle. While Johnson's proposals garnered a modest amount of support, his legislative agenda on overseas travel failed. Proposals to enact new taxes on overseas travel aroused hostility in both liberal and conservative circles, and Congress rejected even mild proposals, such as reducing the duty-free exemption from $100 to $50. The heart of the opposition came from the loose alliance of travel boosters in the media and international travel industry that had grown accustomed to presenting tourism as an extension of U.S. Cold War policy. Faced with the White House's defection from this group of travel boosters, some industry leaders hoped to find a middle ground with the administration. Others articulated a more aggressive rhetoric that claimed overseas vacations as a right of all citizens and placed leisure travel above the government's Cold War policies. These consumer defenders, cheered on by French media and travel industry observers, carried the day.

Johnson received at best tentative support from U.S.-owned international airlines, which scrambled to reconcile transatlantic travel with their long-cultivated ties to U.S. foreign policy. Oklahoma-based Braniff International offered new advertisements in 1966 that announced the company's loyalty to the president while insisting that travel to Europe was still "part of the American Dream." American carriers also used the balance-of-payments crisis as an opportunity to launch "Fly American" campaigns. With roughly one in two American tourists crossing the Atlantic on European airlines, the U.S.-owned carriers argued that if consumers had to visit Europe, the patriotic act was to at least fly with an American company. The White House refused to endorse publicly any such campaign, for fear of inciting foreign government retaliation against U.S. airlines. In private, however, it let the airlines know of its satisfaction with the programs.[44] In 1968, the airlines also initiated a new system of transatlantic fare discounts for round-trip flights originating in Europe to lure more Europeans to the United States. In the months after Johnson's New Year's Day speech, Pan Am president Juan Trippe rushed between the White House and foreign airline executives with characteristic energy, helping bring about an international agreement on these so-called directional fares by April 1968.[45]

Despite some cooperation, U.S. airlines still refused to act on LBJ's call to reduce American travel overseas. Shortly after the New Year's Day speech, TWA's president met with White House officials and apologized for launching a new advertising campaign with the slogan, "There is nothing like Europe." Later that year, TWA developed the new catchphrase "Keep it [the dollar] in the U.S.A. when you go to Europe." Yet even this new slogan revealed that the airline was ultimately not interested in reducing the volume of American tourism in Europe.[46] By May 1968, Pan Am moved further away from the White House position by increasing its transatlantic advertising in the U.S. market. As one Pan Am executive explained to the White House, the airline was losing out to "uninhibited" advertising by the European airlines. In an attempt to preserve its status as an ally of the government, Pan Am stressed that its ads would at least encourage Americans to reduce their expenditures once they got off the planes.[47]

While the airlines tiptoed around the White House's program, others in the industry, especially travel agents, voiced their opposition without apology. Often these travel industry advocates employed their own Cold War rhetoric to justify their defiance of the White House. *ASTA Travel News* politicized the debate by asserting not just a fundamental right to travel overseas but also a more dubious right to bring home souvenirs without U.S. taxation.[48] As early as February 1961, when the Kennedy administration proposed lowering the duty-free limit to $100, the trade journal equated the freedom to cross borders with the freedom to consume: government efforts to increase taxation on tourist expenditures would "contradict the rights of Americans to travel freely about the world."[49] In response to reports in 1965 of a $100 head tax on travel abroad, the trade journal defended "the inalienable right of Americans to travel in the free world unhampered by government restrictions."[50] Guidebook writer Richard Joseph testified to Congress in 1965 that any travel tax resembled Eastern bloc laws.[51] In 1968, when the threat of taxation seemed greatest, ASTA organized letter-writing campaigns to sway Congress while one leading member of the agents' organization amplified the politicized rhetoric by declaring that Johnson's proposals were "as evil as the Berlin Wall."[52]

It's almost embarassing to ask you to thrill to the Rockies as a patriotic gesture to your country.

There was a time in America when patriotism was a very "in" thing.

Today, it's sort of dull. Hokey.

Right now, our President is asking us to be patriotic.

To keep American dollars in America. Temporarily.

To refrain from travel to Europe. Temporarily.

This is not isolationism.

There's nothing *bad* about Europe. In fact, to many of us, a trip to Europe is part of the American Dream.

But our President asks us to hold off. Temporarily.

Is it really that much of a sacrifice for people to see San Francisco? Or New Orleans?

When was the last time they saw the Alamo? Or skied the Colorado "Alps"?

Do they have to be asked to thrill to the majesty of the Pacific Northwest as a patriotic sacrifice to their country?

This message is brought to you by Braniff International, who joins the President in asking people to discover the many wonderful places in America.

Braniff does not fly to all of these places. But this is not an advertisement.

Braniff International

An airline advertisement in response to Johnson's balance-of-payments program. American-owned airlines found themselves in the unfamiliar position of standing outside the national interest. This advertisement typified their somewhat awkward response (from ASTA Travel News, *April 1966).*

More subtly, travel writers and agents advised consumers on how to travel and shop abroad with minimum taxation. Best-selling guidebook author Temple Fielding, after praising Congress for preserving the $100 duty-free exemption in 1965, continued to offer extensive detail on how to evade any duty charges. If traveling with infants, he advised readers, be sure that they too claim their full $100 exemption.[53] As fears of restrictions peaked in early 1968, some agents even began to counsel clients on evasive tactics, such as using Canada as a point of departure to avoid any potential tax on overseas trips.[54] Rejecting LBJ's proposals, the *New York Times* defiantly trumpeted "the sublime faith of the great American tourist who faces down earthquakes and hurricanes, political revolutions, juntas and pocket wars, and threats from his own Government with equal *sang-froid*."[55] In this view, tourists did not serve Cold War interests; they transcended them.

Advocates of tax-free travel also drew on and modified the well-established image of the international traveler as a typical middle-class American. In the late 1940s and 1950s, travel boosters had emphasized, and even exaggerated, the middle-class nature of overseas travel to stress that tourists were more sober-minded and therefore more likely to win friends for the United States abroad. By the late 1960s, however, their rhetoric shifted away from an emphasis on what tourists could do to win the Cold War and adopted bolder proclamations of consumer rights. Travel agents and their supporters suggested that international tourism had become something of a middle-class entitlement. In one of *ASTA Travel News*'s many rebuttals to the White House, the trade journal stressed that tourists should not shoulder added taxes since "most [tourists] correspond more and more closely to the profile of the 'average American.'"[56] Echoing this industry view, *Washington Post* editorial cartoonist Herblock sympathized with the "average tourist" carrying a higher tax burden along with his suitcases. *New York Times* columnist James Reston, who in the 1950s had editorialized on behalf of tourists' Cold War value, once more came to the defense of tourists in 1968 when he opposed Johnson on grounds that "the poor American schoolteacher" might lose the chance to see Europe.[57]

For one African American journalist opposed to Johnson's proposals, travel to Europe represented a particularly essential right for middle-class blacks. In early 1968, Ernest Dunbar, an editor with *Look*, a general-interest magazine, offered a public "Memo to LBJ." Dunbar recast the travel-tax debate to draw readers' attention to blacks' inability to travel safely and comfortably through large parts of the United States. Drawing on a longer tradition in African American writing, he highlighted the importance of Europe as a haven from racism for America's "black middle class." Dunbar then closed the editorial with a call on Johnson to exempt African Americans from any travel tax, a

"TAKE ME ALONG"

A Herblock cartoon showing the consumer backlash against Johnson's travel restriction proposals ("Take Me Along," from ASTA Travel News, *February 1968; © 1968 by Herblock in the Washington Post).*

policy suggestion likely made tongue in cheek but one that underscored a growing sense of European travel as a middle-class right.[58]

Other critics on the left connected the administration's moves against tourism with the war in Vietnam. As early as March 1965, the faculty at Lindenwood College in Missouri wrote Johnson to defend overseas travel, suggesting that the president first reduce military expenses and end the war.[59] Such antiwar arguments, rare in 1965, became more common in 1968 as the war fell in popularity. In response to Johnson's New Year's Day travel announcement, an

Indiana newspaper publisher appealed to the president to "save money by getting us out of the mess in Vietnam" while *Boston Globe* columnist Joseph Kraft criticized Johnson's proposal and faulted instead "the overextended military commitment which finds its chief expression in Vietnam."[60] Norman Cousins, the influential liberal and editor of the *Saturday Review*, likewise called for cutting back the military "before it destroys the principle of freedom of movement for Americans, a basic right that stands far higher, literally, than gold in the order of national importance."[61] In an article for Cousins's magazine, Henry S. Reuss, the Wisconsin Democrat who chaired the Joint Subcommittee on International Exchange and Payments, blamed the monetary crisis on "our military posture overseas."[62] Travel writer Horace Sutton, another liberal, captured the mood by warning of "unpleasant confrontations between superpatriotic groups such as the American Legion, urging support of the President, and militant peaceniks . . . urging the nation to get out of Vietnam and let its people go to Europe."[63]

Attacked from the antiwar left, Johnson's proposals for increased regulation and taxes on private travel also found little support among conservatives. Republican critics of foreign aid programs objected to the notion that American consumers should sacrifice while the U.S. government gave money to other nations. As early as 1961, when Kennedy helped cut the duty-free exemption from $500 to $100, the conservative *National Review* called instead for the abolishment of Kennedy's Alliance for Progress aid program in Latin America.[64] In 1965, congressional critics of foreign aid opposed LBJ's proposal to further reduce the duty-free exemption by invoking the "trade not aid" doctrine popular during the Eisenhower administration.[65] The *St. Charles (Missouri) Banner-News* likewise defended foreign travel as more effective than foreign assistance, since private travel "cuts out the middlemen." Offering an alternative to Johnson's restrictions, the paper proposed a fanciful plan in which the government would subsidize tourist trips abroad. Americans would receive $50 to visit Europe and $500 to visit less common destinations such as South Africa.[66] Republican Thomas Curtin of the House Ways and Means Committee spoke out against a travel tax in 1968, blaming not just Vietnam expenses but also U.S. contributions for foreign aid and the World Bank.[67]

At times, the conservative defense of tourists called into question the need for U.S. troop deployments in Western Europe. In 1965, *Chicago Tribune* columnist Walter Trohan claimed that the United States would be better off if it returned troops from overseas and let tourists roam free without a head tax. Reviving the fiscal-conservative defense doctrine of Eisenhower, Trohan argued that the United States could meet its strategic needs by relying more on the air force and nuclear weapons.[68] NATO troop commitments, in other words, ought to take a back seat to consumer privilege.

Echoing the travel industry press, conservatives also deployed a politicized language that associated unfettered tourism with the Cold War crusade. The Missouri newspaper eager for government subsidies on overseas vacations called the travel tax proposal "undemocratic" and akin to Communism, since "in the Iron Curtain countries [only] the privileged few were able to travel."[69] The *Chicago Tribune* asked in 1968 if LBJ was trying "to reduce us to the status of detainees in a communist state."[70] The next day, a letter from a reader likened Johnson's suggestions to the policies of Nazi Germany and the Soviet bloc.[71] Conservative columnist William F. Buckley Jr., writing from Switzerland in 1968, warned that "the sheer indignity" of Johnson's travel program could cause more damage to "American prestige" in European eyes than the war in Vietnam.[72]

Johnson's measures did attract attention on the other side of the Atlantic, especially in 1968. French opinion that year, drawing on both economic self-interest and foreign policy concerns, generally sided with American consumer advocates. Before 1968, few French tourism observers expressed much concern with U.S. monetary woes. In one rare case, a leading French hotelier in the early 1960s referred to Washington's reduced support of overseas tourism. He argued that this shift in U.S. policy underscored the need for the French state to increase its support of French hotels.[73] In 1968, however, Johnson's tourism agenda created much more public concern in both industry circles and the general media. In part this French attention resulted from the more dramatic proposals and public gestures taken by the White House that year. These new concerns also reflected Johnson's unpopularity in France, where public opinion had grown increasingly opposed to the American war in Vietnam.

The White House's 1968 tourism measures fueled the French media's general opposition to Johnson's handling of foreign affairs. Reporting on Johnson's New Year's Day speech, the Communist *L'Humanité* stressed U.S. militarism as the true source of American monetary problems.[74] For its part, the popular weekly *L'Express* ran a cartoon that lampooned Johnson as a hippy marching under a placard reading, "Make war, not tourism." In a sign of transatlantic protest culture, the liberal and antiwar *Saturday Review* reprinted the cartoon several weeks later for an American audience.[75] Both American and French opponents of Johnson's war in Vietnam shared the notion that American dollars ought to enter the global economy through American consumers, not the U.S. military.

The White House's 1968 proposals to discourage American travel often appeared as an attack on France, even if none of Johnson's measures specifi-

A French critique of Johnson's travel reduction program. In keeping with widespread opposition to the U.S. war in Vietnam, L'Express criticized Johnson's militaristic priorities (Louis Mitelberg cartoon from L'Express, 8–14 January 1968).

cally targeted the nation. Only pockets of French commentary, such as that from the explicitly pro-American *France-U.S.A.* magazine, came to the defense of Johnson.[76] More typical of French responses, *Le Monde* described Johnson's agenda as a thinly veiled move against Western Europe in general and France in particular.[77] The French hotel trade press, already attuned to boycott calls circulating in the United States, likewise stressed the "anti-French" nature of Johnson's program.[78] A skeptical *L'Express* argued that Americans, unable to acknowledge their own economic limits, sought a scapegoat in France.[79]

Other observers emphasized the dangers of the White House proposals for the French travel industry. *Le Monde*'s tourism expert responded to Johnson's speech by stressing that any reduction in American vacationers, who outspent France's other visitors, would upset France's "very precarious" tourism balance.[80] Several days later, the newspaper's Washington correspondent reported widespread support among American politicians for even the most extreme antitravel proposals, including steep taxes to be levied specifically on Americans traveling to France.[81] Devoting a lead editorial to Johnson's New Year's speech, *Paris-Match* warned ominously that European prosperity, which had long depended on "a sea of dollars," risked coming to an end. The editorial included a list of French regions that could suffer most from a loss of American tourist spending.[82] *L'Hôtellerie* responded to the speech by calling for increased marketing and even suggested that French hotels might have to adjust to the new era by focusing on French customers instead of Americans.[83]

Some French voices, however, attempted to minimize the sense of crisis. State Secretary for Tourism Pierre Dumas, initiator of the 1965 smile checks, gave an interview with *Le Figaro* two days after Johnson's 1968 speech. Dumas stressed that Americans valued their "individual liberty" too dearly to accept Johnson's agenda. The next day, Raymond Aron, the prominent intellectual who often wrote in defense of the Atlantic Alliance, echoed the same point and predicted that Americans would not likely be able to resist "the temptation" of travel to Europe.[84] As Johnson's proposals faltered in the United States, other French observers expressed more confidence for the coming tourist season. *France-Soir*, which at first feared a "hard blow" to Europe's travel industry, soon predicted that "the patriotism of American tourists" would decline before the summer started.[85]

In the final analysis, Johnson's tourism campaigns brought little, if any, improvement in the United States' balance of payments. In 1965, after his legislative proposals failed in Congress, the president relied instead on moral appeals to voluntary sacrifice. Still, when compared to the year before, Americans in 1965 made 11 percent more trips abroad and spent another 11 percent more while doing so. The White House's call to patriotic duty might even have backfired.

While some Americans canceled their trips, other consumers may have made a special effort to head overseas before new restrictions or taxes could be imposed.[86] The effectiveness of Johnson's 1968 appeal to stay within the Western Hemisphere for two years is more difficult to measure. American tourist expenditures in Western Europe did fall slightly in 1968, from $944 million to $925 million. That drop, however, also stemmed from the other crises of 1968. Several weeks of general strike and political instability in France in May, the Soviet invasion of Czechoslovakia in August, and widespread hostility among Europeans to the U.S. war in Vietnam weakened the transatlantic travel market that year. By 1969, however, tourist expenditures in Western Europe had more than recovered, exceeding one billion dollars for the first time ever.[87]

Tourists Pay in the End

If saved from making a sacrifice in the 1960s, American tourists finally felt the impact of the United States' monetary problems when Richard Nixon devalued the dollar in 1971. On the campaign trail in 1968, Nixon had used the travel issue to help distinguish himself from the Democrats. He denounced LBJ's tax proposal as "unfair and unnecessary" and defended the ideal middle-class tourist, whom he described as the "school teachers and others who have saved their dollars for a once-in-a-lifetime trip to Europe."[88] Shortly after entering the White House in 1969, Nixon repeated his campaign promise of no taxes and "no restrictions on the American tourist's freedom to travel."[89] Nevertheless, Nixon ultimately had to confront the dollar's continued vulnerability, and his handling of monetary policy ironically proved as bad as any tax for tourists. The nation's balance-of-payments situation deteriorated as Nixon continued the war in Vietnam and as the United States faced persistent trade deficits, inflation, and capital flight. In the face of another monetary crisis in 1971, Nixon completed the break with the Bretton Woods economic system and unilaterally declared that the United States would cease to guarantee a fixed amount of gold for each dollar. No longer pegged to gold, the dollar fell in value against major currencies, including the French franc.[90] Designed in part to promote sales of American goods abroad, Nixon's move also raised prices for Americans traveling overseas. In France, the devalued dollar, when converted into francs, purchased 10 percent less than it did before. By acting unilaterally and unleashing market forces on the dollar, Nixon reduced Americans' overseas buying power to an extent that Johnson never achieved with his open debate on tax policy.

Continuing a pattern set in earlier decades, the popular media after Nixon's devaluation presented American tourists abroad as emblematic of the nation's overall international status. In 1971, the experiences of vacationers in Europe seemed to symbolize the nation's economic woes. When *Time* introduced Americans to "the new economic world" created by the devaluation, it began with photographs of desperate tourists in London selling belongings in the streets to supplement their weakened dollars. Reports circulated of foreign banks and hotels refusing to accept U.S. traveler's checks and offering exorbitant exchange rates for dollars. Several journalists told the story of a French beggar sitting on the steps of Sacré-Coeur cathedral, one of the best locations in Paris for attracting the attention of tourists. Low on cash but not irony, the Frenchman reportedly held a sign announcing that "dollars are no longer accepted."[91] With poor Europeans spurning charity from Americans, the U.S. media's travel reports portrayed a world turned upside down.

In the following years, travel writing frequently reinforced this sense of national decline. At the start of the 1972 travel season, *Newsweek* declared an end to "the good old days" when roving Americans were "kings and queens of the world." "I've never felt more insecure in my whole life," one tourist told the magazine after seeing a European merchant reduce the exchange-rate value of the dollar before her own eyes. *U.S. News and World Report* observed that Americans "can understand now the embarrassment and humiliation" that French and British tourists felt after World War II when their currencies faltered.[92]

Yet American consumerism in Europe proved resilient once more. Rather than reduce the volume of American transatlantic travel, the devaluation reinforced the larger trend toward modest-cost travel. Airlines helped maintain the overseas market by trimming 11 percent from economy-class transatlantic fares. Travel agents in the early 1970s reported a marked shift in their business from luxury to lower-cost tour packages.[93] Arthur Frommer took the new monetary regime in stride by revising the title of his popular *Europe on $5 a Day* guidebook to read *Europe on $5 and $10 a Day*. Frommer's budget tour company, once almost entirely dependent on student travelers, attracted increasing numbers of older Americans.[94] American consumerism and leisure spending, even if less lavish than before, remained a major thread connecting Americans to Europe. For the history of American travel, the lasting legacy of the dollar's decline in the 1960s and early 1970s was an acceleration in the longer-term evolution from elite leisure practices to middle-class travel.

Conclusion

Johnson's efforts to reduce Americans' overseas leisure revealed important changes in U.S. foreign policy and culture in the late 1960s. The campaigns represented one of Americans' first encounters during the Cold War era with the nation's economic limits. As U.S. policymakers came to terms with the relative decline of the United States in the international economy, they attempted to reduce the state's role as a promoter of American travel abroad. In turn, the unpopularity of these measures showed consumerism as a powerful ideology shaping U.S. international relations during the Cold War. The defenders of tourism, within and outside the travel industry, rooted this ideology in a political rhetoric that stressed an inalienable right to travel and shop free from government constraints.

Both sides in the debates over travel taxes assigned Cold War meanings to Americans' overseas leisure. Johnson's definition of Cold War holidays demanded sacrifice from American travelers to maintain the nation's foreign obligations. In contrast, defenders of tourism developed a more successful consumer-friendly version of anti-Communism. This more powerful sense of Cold War holidays presented consumer freedom and privilege as traits that distinguished the United States from the Soviet bloc. Ironically, this widespread sense of entitlement was in part the product of policies and rhetorical positions encouraged by the U.S. government in the late 1940s and 1950s. Yet, as illustrated with the failure of Johnson's travel program, policymakers found more success cultivating rather than containing consumerism.

Conclusion

NATIONS AND GLOBAL HISTORY

At the end of the twentieth century, international tourism represented one of the world's largest industries.[1] Travel's position as a central cultural and economic force in recent world history underscores the need for scholars to understand the causes and consequences of its rise. The history of American tourism in France helps explain this expansion and reveals the many public and private actors engaged in international travel. Tourism's growth did not just happen on its own, especially given the presence within each nation of critics opposed to special efforts on behalf of American tourists. Fueled by American middle-class affluence, mass travel to France also relied on collaboration among government, media, and business elites in each nation. These promoters packaged, sold, and subsidized leisure travel and publicly valorized the activity as beneficial to their nation's foreign policy.

Americans' vacations in France played an important role in some of the most significant issues facing U.S.-French relations during the early Cold War era. Tourist spending, facilitated through the Marshall Plan, contributed substantially to France's postwar economic recovery. Despite some exceptions, the images and discourse generated by tourism solidified Americans' popular commitment to Cold War alliance with Western Europe. Tourism also intensified French debates over Americanization and became one of the principal means by which the French perceived the nature of U.S. influence in their country. During an era of nuclear weapons and decolonization, Americans' leisure in France did not always make front-page news. Nevertheless, tourism held a steady position as one of the main forms of contact between the two nations and thus emerged as a force that policymakers in both countries hoped to control.

Moreover, tourism mattered not just because it attracted policymakers' attention but also because it revealed deeper connections between domestic society and foreign affairs in each nation. Tourism, travel writing, and the act of playing the host compelled members of each nation to ask what it meant to be American or to be French. In France, American visitors intensified internal debates over how to define the nation and how to modernize the economy while still preserving French traditions. As a form of foreign relations that took place within the nation's own borders, tourism also sparked discussion on how to balance domestic consumption and labor practices with the pursuit of foreign currency in a globalizing economy. In the United States, tourism led to a similar blurring of the domestic and international. When Americans attempted to understand the significance of tourism's expansion, they frequently combined domestic debates on the merits of mass culture with foreign policy discussion on strategies for winning world opinion in the Cold War. As a result, American attitudes toward tourism and mass culture, whether positive or negative, reflected and shaped their approaches to cultural diplomacy programs.

Mass tourism's rise and its relationship to the Cold War also shed light on the evolution of globalization. At first glance, the consumer spending of millions of tourists and the worldwide reach of large travel companies might appear as evidence of the increasing inability of states to control international affairs. Certainly, the history of tourism reveals the importance of private actors such as those in the travel industry who made possible greater cross-cultural exchanges and thereby altered the contours of international relations. At times, mass tourism did hamper state sovereignty and Cold War policy agendas. Travel boosters in the 1950s and 1960s were often unable to make tourists adhere to Cold War scripts, as when Americans returned from Europe opposed to U.S. foreign aid. The Johnson administration's futile struggle to reduce travel expenditures in the midst of the 1960s monetary crises provided another example of governments ceding some sovereignty to consumer forces beyond their control.

At the same time, the rise of international tourism also reveals how government authority and Cold War concerns remained crucial factors. These continuities suggest that the best approach for understanding the post-1945 world is to view Cold War policymaking and the growth of globalization not as isolated or competing developments but as two forces that frequently influenced and reinforced each other. For instance, travel industry leaders wrapped themselves in the mantle of patriotic service even as they operated across national borders. Aligning their global operations with national policy goals helped them to defend international tourism from internal critics and to protect subsidies and political support from government officials. Both the U.S. and French governments themselves forged new or expanded roles to make private travel a force behind their own Cold War diplomacy. In the first years of the Cold War, American policymakers, motivated in large part by a fear of Communism, promoted international leisure travel to help rebuild Western Europe's economy. In like fashion, French policies such as the 1949 decision to allow Americans to enter France without visas represented less a withering away of the state than a strategy to exploit consumer behavior to recover from war. Although Washington reduced its support of travel promotion to Europe in the 1960s, de Gaulle's government at the same time intensified its own promotional activity to increase France's economic and cultural standing. As part of its search for a "third way" between the two Cold War superpowers, de Gaulle's Fifth Republic played a critical role in expanding France's hotel industry at a time when private French investors proved incapable or unwilling to place capital into the nation's tourism infrastructure.

The history of American tourism in France thus shows how governments have expanded alongside globalization and, more fundamentally, how governments have eagerly fostered and accelerated globalization's international exchanges.[2] This strategy carried with it some risks for government officials. As Lyndon Johnson discovered during the balance-of-payments crisis, states have had more success when they tried to promote rather than restrict or discipline consumer exchanges. Yet for most of the Cold War era, both French and U.S. government officials were happy to see American tourism expand.

In a cultural corollary to the persistence of nation-state power, this study also suggests that increased exchanges across national borders have reinforced rather than undermined distinct national identities. To be sure, in a few cases, tourism helped foster new transnational identities. For instance, small groups of idealists in the United States, especially in the years immediately after World War II, hoped that tourism would instill in Americans an interest in supranational, one-world government. The travel boosters' rhetoric of purposeful travel, in which Americans were supposed to discover that foreigners were essentially like folks back home, also represented an attempt to have Americans adopt a broader identity emphasizing universal human similarities.[3] However, visions of one-world government and purposeful travel remained relatively marginal. Tourists and members of the travel industry more often sought ways to make France seem culturally different. After all, why spend so much of one's leisure time and money to experience what one could find back home?

Many travel writers did encourage Americans to see themselves as members of a broader Cold War–oriented Atlantic Community, but even here American nationalism prevailed. The Cold War emphasis on a shared Atlantic Community typically offered a new, more expansive way for Americans to envision their national identity. Travel writers frequently put forth the idea that Americans were leaders and caretakers of the Western civilization that bound together this community. Travel discourse also presented the Atlantic Community not as a group of equals but as a union of complementary parts in which the United States provided power and energy while European countries such as France offered history, diversion, and refinement.[4] In other words, travel in

France generally increased Americans' attachment to their nation's leadership role vis-à-vis a European Old World.

Tourism's reification of national difference was also true for the French in their role as hosts, a conclusion that is especially important at a time when many scholars on both sides of the Atlantic associate increased interdependence and globalization with "vanishing" Frenchness.[5] Hosting foreigners created new ways for the French to imagine themselves as French, as when travel promoters launched nationalistic calls for the French to act in public as if they were ambassadors of their nation. When hoteliers recommended serving only traditional French dishes to foreign guests or when technocratic modernizers presented hydroelectric dams as new monuments to French radiance, both sought to use foreign tourism as a vehicle to promote their particular vision of the nation. Tourism officials even launched nationalistic rituals such as the *Fleurir la France* contests, in which thousands of individuals and communities planted flowers to beautify the nation.[6]

The persistence of French national identity becomes even more apparent when we consider the question of Americanization.[7] Although Marshall Plan officials in the late 1940s sought to transform France's travel industry according to American middle-class norms, French authorities and hoteliers made changes on their own terms and at their own pace. Ultimately, the most powerful foreign influence that spurred changes in the French travel industry was not the Marshall Plan but the rise of international competition from Spain and other neighboring nations. American entrepreneur Conrad Hilton did open two hotels in Paris in the mid-1960s, but hotel modernization in France more often resulted in a combination of French traditions of labor-intensive service and Hilton's high-technology and high-comfort approach. Other changes that French hosts adopted were part of a specifically French process of developing a more consumer-oriented society. The French state's push in the 1960s for everything-included bills, a major change in the financial and labor arrangements of hotels, cafés, and restaurants, even if intended to please Americans and other consumers, did not make France more like the United States. In fact, tipping continues to be widespread in the United States while largely abandoned in France. As a tourist environment, postwar France did not necessarily become Americanized but instead followed its own path toward becoming a more consumer-oriented society.

The popular ideology of French "radiance" provides another example of persisting Frenchness. By connecting American tourism to the expansion of French cultural influence, travel promoters in France expressed confidence that national grandeur and international influence would survive in the postwar era. And with good reason. Americans' postwar enthusiasm for Parisian fashions and French cuisine added credence to these boosters' assumptions.[8] "Until then, food had been rather a bore," recalled one American whose outlook on eating changed forever with her 1961 visit to France. She went on to become a French teacher and later led groups of American teenagers through tours of France.[9] Many French did worry about American popular culture and American-derived hotel standards, but such concerns coexisted with more optimistic visions of French national identity, particularly the idea that France had managed what the United States never could: a synthesis of refined civilization and modernity.[10]

Moreover, when Gaullist politicians joined the travel boosters in France, they saw these visitors not as Americanizers but as a means to establish greater independence from U.S. military and economic power. Echoing a French Communist position from the late 1940s, Charles de Gaulle's government became an enthusiastic travel promoter in large part because American consumers represented a source of dollars with relatively few strings attached. Understanding this pragmatic approach helps explain the peculiar phenomenon of de Gaulle evicting U.S. military personnel from France and criticizing American corporations' acquisition of French companies at the same time that his government sought to please American vacationers by funding hotel modernization and friendliness campaigns.

If Charles de Gaulle, often regarded as an anti-American leader, could support American tourism, we might also ask whether tourism helped or hindered U.S.-French understanding and goodwill. A common assumption, even among scholars, is that the legacy of American travel in France has been one of misunderstanding and animosity.[11] Some encounters, of course, support this view. The French hotel and restaurant trade press recorded moments of frustration over the challenges of serving boorish Americans, while other French observers belittled Americans for their uncultured ways. On the other side, many American tourists discovered alarming political views in France or found evidence to confirm the image of rude Parisians.

Yet a closer look reveals a more complex and often more positive picture. This picture, in turn, underscores how American tourism quite often helped preserve closer ties within the Cold War Atlantic Alliance. For instance, many in the French government and travel industry eagerly sought to understand middle-class American tastes, suggesting that not everyone in France looked down on American culture. Even negative stereotypes could, in their own way, solidify relations between the two nations. For some French commentators, caricatures of uncultured Americans took on positive significance by allowing France to instill a sense of civilization in American visitors, thus providing for a degree of reciprocity in the face of a lopsided political, economic, and military relationship. Surveys of French public opinion in the late 1950s asking what kinds of Americans had the most positive influence in their country found that tourists easily outranked other types of Americans, including expatriates, military personnel, and even exchange students.[12] These French responses, although more suggestive than definitive, might even add weight to the theory that Americans' consumer vitality played an important role in winning over European opinion during the Cold War rivalry with the Soviet Union.[13] Armed only with cameras and stuffed wallets, the growing numbers of American tourists presented the United States in a potentially softer light than other manifestations of U.S. power during the Cold War. At the very least, ample evidence exists to cast doubt on any quick condemnation of tourism as a negative force in U.S.-French relations.

In fact, many of the tensions created by tourism did not pit Americans against the French but instead transcended national lines. Major disagreements generally divided advocates of consumer-oriented modernization, whether American or French, against the two nations' defenders of artisanal, elite-oriented traditions. Those American and French observers eager for a more consumer-friendly France valorized middle-class American consumer tastes. They also directed a nearly identical scorn upon allegedly rude Parisian waiters and snobbish hoteliers wedded to older artisanal practices. Meanwhile, old-guard cultural authorities and skeptics of mass culture in both nations defended elite service professionals and looked down on middle-class consumers. With a shared conservative view, many American Francophiles and French traditionalists expressed similar fears that modernization and mass culture would destroy the "Old World" France they loved. Although these American and French groups at times operated in self-conscious alliance, more often they functioned on parallel but separate tracks. The story of American travel in France is thus at once a transnational and a national history. Even as they responded to the same international trends and forged cross-cultural contacts, American tourists and French hosts on the whole remained national in their identity.

This interplay between increased exchanges across borders and reinforced nationalism points to an important lesson on writing the history of the twentieth century. The example of tourism in the Cold War era shows how globalization could occur largely through individuals, businesses, and governments acting according to national identities and on behalf of national concerns. This dynamic suggests that scholars of global or transnational history should not leave behind a focus on national communities and state policy. Likewise, diplomatic historians and other scholars who focus on the Cold War and nation-state concerns need to account for expanding forms of global economic and cultural exchange such as tourism.[14] Although few American tourists left for France aiming to change the nature of international relations, they did bring consumerism and domestic concerns into the global arena. In the process, their pursuits of leisure contributed to a broader reshaping of the post-1945 world.

NOTES

Abbreviations Used in the Notes

AN   Archives nationales, Paris

BDF   Bibliothèque de la Documentation française, Paris

Brewster Papers

                 Ralph Owen Brewster Papers, Bowdoin College, Bowdoin, Maine

CAC   Centre des archives contemporaines, Fontainebleau

CAEF   Centre des archives économiques et financières, Savigny-le-Temple

CRU   Subject Files (Central Files) 1948–53, Communications and Records Units, Administrative Services Division, Director of Administration, Economic Cooperation Administration Files, Record Group 469, Records of the U.S. Foreign Assistance Agencies, 1948–1961, National Archives and Records Administration II, College Park, Maryland

Curtin Files   Subject Files 1948–51, Enos Curtin Files, Office of the Deputy Assistant Administrator, Office of the Assistant Administrator for Operations, Record Group 469, Records of U.S. Foreign Assistance Agencies, Economic Cooperation Administration Files, National Archives and Records Administration II, College Park, Maryland

EU, AM 1944–52

                 États-Unis, Amérique 1944–52, Archives du Ministère des affaires étrangères, Paris

EU, AM 1952–63

                 États-Unis, Amérique 1952–63, Archives du Ministère des affaires étrangères, Paris

FGTO   French Government Tourist Office

FJS   Fonds Jean Sainteny, Archives d'histoire contemporaine, Centre d'histoire de l'Europe du XXe siècle, Fondation nationale des sciences politiques, Paris

FRUS, 1964–1968

                 U.S. Department of State. *Foreign Relations of the United States,1964–68*, vol. 8, *International Monetary and Trade Policy*. Washington: U.S. Government Printing Office, 1998.

Goldstein Files

                 Ernest Goldstein Office Files, Lyndon Baines Johnson Library, Austin, Texas

HCR   Hôtel-Café-Restaurant

HCRB   Hôtel-Café-Restaurant-Brasserie

Files

Subject Files, J. P. Hendrick Files, Office of the Special Assistant to the Administrator, Records of the Office of the Administrator, Economic Cooperation Administration Files, Record Group 469, Records of U.S. Foreign Assistance Agencies, National Archives and Records Administration II, College Park, Maryland

ID-CSF   Country Subject Files, France, 1948–50, Office of the Director, Information Division, Subject Files, Central Secretariat, 1948–52, Records of the Office of the United States Special Representative in Europe, Economic Cooperation Administration Files, Record Group 469, Records of U.S. Foreign Assistance Agencies, National Archives and Records Administration II, College Park, Maryland

ID-GSF   General Subject Files 1948–49, Office of the Director, Information Division, Subject Files, Central Secretariat, 1948–52, Records of the Office of the United States Special Representative in Europe, Economic Cooperation Administration Files, Record Group 469, Records of U.S. Foreign Assistance Agencies, National Archives and Records Administration II, College Park, Maryland

INSEE   Institut national de la statistique et des études économiques

JWT Collection

J. Walter Thompson Collection, John W. Hartman Center for Sales, Advertising, and Marketing History, Rare Book, Manuscript, and Special Collections Library, Duke University, Durham, North Carolina

LBJL   Lyndon Baines Johnson Library, Austin, Texas

LBJL-CF   Confidential Files, Lyndon Baines Johnson Library, Austin, Texas

LBJL-WHCF   White House Central Files, Lyndon Baines Johnson Library, Austin, Texas

MAE   Ministère des affaires étrangères, Paris

NARA   National Archives and Records Administration II, College Park, Maryland

OA   Policy Subject Files 1948–51, Office of the Administrator, Economic Cooperation Administration Files, Record Group 469, Records of U.S. Foreign Assistance Agencies, National Archives and Records Administration II, College Park, Maryland

OEEC   Organization for European Economic Cooperation

OSR   Subject Files, Central Secretariat, 1948–52, Records of the Office of the United States Special Representative in Europe, Economic Cooperation Administration Files, Record Group 469, Records of U.S. Foreign Assistance Agencies, National Archives and Records Administration II, College Park, Maryland

OSR-CSF   Confidential Subject Files 1948–51, Subject Files, Central Secretariat, 1948–52, Records of the Office of the United States Special Representative in Europe, Economic Cooperation Administration Files, Record Group 469, Records of U.S. Foreign Assistance Agencies, National Archives and Records Administration II, College Park, Maryland

Pan Am Records

Pan American World Airways, Inc. Records, Archives and Special

Collections, Otto G. Richter Library, University of Miami, Coral Gables, Florida

Rand Files   Subject Files, William H. Rand, Deputy Director, 1953–54, Office of the Deputy Director, Economic Cooperation Administration Files, Record Group 469, Records of U.S. Foreign Assistance Agencies, National Archives and Records Administration II, College Park, Maryland

RG   Record Group

SR 1953–63   Special Reports 1953–63, Office of Research, Records of the U.S. Information Agency, Record Group 306, National Archives and Records Administration II, College Park, Maryland

SR 1964–82   Special Reports 1964–82, Office of Research, Record Group 306, Records of the U.S. Information Agency, National Archives and Records Administration II, College Park, Maryland

TDS-CSF   Country Subject Files, 1948–51, France, Travel Development and Tourism Section, Export Promotion Division, Office of the Special Representative in Europe, Economic Cooperation Administration Files, Record Group 469, Records of U.S. Foreign Assistance Agencies, National Archives and Records Administration II, College Park, Maryland

TDS-GSF   General Subject Files, Travel Development and Tourism Section, Export Promotion Division, Office of the Special Representative in Europe, Economic Cooperation Administration Files, Record Group 469, Records of U.S. Foreign Assistance Agencies, National Archives and Records Administration II, College Park, Maryland

Wilkinson Records

Records Pertaining to the Chief of the Department of Commerce's Travel Bureau, Herbert A. Wilkinson, 1948–51, Travel Development and Tourism Section, Export Promotion Division, Office of the Special Representative in Europe, Economic Cooperation Administration Files, Record Group 469, Records of U.S. Foreign Assistance Agencies, National Archives and Records Administration II, College Park, Maryland

Introduction

1. "L'Hôtel George V est rendu à sa clientèle civile," *Notre métier: Bulletin du personnel des Hôtels George V—Plaza-Athénée*, April 1946; "Nos hôtels participent à l'histoire," ibid., July 1946.

2. George Kent, "How to Be an American Abroad," *Reader's Digest* 54 (June 1949): 116–18; originally *Travel* 92 (May 1949): 10–11, 32.

3. Ann Rea Craig, interview by author, tape recording, 17 September 2002.

4. Histories of U.S.-French relations typically treat tourism only in passing reference. Frank Costigliola (*France and the United States*, 5), for instance, comments that "although Americans often disregarded or trivialized what the French had to say, many liked spending time in their country." Irwin M. Wall (*United States and the Making of Postwar France*, 181–82) mentions tourism in a list of issues concerning French postwar recovery. Richard Kuisel (*Seducing the French*, 19–20) refers to a U.S. diplomat's complaint in 1949 over

discourteous treatment of tourists, which fed French fears of an overbearing United States. In his diplomatic history textbook, Robert D. Schulzinger (*U.S. Diplomacy since 1900*, 209) refers to travelers' reports of European suffering after the war as a source of the Marshall Plan. A recent exception is McKenzie, "Deep Impact," which includes a chapter on the role of tourism in U.S. cultural diplomacy. See also McKenzie, "Creating a Tourist's Paradise."

5. Recent statements on consumerism include Cohen, *Consumer's Republic*; Strasser, McGovern, and Judt, eds., *Getting and Spending*; Cross, *All-Consuming Century*; and Roberts, "Gender, Consumption, and Commodity Culture." Kristin Hoganson ("Cosmopolitan Domesticity") has also shown how Americans' mass consumption in the late nineteenth century played a revealing role in world affairs.

6. For an overview of recent historical scholarship on tourism in this vein, see Baranowski and Furlough, eds., *Being Elsewhere*. Histories of U.S. or French tourism include Levenstein, *Seductive Journey*; Shaffer, *See America First*; Furlough, "Making Mass Vacations"; and Lavenir, *La Roue et le stylo*. Two indispensable general overviews of earlier tourism scholarship are Crick, "Representations of International Tourism," and Engerman, "Research Agenda for the History of Tourism."

7. Several scholars have paid particular attention to international forces on domestic tourism. See, for instance, Koshar, *German Travel Cultures*, and Löfgren, *On Holiday*.

8. For one of the best essays on this general idea, see Iriye, "Culture and International History." Some historians have begun to develop these connections. For instance, international efforts to attract American tourism are discussed in Merrill, "Negotiating Cold War Paradise," and Schwartz, *Pleasure Island*. On ties between politics and hotels, see Wharton, *Building the Cold War*. It is also worth noting how cultural studies of imperialism have also unveiled political dimensions to travel writing. See, for instance, Pratt, *Imperial Eyes*; Spurr, *Rhetoric of Empire*; and Furlough, "Une leçon des choses."

9. Among the extensive scholarship on globalization, two especially useful works are Held and McGrew et al., *Global Transformations*, and Zeiler, "Just Do It!"

10. This view builds on Akira Iriye's call to go "beyond the Cold War" (*Global Community*, 61–63). See also Connelly, "Taking Off the Cold War Lens."

11. My formulation of this argument has been influenced by Milward, *European Rescue of the Nation-State*, and Buell, *National Culture and the New Global System*. These studies provide a useful corrective to those that present globalization more as an inherent threat to nations, as do Barber, *Jihad vs. McWorld*, and Appadurai, *Modernity at Large*. For further commentary on this subject, see Pérez, "We Are the World."

12. Bender and Altschul, *Chosen Instrument*, 399–402. For more context on "chosen instruments," see Rosenberg, *Spreading the American Dream*.

13. On this theme, see Geyer and Bright, "World History in a Global Age," 1056–57; Helleiner, *States and the Reemergence of Global Finance*; and Weiss, *Myth of the Powerless State*.

14. For a classic statement on this "corporatist" approach, see Hogan, "Corporatism." See also Rosenberg, *Spreading the American Dream*. On public-private cooperation in cultural diplomacy, see Hixson, *Parting the Curtain*.

15. Scholarship on France emphasizing official cultural diplomacy bureaucracy includes Girard and Gentil, *Les Affaires culturelles au temps d'André Malraux*; Lebovics,

Mona Lisa's Escort; Poirrier, *L'État et la culture en France au XXe siècle*; and Urfalino, *L'Invention de la politique culturelle*.

16. Some scholars prefer the terms "transnational" or "global" instead of "international" to describe the history of relations between peoples across national borders, arguing that the term "international" overemphasizes the rigidity of national borders and identities. Although endorsing the value of the "transnational" argument to a degree, this study also employs the more conventional "international history" concept, because almost all of the actors in this study, even as they crossed national borders, still maintained a national identity as either French or American. For more on this semantic issue, see Iriye, *Global Community*, 7–8.

17. For a recent discussion, see *Diplomatic History*'s 2000 roundtable on cultural imperialism, including Gienow-Hecht, "Shame on US?"; Pells, "Who's Afraid of Steven Spielberg?"; and Kuisel, "Americanization for Historians." See also Kuisel, *Seducing the French*, and Pells, *Not Like Us*.

18. On the creation of a transnational Mediterranean travel culture, see Löfgren, *On Holiday*.

19. Among the few scholars to call for more attention to the internationalization of the United States is Pells in "Who's Afraid of Steven Spielberg?"

20. See, for example, LaFeber, *American Age*, 457, and Lundestad, "Empire by Invitation?" 264.

21. "Drafted Report for use by ECA Administration," 3 April 1951, Box 2, Wilkinson Records.

22. For case studies of Hilton and Pan Am, see Wharton, *Building the Cold War*, and Bender and Altschul, *Chosen Instrument*.

23. Harvey Levenstein (*Seductive Journey*, xii) raises this point in his study of U.S. tourism in France up to 1929.

24. George H. Gallup, *The Gallup Poll, Public Opinion, 1935–1971* (New York: Random House, 1972), 2:990.

25. On French images of the United States, see Kuisel, *Seducing the French*; Mathy, *Extrême-Occident*; Pells, *Not Like Us*; Portes, *Une Fascination réticente*; and Strauss, *Menace in the West*.

26. World Tourism Organization, *Yearbook of Tourism Statistics, Vol. 49* (Madrid: World Tourism Organization, 1997), 1: 14–15; *New York Times*, 3 October 1999.

27. A number of social scientists and historians, most often studying lesser-developed countries or regions, have begun to examine these common themes among host societies. Important examples include Enloe, *Bananas, Beaches, and Bases*, 19–41; Lanfant, Allcock, and Bruner, *International Tourism*; Merrill, "Negotiating Cold War Paradise"; Picard and Wood, eds., *Tourism, Ethnicity, and the State*; and Richter, *Politics of Tourism in Asia*. See also Hazbun, "Between Global Flows and Territorial Control," on the Middle East, and Gould-Davies, "Logic of Soviet Cultural Diplomacy," on the Soviet Union.

28. On earlier U.S. travel to Europe, see Levenstein, *Seductive Journey*; Stowe, *Going Abroad*; Green, "Comparative Gaze"; and Dulles, *Americans Abroad*. For earlier French context, see Lavenir, *La Roue et le stylo*.

29. These figures, provided by the French government, are slightly higher than figures from the U.S. government, which did not include Americans entering France from other

countries in Europe. See *International Travel Statistics, 1950* (n.p.: International Union of Official Tourism Offices, 1952): 12; *International Travel Statistics, 1960* (Geneva: International Union of Official Tourism Offices, 1962): 25; and "France," *International Travel Statistics* 24 (1970): 1.

30. This trend continued in later decades, so that by 1996 Americans accounted for under 14 percent of France's earnings from foreign tourists. See INSEE, *Annuaire statistique de la France* 87 (1982): 555; 93 (1988): 271; and 101 (1998): 317.

31. *Saturday Review* 51 (9 March 1968).

32. "Moins de dollars, plus de deutschemarks," *Le Monde*, 29 August 1973, and "Les Américains boudent," *Le Monde*, 2 March 1974, both in Carton 244, 97006, BDF.

33. This trend complements Richard Kuisel's notion that Americanization in the twentieth century represents a specific era in the larger story of the emergence of a more global culture ("Americanization for Historians").

Chapter One

1. Henri Bonnet to Ministère des affaires étrangères, 24 August 1946; "Note pour la Direction des unions," 6 November 1946; and Bonnet to Georges Bidault, 16 September 1946, all in Vol. 73, EU, AM 1944–52; Ludovic Chancel to Bonnet, 10 September 1947, Vol. 74, EU, AM 1944–52. On the 1927 pilgrimage, see Levenstein, *Seductive Journey*, 271–75.

2. Direction d'Amérique to Bonnet, 5 December 1946, Vol. 73, EU, AM 1944–52. On French politics, see Hitchcock, *France Restored*; Wall, *United States and the Making of Postwar France*; and Costigliola, *France and the United States*.

3. Direction d'Amérique to Ministre des anciens combattants et victimes de guerre, 29 May 1947, Vol. 74, EU, AM 1944–52.

4. Paul H. Griffith to Vincent Auriol, 1 March 1947; "Voyage en France de l'American Legion," 20 June 1947; and Christopher Maran to Ludovic Chancel, 3 December 1947, all in Vol. 74, EU, AM 1944–52.

5. "Les délégués de l'American Legion parcourent la voie de la liberté," *Le Monde*, 16 September 1947; ibid., 20 September 1948; "Le pèlerinage en France de l'American Legion," *France Libre*, 13 September 1947.

6. "Extrait d'un rapport établi par le 'Commander' Griffith à la suite de la visite de l'American Legion en France au cours de l'été 1947," Vol. 74, EU, AM 1944–52.

7. Chancel to MAE, 28 August 1947, Vol. 74, EU, AM 1944–52.

8. See Levenstein, *Seductive Journey*; Stowe, *Going Abroad*; and Dulles, *Americans Abroad*.

9. U.S. Bureau of the Census, *Historical Statistics*, 404–5. Statistics by the Bureau of the Census treat Europe and the Mediterranean as one region. On the relationship between tourism and turn-of-the-century international affairs, see Endy, "Travel and World Power."

10. Still valuable on this theme is Strout, *American Image of the Old World*. On Daisy Miller in the 1890s, see Endy, "Travel and World Power," 577, 581.

11. Levenstein, *Seductive Journey*, 271–75.

12. Rodgers, *Atlantic Crossings*; Endy, "Travel and World Power," 578–79.

13. Levenstein (*Seductive Journey*) stresses the rise to prominence of "recreational" or

pleasure-oriented tourism and the relative decline of "cultural tourism." See also Hanna, "French Women and American Men."

14. Andrieu, *Histoire anecdotique des hôtels*, 121; Levenstein, *Seductive Journey*, 91; Watts, *Ritz of Paris*.

15. Levenstein, *Seductive Journey*, 266–70.

16. François Dupré to Fernand de Brinon, 12 March 1941, F60 612, AN. The Nazi minister was Herman Esser, Staatssekretär im Reichsministerium für Volksaufklärung und Propaganda und Leiter des deutschen Fremdenverkehrs. On wartime tourism, see Gordon, "*Ist Gott Französisch?*"

17. Elliot Paul, *The Last Time I Saw Paris* (New York: Random House, 1942); *Casablanca* (Warner Brothers, 1942).

18. "Out of a Book," *Time* 44 (14 August 1944): 55.

19. Ben Hibbs, "Preview of Your Atlantic Flight," *Saturday Evening Post* 218 (14 July 1945): 6.

20. William Walton, "The Liberation of Montmartre," *Life* 17 (11 September 1944): 38; "Paris," ibid., 25–37.

21. "Paris: The City of Lights Comes out of the Darkness Again," *Life* 17 (2 October 1944): 87–95; Charles Wertenbaker, "The Streets and People," *Life* 17 (11 September 1944): 38; George Sessions Perry, "Riviera Picnic," *Saturday Evening Post* 217 (9 December 1944): 17, 89–92.

22. Henry R. Luce, "The American Century," *Life* 10 (17 February 1941): 61–65.

23. Franklin G. Smith, "Military Travel Market," *ASTA Travel News* 26 (April 1957): 52–53; Schrijvers, *Crash of Ruin*; Linderman, *World within War*.

24. Christopher Blake, "France to Me," *France-U.S.A.*, no. 3 (June 1947). After the war, the soldier stayed in Paris to live as an expatriate writer.

25. Bill Mauldin, *Up Front* (New York: Henry Holt, 1945), 63, 179, 189.

26. Schrijvers, *Crash of Ruin*, 107.

27. Bill Mauldin, *Back Home* (New York: William Sloane, 1947), 43.

28. "G.I. 'Heaven,'" *Time* 45 (18 June 1945): 19.

29. Beverly Smith, "Yanks on the Riviera," *American Magazine* 140 (August 1945): 103–6; Frederick Simpich Jr., "Paris Freed," *National Geographic* 87 (April 1945): 385–412; "Paris on a 48-Hour Pass," *National Geographic* 87 (January 1945): 79–86.

30. Tom Siler, "Paris: The G.I.'s Silver Foxhole," *Saturday Evening Post* 148 (September 1945): 26–27, 66.

31. Torrent, "L'Image du soldat américain en France."

32. Baum, "Marshall Plan and French Foreign Trade," 395. See also Mary Burnet, "Planning to Visit France?" *Harper's* 194 (May 1947): 465.

33. Joe Weston, "The GIs in Le Havre," *Life* 19 (10 December 1945): 19–20. See also "The Idle GI and Liberated France are Mighty Tired of Each Other," *Newsweek* 26 (19 November 1945): 56–58.

34. C. G. Paulding, "The Returning Soldiers: Mistrust of What They Tell about Europe," *Commonweal* 42 (28 September 1945): 566–69.

35. Charles J. Rolo, "Innocents Abroad," *Saturday Review* 28 (6 April 1946): 5–6, 20–23.

36. John Dos Passos, "Americans are Losing the Victory in Europe," *Life* 20 (7 January 1946): 23–24.

37. COFBA also catered to British and Canadian soldiers. See Lt. H. P. Boucher, "Memorandum on Franco-American Relations," 19 February 1946, Vol. 78, EU, AM 1944–52, and Bonnet to Ministère des affaires étrangères, 17 January 1945, Vol. 77, EU, AM 1944–52.

38. Details on COFBA activities can be found in Vol. 78, EU, AM 1944–52. For an insightful discussion of tourism by U.S. soldiers after World War I, see Meigs, *Optimism at Armageddon*.

39. COFBA, "Rapport d'activité au 1er octobre 1945," Vol. 79, EU, AM 1944–52.

40. Commissariat général au tourisme, "How to See Paris: For the Soldiers of the Allied Armies," 1946 booklet, Article 30, 790549, CAC.

41. COFBA, *France* (Paris: Gaston Maillet, 1947), 26.

42. Emile Servan-Schreiber, "Miami ou Pompeï," *Les Échos*, 31 July 1945. Servan-Schreiber also represented France as an economic expert at the May 1945 United Nations conference in San Francisco and was father to future *L'Express* editor Jean-Jacques Servan-Schreiber.

43. Léon Guerdan, "Lettre de New York," *L'Ordre*, 23 January 1947, Reel 6, Problèmes généraux 1944 à 1952, Relations diplomatiques, France–États Unis, BDF. *L'Ordre* was reestablished after the war by Emile Buré, who spent the war in New York publishing *France-Amérique*, an outlet for Charles de Gaulle's Free French forces.

44. Fichtenbaum, *Passport to the World*, 58.

45. "Going Abroad? Here's How," *Business Week*, 5 January 1946, pp. 17–18.

46. "European Travel Boom On," *Business Week*, 29 March 1947, pp. 19–20.

47. U.S. Bureau of the Census, *Historical Statistics*, 404.

48. Hugh A. Harter, *Return to Patton's France: 1944's Odyssey Retraced* (London: Janus, 1999), 199–200.

49. Pan American World Airways, press release, 19 December 1946, Box 357, Pan Am Records.

50. Commissariat général au tourisme, "Note sur les possibilités du tourisme américain en France et les conditions faites aux touristes," 5 June 1946, Vol. 264, EU, AM 1944–52.

51. Maurice Carisey, "Les États-Unis et nous," *XXe Siècle*, 8 May 1946.

52. Olivier Merlin, "Le Tourisme au service du relèvement français," *Le Monde*, 18 April 1946.

53. Commissariat général au tourisme, "Note sur les possibilités du tourisme américain en France."

54. Jules Moch, "Conférence de presse sur le Tourisme," 15 March 1946, Carton 242, 97006, BDF.

55. Marcel Cuau, "Le Tourisme et le relèvement de la France," *L'Evènement*, 27 April 1946, Carton 242, 97006, BDF.

56. Merlin, "Le Tourisme au service du relèvement français."

57. "Suppression de la carte de touriste," *L'Hôtellerie*, 1 September 1947; Burnet, "Planning to Visit France?" 465.

58. Rioux, *Fourth Republic*, 80, 113.

59. Advertisement for French Government Tourist Office, *United Nations World* 1 (February 1947).

60. Laura Vitray, "France Polishes the Bars, Makes Children Visitor-Conscious, Sweats over Souvenirs, Rolls out the Red Carpet for Spring's Tourists," *United Nations World* 1 (February 1947): 71–73.

61. Commissariat général au tourisme, "On Solid Foundations of Past and Present Achievements, FRANCE Is Now Building for the Future," 1947 pamphlet, Article 30, 790549, CAC. See also Commissariat général au tourisme, "France," 1947 pamphlet, Article 30, 790549, CAC.

62. "Britain Warns off Tourists Till 1948," *New York Times*, 12 April 1947.

63. Bonnet to Georges Bidault, 18 April 1947, Vol. 264, EU, AM 1944–52.

64. "Warning to Tourists," *Washington Post*, 14 April 1947.

65. "Tourists to Europe," *New York Times*, 13 April 1947.

66. Sydney Clark, *All the Best in France* (New York: Dodd, Mead & Co., 1947), 3, 6.

67. Carl de Suze, "Tourist in France," *Atlantic Monthly* 180 (September 1947): 106–8. On rations, see Rioux, *Fourth Republic*, 113.

68. Horace Sutton, *Footloose in France* (New York: Rinehart and Co., 1948), 5.

69. Horace Sutton, "Tourists' Dollars for ERP," *Nation* 166 (14 February 1948): 184.

70. Hogan, *Cross of Iron*.

71. *Congressional Record*, 80th Cong., 1st sess., 24 November 1947, vol. 93, pt. 9:10806.

72. Ibid., 2 December 1947, vol. 93, pt. 13:A4320–21.

73. Ibid., 18 November 1947, vol. 93, pt. 9:10648.

74. James Marshall, "The Europe We Are Fleeing From," *Saturday Review* 16 (16 February 1946): 23–25. See also "Paris in the Summer," *Fortune* 36 (August 1947): 120, and Michael Straight, "The Streets of Rome," *New Republic* 117 (17 November 1947): 10–11.

75. Anne Morrow Lindbergh, "The Flame of Europe," *Reader's Digest* 52 (January 1948): 141–46. Charles, too, converted from isolationism during World War II and publicly supported the Truman Doctrine in 1947 (Berg, *Lindbergh*, 477, 482–83).

76. Stephen Spender, "Wilson among the Ruins," *Nation* 165 (29 November 1947): 592–95. Spender became active in the Congress for Cultural Freedom, a group of non-Communist, left-leaning intellectuals in the United States and Europe that, unbeknownst to most participants, received funding from the Central Intelligence Agency (Coleman, *Liberal Conspiracy*).

77. For an insightful analysis of how earlier Americans used the concept of civilization, see Bederman, *Manliness and Civilization*, especially the methodological discussion on pp. 23–24. See also Ninkovich, *Modernity and Power*, xi; Robert Young, "In the Eye of the Beholder"; and Federici, "God that Never Failed."

78. Janet Flanner [Gênet], *Paris Journal*, vol. 1, *1944–1955*, ed. William Shawn (New York: Harcourt Brace Jovanovich, 1988), 15.

79. Anne Fremantle, "France Forever," *Commonweal* 47 (7 November 1947): 90.

80. Cyril Connolly, "Paris Regained," *Nation* 160 (2 June 1945): 626.

81. Quoted in Price, *Marshall Plan and Its Meaning*, 47.

82. Scholars of nationalism such as Benedict Anderson (*Imagined Communities*) have suggested that nations are "imagined communities" that depend on media and cultural constructions to convey a sense of common bonds among people with no direct personal ties to each other. I emphasize here that a similar process held for other community-

building projects such as the postwar "Atlantic Community." For a fruitful analysis of community-building on an international level, see Rupp, *Worlds of Women*.

83. Lindbergh, "Flame of Europe."

84. Tibor Koeves, "The First Time You'll See Paris," *United Nations World* 2 (May 1948): 47; Sutton, *Footloose in France*, 87; Elliot Paul, *Paris* (Chicago: Ziff Davis Publishing, 1947).

Chapter Two

1. "Tourist Planes for Europe," *Indianapolis Star*, 16 November 1951, Box 357, Pan Am Records; Horace Sutton, "Tourists' Dollars for ERP," *Nation* 166 (14 February 1948): 184.

2. Herbert Wilkinson, speech before "European Technical Mission to the United States for the Study of Techniques in Travel, Hotels, and Allied Activities," 19 January 1950, Box 9, Curtin Files.

3. For general accounts of government-business cooperation, see Rosenberg, *Spreading the American Dream*, and McQuaid, *Uneasy Partners*. Several books and books-in-progress shed light on the tourism dimension of U.S.-Latin American relations. On Hilton, see Wharton, *Building the Cold War*. See also Dennis Merrill's forthcoming book on tourism in the Spanish-speaking Caribbean and Christine Skwiot, "Itineraries of Empire."

4. Heppenheimer, *Turbulent Skies*.

5. "International Conference of National Tourist Organizations, 1–4 October 1946," Box 26, Committees, October 1945 to December 1949, Central Files, Office of International Trade, Records of the Bureau of Foreign and Domestic Commerce, RG 151, NARA.

6. Fichtenbaum, *Passport to the World*, 23, 31–32.

7. Grossman, *American Express*, 253.

8. Levenstein, *Seductive Journey*, 235–36.

9. Travel Branch, Office of International Trade, "Summary Statement," 31 January 1949, Box 9, Curtin Files.

10. "U.S. Lines Resists Edict by Truman," *New York Times*, 17 December 1952; "Sawyer 'Childish,' Controller Snaps in Controversy over Liner Subsidy," ibid., 2 July 1952; "Subsidies to Liner Called Excessive," ibid., 1 June 1952; Charles Sawyer, "U.S. Government Pushes Policy to Encourage Travel Abroad," *ASTA Travel News* 18 (January 1948): 12–13.

11. "Invasion, 1952," *Time* 59 (23 June 1952): 78–88.

12. On the centrality of militarization, see Sherry, *In the Shadow of War*.

13. Bilstein, *Enterprise of Flight*, 135–39; Miller, "'Air Power Is Peace Power.'"

14. Bender and Altschul, *Chosen Instrument*, 288, 404; Fichtenbaum, *Passport to the World*, 25. See also Solberg, *Conquest of the Skies*, and, for a more general discussion, Rosenberg, *Spreading the American Dream*, 105–7, 198–99.

15. In 1948, Pan American offered 96,724 seats across the Atlantic, ahead of its nearest rival, Trans World Airlines, with 81,040. The third largest carrier was American Overseas Airlines. British Overseas Airways Corporation was sixth, with 33,540, and Air France, seventh, with 31,356 (Travel Branch, Office of International Trade, "Summary Statement," 31 January 1949, Box 9, Curtin Files). See also Herbert Wilkinson, "The Mass Market for Air Travel," *United Nations World* 3 (September 1949): 44–50.

16. Advertisement in *United Nations World* 1 (February 1947): inside front cover.

17. Curtis Publishing, *The Vacation Travel Market of the United States: A Nationwide Survey* (Philadelphia: Curtis Publishing, 1950), Carton 8, 760351, CAC.

18. Information on "press flights" from Boxes 320–23, Pan Am Records. For an example of this promotional technique on a TWA flight, see Paul J. C. Friedlander, "Report from a Flying Tourist," *New York Times*, 11 May 1952.

19. Wittner, *Rebels against War*; Wooley, *Alternatives to Anarchy*; Graebner, *Age of Doubt*.

20. Wendell L. Willkie, *One World* (New York: Simon and Schuster, 1943); Norman Cousins, *Who Speaks for Man?* (New York: Macmillan, 1953), 67. See also Ralph Barton Perry, *One World in the Making* (New York: Current Books, 1945), 13, and Selig Adler, *Isolationist Impulse*, 307–8. On travel and the peace movement in an earlier era, see Endy, "Travel and World Power," 589–90.

21. Peterson, *Magazines in the Twentieth Century*, 110.

22. Pearl S. Buck, "Americans in Distress," *United Nations World* 1 (April 1947): 26–29. Although Buck was not a member of the UWF, she did oppose the anti-Communist hardening of U.S. foreign policy in the late 1940s (Conn, *Pearl S. Buck*).

23. Norman Cousins, "Expanded Travel Called Key to U.S. Leadership Role," *ASTA Travel News* 18 (December 1949): 12, 20. For more on the *Saturday Review*'s worldview, see Klein, *Cold War Orientalism*.

24. Trippe quoted in Bender and Altschul, *Chosen Instrument*, 377.

25. Juan Trippe, speech before the American Tariff League, 27 October 1948, Box 460, Pan Am Records.

26. Advertisement in *United Nations World* 1 (May 1947): inside front cover. John Fousek observes a similar theme in postwar advertising in his *To Lead the Free World*, 73–74, 91–102.

27. A. L. Simons, "Cutting the Red Tape," *New York Times*, 26 October 1952.

28. "P.A.A. Cancels Mid-European Service," 11 October 1946, Box 357, Pan Am Records.

29. Wittner, *Rebels against War*, 199; Wooley, *Alternatives to Anarchy*, 60.

30. Wilkinson, "Mass Market for Air Travel," 44–50, esp. 50. American Overseas Airlines was the international division of American Airlines. On Pan Am's participation in Cold War crises, see Juan Terry Trippe, Executive System Memo No. 120, 15 February 1951, Box 71, Pan Am Records.

31. "Former War Correspondents to See Europe Ten Years after Invasion," [June 1954?], Box 321, Pan Am Records; Pan Am press release, 15 October 1947, Box 357, ibid.

32. Juan Trippe, "America in the Air Age," speech at University of California Charter Week Ceremonies, 23 March 1944, Box 252, Pan Am Records; Juan Trippe, speech before the Foreign Traders Association of Philadelphia, 25 September 1951, Box 460, ibid.; Juan Trippe, "Now You Can Take That Trip Abroad," *Reader's Digest* 54 (January 1949): 69–72; Juan Trippe, "Space-Time . . . for Sale," *United Nations World* 2 (December 1948): 36–40.

33. Committee on Foreign Travel, Business Advisory Council, "Reducing American Credit Losses Abroad Through Increased Foreign Travel," n.d., Box 9, Curtin Files. On the Business Advisory Council, see Hogan, *Marshall Plan*, 15.

34. Wall, *United States and the Making of Postwar France*; Hogan, *Marshall Plan*; Hitchcock, *France Restored*.

35. Ralph T. Reed to Paul Hoffman, 9 April 1948, Box 117, CRU. As early as 1944, some

economists suggested that the government could subsidize overseas tourism costs as one way to stabilize war-damaged economies. See Bernard B. Smith, "Our International Money's Worth," *Harper's* 189 (October 1944): 415–17.

36. Travel Policy Committee, "Proposed Plan for Expanding U.S. Tourist Travel to Europe Submitted by Mr. Robert Grant Efteland," n.d., with covering letter Morse to Department of State, 9 August 1947, Box 126a, Travel Policy Committee 1947–50, Records of Interdepartmental and Intradepartmental Committees, RG 353, NARA.

37. Hitchcock, *France Restored*, 65.

38. Wall, *United States and the Making of Postwar France*, 159.

39. Hogan, *Marshall Plan*, 95–97; Patterson, *Mr. Republican*, 385. Hogan's more recent study on the period (*Cross of Iron*) places even greater emphasis on widespread concern in the United States over expanding government spending.

40. *Congressional Record*, 80th Cong., 2nd sess., 11 March 1948, vol. 94, pt. 2:2546. The amendment appeared as Section 117-B of the Foreign Assistance Act. Brewster's provision also became part of the U.S.-French bilateral accord of June 1948 that set the terms for French participation in the Marshall Plan ("Tourisme et Plan Marshall," *L'Aide américaine à la France* [15 August 1948]).

41. Congress raised the limit to $400 in 1948 and then $500 in 1949. See *Congressional Record*, 83rd Cong., 2nd sess., 15 March 1954, vol. 100, pt. 3:263.

42. "Tourist Is Europe's Man of Year," *Christian Science Monitor*, 14 February 1950; *Congressional Record*, 80th Cong., 2nd sess., 11 March 1948, vol. 94, pt. 2:2548; Owen Brewster to Paul Hoffman, 14 May 1948, Box 117, CRU.

43. Bender and Altschul, *Chosen Instrument*, 366–67, 387, 426; Solberg, *Conquest of the Skies*, 288–89, 302–4. On Brewster, see also "Payne Has Stood as a Progressive," *New York Times*, 18 June 1952; "Exit Brewster," ibid., 22 June 1952; and "Owen Brewster, Ex-Senator Dies," ibid., 26 December 1962.

44. Harry M. Paulson to Paul G. Hoffman, 14 April 1948; Ralph T. Reed to Hoffman, 9 April 1948, with covering letter, Hoffman to Reed, 19 April 1948; and Hoffman to Howard Bruce, 5 May 1948, all in Box 117, CRU.

45. ECA Press Release No. 101, 21 July 1948, Box 117, CRU.

46. Aubrey H. Harwood to Norman S. Taber, 4 November 1948, Box 117, CRU.

47. Travel Advisory Council documents, Box 3, Rand Files.

48. Donald C. Stone to the Administrator, 24 August 1948, Box 5, OA.

49. On staffing the TDS, see Harwood to Norman S. Taber, 4 November 1948, Box 117, CRU; Th. McKittrick to W. Averell Harriman, 30 August 1948, Box 1, TDS-GSF; "Schedule of Positions," Box 2, TDS-GSF; and Théo J. Pozzy to Ralph I. Straus, 8 December 1950, Box 5, TDS-GSF.

50. Peter M. Pozzy, interviews by author, tape recording, 3 and 4 August 1999; Pozzy family scrapbooks, courtesy of Peter M. Pozzy. On Théo Pozzy at the Plaza-Athénée hotel, see Herbert Wilkinson to Samuel S. Board, 15 October 1948, Box 9, Curtin Files.

51. ECA press release, 24 February 1950, Box 4, TDS-GSF.

52. Wilkinson to Harwood, 16 October 1948, Box 9, Curtin Files.

53. Robertson, *International Herald Tribune*.

54. Julian Street to Pozzy, 22 February 1949, Box 32, OSR; "Personal History—Julian Street, Jr.," n.d., Box 4, TDS-GSF.

55. Wilkinson to Harwood, 16 October 1948, Curtin Files.

56. ECA Press Release, 2 August 1950, Box 5, TDS-GSF.

57. Donald C. Stone to the Administrator, 24 August 1948, Box 5, OA.

58. Harriman to Henri Ingrand, 12 October 1948, Box 1, TDS-GSF. For more on TDS relations with Europeans, see Chapters 3 and 4.

59. On the classless ideal in postwar America, see Marchand, "Visions of Classlessness," and Lears, "Matter of Taste."

60. Wilkinson, note, 15 April 1949, Box 2, Wilkinson Records; Harwood to David Bruce, 6 October 1948, Box 9, Curtin Files.

61. Jean Médecin, "Rapport au Comité national," March 1952, Article 15, 790205, CAC.

62. U.S. Bureau of the Census, *Historical Statistics*, 289; "What a European Tour Will Cost," *U.S. News and World Report* 32 (4 April 1952): 26.

63. TDS, "Report for OEEC: American Student Travel to Europe," 30 June 1949, Box 2, TDS-GSF; Ernest O. Hauser, "G.I. Jim's in Love with Paris," *Saturday Evening Post* 222 (6 August 1949): 24–25, 48–58.

64. Zunz, *Why the American Century?* 109.

65. C. V. Whitney, speech before the International Union of Official Travel Organizations, 20 September 1949, Box 10, Hendrick Files; Pozzy to Franz Seiler, 14 October 1949, Box 5, TDS-GSF; Herbert A. Wilkinson, "Background for Technical Studies of the Travel Plant and Market," Speech before the European Technical Mission to the United States for the Study of Techniques in Travel, Hotels, and Allied Activities, 19 January 1950, Box 5, M200.5.1, Brewster Papers.

66. Minutes, Travel Advisory Committee, 17 November 1949, Box 1, TDS-GSF.

67. TDS, confidential report: "American Travel Abroad: A Key to World Peace and Prosperity," n.d., Box 32, OSR.

68. Eric N. Tuffier to Julian Street, "1950 Modernization and Development Program for Tourism," 13 December 1949, Box 3, TDS-CSF. On public relations, see Fox, *Mirror Makers*, 176.

69. Minutes, European Travel Commission, 23/24 June 1950, Box 3, TDS-GSF.

70. See, for instance, Pozzy to Wilkinson, 5 May 1950, Box 3, TDS-GSF.

71. Leff, "Politics of Sacrifice."

72. Pozzy to George Blowers, "Stronger Travel Development Campaign," 9 March 1949, Box 2, TDS-GSF.

73. On relations between the ECA and the ETC, see Boxes 3 and 4, TDS-GSF. More information on the ETC appears in Chapters 3 and 5.

74. Expense statements, "Budget and Fiscal" folder, Box 2, TDS-GSF.

75. Native-born U.S. tourists in 1948 on average spent $845 per trip while visiting 3.5 countries, in contrast to the $541 spent in 1.4 countries on average by immigrants or naturalized Americans revisiting Europe. Promoting tourism in the foreign-language U.S. media was low on the list of TDS objectives in 1950 (OEEC, *Tourism and Economic Recovery*, C [51] 26 [Paris: OEEC, 1951], 20–21). The European Travel Commission, funded by the Marshall Plan, devoted under 5 percent of its advertising resources to the foreign-language press, although immigrants and first-generation U.S. citizens made up about half of the transatlantic travel market.

76. Minutes, Travel Advisory Committee, 17 November 1949, Box 1, TDS-GSF.

77. Ibid.

78. Paul Hoffman to General Philip R. Fleming, 8 February 1950, and Enos Curtin to Hoffman, 3 February 1950, both in Box 9, Curtin Files.

79. Trippe claimed that a tourist fare would bring 75,000 more tourists and $60 million more dollars to Europe. See "Tourist Air Fares," Box 1, Wilkinson Records, and "Pan American Sets Air Tourist Fares," *New York Times*, 22 September 1951.

80. On the CAB's resistance, see Joseph J. O'Connell to Paul Hoffman, 27 April 1949, Box 9, Curtin Files; Juan Trippe to Hoffman, 10 March 1949, Box 117, CRU; Hoffman to Joseph J. O'Connell Jr., 15 April 1949, Box 32, OSR; and Harriman to Hoffman, 7 April 1949, Box 117, CRU. For a discussion of the eventual adoption of tourist-class flights, see Chapter 6.

81. Clinton S. Golden and Bert M. Jewell to Enos Curtin, 14 February 1950, and Associated Council for Economic Co-operation, Inc., "Proposal," 1 February 1950, both in Box 9, Curtin Files. For background on the two labor advisers and their somewhat limited role in the Marshall Plan, see Romero, *United States and the European Trade Movement*, 85, 120.

82. Travel Branch—Office of International Trade, "Employee Travel," 8 March 1950, Box 10, Hendrick Files.

83. Minutes, Travel Advisory Committee, 19 May 1949, Box 1, TDS-GSF.

84. George Ball, "Draft Proposal for the Installment Sale of French Tourism," B 33 924, Fonds Trésor, CAEF.

85. Minutes, Travel Advisory Committee, 19 May 1949, Box 1, TDS-GSF.

86. B. de Margerie to Guillaume Guindey, 24 June 1949, B 33 924, Fonds Trésor, CAEF. Another cause for the Ministry of Finance's opposition was a concern that such a measure would violate the Bretton Woods injunction against multiple currency practices.

87. "Predict Major Increase in Travel to Europe," *Travel Agent* 56 (10 October 1964): 82–85. For a broader context but mostly from the 1920s and 1930s, see Calder, *Financing the American Dream*.

88. "Travel to the United States," Hearing before the Committee on Interstate and Foreign Commerce, 80th Cong., 2nd sess., House, 21 May 1948.

89. Charles Sawyer to Samuel A. Wallace, 16 November 1948, Box 26, Committees, October 1945 to December 1949, Central Files, Office of International Trade, Records of the Bureau of Foreign and Domestic Commerce, RG 151, NARA.

90. Paul Hoffman to Frank Pace, Box 9, Curtin Files; Théo J. Pozzy, speech before European Travel Commission in Paris, September 1950, Box 3, TDS-GSF. Herbert Wilkinson also found encouragement in Congress's 1949 rejection of a U.S. Travel Division, noting that it "gives us a free hand" to promote U.S. travel to Europe. See Wilkinson, 15 July 1949, "Interior Dept Travel," Box 2, Wilkinson Records.

91. Harriman to the Secretary of State for Cooley and Curtin, 24 May 1949, Box 1, Wilkinson Records; Walter C. Nye to Mike Mansfield, 9 December 1949, Box 10, Hendrick Files. This interpretation of Brewster's action as an attempt to preserve the larger program also draws on comments to Pozzy by a Commerce Department official in Washington, who apologized that the ECA was cautious about pressing too hard on advertisement funding for fear that the larger ECA appropriations bill would not pass (Fowler W. Barker to Pozzy, 15 April 1949, Box 1, Wilkinson Records).

92. J. P. Hendrick, memorandum to file, 28 December 1949, and Wilkinson to Hendrick and Curtin, 9 June 1950, both in Box 10, Hendrick Files.

93. Hoffman to American embassy in Paris, 13 March 1950, Box 10, Hendrick Files.

94. Pozzy to Robert Hopkins, 29 November 1950, Box 5, TDS-GSF.

95. J. William Fulbright, "Promotion of Tourism Can Supply Europe with Dollars," *Congressional Record*, 81st Cong., 2nd sess., 26 April 1950, vol. 96, pt. 15:A3003–3004; Wall, *United States and the Making of Postwar France*, 181–82.

96. U.S. Bureau of the Census, *Historical Statistics*, 405; "Summary Report: Survey among American Tourists Leaving Europe," Box 2, TDS-GSF. U.S. statistics treated Europe and the Mediterranean as a single region.

97. "Tourism Earns Western Europe $272 Million in 1949," *Department of Commerce Travel Vistas* (February 1950), M200.5.1, Brewster Papers.

98. Joseph B. Barry, "Most Visible of Invisibles," *New York Times Magazine*, 23 April 1950, p. 17.

99. U.S. tourist receipts as a percentage of France's total dollar earnings dropped as French exports recovered. Yet even in 1951, American visitors gave France the equivalent of 51 percent of all its exports to the United States ("Drafted Report for Use by ECA Administration," 3 April 1951, Box 2, Wilkinson Records).

100. OEEC, *Tourism and Economic Recovery*, 22; Direction générale au tourisme, *Le Tourisme étranger en France* (1953): 28. This $214 million dollar figure almost certainly underestimated tourist expenses, since many tourist currency exchanges took place through unlicensed exchanges that escaped French government accounting. At times, such as in late 1948, the French and U.S. governments suspected that over half of all U.S. tourists' currency exchanges in France escaped official French channels. On the black market, see "French Tourism," 24 November 1948, Box 3, TDS-CSF. On France's share of the Marshall Plan, see Costigliola, *France and the United States*, 63. Michel Margairaz ("Les Finances, le Plan Monnet et le Plan Marshall," 154) lists a slightly higher figure of $2.7 billion.

101. On the rapid recovery of production, see Milward, *Reconstruction of Western Europe*. More recently, Milward's seminal work has come under criticism for underestimating the dangers to recovery posed by Western Europe's trade deficits and dollar gap. See, for example, Killick, *United States and European Reconstruction*, 8. William Hitchcock also emphasizes monetary and trade balance issues in *France Restored*, 64–66.

Chapter Three

1. Alfred Jules-Julien, preface to *Tourisme: Facteur essentiel de redressement de l'économie nationale*, by Georges Villette (n.p., 1950), 5. Jules-Julien, a Radical-Socialist (moderate) member of the 1930s Popular Front government, was after the war president of the Comité républicain du commerce, de l'industrie et de l'agriculture. On travel boosters at the start of the century, see Harp, *Marketing Michelin*; Lavenir, *La Roue et le stylo*; and Patrick Young, "*La Vieille France* as Object of Bourgeois Desire."

2. See the conclusion of Chapter 2 for more on tourism's role in French trade and currency balances.

3. "Note sur l'activité du Commissaire général au tourisme de mars à octobre 1946,"

Article 15, 790205, CAC. One newspaper erroneously claimed that tourism employed 1.5 million French people, compared to only 280,000 in metallurgy and 520,000 in mining. See "Le Tourisme," *Professions*, 11 May 1946, Carton 242, 97006, BDF.

4. Institut national de la statistique et des études économiques, *Annuaire statistique de la France* 69 (1963), 89; "# of Persons Employed in Travel Industry in ERP Countries," August 1949, Box 1, TDS-GSF; Gautier, *Métiers et main-d'oeuvre*, 13.

5. Gautier, *L'Industrie hôtelière*, 63; Rousseau, *Le Facteur travail dans l'industrie du tourisme*, 125–27.

6. Centre national du tourisme, *Annuaire* (1950): 48; "Il faut savoir que . . . ," *George V: Bulletin du personnel de l'Hôtel George V*, July 1948.

7. Gautier, *L'Industrie hôtelière*, 32.

8. Robert Krier, "M. Ingrand, Réorganisateur du Tourisme," *Revue officielle de l'hôtellerie, de la restauration et du commerce des boissons*, no. 11 (June 1946): 15. See also Robert Krier, "Profits illicites," ibid. (January 1946): 6; and Jack Handrey, "Réquisitions et profits illicites," ibid., no. 1 (July 1945): 7.

9. Bourseau, *Traité pratique*, 1079–80.

10. Ibid., 558.

11. Watts, *Ritz of Paris*, 10, 22.

12. Harp, *Marketing Michelin*, 54–88; Lavenir, *La Roue et le stylo*, 96–102, 217–39, 259–60.

13. Jocard, *Tourisme et l'action de l'état*, 20–21; Réné Duchet, *Le Tourisme à travers les ages, Sa place dans la vie moderne* (Paris: Vigot Frères, 1949), 183; Georges Mathiot, *Le Tourisme réceptif français: Sa place dans l'économie nationale et internationale, sa position devant la nouvelle réglementation de 1942–1943* (Nancy: Société d'impressions typographiques, 1945), 82.

14. Madame [Elisabeth] Dussauze-Ingrand, *Étude sur le tourisme en France de 1946 à 1948, Supplément au Bulletin d'informations touristiques* (Paris: Commissariat général au tourisme, 1948), 14; Direction générale du tourisme, "Étude historique et critique de l'organisation officielle du tourisme français—1951," Article 2, 760351, CAC.

15. Muron, *Pompidou*, 34.

16. "Note sur l'activité du Commissaire général au tourisme de mars à octobre 1946," Article 15, 790205, CAC.

17. "Les débats du Congrès national 1946," *L'Hôtellerie*, 1 December 1946.

18. "Rapport de M. Arthur Haulot," n.d., Box 3, TDS-GSF.

19. "ETC Coordination Committee Meeting," 21 February 1951, Box 3, TDS-GSF.

20. Although the standard narrative of European integration stresses the coal and steel agreements, this focus on industrial and military affairs should not distract us from the consumer dimensions and sources of integration.

21. Michel Dumont to Georges Bidault, 15 June 1948, Carton 126, sous-série 1948–55, Rélations culturelles 1945–59, MAE. These titles refer to the noncommercial films screened in New York by the embassy in May 1948.

22. François Briere to Henri Bonnet, 29 September 1952, Vol. 346, EU, AM 1952–63; J. J. Viala to Bonnet, 28 June 1949, with covering letter, Bonnet to Robert Schuman, 7 July 1949, Vol. 264, EU, AM 1944–52; Albert Chambon to Bonnet, 24 May 1950, and Bonnet to Schuman, 22 June 1950, Vol. 264, EU, AM 1944–52.

23. André Siegfried, "Le tourisme recette 'invisible,'" *Le Figaro*, 2 June 1948. See also Siegfried, "La Grande transformation des voyages," *Le Figaro*, 11–12 August 1951, and Siegfried, *Aspects du XXe siècle* (Paris: Hachette, 1955), 107, 147. On Siegfried as an antitourist, see Furlough, "Making Mass Vacations."

24. "Le Tourisme," *Professions*, 11 May 1946, Carton 242, 97006, BDF.

25. Georges Villette, *Tourisme: Facteur essentiel de redressement de l'économie nationale* (n.p., 1950), 9–11.

26. *Rapport général de la Commission de modernisation du tourisme* (Paris: Commission générale de modernisation et d'équipement, 1948), 214, in 80 AJ 12, AN. See also Christian Pineau, speech at Centre national du tourisme, 11 May 1950, Carton 245, 97006, BDF.

27. "Une Industrie qui vaut de l'or: Le Tourisme," *La Vie française*, 15 December 1945, Carton 242, 97006, BDF; G. Mortier, "Instruction et éducation touristiques," *L'Hôtellerie*, 15 June 1954; André Billy, "Tourisme et monnaie," *Le Figaro*, 5 January 1946; Orville, "Le Point de vue du client," *L'Hôtellerie*, 1 February 1946.

28. Hecht, *Radiance of France*, 2.

29. Robert Frank, *La Hantise du déclin*, 229.

30. Martel, press conference, 20 October 1950, Carton 246, 97006, BDF.

31. Dussauze-Ingrand, *Étude sur le tourisme*, 12. See also Georges Bernier, "Venez en France," *Rapports France–États Unis*, no. 71 (February 1953): 37–44; Centre national du tourisme, "Organisation administrative du tourisme en France," 19 October 1950, Article 15, 790205, CAC; and "Le Budget du Commissariat au tourisme," *L'Hôtellerie*, 1 April 1947.

32. Vincent Auriol, speech before the Touring Club de France, 4 June 1950, Box 3, TDS-CSF.

33. "Les Perspectives d'après-guerre de l'industrie hôtelière," *La Tribune économique*, 11 January 1946.

34. J. Pouget, "Une Industrie primordiale: Le Tourisme," *Les Échos*, 21 August 1945.

35. On French reactions to the war and collaboration, see Rousso, *Vichy Syndrome*. Adding to the irony, Vichy sympathizers during the war turned out similar paises of the French landscape to argue that an eternal French nation persisted under the Vichy government (Lebovics, *True France*).

36. Roger Dusseaulx, "Le Tourisme au secours du franc," *La Voix de l'hôtellerie*, February 1947.

37. Centre national du tourisme, *Annuaire* (1950): 123.

38. Paul B. Métadier, *Propos sur le tourisme* (Tours: n.p., 1952), 64. Métadier was president of the Syndicat d'initiative de Touraine.

39. *Congrès national du tourisme* (Vichy: Congrès national du tourisme, 1948), 20. The speaker was J. Pouget, who was also president of the Centre national du tourisme.

40. Henri Ingrand, speech at Comité national du tourisme, 17 November 1950, Box 3, TDS-CSF.

41. "Si nous reprenions nos bonnes vieilles habitudes," *Tourisme*, September 1949, in VI-8.00 (3), Archives de la Chambre de commerce et d'industrie de Paris, Paris.

42. Jean Sarlat, "La Propagande touristique par notre littérature," *L'Hôtellerie*, 1 November 1948; "La Propagande par la table," ibid., 15 January 1948.

43. On the relative decline of this tradition, see Levenstein, *Seductive Journey*.

44. Jean Sarlat, "Une Propagandiste du tourisme: La Langue française," *L'Hôtellerie*, 15 February 1950.

45. "Les Yeux de l'étranger," *Le Figaro*, 1 September 1949, Carton 242, 97006, BDF.

46. Robert Krier, "Plus ça change . . . !" *Revue générale de l'hôtellerie, de la gastronomie, et du tourisme*, no. 68 (March 1951).

47. Villette, *Tourisme*, 9–11.

48. "Alerte aux syndicats!" *L'Hôtellerie*, 1 November 1947; Jean Sarlat, "L'Invitation à la valse," ibid., 15 October 1948.

49. Minutes, Commission des investissements, 21 December 1948, B 42 268, Fonds Trésor, CAEF. On the CGP, see Cazes and Mioche, *Modernisation ou décadence*; Kuisel, *Capitalism and the State in Modern France*, 219–47; and Wall, *United States and the Making of Postwar France*, 175.

50. Minutes, Commission des investissements, 5 June 1950, B 42 268, Fonds Trésor, CAEF.

51. R. Marjolin, "Programme et objectifs de production et d'investissements 1946–1950," September 1946, p. 18, in 80 AJ 1, AN; Monnet quoted in Kuisel, *Capitalism and the State in Modern France*, 241.

52. Ministère des affaires économiques, "Note sur la situation de l'industrie au début de 1952," 25 January 1952, in 80 AJ 17, AN; and Minutes, Commission des investissements, 27 October 1952, B 42 269, Fonds Trésor, CAEF.

53. Louis Terrenoire, "Il faut complèter le plan Monnet qui n'a rien prévu pour le tourisme," *La Voix de l'hôtellerie*, November 1947.

54. Gilles Gozard, "La Représentation des industries touristiques au sein du Conseil économique," in Centre national du tourisme, *Annuaire* (1950): 51.

55. Jean Médecin's son, Jacques, continued the family tradition of Riviera tourism promotion when he became mayor of Nice in the 1960s. For a sketch of the Médecin dynasty, see Blume, *Côte d'Azur*.

56. *Congrès national du tourisme*, 21.

57. Jean Gemaehling, "Pour développer le tourisme populaire il faut d'abord moderniser le 'tourisme à devises,'" newspaper clipping, 6 January 1949, Carton 245, 97006, BDF.

58. "La Dernière étape," *Information hôtelière, touristique, et gastronomique*, 10 May 1950.

59. Marcel Bourseau, "Le Plan de modernisation du tourisme est-il menacé?" *La Voix de l'hôtellerie*, 10 January 1950. See also "Autour de la modernisation et des investissements," ibid., 10 March 1950.

60. On French working-class vacations, see Furlough, "Making Mass Vacations," 254, 258–59, 273. Furlough notes that a similar bias in favor of developing luxury tourism existed in the 1930s as well.

61. See comments by Lienart in Minutes, Commission de modernisation du tourisme, 30 April 1953, in 80 AJ 67, AN.

62. Merlin, "Le Tourisme au service du relèvement français," *Le Monde*, 21 April 1946; "Les Yeux de l'étranger," *Le Figaro*, 1 September 1949.

63. Jocard, *Tourisme et l'action de l'état*, 184.

64. *Rapport général de la Commission de modernisation du tourisme*, 7–10.

65. See, for example, the comments by cabinet minister Christian Pineau in Centre national du tourisme, *Annuaire* (1950): 129.

66. *Rapport général de la Commission de modernisation du tourisme*, 305, 170–71, 258.

67. Pierre Montfajon, "Le Tourisme: Première industrie française d'exportation," in Centre national du Tourisme, *Annuaire* (1950): 28–38.

68. Minutes, Commission de modernisation du tourisme, 10 July 1953, in 80 AJ 67, AN.

69. André Leveuf, "Quelles régions touristique faut-il développer par priorité," *Le Monde*, 21 October 1953.

70. Georges Devaux, "Chronique syndicale," *Notre métier: Bulletin du personnel des Hôtels George V—Plaza-Athénée*, April 1946.

71. "Nouvelles syndicales," *George V: Bulletin du personnel de l'Hôtel George V*, February 1949. Within the CGT, the Fédération nationale des travailleurs de l'alimentation et des hôtels, cafés, et restaurants represented an assortment of professions from hotel and restaurant workers to bakers.

72. Minutes, Fédération nationale des travailleurs de l'alimentation et des hôtels, cafés, et restaurants de France, des colonies et des pays de protectorat et sous mandat, 9–10 January 1946, in *Bulletin spécial d'information et d'éducation syndicales* (numéro spécial, March 1946): 19.

73. A. Mariani quoted in "Les Cabarets dancing-spectacles," *L'Hôtellerie*, 1 October 1947.

74. Gautier, *Métiers et main-d'oeuvre*, 151–52; Marcel Cacciolato, *Le Hall: Commentaires sur le service du hall dans les palaces et grands hôtels* (Paris: Organisation du travail dans l'hôtellerie, 1945), 101–2.

75. Cacciolato, *Le Hall*, 17.

76. "Parlons un français correct," *Notre métier: Bulletin du personnel des Hôtels George V—Plaza-Athénée*, October 1945.

77. La Bonne plume [pseudonym], "Notre métier est le plus beau du monde," *Notre métier: Bulletin du personnel des Hôtels George V—Plaza-Athénée*, April 1945; untitled article, ibid., January 1945.

78. Henry Marion, "Do You Speak English," *George V: Bulletin du personnel de l'Hôtel George V*, October 1948.

79. Louis Pucheu, "La Semaine en cinq jours," *Le Trait d'union des hôtels-cafés-restaurants et cantines*, February 1950; "Les Travailleurs des hôtels, cafés, restaurants," ibid., April 1950.

80. See Virgile Barel in *Journal officiel de la République française, Assemblée nationale, Débats* (17 November 1950): 7875.

81. See, for example, L. Charton, "Mise au point sur l'avenir de la profession hôtelière," *Cadres alimentation*, January 1951, and Gautier, *L'Industrie hôtelière*, 83.

82. "La Lutte contre le complot," *Le Militant de l'alimentation et des H.C.R.*, 15–28 February 1953.

83. Maurice Simonin, "Les Victimes de la course aux dollars," *Le Trait d'union des hôtels-cafés-restaurants et cantines*, October–December 1948; R. Bonnet, "Bas les pattes!" *L'Hôtel-Café-Restaurant et le travailleur des H.C.R.B. réunis de la région parisienne*, no. 34 (April–May 1949).

84. Virgile Barel, "Tourisme et Plan Marshall," *L'Hôtel-Café-Restaurant et le travailleur des H.C.R.B. réunis de la région parisienne*, no. 33 (March 1949). See also Barel, "Développons notre industrie hôtelière," *Le Travailleur des hôtels, cafés, restaurants et bars* (Marseille), no. 13 (November 1946).

85. Julian Livi, "Le Personnel a son mot à dire," *L'Hôtel-Café-Restaurant et le travailleur des H.C.R.B. réunis de la région parisienne*, no. 45 (October–November 1950). See also L. Fascio, "Oeuvrons à la renaissance de la France," *Le Travailleur des hôtels, cafés, restaurants et bars* (Marseille), no. 2 (September 1945).

86. Minutes, Commission de modernisation du tourisme, 30 November 1953, 17 March 1953, and 28 April 1953, in 80 AJ 67, AN.

87. On associations between travelers and power over others, see Pratt, *Imperial Eyes*, and Spurr, *Rhetoric of Empire*.

88. On French fears that American influence would lead to "colonization," see Kuisel, *Seducing the French*, and Kristin Ross, *Fast Cars, Clean Bodies*.

89. On missionaries, see MAE Direction des conventions administratives et sociales, "Note pour la Direction d'Amérique," 19 June 1947; Ministère des départements d'outre-mer (DOM) to MAE Direction des conventions administratives et sociales, 29 May 1947; and Ministère de l'Intérieur, Direction générale de la sureté nationale, to MAE-Amérique, 3 January 1950, all in Vol. 300, EU, AM 1944–52. On African Americans, see Théo Pozzy to Herbert Wilkinson, 9 August 1949, Box 9, TDS-GSF. The French embassy in Washington also monitored reports in the American media of American missionaries agitating for independence in West Africa. See Henri Bonnet (Francis Lacoste) to Direction d'Afrique-Levant, 28 April 1947, Vol. 300, EU, AM 1944–52.

90. Ministère DOM to MAE Direction des conventions administratives et sociales, 29 May 1947; MAE Direction d'Amérique to MAE Direction des conventions administratives et sociales, 25 June 1947; and MAE Direction des conventions administratives et sociales to Agents diplomatiques et consulaires de la République française, 4 April 1949, all in Vol. 300, EU, AM 1944–52. See also "Visas," Box 9, TDS-GSF.

91. On U.S. travel restrictions in the age of McCarthy, see Dowty, *Closed Borders*.

92. "Les Américains viendront en France sans visa," *L'Humanité*, 26 January 1949; Pierre Courtade, "La 'Porte ouverte,'" ibid., 27 January 1949.

93. Note par la Direction générale politique d'Amérique, 8 August 1957, Vol. 358, EU, AM 1952–63.

94. Courtade, "La 'Porte ouverte'"; "Les Américains viendront en France sans visa."

95. "L'Hôtellerie est, pour la France, une des premières et de plus régulières parmi les industries exportatrices," *Information*, 16 December 1952, Carton 242, 97006, BDF.

96. Raoul Bertrand to Henri Bonnet, 4 November 1952, Vol. 328, EU, AM 1952–63.

97. Kuisel, *Seducing the French*, 37–69.

98. John L. Brown, "Report on Activities June 1–31, 1949," Box 3, ID-CSF. For an analysis of the magazine, see McKenzie, "Deep Impact," 274–88.

99. "Le Plan Marshall et le développement du tourisme," special supplement to 1 May 1949 issue of *L'Aide américaine à la France*, 1. The Commissariat général au tourisme helped the ECA produce the supplement. The ECA's cartoon was reproduced in the French press, as well as in *Le Matin*, 9 July 1949.

100. Editorial note, *Rapports France–États Unis* (February 1950): 1.

101. On the circulation figure, see Kuisel, *Seducing the French*, 25.

102. ". . . Lorsque cet Américain est bourguignon," *Rapports France–États Unis* (August 1950): 46–49; Henriette Nizan, "Quand la jeunesse américaine vient respirer l'air de Paris," ibid. (September 1950): 45–50.

103. James Donnadieu, "Quand Américains et Français échangent maîtres et professeurs," *Rapports France–États Unis* (September 1950): 37–43.

104. "Propos, en guise d'éditorial," *Rapports France–États Unis* (June 1950): 1.

105. Georges Ravon, "Les Américains chez nous," in "Le Plan Marshall et le développement du tourisme," special supplement to 1 May 1949 issue of *L'Aide américaine à la France*. The film, a French-British production, was titled *Fantôme à vendre* (Ghost for sale) in French and *The Ghost Goes West* in English (Charensol and Regent, *50 ans de cinéma avec René Clair*, 107, 113–15).

106. John L. Brown, "Report on Activities June 1–31, 1949," Box 3, ID-CSF.

107. Frank Shea to John Brown, 2 May 1950, Box 3, ID-CSF; Wilkinson to Pozzy, 26 May 1949, Box 2, Wilkinson Records.

108. "Touristes ou amis," *Rapports France–États Unis* (October 1951): 79.

109. Pierre Ladune, "Qui est cet américain?" *Rapports France–États Unis* (August 1950): 38–45.

110. Renée-Pierre Gosset, "Les Touristes à Paris," *Rapports France–États Unis* (April 1950): 32–33.

111. See, for example, *Des Dollars qui coûtent cher: La Vérité sur l'aide américaine à la France* (Paris: Parti communiste français, 1952), 8. Thanks to Richard Kuisel for help in unpackaging the anti-Bolshevik imagery.

112. ECA, " 'L'Homme au cigare entre les dents': Les 1000 et 1 méfaits du plan Marshall" (drawings by "Curry"), supplément hors-série de *Rapports France–États Unis*, 1950.

Chapter Four

1. *Rapport général de la Commission de modernisation du tourisme* (Paris: Commission générale de modernisation et d'équipement, 1948), 214, in 80 AJ 12, AN.

2. L. Charton, "Mise au point sur l'avenir de la profession hôtelière," *Cadres alimentation*, January 1951.

3. See especially Kuisel, *Seducing the French*; Maier, "Politics of Productivity"; and Boltanski, "America America."

4. Théo J. Pozzy to Barry Bingham, 2 May 1950, Box 3, TDS-CSF. See also Pozzy to Herbert Wilkinson, 10 February 1950, Box 3, TDS-GSF.

5. Yvonne Henderson to George B. Ingram, 9 February 1950, Box 3, TDS-GSF.

6. See Esposito, *America's Feeble Weapon*, and Bossuat, "Le Plan Marshall dans la modernisation de la France."

7. Théo Pozzy, brief relating to OEEC Inland Transport Committee, 16 February 1951, Box 1, TDS-GSF. See also Pozzy to Henri Ingrand, 31 August 1949, and Pozzy to Ingrand, 13 June 1949, both in Box 3, TDS-CSF.

8. "Summary Report: Survey among American Tourists Leaving Europe," November 1950, Box 2, TDS-GSF.

9. Centre national du tourisme, *Annuaire* (1950): 48.

10. Peter M. Pozzy, interview by author, tape recording, 4 August 1999.

11. Pozzy to Ingrand, 12 June 1950, Box 3, TDS-CSF.

12. Pozzy to Ingrand, 6 April 1949, Box 2, TDS-GSF.

13. Peter M. Pozzy, interviews by author, tape recording, 3–4 August 1999. One French newspaper, making no reference to Pozzy's original French citizenship, praised him as a "great friend of our country" who "admirably speaks our language" (Jacques Zenner, "Tourisme américain," unidentified newspaper clipping, 17 December 1948 in Pozzy family scrapbook "Marshall Plan 1948–1951" [courtesy of Peter M. Pozzy]). For a discussion of the skills of U.S. diplomats with foreign origins, see Gienow-Hecht, "Art Is Democracy and Democracy Is Art."

14. "Tourist Plant Programs and Hotel Facilities of the ERP Countries," [21 June 1950?], Box 101, CRU.

15. Wall, *United States and the Making of Postwar France*, 181–82.

16. ECA booklet, "Tourism in the European Recovery Program," June 1950, Carton 8, 760351, CAC.

17. Bruno Luzzato to George A. King, 11 October 1948; James R. Brooks to Arthur Smithies, 3 November 1948; and Dean Acheson to diplomatic posts, 22 April 1950, all in Box 117, CRU; Paul G. Hoffman to Averell Harriman, 3 May 1949, and Harriman to Hoffman, 7 May 1949, both in Box 32, OSR. See also Enos Curtin memorandum to files, "Inter-Continental Hotels Corp.," 2 September 1949, Box 9, Curtin Files; IHC President, "Memorandum Re: Section 117(b) of the Foreign Assistance Act of 1948 and Recommendations for Action Thereunder," 1 September 1949, Box 8, TDS-GSF; and the folder "Intercontinental Hotel Corporation" in Box 5, TDS-GSF.

18. Harriman to Francis Towle, 5 December 1949, Box 32, OSR.

19. Wharton, *Building the Cold War*.

20. R. John Bay to Department of State, 11 December 1951, 851.181/12-11-51, Decimal File, 1950–54, State Department Central Files, RG 59, NARA.

21. Eric N. Tuffier to Julian Street, "1950 Modernization and Development Program for Tourism," 13 December 1949, Box 3, TDS-CSF. With its emphasis on U.S. consumption, the TDS's plan was atypical among most Marshall Plan programs. Marshall Plan officials as a whole encouraged French social projects such as public housing, which U.S. diplomats saw as essential for stopping Communism. On the ECA and French social funding, see Wall, *United States and the Making of Postwar France*. One French official later recalled that the French sometimes expressed puzzlement with the ECA's belief that Communism appealed only to those in miserable social conditions. See Bloch-Lainé and Bouvier, *La France restaurée*, 188.

22. Tuffier to Street, "1950 Modernization and Development Program for Tourism."

23. "Tourist Plant Programs and Hotel Facilities of the ERP Countries," [21 June 1950?], Box 101, CRU. See also Pozzy to Franz Seiler, 14 October 1949, Box 5, TDS-GSF.

24. C. V. Whitney, Speech before the International Union of Official Travel Organizations, 20 September 1949, Box 10, Hendrick Files.

25. Jackle, Sculle, and Rodgers, *Motel in America*; Belasco, *Americans on the Road*; Wharton, *Building the Cold War*.

26. Lears, *Fables of Abundance*, 247, 252.

27. Jackle, Sculle, and Rodgers, *Motel in America*; Belasco, *Americans on the Road*.

28. Jackle, Sculle, and Rodgers, *Motel in America*.

29. Centre national du tourisme, "Organisation administrative du tourisme en France," 19 October 1950, Article 15, 790205, CAC.

30. Willi Frischauer, *An Hotel Is like a Woman . . . The Grand Hotels of Europe* (London: Leslie Frewin, 1965), 12. See also Marcel Cacciolato, *Le Hall: Commentaires sur le service du hall dans les palaces et grands hôtels* (Paris: Organisation du travail dans l'hôtellerie, 1945).

31. "Summary Report: Survey among American Tourists Leaving Europe," November 1950, Box 2, TDS-GSF.

32. Stanley Frank, "They Drive Travel Agents Crazy!" *Saturday Evening Post* 225 (24 January 1953): 26–27, 115–18.

33. Lavenir, *La Roue et le stylo*, 226.

34. Centre national du tourisme, *Annuaire* (1951): 36.

35. Maier, "Politics of Productivity"; Kuisel, *Seducing the French*; Hogan, *Marshall Plan*.

36. Pozzy to M. Mange, n.d., Box 32, OSR.

37. Pozzy to William Wise, 25 July 1950, Box 2, TDS-GSF.

38. Theodore [Théo] J. Pozzy, "Modernization Program Outlined for European Hotel Operators," *ASTA Travel News* 19 (October 1950): 76–84.

39. When Pozzy took to French radio to condemn Riviera hotels that overcharged Americans, the Comité Regional de Tourisme launched an official complaint ("Le Comité régional de tourisme s'emeut d'une certaine émission radiophonique," *L'Espoir de Nice*, 15 October 1949). See also "Extrait d'un article: L'Espoir du 15 Octobre" in Box 3, TDS-CSF.

40. Pozzy to P. Depret, 8 August 1950, Box 5, TDS-GSF.

41. Pozzy to Ingrand, 21 April 1949, Box 3, TDS-CSF.

42. Art Buchwald, *Paris after Dark* (Paris: Imprimerie du Centre and New York Herald Tribune, 1950), 10.

43. John Walker, "Interviewer's Impressions on American Tourists Being Interviewed," Box 2, Wilkinson Records.

44. John H. Humpstone to Wilkinson, 25 January 1951, Box 3, TDS-CSF.

45. J. G.-D., "Ce qu'il faut savoir des États-Unis," *Notre métier: Bulletin du personnel des Hôtels George V—Plaza-Athénée*, April 1945.

46. Gérard Louchet, "Apprenez à connaître les gouts des touristes étrangers à l'hôtel," *L'Hôtellerie*, 15 July 1950. This hotelier's views of U.S. and British motives for traveling in France contradicted studies done by the French government a few years later. In the latter studies, Americans appeared more likely than the British to list France's cultural heritage as their primary motive (Direction générale du tourisme, *Le Tourisme étranger en France* [1955]: 12).

47. C.-V. Gruat, " 'Je ne puis recevoir de noirs dans mon hôtel,' " *Le Populaire de Paris*, 19 June 1950; Henri Sacha Dillot, "Comment des mercantis dénaturent le visage de la France," *Le Droit de vivre*, 15 July–15 August 1950; Dillot, "Les Noirs auront accès dans touts les hôtels de Paris," ibid., 15 October–15 November 1950. On the small size of African American tourism to France, see Chapter 6. Historian Tyler Stovall (*Paris Noir*, 232) estimates that just 500 African American expatriates lived in Paris in the early 1950s, in contrast to the 1,500 a decade later.

48. "Une Nouvelle question orale à propos des 'discriminations raciales,' " *Le Monde*, 21

July 1950; *Journal officiel de la République française, Assemblée nationale, Débats* (21 July 1950): 5634–35.

49. *Journal officiel de la République française, Assemblée nationale, Débats* (21 July 1950): 5634–35.

50. "Discrimination raciale," *Revue générale de l'hôtellerie, de la gastronomie, et du tourisme*, no. 62 (September 1950): 8.

51. Henry Marion, "L'Actualité vue du George V," *George V: Bulletin du personnel de l'Hôtel George V*, September 1948.

52. Wharton, *Building the Cold War*, 28.

53. *Rapport général de la Commission de modernisation du tourisme*, 214.

54. Minutes, Commission des investissements, 21 December 1948, B 42 268, Fonds Trésor, CAEF.

55. "Outline of Program for Study of Techniques in Travel, Hotels and Allied Activities," Box 8, TDS-GSF. For an overview of Marshall Plan productivity tours, see Kuisel, *Seducing the French*, 70–102.

56. Herbert A. Wilkinson, "Background for Technical Studies of the Travel Plant and Market," Speech before the European Technical Mission to the United States for the Study of Techniques in Travel, Hotels, and Allied Activities, 19 January 1950, Box 5, M200.5.1, Brewster Papers.

57. André Singer, "Devant le développement des classes moyennes américaines, nos industries touristiques et hôtelières doivent réviser leurs conceptions," *France-U.S.A.*, no. 32 (August 1950): 6.

58. Lucien Serre, "Voyage d'études aux États-Unis organisé sous les auspices de l'E.C.A.," [May 1950?], Box 5, TDS-GSF. Quotations from this report come from an English translation of the report located in the same archive folder.

59. Ibid.

60. Ibid.

61. B. E. L. Timmons to Department of State, 12 July 1950, Box 3, TDS-CSF; Stafford Derby, "Europe Looks to United States at Pattern for Hotels," *Christian Science Monitor*, 1 April 1950.

62. M. Jeanne, "Le Point de vue de l'enseignement touristique," in "Le Plan Marshall et le développement du tourisme," special supplement to 1 May 1949 issue of *L'Aide américaine à la France*, 8–11; Christine de Rivoyre, "Paris-Vacances," *Rapports France–États Unis*, no. 65 (August 1952): 23–32.

63. Pierre Daninos, "Le Touriste et vous: Suggestions et conseils," *Rapports France–États Unis* (July 1950): 33–41.

64. Jean Bertrand, "L'Évolution des problems fiscaux intéressant l'hôtellerie et leur incidence sur l'équipement touristique," Assemblée générale de la Fédération nationale de l'industrie hôtelière, 13–15 November 1950, Carton 245, 97006, BDF. See also "Que demande le touriste américain," *Revue générale de l'hôtellerie, de la gastronomie, et du tourisme*, no. 64 (November 1950).

65. Orville, "Le Point de vue du client," *L'Hôtellerie*, 2 May 1950. Responding to criticism over the column from at least two hoteliers, Orville stood his ground against the "monster hotels of the New World" (Orville, "Le Point de vue du client," *L'Hôtellerie*,

15 May 1950). On the stereotype of U.S. culture as the domain of women, see Joseph Folliet, "L'Opinion américaine et la France," *La Croix*, 12 February 1953.

66. Orville, "Le Point de vue du client," *L'Hôtellerie*, 2 May 1950.

67. "A La Veille d'une réalisation: L'Organisation du tourisme européen," *L'Hôtellerie*, 1 April 1949.

68. R. John Bay to State, 11 December 1951, 851.181/12–1151, Decimal File, State Department Central Files, RG 59, NARA.

69. Information from press photograph and unidentified newspaper clipping in Pozzy family scrapbook, "Marshall Plan 1948–1951" (courtesy of Peter M. Pozzy). See also Travel Advisory Committee, 17 November 1949 meeting minutes, 32, Box 1, TDS-GSF.

70. Although this example came from early 1953, it revealed the basic long-term outlook of the various French actors. See Commission de modernisation du tourisme, CGP, 30 April 1953 meeting minutes, 80 AJ 67, AN.

71. Marshall Plan archives hold no correspondence between the TDS and travel industry labor federations. Nor do labor newsletters refer to any such interaction. Théo Pozzy's son, in Paris during the Marshall Plan years, likewise did not recall any contacts between his father and hotel labor organizations (Peter M. Pozzy, interview by author, tape recording, 4 August 1999).

72. "On n'obtient rien sans lutte," *L'Hôtel-Café-Restaurant et le travailleur des H.C.R.B. réunis de la région parisienne*, no. 36 (September 1949); "Les H.C.R. à l'action," ibid., no. 34 (April–May 1949).

73. Pozzy to Depret, 6 October 1949, Box 5, TDS-GSF.

74. Virgile Barel, "Tourisme et Plan Marshall," *L'Hôtel-Café-Restaurant et le travailleur des H.C.R.B. réunis de la région parisienne*, no. 33 (March 1949). Although one of the official tasks of the ECA was to provide guarantees for U.S. companies that invested in Western Europe, this aspect of the Marshall Plan remained only a minor feature of the ECA's activity (Bossuat, *La France, l'aide américaine et la construction européenne*, 374–75).

75. "Un An d'activité syndicale," *L'Hôtel-Café-Restaurant et le travailleur des H.C.R.B. réunis de la région parisienne*, no. 34 (April–May 1949); *Journal officiel de la République française, Assemblée nationale, Débats* (17 March 1950): 2143–44. See also R. Bonnet, "Comme pendant l'occupation: Un aspect de l'application du Plan Marshall," *L'Hôtel-Café-Restaurant et le travailleur des H.C.R.B. réunis de la région parisienne*, no. 33 (March 1949).

76. R. Nollet, "Un Curieux nouveau venu dans notre presse professionelle," *L'Hôtel-Café-Restaurant et le travailleur des H.C.R.B. réunis de la région parisienne*, no. 39 (January–February 1950). In the original article, the Paris director of American Express, Harry Hill, had called his company the "principal client" of French hotels and suggested that French hotels set aside several rooms or a floor "to the American taste." See Robert Boucard, "M. Harry Hill, Directeur Général de l'American Express," *Hôtels-Restaurants-Bars brasseries et limonadiers de France*, November 1949.

77. Sulpice Dewez, "Bienvenue et longue vie," *L'Hôtellerie syndicaliste indépendante*, February 1952.

78. Maurice Magné, "L'Indépendance syndicale," *L'Hôtellerie syndicaliste indépendante*, May 1952. See also "Les Deux tiers de touristes étrangers venus en France ont été les clients de l'hôtellerie moyenne," ibid., February 1952.

79. For complementary analyses of other European industries, see Kipping and Bjarnar, *Americanisation of European Business*.

Chapter Five

1. Henry Wales, "U.S. Farmers Eye Paris Night Life on Europe Tour," *Chicago Daily Tribune*, 15 September 1949.

2. "U.S. Citizens Look at Europe," *Life* 23 (20 October 1947): 35.

3. Draft version of Friendly to W. Averell Harriman, 28 October 1948, Box 13, ID-GSF.

4. J. J. Viala to Henri Bonnet, 19 September 1949, Carton 126, Échanges culturels 1948–55, Rélations culturelles 1945–59, MAE.

5. This focus on French difference as a bond of affection for Americans builds on Costigliola, "Nuclear Family."

6. See, for instance, Fousek, *To Lead the Free World*; Elaine May, *Homeward Bound*; and Holsti, *Public Opinion and American Foreign Policy*.

7. Joseph A. Barry and Naomi Jolles Barry, "A Primer on Etiquette for Innocents Abroad," *New York Times Magazine*, 23 July 1950, p. 12.

8. "Invasion, 1952," *Time* 59 (23 June 1952): 79.

9. "Paris Preens for 2000th Birthday, But Isn't Sure Who's Coming to the Party," *Attleborough Sun*, 9 March 1951; "Wanderlust Is Still Strong," *Business Week*, 7 April 1951, p. 152.

10. Marie Bennett Alsmeyer, *Six Years after D-Day: Cycling through Europe* (Denton: University of North Texas Press, 1995), 2. On postwar domesticity, see May, *Homeward Bound*.

11. "Brief on C(50) 296," Box 1, TDS-GSF. See also Herbert Wilkinson, "The Mass Market for Air Travel," *United Nations World* 3 (September 1949): 44–50.

12. On the importance of difference in tourism, see Urry, *Tourist Gaze*, 1–2, 11.

13. Direction générale du tourisme, *Le Tourisme étranger en France* (1955): 12; William D. Toomey to State Department, "For Commerce," 10 February 1954, 851.181/2–1054, Decimal File 1950–54, State Department Central Files, Record Group 59, NARA.

14. *Time* 58 (8 October 1951): 108.

15. Anne Fremantle and Bryan Holme, *Europe: A Journey with Pictures* (n.p.: Studio Publications, 1954), 11; Horace Sutton, *Footloose in France* (New York: Rinehart and Co, 1948), 137; George Kent, "How to Be an American Abroad," *Travel* 92 (May 1949): 10–11, 32, reprinted under same title in *Reader's Digest* 54 (June 1949): 116–18.

16. John L. Brown, "Paris 1939–1947," in Clara E. Laughlin, *So You're Going to Paris!*, 8th ed. (Boston: Houghton Mifflin, 1948), vi; Melvin Hall, "Vézelay, Hill of the Pilgrims," *National Geographic* 103 (February 1953): 229.

17. Donald William Dresden, "Paris, Home Town of the World," *National Geographic* 101 (June 1952): 767–804; Horace Sutton, "400,000 'Diplomats' on the Loose," *Saturday Review* 34 (13 January 1951): 70–77.

18. Marvin Barrett, "We Cruised Through Paris," *American Magazine* 158 (October 1954): 98–102; Rose Grieco, "The Heart of Italy," *Commonweal* 59 (6 November 1953): 118; Elliot Paul, *Understanding the French* (New York: Random House, 1954), 111.

19. This romanticism even circulated in intellectual circles, as when Dwight Mac-

donald claimed in 1958 that the poor in Europe had more joy than wealthy Americans (Pells, *Liberal Mind*, 189). In fairness to the genre of travel writing, a few writers rejected the temptation to depict poverty as picturesque. *Grapes of Wrath* author John Steinbeck, who wrote numerous travel articles from Europe after World War II, described Paris's poor as those who "keep the picture in true perspective" (John Steinbeck, "Paris," *Saturday Review* 38 [16 April 1955]: 41).

20. For commentary on similar ironies, see Lears, *Fables of Abundance*, 382–83, and Marchand, *Advertising the American Dream*, 223–26.

21. David Greenberg and Marian Greenberg, *The Shopping Guide to Europe* (New York: Harper and Brothers, 1954), 4; Temple Fielding, *Fielding's Travel Guide to Europe* (New York: William Sloane, 1955), 322. See also, Clara E. Laughlin, *So You're Going to Italy!* (Boston: Houghton Mifflin, 1950), xx.

22. Harry Hill, "Things Happen in Paris," *American Magazine* 154 (December 1954): 98–102.

23. "Les Cabarets dancing-spectacles," *L'Hôtellerie*, 1 October 1947.

24. Art Buchwald, *Paris after Dark* (Paris: Imprimerie du Centre and New York Herald Tribune, 1950), 18. See also Jarrett, *Stripping in Time*.

25. "An Artist's Impressions of American Tourists," *New York Times*, 7 May 1950.

26. Corbin, *Les Filles de noce*, 506–10.

27. Sanford Gottlieb, "Brothels into Dormitories," *Nation* 171 (22 July 1950): 85; William Attwood, *The Man Who Could Grow Hair* (New York: Alfred A. Knopf, 1949), 24.

28. Lucy H. Hooper, "French Society and Parisianized Americans," *Appleton's Journal* 11 (1874): 395.

29. Advertisement for *Ladies' Home Journal*, *ASTA Travel News* 18 (May 1949): 4. The 40 percent figure comes from an OEEC study cited in "Brief on C(50) 296," Box 1, TDS-GSF. On the 1920s, see Levenstein, *Seductive Journey*, 245–50.

30. Allan Nevins, "The Meaning of Europe," *Holiday* 15 (January 1954): 30–31, 96; Erik Sjögren, "Human Interest Travel," in *Travel Key to Europe* (New York: This Week Magazine, 1952), 36. This discourse parallels rhetoric used at the time by Americans of a rational, masculine United States protecting an irrational, feminine Western Europe. See Costigliola, "Nuclear Family."

31. Frederic Prokosch, "Italy: Renascence from Rubble," *House and Garden* 93 (June 1948): 112, 176. See also Costigliola, "Culture, Emotion and the Creation of the Atlantic Identity," 29.

32. Attwood, *Man Who Could Grow Hair*, vii–ix, 8. Attwood was more oriented toward politics than this passage would suggest. A longtime intimate of Democrat Adlai Stevenson, he later became a speech writer and then an ambassador for the Kennedy and Johnson administrations.

33. Dan W. Mankiewicz, *New York Times Book Review*, 24 July 1949.

34. Quoted in William Attwood, "Paris Plans a Party!" *This Week*, 12 November 1950, Vol. 280, EU, AM 1944–52; Paris 2,000th Birthday Coordinating Committee, "Paris 2000th Birthday Events and Publicity in America in 1951," Box 3, TDS-CSF.

35. "14 Parises in USA Get Invite to Paris, France," *Lowell (Mass.) Sunday Sun*, 22 April 1951, Vol. 281, EU, AM 1944–52.

36. Henri Bonnet to Ministère des affaires étrangères, 21 December 1950, Vol. 280, EU,

AM 1944–52; Paris 2,000th Birthday Coordinating Committee, "Paris 2000th Birthday Events and Publicity in America in 1951," Box 3, TDS-CSF.

37. "Swell Trip to France—If Town Had a Mayor," *Boston Herald*, 26 April 1951; "14 Parises in USA Get Invite to Paris, France."

38. Bonnet to M. A. de Manziarly, 20 August 1951, and Bonnet to Robert Schuman, 11 July 1951, both in Vol. 280, EU, AM 1944–52.

39. "Relations franco-américaines," USA no. 649 (24 August 1948), reel 7, France–États Unis, BDF.

40. Commissariat général au tourisme, "Cathedrals and Churches of France," 1949 booklet, and "France: Pèlerinages," 1949 brochure, both in Article 33, 790549, CAC.

41. Commissariat général au tourisme, "Protestant Itineraries," 1951 brochure, Article 34, 790549, CAC. The brochures were reprinted in 1952 and 1954.

42. Jocard, *Le Tourisme et l'action de l'état*, 179; Direction générale du tourisme, *Le Tourisme étranger en France* (1953): 12; (1954): 101; Conseil d'administration de la Caisse nationale des monuments historiques, Article 72, 890537, CAC.

43. On tourists' special interest in modern Paris in the late nineteenth century, see Levenstein, *Seductive Journey*, 92, and MacCannell, *Tourist*, 57–76.

44. "Le Tourisme industriel," *Hommes et techniques* 320–21 (June–July 1971): 558.

45. "Le Développement du tourisme étranger en France," *Bulletin du Conseil national du patronat français* 42 (January 1950): 11.

46. "Visites d'usines," *L'Hôtellerie*, 15 October 1954, p. 4; "Le Tourisme industriel," 558; Ginier, *Les Touristes étrangers*, 567.

47. TDS, "Results of 'Pilot' Survey of Travelers Made by OSR Travel Development Section, Paris," Box 1, Wilkinson Records. The tourists in the survey were largely wealthy white northeasterners who might have been more inclined to fiscal conservative views like these. Still, as well-off elites from the Northeast with an interest in transatlantic travel, they might also have been expected to support one of the government's keystone policies in the Marshall Plan.

48. *Congressional Record*, 81st Cong., 2nd sess., 11 April 1950, vol. 96, pt. 4:5020–21.

49. "French Attitudes toward the United States," 11 September 1953, Box 2, SR 1953–63; see also "Sightseeing with Insults," *Business Week*, 26 September 1953, 200.

50. André Morice, press statement, 27 March 1953, Vol. 242, 97006, BDF; "Discours de M. André Morice," *L'Hôtellerie*, 1 December 1952.

51. "Anti-Americanism Aids Airline," *New York Times*, 13 May 1952.

52. *Congressional Record*, 81st Cong., 2nd sess., 21 July 1950, vol. 96, pt. 16:A5291.

53. Ibid., 82nd Cong., 2nd sess., 19 June 1952, vol. 98, pt. 11:A4076–77.

54. Ibid., 82nd Cong., 2nd sess., 15 May 1952, vol. 98, pt. 10:A9275–76.

55. On criticism of foreign aid, see Hogan, *Marshall Plan*, 380–93.

56. George F. Kennan, *Memoirs, 1925–1950* (Boston: Little, Brown, 1967), 277; Kennan, *Memoirs, 1950–1963* (Boston: Little, Brown, 1972), 82; Kennan, *American Diplomacy* (1951; Chicago: University of Chicago Press, 1984), 93–94. On Lippmann's "anti-majoritarian" outlook, see Steel, *Walter Lippmann*, 492–93.

57. Thomas A. Bailey, *The Man in the Street: The Impact of American Public Opinion on Foreign Policy* (New York: Macmillan, 1948), 223, 319.

58. Joseph W. Furnas, "What Tourists Learn Abroad Is Often Short of the Truth,"

Saturday Evening Post 222 (6 August 1949): 12; O. Walter Wagner, "Must We Misrepresent Europe's Misery?" *Christian Century* 65 (17 November 1948): 1238–39.

59. Wagner, "Must We Misrepresent"; Donovan Richardson, "An Air-Conditioned Look at France," *Christian Science Monitor*, 15 December 1950.

60. This rhetorical position possessed a long tradition with travel writers from other time periods and countries. As Jonathan Culler (*Framing the Sign*, 156) has put it, "The desire to distinguish between tourists and real travelers is part of tourism—integral to it rather than outside it or beyond it." See also Buzard, *Beaten Track*, and MacCannell, *Tourist*.

61. Henry C. Wolfe, "Innocents Abroad and World Peace," *Saturday Review* 31 (4 September 1948): 18–19.

62. Cornelia Otis Skinner, " 'It's Ridiculous!' " *Reader's Digest* 64 (April 1954): 105–8.

63. M. L. Deyo, " 'Hate America'—A Corrective Measure," Box 3, Rand Files. See also Victor Riesel, "Moola-Laden American Tourists Making Frenchmen Turn Red," *Los Angeles Daily News*, 20 July 1953, in Vol. 328, EU, AM 1952–63.

64. "The American as International Traveler and Host: A Discussion Outline and Work Paper Prepared for Citizen Consultations Initiated by the U.S. National Commission for UNESCO," S1.70.4: Un34, no. 25 (December 1954).

65. On 1950 as a pivotal year in the rise of Cold War anxiety in the U.S. public, see Rose, *Cold War Comes to Main Street*.

66. Although presented as a new concept, this desire to make vacations uplifting had deeper roots in U.S. culture, as Cindy S. Aron shows in her book *Working at Play*.

67. Irwin Robinson, "Profits or Prophets (of Doom)?" *ASTA Travel News* 19 (September 1950): 12.

68. "Million Americans Yearly May Visit Europe," *Christian Science Monitor*, 10 October 1950.

69. TDS, press release, 31 October 1950, Box 6, TDS-GSF.

70. "Le Congrès de l'ASTA a été à la taille de l'époque," *L'Hôtellerie*, 1 November 1951.

71. Stanley Frank, "They Drive Travel Agents Crazy!" *Saturday Evening Post* 225 (24 January 1953): 118.

72. Birger Nordholm, " 'Purposeful' Travel Is Stressed by ETC," *ASTA Travel News* 19 (November 1950): 26, 30; Office of Educational Exchange, Department of State, *Building Roads to Peace: Exchange of People Between the United States and Other Countries* (Washington: U.S. Government Printing Office, 1950), 48.

73. University of Vermont, "Marshall Plan in Action," brochure, 811.42751/8–2448, Box 4804, Decimal File 1945–49, State Department Central Files, RG 59, NARA; Benjamin Fine, "Education in Review," *New York Times*, 16 May 1948; Advertisement for University of Vermont 1949 Foreign Study Program, Box 9, Curtin Files.

74. Francis J. Colligan, "Americans Abroad," *U.S. Department of State Bulletin* 30 (3 May 1954): 663–68.

75. Fichtenbaum, *Passport to the World*, 71.

76. Advertisement in *United Nations World* 3 (March 1949): 1.

77. Advertisement in *Saturday Review* 37 (2 January 1954): 33.

78. U.S. Senate, Judiciary Committee, *Unauthorized Travel of Subversives Behind the Iron Curtain on United States Passports*, 82nd Cong., 1st sess., 1951 (Washington: U.S.

Government Printing Office, 1951). Not until *Aptheker v. Secretary of State*, in 1964, did the Supreme Court strike down a 1950 law that allowed for the refusal of passports to Communists (Dowty, *Closed Borders*). See also Klein, *Cold War Orientalism*, 135–37.

79. Ruth Dowling Wehle to Thomas W. Wilson, 21 March 1949, Box 13, ID-GSF; Minutes, Travel Advisory Committee, 19 May 1949, p. 82, Box 1, TDS-GSF.

80. Sutton, "400,000 'Diplomats' on the Loose," 70–77; "Meeting with Representatives in the United States of ETC," 22 November 1949, Box 3, TDS-GSF.

81. Marquis Childs, "Americans Abroad," *Washington Post*, 18 April 1949, Box 2, Wilkinson Records.

82. Ernest O. Hauser, "G.I. Jim's in Love with Paris," *Saturday Evening Post* 222 (6 August 1949): 24–25, 48–58. See also Paul F. Kneeland, "Massachusetts Girl Says French Break Backs with Two-Foot Hoe," *Boston Globe*, 7 January 1951.

83. John W. Mowinckel, "U.S. Tourists Rush to France Again, But There's a Difference—They Talk Politics, Look for Bargains, Cut Down on Size of Tips," *U.S. News and World Report* 27 (16 September 1949): 39.

84. "Un Américain raconte . . . ," *Le Monde*, 16–17 October 1949.

85. Andrew H. Berding to Théo Pozzy, 2 February 1951, Box 2, TDS-GSF; William Nichols to Arthur Haulot, 23 February 1951, Box 3, TDS-GSF. For more information, see Box 4, TDS-GSF.

86. Sjögren, "Human Interest Travel," 21–61.

87. Leland Stowe, "The Knack of Intelligent Travel," *Reader's Digest* 61 (September 1952): 103–6.

88. "Rapport de M. Arthur Haulot," Box 3, TDS-GSF.

89. Herbert Wilkinson to Pozzy, 17 December 1948, Box 2, Wilkinson Records; "Meeting with Representatives in the United States of ETC," 22 November 1949, Box 3, TDS-GSF.

90. "Meeting with Representatives in the United States of ETC," 22 November 1949, Box 3, TDS-GSF.

91. Minutes, Working Committee for the Coordinated Promotion of European Travel, 14 February 1951, Box 3, TDS-GSF.

92. Advertisement, *New York Times*, 19 February 1950.

93. Roscoe Drummond to Milton Katz, 28 November 1949, Box 13, ID-GSF.

94. Kuisel, *Seducing the French*, 74–75.

95. Roscoe Drummond to Milton Katz, 28 November 1949, Box 13, ID-GSF.

96. Friendly to Harriman, 3 November 1948, Box 4, OSR-CSF; Draft version of Friendly to Harriman, 28 October 1948, Box 13, ID-GSF. See also Wagner, "Must We Misrepresent."

97. ECA, *The European Recovery Program: Information for Americans Going Abroad*, pamphlet, 1st ed., 1948, and 2nd ed., 11 August 1948, Library of Congress, Washington, D.C.

98. ECA, *The Marshall Plan: Information for Americans Going Abroad*, 1 June 1949, Library of Congress, Washington, D.C.; "How to Help Your Clients Preserve Democracy," *ASTA Travel News* 18 (June 1949): 12.

99. TDS, "Tips for Your Trip," pamphlet, June 1950, Box 10, Hendrick Files.

100. Hixson, *Parting the Curtain*.

101. "What Should I Know When I Travel Abroad?" 1952 edition, and "Traveling Americans Appreciate Advice," 27 July 1952 (S-36-54), both in Box 9, SR 1953–63.

102. "What Should I Know When I Travel Abroad?" 9–11, 14–16.

103. Ibid., 21, 22.

104. "Traveling Americans Appreciate Advice"; "What Should I Know When I Travel Abroad?: Reactions of Tourists to an Orientation Booklet," June 1954 (S-45-54), 26, Box 9, SR 1953–63.

105. "Traveling Americans Appreciate Advice"; "What Should I Know When I Travel Abroad?" June 1954 (S-45-54), 26.

106. "What Should I Know When I Travel Abroad?" June 1954 (S-45-54), x, 42, 43, 52.

107. Joseph Folliet, "L'Opinion américaine et la France," *La Croix*, 12 February 1953, and Henry Bénazet, "Les Outrances d'un magazine américain," *L'Aurore*, 26 January 1953, both in Reel 6, BDF. For the offending editorial, see "France: New Government," *Life* 34 (26 January 1953): 34.

108. Hogan, *Marshall Plan*, 380.

109. Pozzy to J. P. Hendrick, 1 December 1950, Box 4, TDS-GSF. See also Statement by Ralph I. Straus to Mission Heads, 25 September 1950, Box 4, TDS-GSF.

110. Pozzy to Roscoe Drummond, 6 November 1950, Box 5, TDS-GSF.

111. Milton Katz to Georges Marquet, [March 1951?], and Pozzy to Straus, 8 December 1950, both in Box 5, TDS-GSF; Minutes, Collective Publicity Coordinating Committee, 21 February 1951, Box 32, OSR.

112. For a more extended discussion on the merits and limits of Cold War culture, see Kuznick and Gilbert, eds., *Rethinking Cold War Culture*, especially Peter Filene's essay, " 'Cold War Culture' Doesn't Say It All."

Chapter Six

1. On tourist-class flights, see Box 357, Pan Am Records; Paul J. C. Friedlander, "Report from a Flying Tourist," *New York Times*, 11 May 1952; and Heppenheimer, *Turbulent Skies*, 192–93.

2. Gill Robb Wilson, "Lower Tourist Fares Called Next Problem for Industry," *New York Herald Tribune*, 4 October 1951; and "This Is No Dream," *Call Bulletin* (San Francisco), 16 November 1951, in Box 357, Pan Am Records; Ingrand quoted in Pan Am press release, "Record Tourist Exodus Is Underway to Europe," 1 May 1952, ibid.

3. For an overview of this intellectual debate, see Pells, *Liberal Mind*, 182–232, and Berghahn, *America and the Intellectual Cold Wars in Europe*, 95–103.

4. On the concept of a travel boom, see "The Biggest Season," *Time* 65 (16 May 1955): 94; "Millions of Foot-Loose Americans," *U.S. News and World Report* 38 (13 March 1955): 80–81; and "Gloom Amid a Boom," *Newsweek* 48 (24 December 1956): 57.

5. U.S. Bureau of the Census, *Historical Statistics*, 404–5.

6. Figures derived from information in ibid., 316–19. These figures are based on the category "foreign travel and other" expenses, with the precise nature of the "other" expenses left unfortunately undefined. Statistics on what Americans spent in France alone are shaky, given the large amount of currency exchanged outside institutions approved and monitored by the French government.

7. "Pan American Set on Europe Tourist Service," *New York Herald Tribune*, 22 September 1951; "Pan American Sets Air Tourist Fares," *New York Times*, 22 September 1951. On

Trippe's sense of history, see Solberg, *Conquest of the Skies*, 345–47. See also Hudson and Pettifer, *Diamonds in the Sky*. Although Harvey Levenstein (*Seductive Journey*) effectively traces the emergence of middle-class travel to the mid-nineteenth century, I would make the case that it took almost a full century to complete the transition from upper- to middle-class predominance.

8. Nancy Greenwood, interview by author, tape recording, 27 August 2002; Sally Wimbrow, interview by author, tape recording, 23 September 2002.

9. Flo Hinz, "Washington Window," *ASTA Travel News* 27 (March 1959): 39; "Predict Major Increase in Travel to Europe," *Travel Agent* 56 (10 October 1964): 82–85; Solberg, *Conquest of the Skies*, 347.

10. Solberg, *Conquest of the Skies*, 349; "Millions of Foot-Loose Americans," 80–81; Advertisement, *ASTA Travel News* 25 (January 1956): 59. See also Calder, *Financing the American Dream*. Paying for travel by installments worked for innovative tour operator Thomas Cook in nineteenth-century Britain, perhaps because his British clients did not have any large ocean to cross to reach their destination. See Buzard, *Beaten Track*.

11. "Millions of Foot-Loose Americans," 80–81. For general context, see Kaufman, *Trade and Aid*.

12. Clarence B. Randall, "U.S. Encouragement of International Travel," *U.S. Department of State Bulletin* 30 (28 June 1954): 997–99.

13. Dwight D. Eisenhower, "Recommendations Concerning U.S. Foreign Economic Policy," *U.S. Department of State Bulletin* 30 (19 April 1954): 606; Eisenhower, "Further Developing the Foreign Economic Policy of the United States," ibid., 32 (24 January 1955): 119–22; House Committee on Ways and Means, *Increase of Duty-Free Allowance to American Tourists: Hearings on H.R. 8352*, 83rd Cong., 2nd sess., 1954; Sinclair Weeks, "Importance of International Travel in Advancing World Peace," *U.S. Department of State Bulletin* 33 (18 July 1955): 106–9; "Development of International Travel, Its Present Increasing Volume and Future Prospects," ibid., 32 (21 March 1955): 491–95.

14. See, for instance, Juan Trippe, "Aviation and the Cold War," speech at the Aero Club of Washington, 17 December 1954, Box 461, Pan Am Records.

15. Sutton, *Travelers*, 223.

16. This list includes *An American in Paris* (1951), *April in Paris* (1952), *Lovely to Look At* (1952), *Moulin Rouge* (1952), *Gentleman Prefer Blondes* (1953), *Ma and Pa Kettle on Vacation* (1953), *The French Line* (1954), *The Last Time I Saw Paris* (1954), *Sabrina* (1954), *To Paris with Love* (1954); *To Catch a Thief* (1955), *Silk Stockings* (1957), *French Can-Can* (1955), *Funny Face* (1957), *Paris Holiday* (1957), *Gigi* (1958), *Perfect Furlough* (1959), *Can Can* (1960), *Paris Blues* (1961), *Bon Voyage* (1962), *Ladies' Man* (1962), *Bedtime Story* (1963), *Paris When It Sizzles* (1964), *Boeing, Boeing* (1965), and *Dear Brigitte* (1965). This catalog was compiled with the help of Connors and Craddock, *VideoHound's Golden Movie Retriever*. For a general survey of France in the U.S. print media, see Gordon, "Decline of a Cultural Icon."

17. Ann Rea Craig, interview by author, tape recording, 17 September 2002.

18. "1st Transatlantic Tourist," 1 May 1952, Box 320, Pan Am Records; "Plane Load of Passengers That Left for London," *New York Times*, 2 May 1952.

19. Pan Am Press Release, 26 October 1958, Box 323, Pan Am Records.

20. "Travel—The New Status Symbol," *Ebony* 17 (March 1962): 84–85. This 1 percent

estimate comes from Claude Lewis, "Blacks Roam the Globe with Little Anxiety," *Saturday Review* 55 (27 May 1972): 16–18. Given this low percentage, airlines and other travel promoters paid little attention to the African American market until the early 1970s. See also Horace Sutton and David Butwin, "Will It Be the Soaring Seventies?" *Saturday Review* 53 (3 January 1970): 48–49.

21. Fred Baum, "Women's Promotion Reps Spark Airline Sales," *Travel Agent* 43 (25 April 1958): 22–24.

22. As early as 1886, low-budget "tramping" guidebooks appeared in the United States. See, for example, Lee Meriwether, *A Tramp Trip: How to See Europe on Fifty Cents a Day* (New York: Harper and Brothers, 1886). For an insightful essay on the history of tourism from the bottom up, see Judith Adler, "Youth on the Road."

23. John L. Offner, interview by author, tape recording, 9 September 1998.

24. Nancy Greenwood, interview by author, tape recording, 27 August 2002.

25. Harry Hill, "Things Happen in Paris," *American Magazine* 154 (December 1952): 98–102; "Travel to Europe among U.S. College Students," *Travel Europe* 3 (November 1965): 29–36.

26. *ASTA Travel News* 28 (January 1959): 63; "Fall Business Builder," ibid., 25 (August 1956): 48–49; Frances Kolton, "Have Job–Will Travel Say Working Gals," *Travel Agent* 43 (10 March 1958): 31–32; Playboy Advertisement, *ASTA Travel News* 29 (December 1960): 23. With its emphasis on breaking away from rules, *Playboy* echoed the successful formula of France's Club Méditerranée, which at the same time was becoming popular among young European travelers seeking an escape from social norms. Indeed, in 1968, Club Med signed a promotional agreement with American Express to expand into the U.S. market. Club Med opened its first U.S. office in the early 1970s. See Furlough, "Packaging Pleasures."

27. Sally Wimbrow, interview by author, tape recording, 23 September 2002.

28. "Predict Major Increase in Travel to Europe," *Travel Agent* 56 (10 October 1964): 82–85; see also *Étude du marché touristique américain pour la France* (1959), Article 7, 760351, CAC.

29. "What's in It for You," *Travel Europe* 5 (June 1966): 1; "Next Time, We'll See an ASTA Travel Agent," *ASTA Travel News* 28 (March 1959): 56; " 'Innocents Abroad,' " ibid., 27 (April 1958): 52–54. Airlines such as Air France pitched in with the campaign by endorsing the professional expertise of travel agents in its own advertisements. See "News Section," ibid., 29 (May 1960): 11.

30. "Topics," *New York Times*, 17 November 1960. This trend confirms the analysis of William H. Whyte Jr., who in 1956 described the tendency of middle-class Americans to revise upward their definition of the good life. See Whyte, *The Organization Man* (New York: Simon and Schuster, 1956), 316–19.

31. Ithiel de Sola Pool, Suzanne Keller, and Raymond A. Bauer, "The Influence of Foreign Travel on Political Attitudes of American Businessmen," *Public Opinion Quarterly* 20 (Spring 1956): 161–75.

32. "No. 1 Travel Guide," *Time* 71 (21 April 1958): 90; "A Guide to Temple Fielding," *Time* 93 (6 June 1969): 79–87.

33. John McPhee, "Templex," *New Yorker* 43 (6 January 1968): 32–67.

34. "Guide to Temple Fielding."

35. Temple Fielding, *Fielding's Travel Guide to Europe* (New York: William Sloane, 1955–56), x.

36. McPhee, "Templex."

37. Fielding, *Fielding's Travel Guide to Europe* (1955–56), ix, 271; McPhee, "Templex," 66.

38. Horace Sutton, "Duffel Stuffers," *Saturday Review* 41 (14 June 1958): 32–33. See also "What You Should Know about Travel Guides," *ASTA Travel News* 32 (July 1963): 56–57, 120–22.

39. Buzard, *Beaten Track*, 65–77; Levenstein, *Seductive Journey*, 246.

40. Fielding, *Fielding's Travel Guide to Europe* (1955–56), 323.

41. "Tourists' 'Likes and Dislikes,'" *ASTA Travel News* 25 (October 1956): 72, 116–18. In France, one newspaper mocked *Playboy*'s entry into travel writing, criticizing the magazine's 1962 travel feature on Paris for imagining the city as nothing more than a place for prostitution or, for those who bothered to enter museums, as a place to ogle female nudes. See Walter Lewino, "Les Américains à Paris," *France Observateur*, 19 April 1962, pp. 15–16.

42. "News of the Month," *ASTA Travel News* 34 (May 1965): 23; "News Digest," *Travel Europe* 2 (October 1964): 9; *L'Équipement touristique de la France* (19 April 1972), Annexe XII, in Article 8, 880559, CAC; "David Ogilvy on Selling the New Tourism," *Travel Europe* 6 (December 1966): 30–31. Ogilvy, arguably the leader in his field, was involved in tourism through his firm's accounts with Great Britain, Puerto Rico, and KLM airlines.

43. Levenstein's history of tourism in France up to 1929 (*Seductive Journey*) skillfully traces the fusion of pleasure and high culture in the motives of nineteenth-century travelers.

44. "Beyond the Horizon," *Time* 77 (19 May 1961): 70–81.

45. "Europe Plain & Simple," *Time* 82 (26 July 1963): 6; Stanley Elkin, "The World on $5 a Day," *Harper's* 245 (July 1972): 41–46.

46. "Operator Says $5-a-Day Tours Are Big Value," *Travel Agent* 57 (25 December 1964): 53–54, 68; Elkin, "World on $5 a Day"; Norman Mailer, *The White Negro* (San Francisco: City Lights Books, 1970).

47. Roger Craig, interview by author, tape recording, 19 September 2002.

48. On this theme, see Thomas Frank, *Conquest of Cool*.

49. Juan Terry Trippe, speech at American International College in Springfield, Mass., 3 June 1956, Box 460, Pan Am Records; "Guide to Temple Fielding," 81.

50. On foreign service personnel, see Clare Boothe Luce, "The Ambassadorial Issue: Professionals or Amateurs?" *Foreign Affairs* 26 (October 1957): 105–21, and William J. Lederer and Eugene Burdick, *The Ugly American* (New York: W. W. Norton, 1958). On jazz musicians, see Von Eschen, "Who's the Real Ambassador?"

51. Edward L. Bernays, "Unpopularity Is Unnecessary," *Saturday Review* 38 (17 September 1955): 11–12. Bernays was chairman of the National Committee for an Adequate Overseas U.S. Information Program. For more on Bernays's political views, see Tye, *Father of Spin*, 105.

52. Robert Coughlan, "How We Appear to Others," *Life* 43 (23 December 1957): 150–55.

53. R. L. Duffus, "Still 'The Innocents Abroad,'" *New York Times Magazine*, 2 August 1959, pp. 14, 26. See also Cuordileone, "'Politics in an Age of Anxiety,'" and Dean, *Imperial Brotherhood*.

54. William D. Patterson, "In Defense of the Tourist," *Saturday Review* 40 (12 January 1957): 16; Patterson, "The Fortunate Diversity," ibid., 39 (7 January 1956): 16.

55. Norman Cousins, "Everyman as Reporter," *Saturday Review* 39 (20 October 1956): 28.

56. Lederer and Burdick, *Ugly American*; "The Articulate American," *Time* 74 (31 August 1959): 34; "The U.S. Student Abroad," *Newsweek* 54 (21 December 1959): 90; Frances Knight, "Don't Be an 'Ugly American,'" *Parade*, 5 June 1960, p. 4. *Parade* appeared throughout the country in local Sunday newspapers such as the *Boston Sunday Globe*.

57. Knight, "Don't Be an 'Ugly American'"; House Committee on Interstate and Foreign Commerce, *Office of International Travel*, 86th Cong., 2nd sess., 24 June 1960, p. 48. The representative was Robert W. Hemphill.

58. Sally Wimbrow, interview by author, tape recording, 23 September 2002.

59. Ann Rea Craig, interview by author, tape recording, 17 September 2002.

60. Henry E. Mattox, interview by author, tape recording, August 20, 1998.

61. Daniel J. Boorstin, *The Image, or What Happened to the American Dream* (New York: Atheneum, 1962), 6, 77–117. See also Whitfield, "Image."

62. Horace Sutton, "Leave It to the People," *Saturday Review* 38 (17 September 1958): 38–41. The liberal Sutton and his populist rhetoric complicates historian Michael Kazin's emphasis on early Cold War populism as the domain of red-baiting conservatives such as Joseph McCarthy. See Kazin, *Populist Persuasion*, 165–93.

63. Whitfield, *Culture of the Cold War*, 132–33; Sayre, *Running Time*, 54–56; Lary May, "Making the American Consensus."

64. Carl N. Clausen, "Red Propaganda," letter to the editor, *New York Times*, 8 February 1953. For a rebuttal, see Daisy Blume, "No Red Propaganda," letter to the editor, ibid., 15 February 1953.

65. McCarthy quoted in Fried, *McCarthyism*, 89.

66. "Fort Wayne Flies to Paris," *Fortune* 47 (June 1953): 111, 224; "The 'Innocents'— 1954," *Newsweek* 44 (27 September 1954): 94–97.

67. James Reston, "Bruges, Belgium," *New York Times*, 15 September 1957.

68. "Millions of Foot-Loose Americans," 80–81.

69. Abram Chasins, "In Defense of Americans," *New York Times*, 6 October 1957; Mrs. Charles Moselle, letter, *New York Times*, 13 October 1957.

70. Russell Porter, "Inquiry Charges Red Link in Music," *New York Times*, 10 April 1957; "Reds Said to Run School of Music," ibid., 30 June 1957.

71. Robert Griffith, "Dwight D. Eisenhower and the Corporate Commonwealth," *American Historical Review* 87 (February 1982): 87–122. On the USIA under Eisenhower, see Hixson, *Parting the Curtain*, 133.

72. Dwight D. Eisenhower, "U.S. Dependence on Foreign Trade," *U.S. Department of State Bulletin* 29 (26 October 1953): 539–41. See also Eisenhower, "Recommendations Concerning U.S. Foreign Economic Policy," and Eisenhower, "Further Developing the Foreign Economic Policy of the United States."

73. Colligan, "Americans Abroad," 663–68.

74. "Better Goodwill Ambassadors," *ASTA Travel News* 24 (1955): 76, 136–38; Ralph T. Reed, "The New Role of U.S. Tourism Abroad," ibid., 25 (February 1956): 41–45, 89–96.

75. Colligan, "Americans Abroad," 665.

76. Charles Edward Wilson should not be confused with Charles Erwin Wilson, the General Motors executive who served as Eisenhower's secretary of defense from 1953 to 1957. For background on the foundation, see Dan Wakefield, "People to People," *Nation* 186 (25 January 1958): 74–76.

77. "People-to-People Now Private Unit," *New York Times*, 26 September 1957.

78. Charles E. Wilson, "Quotes," *ASTA Travel News* 27 (July 1958): 26.

79. "Tourists Get Plea," *New York Times*, 21 May 1957.

80. Charles E. Wilson, "Peace through Understanding," *ASTA Travel News* 27 (July 1958): 26–28.

81. "Dollars for Peace," *New York Times*, 13 February 1958; "U.S. Travelers to Get Missions as Goodwill Envoys Overseas," ibid., 26 July 1957.

82. Robert Coughlan, "How We Appear to Others," *Life* 43 (23 December 1957): 150–55.

83. "Every Tourist an Envoy," *New York Times*, 27 July 1957. See also "U.S. Tourists: Good or Ill Will Envoys?" *New York Times Magazine* (1 September 1957): 8, 45–47.

84. Thomson and Laves, *Cultural Relations*, 132.

85. William D. Patterson, "The Big Picture," *ASTA Travel News* 27 (May 1958): 140; Coombs, *Fourth Dimension*, 42–43.

86. Hixson, *Parting the Curtain*, xiii–xiv.

87. Francis Pickens Miller, "Americans at Home and Abroad," *U.S. Department of State Bulletin* 45 (21 August 1961): 331–33. On masculine rhetoric in the Kennedy administration's approach to foreign affairs, see Dean, *Imperial Brotherhood*.

88. John F. Kennedy, *Public Papers of the Presidents of the United States, 1961–1963* (Washington: U.S. Government Printing Office, 1962–64), 1961: 135, 146; 1962: 164; 1963: 555. See also Elizabeth Hoffman, *All You Need Is Love*.

89. Johnson and Colligan, *Fulbright Program*, 343–46; Coombs, *Fourth Dimension*, 33–36, 43. The Fulbright Program sent more Americans to France than to any other country.

90. Elaine May, *Homeward Bound*, 26; Herman, *Romance of American Psychology*; Kazin, *Populist Persuasion*. Ole R. Holsti (*Public Opinion and American Foreign Policy*) also writes of a postwar "consensus" critical of the public's role in foreign policy.

91. On consumerism and traditional cultural diplomacy, see Hixson, *Parting the Curtain*; Elaine May, *Homeward Bound*; and Haddow, *Pavilions of Plenty*.

Chapter Seven

1. "La Campagne nationale d'accueil et d'amabilité," *L'Hôtellerie*, 15 April 1965; "French Try Smiles and Roses," *Travel Europe* (May 1965): 10; "French 'Smile Campaign' Under Way—in Bid to Woo International Tourist," *ASTA Travel News* 34 (June 1965): 28.

2. For a discussion of tensions between U.S. tourists and French hosts in the 1920s, see Levenstein, *Seductive Journey*.

3. See, for instance, "Pour combattre la crise du tourisme français," *Le Monde*, 4 June 1955; Claude Estier, "Voici les vraies raisons de la crise du tourisme en France," *Libération*, 2 September 1964; Edouard Bonnefous, "La Grande pitié du tourisme français," *Revue politique et parlementaire*, no. 747 (July–August 1964): 15–23; and Gilles Roche, "La Cause du marasme de notre industrie touristique," *Carrefour*, 28 July 1965.

4. "Reprise de la campagne pour l'accueil et l'étalement," *L'Hôtellerie*, 2 May 1966.

5. Orvar Löfgren offers an insightful essay on transnational leisure trends around the Mediterranean after World War II in *On Holiday*. On Spanish promotion efforts, see Poutet, *Images touristiques de l'Espagne*.

6. The state's response to the tourism crisis confirms Richard F. Kuisel's analysis of the 1960s as a time when the state increasingly "took charge" of the French economy. See his *Capitalism and the State in Modern France*.

7. For complementary analyses of this Gaullist tension between tradition and modernity, see Kuisel, *Seducing the French*, 149; Lebovics, *Mona Lisa's Escort*, 5–6, 105; and George Ross, "Introduction: Janus and Marianne," 3.

8. This chapter joins Ellen Furlough and Rosemary Wakeman ("Composing a Landscape") in identifying the early Fifth Republic as a turning point in state involvement in France's travel industry.

9. That sum of gold demanded by de Gaulle represented around half of all U.S. gold releases during those six months. See "Report to the President from Cabinet committee on Balance of Payments," 7 June 1965, Box 49, FO 4-1, LBJL-CF. For more on Gaullist policy toward the United States, see Costigliola, *France and the United States*; Kuisel, *Seducing the French*; Kunz, *Butter and Guns*; and Grosser, *Affaires extérieures*.

10. See especially Kuisel, *Seducing the French*, 154–84.

11. France's tourism bureaucracy changed names from the Commissariat générale au tourisme to the Direction générale au tourisme in 1949 and then back to the Commissariat in 1959. See Jocard, *Le Tourisme et l'action de l'état*, 22.

12. For background on Sainteny, see Eric Mann, "Men Who Make Tourism—Jean Sainteny," *ASTA Travel News* 29 (October 1960): 59–60, 122–26. For comments on his appointment, see J. M. R., "La France regagnera-t-elle la faveur première qu'elle connaissait auprès des touristes américains?" *Combat*, 7 April 1959; "Le Tourisme sera l'une des préoccupations majeures du gouvernement," *La Croix*, 5 June 1959; and "M. Sainteny, Commissaire général au tourisme," *Le Journal du Parlement*, 4 June 1959.

13. The result was the Interministerial Committee on Tourism, which united five key ministers whose domains had a part in French tourism: Foreign Affairs, Cultural Affairs, Finance, Interior, and Public Works–Transports-Tourism. For its part, André Malraux's newly created Ministry of Cultural Affairs informed Sainteny that it wished to work closely with the Tourism Commissariat, particularly when it came to promoting France's reputation abroad. See Georges Loubet to Jean Sainteny, 23 May 1959, 3SA2, FJS.

14. "Note préliminaire sur une structure financière du tourisme," 2 May 1959, 3SA2, FJS; Jocard, *Le Tourisme et l'action de l'état*, 191; see also Commissariat général au tourisme, Conférence de presse du 30 mars 1962, Article 6, 760351, CAC.

15. François Dupuis, "L'Hôtellerie dans de beaux draps," *Le Nouvel observateur*, 15 September 1975, Carton 246, 97006, BDF. On Mediterranean resorts, see Furlough and Wakeman, "Composing a Landscape," and Furlough and Wakeman, "La Grande Motte."

16. "M. Sainteny satisfait de son voyage en Amérique," *Combat*, 4 January 1961, 3SA3, FJS; André Alphand, "France," *ASTA Travel News* 29 (November 1960): 124–26.

17. Conseil superieur du tourisme, "Procès-verbal de la réunion du Comité permanent," 5 July 1960, Article 17, 790205, CAC.

18. O. Segalat to Représentatif général des services français du tourisme aux États Unis et au Canada, 15 May 1963, Article 3, 910748, CAC.

19. "Compte-rendu de la réunion des représentants du tourisme français à l'étranger— et des secrétaires généraux des comités régionaux de tourisme," 12 February 1959, Article 7, 760351, CAC.

20. "This Is How It Is?" *Advertising Age*, 2 March 1959 (see also "Second Thoughts on Tourist Ads," *Knickerbocker (Albany, N.Y.) News*, n.d., Article 4, 910748, CAC); Advertisements for the FGTO, *New Yorker* 35 (21 March 1959): 75. All ads cited in this chapter are also located in the JWT Collection.

21. André Alphand to the Commissaire général au tourisme, 13 April 1959, Article 4, 910748, CAC.

22. Myron Clement to André Alphand, "Choix d'une nouvelle agence de publicité," 1 June 1959, and Jean Sainteny to RGSFTAN (Alphand), 17 June 1959, both in Article 4, 910748, CAC.

23. Thomas Frank, *Conquest of Cool*, 55–72.

24. The French government replaced DDB in 1969 with Ogilvy and Mather, another well-known firm but one with a reputation for more traditional approaches to advertising.

25. Advertisement for the FGTO, *New Yorker* 37 (11 March 1961): 86–87.

26. Advertisements for the FGTO, *New Yorker* 35 (31 October 1959): 21, and ibid., 38 (16 February 1963): 82–83.

27. For a helpful essay and bibliography on cultural conservation in France, see Bachelier, "La Notion de patrimoine."

28. J.-F. Simon, "La France fleurie et propre," *Le Monde*, 10 February 1965.

29. Roger Parment, "Pour retenir les touristes les Français doivent être souriants," *Paris-Normandie*, 18 March 1960, 3SA3, FJS. The frequent references to recovering France's good humor suggests that Pierre Nora's project of mapping the nation's "realms of memory" could also include a discussion of the "French smile" as a specific site of memory (Nora, ed., *Realms of Memory*).

30. "M. Sainteny fera la politique du sourire," *Paris-Presse*, 4 June 1959, and "200 milliards de devises chaque année grâce au tourisme," *Sud-Ouest*, 4 June 1959, both in 3SA2, FJS.

31. "Compte-rendu de la réunion des représentants du tourisme français à l'étranger."

32. Eric Mann, "Men Who Make Tourism—Jean Ravenel," *ASTA Travel News* 34 (January 1965): 55, 112; "T.V.—radio," *L'Écho touristique*, June 1965.

33. "La Campagne nationale d'accueil et d'amabilité," *L'Hôtellerie*, 15 April 1965.

34. "Étude de l'opinion des touristes étrangers sur l'accueil qui leur est réservé en France," study conducted by Synergie-ROC for the Direction générale de tourisme (Paris: 1958), Article 15, 850559, CAC.

35. INSEE, *Annuaire statistique de la France* 74 (1968): 466. See also Direction générale du tourisme, *Le Tourisme étranger en France* (1955), 19, and ibid. (1957), 41. Half of the Americans visiting France stayed in four-star or four-star-deluxe hotels, a figure that helps explain much of Americans' high rate of consumption in France (Ginier, *Les Touristes étrangers*, 256).

36. The survey's results on American tourists were nearly identical to its findings on all foreigners visiting France. Among foreigners in general, 85 percent were "very satisfied" with their trips and only 3 percent were "not very satisfied" or "unhappy" ("Étude de l'opinion des touristes étrangers").

37. Service d'étude du marché d'Air France (for the Commissariat général au tourisme), "Les Voyageurs aériens étrangers et les hôtels français," December 1961, Article 8, 850559, CAC.

38. Ginier, *Les Touristes étrangers*, 261.

39. Vincent Planque, "Les Marchés touristiques," January 1957, 80 AJ 153, AN; William D. Patterson, "The Big Picture," *ASTA Travel News* 26 (June 1957): 46–50.

40. "Étude de l'opinion des touristes étrangers"; Drew Middleton, "Foreigners Begin to Avoid France," *New York Times*, 10 September 1964, Carton 243, 97006, BDF.

41. Roger Craig, interview by author, tape recording, 19 September 2002.

42. INSEE, *Annuaire statistique de la France* 70 (1964): 344; 74 (1968): 466.

43. Stewart Alsop, "Let's Relax about Europe," *Saturday Evening Post* 238 (16 January 1965): 16.

44. *Congressional Record*, 89th Cong., 1st sess., 28 July 1965, vol. 111, pt. 14: 18544–45.

45. Robert Daley, "I Hate Paris in the Springtime," *Saturday Evening Post* 239 (5 June 1965): 10.

46. *Congressional Record*, 89th Cong., 1st sess., 4 March 1965, vol. 111, pt. 3: 4189–90.

47. "The Worm Turns," *Newsweek* 64 (7 September 1964): 43–46. See also "Garçon! Souriez!" *Time* 85 (23 April 1965): 37. For a useful overview of U.S. press coverage of France's tourism industry, see Gordon, "Decline of a Cultural Icon," 633. Gordon's study of the *Readers' Guide to Periodical Literature* confirms this sharp increase in U.S. articles on the tourist trade in France during the 1960s.

48. *Le Monde*, 31 July 1965; "French Reprint Card Urging Americans to Shun France," *New York Times*, 31 July 1965.

49. Georges Mazoyer, " 'Touristes américains, évitez la France,' " *Paris Match*, no. 805 (12 September 1964): 38–41; " 'Touristes américains, évitez la France,' " ibid., no. 808 (3 October 1964): 17, 21–22; *Journal officiel de la République française, Sénat, Débats parlementaires*, 17 November 1964, p. 1610. See also "L'Affaire Fielding une baudruche dégonflée!" *L'Hôtellerie*, 1 November 1964.

50. More than most macroeconomic concepts, the idea of a tourist balance deserves to be seen as a cultural construction. Although a tourist balance can affect a nation's balance of payments, the state of a nation's tourist balance itself has no direct macroeconomic consequences, in contrast to other phenomena such as inflation.

51. William D. Patterson, "The Big Picture," *ASTA Travel News* 35 (June 1966): 112, 118; ibid., 36 (April 1967), 51. For an excellent study of French vacations, see Furlough, "Making Mass Vacations."

52. Bonnefous, "La Grand pitié du tourisme français," 16. *Paris Match* repeated Bonnefous's "paradox of paradoxes" argument in Mazoyer, " 'Touristes américains.' " See also Christian Guy, "La France a perdu la bataille des vacances," *L'Aurore*, 1–3 September 1964, and G. de Beaurepaire, "Le Tourisme français: L'Homme malade de l'économie française," *Perspectives*, no. 876 (29 February 1964), both in Carton 243, 97006, BDF.

53. William D. Patterson, "The Big Picture," *ASTA Travel News* 26 (June 1957): 46–50; ibid., 33 (June 1964): 46.

54. "Garçon! Souriez!" 37.

55. Mme Raynard, "Un Américain à Paris," *Paris-Presse*, 7 October 1964. Although the

newspaper labeled the tourist an American, the letter writer herself described him as either British or American.

56. Cabu, cartoons, *Paris-Presse*, 15 and 20–21 September 1964; "Les Employés d'hôtel sont déjà payés," ibid., 22 September 1964; "A qui va le service que vous payez à l'hôtel," ibid., 20–21 September 1964.

57. On Godard, youth culture, cars, and decolonization, see Kristin Ross, *Fast Cars, Clean Bodies*. See also Kuisel, *Seducing the French*, and Weiner, *Enfants Terribles*.

58. *Bulletin municipal officiel de la Ville de Paris, Débats des Assemblées*, 1 December 1964, p. 837.

59. Lucien Junillon, "L'État de l'hôtellerie en France et ses incidences sur le tourisme," *Journal officiel de la République française, Avis et rapports du Conseil économique et social*, 24 January 1967, p. 39.

60. *Bulletin municipal officiel de la Ville de Paris, Débats des Assemblées*, 1 December 1964, p. 837.

61. Georges Dupont, "Les Exigences du tourisme," in *Le District de la région de Paris*, ed. Alfred Mallet (Paris: Éditions Friedland, 1964).

62. "Étude de l'opinion des touristes étrangers."

63. Jean-Marie Le Pen, "Jean-Marie Le Pen, Deputé de Paris et la 'réorganisation' du tourisme," *L'Écho touristique*, 10 July 1959.

64. Kristin Ross, *Fast Cars, Clean Bodies*; Evanson, *Paris*.

65. André Courbez, "La Chasse aux dollars est ouverte: Safari-touristes à Paris," *L'Humanité*, 13 July 1965. For all its criticism of U.S. foreign policy and its emphasis on social tourism for the French, *L'Humanité* declared itself "happy" to receive U.S. tourist dollars, since every dollar earned by a traveling American was one dollar fewer that the French needed to borrow from U.S. financiers.

66. E. Plumon, "La Courtoisie et la gastronomie," *L'Hôtellerie*, 15 July 1954.

67. A. M., "Nous devons tout mettre en oeuvre pour vaincre le chômage," *L'Hôtellerie syndicaliste indépendante*, January–February 1953.

68. J. O. Retel, *Les Gens de l'hôtellerie* (Paris: Éditions ouvrières, 1965), 47, 112.

69. C. Danville, "Être client nécessite aussi . . . un apprentissage," *L'Hôtellerie*, 1 September 1964; C. Danville, "Et pourquoi ne pas classer les clients?" ibid., 1 July 1968.

70. Kuisel, *Seducing the French*; Kristin Ross, *Fast Cars, Clean Bodies*.

71. The average French hotel in 1966 had twenty-seven rooms and 7.1 salaried employees. One- and two-star tourist-class hotels averaged just 4.2 and 6.5 employees each, respectively, making such enterprises family-centered operations. The majority of French hotels that did not qualify as tourist-class employed even fewer salaried workers, on average just 2.6 per hotel. At the other end of the spectrum, the more luxurious hotels were larger but also labor intensive, with one industry expert citing a ratio of three employees for every two guests as the norm. See Rousseau, *Le Facteur travail dans l'industrie du tourisme*, 125–27, and Bourseau, *Traité pratique*, 503.

72. Roger Prain, "Note pour memoire sur la réunion tenue par M. Giscard d'Estaing le 17.11.64 au sujet de 'l'Opération vacances,' " Article 1, 760351, CAC.

73. At first, *L'Hôtellerie* and the Fédération nationale de l'industrie hôtelière, both Paris-based industry leaders, treated Poujade as a threat to their own leadership role and criticized him as a demagogue. The growing popularity of *poujadisme* among hoteliers,

however, led the FNIH to announce in 1955 that there was "no incompatibility" in membership in the hotel organization and in Poujade's own organization (Hoffmann, *Le Mouvement poujade*, 151–52, 319–20). For a more general study of artisanal politics, see Zdatny, *Politics of Survival*.

74. "Note de M. CHARPENTIER, Inspecteur des finances sur les problèmes de l'hôtellerie," 23 December 1964, and "Note établie par M. Lion, Inspecteur des finances sur le regime fiscal de l'hôtellerie," 30 August 1964, both in 251–64, CAEF.

75. "Compte-rendu de la réunion des représentants du tourisme français à l'étranger," 7 November 1963, Carton 7, 760351, CAC; "L'Équipement hôtelier préoccupe Pompidou," *Les Échos*, 8 November 1963.

76. On technology and national radiance in the 1960s, see Hecht, *Radiance of France*.

77. De Beaurepaire, "Le Tourisme français"; "Avec C. Hilton, la gestion industrielle remplace la pratique de l'artisanat," *Entreprise*, no. 456 (6 June 1964), Carton 246, 97006, BDF; Mazoyer, "'Touristes américains.'"

78. André Alphand, "Les Courants touristiques Amérique-Europe," [1960?], Article 6, 760351, CAC.

79. Jocard, *Le Tourisme et l'action de l'état*, 93, 106–7.

80. *Enquête dans les aéroports d'Orly et du Bourget sur l'opinion des visiteurs étrangers à l'issue de leur séjour en France*, January 1967, Bibliothèque administrative de la Ville de Paris.

81. Procès-verbal, Syndicat d'initiative de Paris, 28 March 1958 and 11 April 1961, Article 1, CTP/A, Archives du Chambre de commerce et d'industrie de Paris; "News of the Month," *ASTA Travel News* 30 (February 1961): 10. Although largely the initiative of private booster groups such as the Paris Chamber of Commerce and Industry, these tourism activities also drew on support from the Tourism Commissariat (*Bulletin municipal officiel de la Ville de Paris: Débats du Conseil de Paris*, 28 March 1969, p. 82).

82. G. d'Orgeville, "Accueillir . . . c'est sourire!" *L'Hôtellerie*, 1 July 1960.

83. Jocard, *Le Tourisme et l'action de l'état*, 247; Rousseau, *Le Facteur travail dans l'industrie du tourisme*, 177. See also Nielson, *From Sky Girl to Flight Attendant*, 1–13.

84. Jocard, *Le Tourisme et l'action de l'état*, 247; C. Danville, "Le Point de vue du client," *L'Hôtellerie*, 1 June 1954.

85. The impetus for the 1959 campaign came from the Direction générale du tourisme, the state bureaucracy that preceded Sainteny's more powerful commissariat. On earlier contests, see Lavenir, *La Roue et le stylo*, 250.

86. Images of these and other posters can be found in Articles 4 and 11, 910166, CAC.

87. "La Campagne pour fleurir la France," *L'Hôtellerie*, 1 December 1961; "Conférence de presse de Monsieur le Commissaire général au tourisme," 30 March 1962, 3SA3, FJS; Simon, "La France fleurie et propre."

88. Gautier, *Métiers et main-d'oeuvre*, 81.

89. Ibid., 81, 89.

90. Pierre Chanlaine, "L'Habitude du pourboire nuit à notre tourisme," *L'Écho touristique*, November 1961.

91. On tax and salary regulations, see Bourseau, *Traité pratique*, 913, 952, 961. For a labor point of view, see "A l'appreciation de la clientele," *F.O. dans les H.C.R. de la région parisienne*, no. 24 (1963): 6–8.

92. " 'Nous ne voulons pas mendier notre paie," *Paris-Presse*, 8 October 1964; "L'Opéra-tion 'baton de craie,' " ibid., 10 October 1964. Although owners represented the principal source of opposition to *tout compris*, some hotel-restaurant-café labor unions, especially those affiliated with the Communist-led CGT, also expressed reservations with the system on grounds that corrupt bosses too often kept parts of the 15 percent service-included receipts for themselves. See "Grève au Royal Monceau," *L'Hôtel-Café-Restaurant et le travailleur des H.C.R.B. réunis de la région parisienne*, no. 113 (July 1962), and *Le Militant de l'alimentation et des H.C.R.: Rapport général pour la conférence nationale*, 11–14 May 1958, p. 59.

93. "Des décisions en faveur du tourisme et de l'hôtellerie sont prises en conseil interministériel," *Le Monde*, 23 July 1965; J.-F. Simon, "La Suppression du couvert dans les restaurants gênera d'avantage les 'palaces' que les 'bistrots,' " ibid., 12 January 1966, Carton 244, 97006, BDF.

94. Simon, "La Suppression du couvert dans les restaurants."

95. "Vingt-sept départements participeront à 'l'opération vacances' de contrôle des prix," *Le Monde*, 3 June 1965; J.-F. Simon, "M. Giscard d'Estaing fait le point de 'l'opéra-tion vacances,' " ibid., 28 August 1965; J.-F. Simon, "Tourisme," ibid., 18 June 1966; and "Le Tourisme doit être considéré comme une branche de commerce extérieur," *Le Figaro*, 27 August 1965, all in Carton 243, 97006, BDF.

96. Jean Duffaud, "Les Équipements d'hébergement touristique," *Notes et études docu-mentaires*, no. 4100–4101 (27 June 1974): 7–13.

97. J. M. Duran-Souffland, "La Mort des petits établissements," *Le Monde*, 15 February 1972, Carton 246, 97006, BDF.

98. "News of the Month," *ASTA Travel News* 30 (February 1961): 10.

99. " 'Le Gouvernement américain m'a encouragé à construire des hôtels à l'étranger notamment au titre du plan Marshall,' nous déclare M. Conrad Hilton," *Le Monde*, 3 May 1966; "Avec C. Hilton, la gestion industrielle remplace la pratique de l'artisanat," *En-treprise*, no. 456 (6 June 1964), Carton 246, 97006, BDF.

100. Jean-Pierre Quélin, "Cet hôtel qui ne plaît pas aux Français," *Le Monde*, 24 October 1970. The Continental Hotel reopened as the Intercontinental, a name more in keeping with Pan American's hotel subsidiary, the Intercontinental Hotel Corporation.

101. Jean-Jacques Servan-Schreiber, *The American Challenge*, trans. Ronald Steel (New York: Atheneum, 1968); see also Kuisel, *Seducing the French*, 178–80.

102. Pierre Bernard-Danay, "Le Premier grand hôtel construit à Paris depuis 37 ans est américain," *Les Échos*, 21 May 1965.

103. "L'Hôtel d'Orsay 'aux oubliettes,' " *Le Monde*, 14 July 1965. See also Schneider, *Creating the Musée d'Orsay*.

104. The dynamic between foreign and French investment in the hotel industry of 1960s France corresponds to the more general pattern traced by Richard Kuisel. The Gaullist state promoted foreign investment as essential for the modernization of the French economy and then faced additional pressure from economic nationalists to ensure that some of these modernization programs were controlled by the French themselves. See Kuisel, *Seducing the French*.

105. "Les Appareils géants obligent les compagnies aériennes à étudier de plus près l'industrie des vacances," *Le Monde*, 6 May 1968; Maurice Guillon, "Création en France

d'une chaine d'hôtels trois étoiles: La Frantel," *Le Figaro*, 17 January 1966; "Des hôtels d'état en France?" *L'Hôtellerie*, 15 July 1963. See also Ginier, *Les Touristes étrangers*, 250, and Rauch, *Vacances en France*, 165.

106. Jean Bellandini, "A Paris, l'hôtel le plus moderne du monde," *Le Figaro*, 17 February 1972; "Les palaces parisiens des années 70," *Le Monde*, 22 April 1972; and Duran-Souffland, "La Mort des petits établissements," all in Carton 246, 97006, BDF.

107. "A France-Inter, un exposé du Président Bourseau," *L'Hôtellerie*, 1 January 1965. Bourseau, who directed several luxury hotels in Paris and the Riviera, led the Fédération nationale de l'industrie hôtelière, the most prominent hotel trade organization and one that emphasized luxury hotel interests.

108. "Les Hôteliers savoyards manifestent très vivement leur mécontentment," *Le Monde*, 14 September 1964, Carton 246, 97006, BDF; Ginier, *Les Touristes étrangers*, 261.

109. Robert Krier, "Ce qu'il faut dire," *Revue générale de l'hôtellerie de la gastronomie et du tourisme*, no. 234 (January 1965); Robert Krier, "La main passe . . . ," ibid., no. 238 (May 1965).

110. See caption and photograph in *L'Hôtel-Café-Restaurant et le travailleur des H.C.R.B. réunis de la région parisienne*, no. 134 (March 1968): 1; see also Serge Richard, "L'Avion cherche des lits," *L'Express*, no. 874 (18–24 March 1968): 10–11, and François Beslu, "La Discrète prospérité des vieux palaces," *Entreprise*, no. 1020 (28 March 1975).

111. André Siegfried, *Aspects du XXè siècle* (Paris: Hachette, 1955): 123, 148.

112. *Bulletin municipal officiel de la Ville de Paris, Débats des Assemblées*, 1 December 1964, p. 834. On Frédéric-Dupont's politics in the 1950s, see Stanley Hoffmann, *Le Mouvement poujade*, 358, 372.

113. Heim's phrase, "french way of life," appeared in English, suggesting that Heim emphasized the importance of Francophilia in Anglophone countries (Jacques Heim, "Sacrifier la qualité?" *Le Monde*, 3 November 1965); Kristin Ross, *Fast Cars, Clean Bodies*.

114. "Les Palaces parisiens des années 70," *Le Monde*, 22 April 1972, Carton 246, 97006, BDF.

115. The frenetic pace of *Playtime* contrasted with Tati's more sedate portrait of tourism in *Les vacances de Monsieur Hulot* (1953), which featured slower-paced U.S., British, and French vacationers.

116. "The Coup de Grâce," *Newsweek* 71 (3 June 1968): 74.

117. Charles Vanhecke, "Une Expérience d'occupation des sites," *Le Monde*, 1 July 1968. On Club Med's role in French consumer culture, see Ellen Furlough, "Packaging Pleasures."

118. J.-F. Simon, "Le Tourisme est devenu une industrie majeure," *Le Monde*, 3 November 1961; J.-F. Simon, "Les Vacances vont devenir des marchandises," ibid., 3 June 1968.

119. "Il faut pouvoir vendre le tourisme comme une automobile ou un réfrigérateur," *Le Monde*, 13–14 October 1968; Jean Barraud, "Le Tourisme français à l'école de l'industrie," *Le Figaro*, 5 February 1969. The French state also continued to develop massive tourist resorts aimed primarily at French vacationers. See Furlough and Wakeman, "Composing a Landscape."

120. Temple Fielding, *Fielding's Travel Guide to Europe* (New York: Fielding Publications, 1966), 816, 828.

121. " 'Offensive' French Are Now on the Defensive," *New York Times*, 28 February 1965;

Henry Kamm, "France Turns on a Radiant Smile," *New York Times*, 18 May 1965; Andreas Freund, " 'Welcome and Amiability,' " *New York Times*, 23 May 1965.

122. "The Worm Turns," *Newsweek* 64 (7 September 1964): 43–46.

123. *Enquête dans les aéroports d'Orly et du Bourget.*

124. Timothy Foote, "The French Smile—at Americans!" *New York Times Magazine*, 20 June 1965, pp. 24–32.

125. Laurence Wylie, "Social Change at the Grass Roots," in *In Search of France*, ed. Stanley Hoffmann et al. (Cambridge, Mass.: Harvard University Press, 1963), 159–60.

126. "Sticks and Stones," *New York Herald Tribune*, 5 March 1968, Reel 7, France–États Unis, BDF.

127. In 1967, ongoing monetary tensions, differing Middle East policies, and growing French criticism of the war in Vietnam were among the most important tensions troubling the alliance. See Costigliola, *France and the United States*, and Thomas Schwartz, *Lyndon Johnson and Europe*.

128. "Les Manifestations anti-américaines de Paris provoquent la colère d'un dirigeant de l'Américan Legion," *Le Monde*, 11 April 1967; "Galled by de Gaulle," *Business Week*, 30 December 1967, p. 22.

129. "Bill Asks Tax on Tourists," *New York Times*, 14 December 1967.

130. "Gaullism Empties Bistros," *Business Week*, 2 September 1967; Gloria Emerson, "U.S. Tourists Shun French Vacations," *New York Times*, 28 August 1967.

131. Marcel Tilloy, "Dans le Middle West, les Américains qui iront passer leurs vacances en Europe seront-ils montrés du doigt?" *L'Hôtellerie*, 1 February 1968; Marcel Tilloy, "La Grande leçon de mon voyage aux U.S.A.," ibid., 15 February 1968.

132. Robert Craig, "The Truth about Travel in France," *ASTA Travel News* 37 (June 1968): 57, 136–37.

133. Advertisement for the FGTO, *New Yorker* 41 (24 April 1965): 100–101. Other ads from the second half of the 1960s reveal this shift to "old world" images. An excellent collection of these advertisements is located in the JWT Collection.

134. Craig, "Truth about Travel in France," 57, 136–37.

135. Hugh Moffett, "How to Hurt a Frenchman," *Life* 64 (19 January 1968): 34–35.

136. "Contribution to France," *New York Times*, 9 December 1967.

137. On Lyndon Johnson's improved relations with de Gaulle after May 1968, see Schwartz, *Lyndon Johnson and Europe*, 230. Statistics come from INSEE, *Annuaire statistique de la France* 74 (1968): 466; 77 (1972): 441, 445; and *International Travel Statistics* (Geneva: International Union of Official Travel Organizations, 1967), 30.

138. World Tourism Organization, *Yearbook of Tourism Statistics, Vol. 49* (Madrid: World Tourism Organization, 1997), 1:14–15; *New York Times*, 3 October 1999.

139. In line with Ellen Furlough's scholarship on French tourism, my emphasis on the historical specificity of France's foreign tourism infrastructure suggests that leisure patterns did not emerge inevitably with increased prosperity but were shaped by specific circumstances, pressure groups, and government actions. See Furlough, "Making Mass Vacations," 249, 283.

140. This view of de Gaulle as pragmatic when it came to imitating the United States confirms Richard Kuisel's argument in his essay "Was de Gaulle Anti-American?"

1. Quoted in "LBJ Calls for Travel Curbs," *ASTA Travel News* 37 (January 1968): 17.

2. Lyndon B. Johnson, Special Message to Congress on International Balance of Payments, 10 February 1965, *Public Papers of the Presidents of the United States, Lyndon B. Johnson, 1965*, vol. 1 (Washington: U.S. Government Printing Office, 1966), 175–76; Lyndon B. Johnson, Statement by the President Outlining a Program of Action to Deal with the Balance of Payments Problem, 1 January 1968, *Public Papers of the Presidents of the United States, Lyndon B. Johnson, 1968–69*, vol. 1 (Washington: U.S. Government Printing Office, 1969), 2; Lyndon B. Johnson, *The Johnson Presidential Conferences*, vol. 2 (New York: Earl M. Coleman Enterprises, 1978), 886.

3. John Black, interview by Paige Mulhollan, 18 October 1968, 12, AC 74–175, LBJL. Black was director of the U.S. Travel Service.

4. Gardner Ackley to Lyndon Johnson, 6 January 1968, Box 50, FO 4-1, LBJL-WHCF.

5. See Collins, "Economic Crisis of 1968"; Gavin, "Gold Battles within the Cold War" and "Defending Europe and the Dollar"; and Schwartz, *Lyndon Johnson and Europe*. All of these insightful works offer brief reference to but no sustained analysis of the role of tourism in the crisis. In fact, the critical reception of LBJ's tourism proposals complicates Collins's claim that "the initial public response [to Johnson's New Year's Day announcement] was strongly positive" ("Economic Crisis of 1968," 406).

6. The U.S. government's Cold War cultural diplomacy programs overseas also stressed a connection between consumerism and anti-Communism. The travel-tax debates, however, represent a moment when consumerism clashed with the Cold War state. On cultural diplomacy, see Hixson, *Parting the Curtain*, and Haddow, *Pavilions of Plenty*.

7. Gardner Ackley, Johnson's chief economic adviser, informed the president of a sharp slump in France's 1967 tourist trade, adding that the French "have some reminders right at home that being nasty can pinch their pocketbooks where it hurts" (Ackley, Memorandum for the President, 26 August 1967, Box 50, FO 4-1, LBJL-CF). See also Ackley, Memorandum for the President, 22 May 1965, Box 33, FO 4-1, LBJL-WHCF.

8. Gavin, "Legends of Bretton Woods"; Schwartz, *Lyndon Johnson and Europe*, 64; LaFeber, *American Age*, 644.

9. Flo Hinz, "Washington Window," *ASTA Travel News* 30 (February 1961): 37, 122; Dwight D. Eisenhower, News Conference at August, Georgia, 16 November 1960, *Public Papers of the Presidents of the United States, Dwight D. Eisenhower* (Washington: U.S. Government Printing Office, 1971), 362.

10. "U.S. Travel Policy Is Being Shaped," *Travel Agent* 43 (25 March 1958): 76–81.

11. Flo Hinz, "Washington Window," *ASTA Travel News* 30 (April 1961): 33l; (May 1961): 39.

12. *Congressional Record*, 86th Cong., 2nd sess., 18 March 1960, vol. 106, pt. 5:5978.

13. LaFeber, *American Age*, 561, 645.

14. U.S. Bureau of the Census, *Historical Statistics*, 864.

15. Black interview; Department of Commerce, Press Release G-63-11, 18 January 1963, Box 57, Pan Am Records.

16. *Congressional Record*, 89th Cong., 1st sess., 29 June 1965, vol. 111, pt. 11:15084–88; U.S.

House of Representatives, House Committee on Ways and Means, *Duty Exemption for Returning American Residents: Hearings before the House Committee on Ways and Means on H.R. 7368,* 89th Cong., 1st sess., 1965, p. 40.

17. Flo Hinz, "Washington Window," *ASTA Travel News* 30 (February 1961): 37, 122.

18. Howard Apter, "A Lesson from a Hotel Squeeze," *Travel Agent* 56 (10 August 1964): 76–68.

19. Trevor L. Christie, "Tourism and the Common Market," *ASTA Travel News* 33 (February 1963): 56–57.

20. Report of the President's Task Force on Foreign Economic Policy, *FRUS, 1964–1968,* 8:34–51.

21. Minutes of the Meeting on Travel Tax, 4 May 1966, *FRUS, 1964–1968,* 8:264–68. See also Paper Prepared for the Cabinet Committee on Balance of Payments, 9 December 1964, ibid., 8:56–60. Ball himself had old ties to tourism boosters. As a lawyer in Paris in the early 1950s, he had worked with French business leaders to promote U.S. tourism to France. See Chapters 2 and 5.

22. Memorandum from the President's Special Assistant for National Security Affairs (Bundy) to President Johnson, 22 January 1965, *FRUS, 1964–1968,* 8:83–84. See also Gavin, "Defending Europe and the Dollar," 365.

23. "Reasons for Supporting a Western Hemisphere Exemption to Limitations on Tourist Travel," 18 January 1968, Box 12, Goldstein Files. See also Council of Economic Advisors Staff Paper, "Balance of Payments Aspects of CAB's Proposals on Supplemental Air Carriers," 25 August 1966, with covering letter, Ackley to McPherson, 25 August 1966, Box 17, CA/7, LBJL-WHCF.

24. House Committee on Ways and Means, *Duty Exemption for Returning American Residents,* 32. See also Gardner Ackley, Memorandum for the President, 12 June 1965, Box 33, FO 4, LBJL-WHCF, and Stanley Surrey, speech before the Tax Executives Institute, Inc., 26 February 1968, Box 44, FO 5, LBJL-WHCF.

25. "And Now, a Tax on Tourists," *Waukegan New-Sun,* 17 February 1965, in *Congressional Record,* 89th Cong., 1st sess., 17 February 1965, vol. 111, pt. 24:A844–45.

26. *Congressional Record,* 89th Cong., 1st sess., 29 June 1965, vol. 111, pt. 11:15086.

27. Report from the Cabinet Committee on Balance of Payments, [January 1965?], *FRUS, 1964–1968,* 8:94. See also Memorandum of Conversation, 27 October 1965, ibid., 8:221.

28. Joseph Califano, Memorandum for the President, 30 May 1968, Box 44, FO 5, LBJL-WHCF.

29. E. Ernest Goldstein, interview by T. H. Baker, 19 December 1968, 10, 15, AC 74–81, LBJL.

30. Memorandum of Conversation, 27 October 1965, *FRUS, 1964–1968,* 8:221.

31. Gardner Ackley, Memorandum for the President, 23 December 1967, with covering letter, Joseph Califano to the President, 23 December 1967, Box 50, FO 4-1, LBJL-CF; Gardner Ackley, Memorandum for the President, 10 January 1968, Box 50, FO 4-1, LBJL-CF; Telegram from the President's Special Assistant (Califano) to President Johnson in Thailand, 22 December 1967, *FRUS, 1964–1968,* 8:465–69, esp. 468.

32. Henry Hamill (Joe) Fowler, interview by David G. McComb, 22 April 1969, AC 74–98, LBJL.

33. Ernest Goldstein, Memorandum for the President, 8 January 1968, with covering letter, Gardner Ackley, Memorandum for the President, 19 January 1968, Box 50, FO 4-1, LBJL-CF.

34. On the broader transformation of U.S. economic relations with Western Europe, see Kunz, *Butter and Guns*, 177–78, and Gavin, "Defending Europe and the Dollar" and "Gold Battles within the Cold War."

35. U.S. Bureau of the Census, *Historical Statistics*, 404. On the administration's focus on limiting travel expenses in Western Europe, see Report from the Cabinet Committee on Balance of Payments, [January 1965?], *FRUS, 1964–1968*, 8:94.

36. *Congressional Record*, 89th Cong., 1st sess., 4 March 1965, vol. 111, pt. 3:4189–90.

37. Quoted in James G. Morton to Jack Valenti, 31 March 1965, Box 41, FO 5, LBJL-WHCF. Although an advocate of free trade, Porter also tended to place national interest over economic theory, as in 1959 when she endorsed "Buy American" consumer habits. See Dana Frank, *Buy American*, 115.

38. *Congressional Record*, 89th Cong., 1st sess., 4 August 1965, vol. 111, pt. 28:A4298–99.

39. Lyndon B. Johnson, for *Parade* magazine, 1 April 1965, Box 41, FO 5, LBJL-WHCF.

40. Ed Dodd, *Mark Trail* (New York: The Hall Syndicate), release for the week of August 1, 1966, with covering letter, Morton to Bob Kinter, 8 July 1966, Box 42, FO 5, LBJL-WHCF.

41. Johnson to William Randolph Hearst Jr., 17 January 1968, Box 44, FO 5, LBJL-WHCF.

42. Sylvia Meredith, telegram to Lyndon B. Johnson, 3 January 1968, Box 35, FO 4-1, LBJL-WHCF.

43. B. B. McGimsey to Lyndon B. Johnson, 2 January 1968, and Johnson to B. B. McGimsey, 13 January 1968, both in Box 35, FO 4-1, LBJL-WHCF.

44. Ernest Goldstein, Memorandum for the President, 3 January 1968, and Frank E. Lay to Mr. Solomon, 3 January 1968, both in Box 1, Goldstein Files.

45. Ernest Goldstein, Memoranda for the President, 25 and 31 January 1968, Box 44, FO 5, LBJL-WHCF.

46. Ernest Goldstein, Memorandum for the President, 8 January 1968, Box 1, Goldstein Files; "News of the Month," *ASTA Travel News* 37 (February 1968): 26.

47. Ernest Goldstein, Memorandum for the President, 23 May 1968, Box 44, FO 5, LBJL-WHCF.

48. None of the important U.S. court rulings on travel restrictions established a right to travel without taxation or duty fees. The right to leave the country had been established through a series of court decisions beginning in the early Cold War in the wake of the State Department's refusal to grant passports to real or suspected Communists. The 1952 *Bauer v. Acheson* case established an individual's constitutional right to due process before his or her passport could be revoked. *Kent v. Dulles* in 1958 determined that the Fifth Amendment secured "freedom of movement" for individuals but not necessarily for travel to countries deemed threats to U.S. national security. The 1964 case of *Aptheker v. the Secretary of State*, prompted by the travels of Communist intellectual Herbert Aptheker, struck down a 1950 law justifying the barring of travel by Communists. See Dowty, *Closed Borders*, and " 'The Very Essence of Our Free Society,' " *Chicago Tribune*, 5 January 1968.

49. Flo Hinz, "Washington Window," *ASTA Travel News* 30 (February 1961): 37, 122.

50. "$100 Head Tax on Travel," *ASTA Travel News* 34 (February 1965): 9.

51. House Committee on Ways and Means, *Duty Exemption for Returning American Residents*, 134.

52. "Is This Trip Necessary?" *Newsweek* 71 (19 February 1968): 65–66; "Fowler Revives Tax in Senate," *ASTA Travel News* 37 (July 1968): 25.

53. Temple Fielding, *Fielding's Travel Guide to Europe* (New York: Fielding Publications, 1966).

54. "Is This Trip Necessary?"

55. Paul J. C. Friedlander, [caption], *New York Times*, 25 February 1968 (International Travel Special).

56. "Travel Spending and the U.S. Balance of Payments," *ASTA Travel News* 34 (June 1965): 42–43, 122.

57. James Reston, "Washington: How You Gonna Keep 'em Down on the Farm," *New York Times*, 3 January 1968. See also "And Now, a Tax on Tourists."

58. Ernest Dunbar, "Memo to LBJ: See America First . . . If You Can," *Look* 32 (16 April 1968): 48. Dunbar continued a longer tradition of African Americans referring to European openness as a form of critiquing the United States. See, for instance, Stovall, *Paris Noir*.

59. Douglass Cater to Agnes Sibley of Lindenwood College, MO, 8 March 1965, Box 36, FO 4-1, LBJL-WHCF.

60. Wade Mann to President Johnson, [January 1968], Box 37, FO 4-1, LBJL-WHCF; Joseph Kraft, "Living with Gold," *Boston Globe*, 5 January 1968.

61. Norman Cousins, "The President's Closed-Door Policy," *Saturday Review* 51 (20 January 1968): 16.

62. Henry S. Reuss, "Is This the Year of the Pumpkin?" *Saturday Review* 51 (9 March 1968): 41–42, 85.

63. Horace Sutton, "Does He Still Own the World?" *Saturday Review* 51 (9 March 1968): 39–40, 81–83.

64. "Tourists, Go Home!" *National Review* 11 (26 August 1961): 113.

65. *Congressional Record*, 89th Cong., 1st sess., 20 May 1965, vol. 111, pt. 8:11157.

66. Louise Thompson, "On Taxing Travel," *St. Charles (Missouri) Banner-News*, in *Congressional Record*, 89th Cong., 1st sess., 12 April 1965, vol. 111, pt. 6:7777–78.

67. "Hartke and Curtis Criticize Fowler Tax Proposal," *ASTA Travel News* 37 (March 1968): 23.

68. Walter Trohan, quoted in *Congressional Record*, 89th Cong., 1st sess., 8 February 1965, vol. 111, pt. 24:A495. In like fashion, *Aviation Week and Space Technology* argued that the monetary crisis stemmed less from tourism than from "obsolete U.S. military commitments abroad" (Robert Hotz, "An Unnecessary Blow," *Aviation Week and Space Technology* [8 January 1968]: 11).

69. Thompson, "On Taxing Travel."

70. "The Very Essence of Our Free Society," " *Chicago Tribune*, 5 January 1968.

71. George Murray, "Banning Travel," *Chicago Tribune*, 6 January 1968.

72. William F. Buckley Jr., "On the Right," *National Review* 20 (27 February 1968): 206.

73. Marcel Bourseau, "A Propos d'une concurrence," *L'Écho touristique*, 3 February 1961.

74. Jacques Kahn, "Johnson annonce des économies de dollars," *L'Humanité*, 3 January 1968.

75. "Le Plan Johnson fait trembler l'Europe," *L'Express*, no. 864 (8–14 January 1968): 17–18. The cartoon appeared in the 9 March 1968 issue of the *Saturday Review*.

76. C. Makinsky, "Retour de Baton," *France-U.S.A.*, no. 185 (January–February 1968): 1.

77. J.-F. Simon, "Les Conséquences du plan Johnson," *Le Monde*, 5 January 1968. See also Alain Clémont, "L'Opinion américaine rêve de 'représailles' pour punir la France de son 'ingratitude,' " ibid., 10 January 1968.

78. Marcel Tilloy, "Dans le Middle West, les Américains qui iront passer leurs vacances en Europe seront-ils montrés du doigt?" *L'Hôtellerie*, 1 February 1968.

79. Marc Ullmann, "Amérique: Pourquoi de Gaulle se tait," *L'Express*, no. 871 (26 February–3 March 1968): 4–7.

80. Simon, "Les Conséquences du plan Johnson."

81. Clémont, "L'Opinion américaine."

82. "Les Dollars quittent l'Europe," *Paris Match*, no. 979 (13 January 1968): 4.

83. G. d'Orgeville, "Visitez la France," and Marcel Tilloy, "La Grande leçon de mon voyage aux U.S.A," both in *L'Hôtellerie*, 15 February 1968.

84. Raymond Aron, "La Défense du dollar," *Le Figaro*, 4 January 1968.

85. Gabriel Farkas, "Difficultés attendues pour l'économie mondiale," *France-Soir*, 3 January 1968; A. de Segonzac, "Les Américains mécontents d'avoir à réduire leurs vacances à l'étranger," ibid., 6 January 1968.

86. "Big Leak in Dollars as Americans Rush Abroad," *U.S. News & World Report* 59 (12 July 1965): 40–41; U.S. Bureau of the Census, *Historical Statistics*, 403–4.

87. U.S. Bureau of the Census, *Historical Statistics*, 404.

88. William D. Patterson, "The Big Picture," *ASTA Travel News* 38 (March 1969): 40–41.

89. Richard Nixon, Statement on the Balance of Payments, 4 April 1969, *Public Papers of the Presidents of the United States, Richard Nixon, 1969* (Washington: U.S. Government Printing Office, 1971): 266.

90. Costigliola, *France and the United States*, 170–72.

91. "Exploring the New Economic World," *Time* 98 (30 August 1971): 10; " 'They Look at Our Dollars as If They Were Germ Carriers,' " *Newsweek* 71 (30 August 1971): 24.

92. "The Buck Stops Here," *Newsweek* 79 (12 June 1972): 92; "Going Abroad? You Will Pay More or See Less," *U.S. News and World Report* 74 (2 April 1973): 58.

93. "Traveling More but Spending Less," *Business Week*, 29 July 1972, p. 21; "If You're Going Abroad—Tips for Travelers," *U.S. News and World Report* 72 (17 January 1972): 24.

94. Stanley Elkin, "The World on $5 a Day," *Harper's* 245 (July 1972): 41–46.

Conclusion

1. See, for instance, Goldstone, *Making the World Safe for Tourism*.

2. See note 13 of the Introduction for scholarship on the persistence of nation-states amid globalization.

3. Christina Klein (*Cold War Orientalism*) locates a similar emphasis on similarities in middlebrow Americans' sentimental travel writing about Asia and Asians.

4. This point builds from Frank Costigliola's discussion of how U.S. policymakers saw the Western alliance in terms of a heterosexual relationship, with the United States as the patriarch ("Nuclear Family").

5. For an insightful discussion of these concerns, see Kuisel, "American Historians in Search of France."

6. This nationalistic dynamic in postwar France has also been true in developing countries, where hosting foreigners has offered a way to heighten national identity among individuals or local communities. See Picard and Wood, eds., *Tourism, Ethnicity, and the State*, and Lanfant, Allcock, and Bruner, eds., *International Tourism*.

7. See note 17 of the Introduction for references to scholarship on adaptation and Americanization.

8. Basing his view on a quantitative analysis of U.S. media coverage of France, Bertram M. Gordon sees the 1960s as the peak in American popular interest in France. See his "Decline of a Cultural Icon."

9. Ann Rea Craig, interview by author, tape recording, 17 September 2002.

10. On radiance, see Hecht, *Radiance of France*.

11. Richard Pells's recent synthesis on U.S.–Western European cultural relations describes U.S. tourists as "proud of their parochialism" and as contributors to international misunderstanding. Jean-Baptiste Duroselle went even further, characterizing American tourism as an important cause of French anti-Americanism. While Pells and Duroselle deserve credit for considering tourism a part of international relations, their disparagement of mass leisure travel misses the more complex and often more positive roles that tourism played in U.S.-French relations. See Pells, *Not Like Us*, 135–38, and Duroselle, *France and the United States*, 198–99.

12. "The Image of America: Some Dimensions of International Perception as Revealed in USIA Survey Data from Western Europe and Japan," S-19-67, Box 4, SR 1964–82.

13. For one assessment of consumerism's role in "winning" the Cold War, see Wagnleitner, "Empire of Fun."

14. For a similar argument on the value of this kind of synthesis, see Thomas Bender's introductory essay in Bender, ed., *Rethinking American History in a Global Age*.

SELECTED BIBLIOGRAPHY

Archival Collections in the United States

Austin, Texas
  Lyndon Baines Johnson Library
    Confidential Files
    White House Central Files
Bowdoin, Maine
  Bowdoin College
    Ralph Owen Brewster Papers
College Park, Maryland
  National Archives and Records Administration II
    Record Group 59, Records of the Department of State
    Record Group 151, Records of the Bureau of Foreign and Domestic Commerce
    Record Group 306, Records of the U.S. Information Agency
    Record Group 353, Records of Interdepartmental and Intradepartmental
      Committees
    Record Group 469, Records of U.S. Foreign Assistance Agencies
      Economic Cooperation Administration Files
Coral Gables, Florida
  Archives and Special Collections, Otto G. Richter Library, University of Miami
    Pan American World Airways Inc. Records
Durham, N.C.
  Rare Book, Manuscript, and Special Collections Library, Duke University
    John W. Hartman Center for Sales, Advertising, and Marketing History

Archival Collections in France

Fontainebleau
  Centre des archives contemporaines
Paris
  Archives d'histoire contemporaine, Centre d'histoire de l'Europe du XXe siècle,
    Fondation nationale des sciences politiques
    Fonds Jean Sainteny
  Archives nationales
    80 AJ, Commissariat général du plan
    F14, Archives du cabinet de M. Jules Moch
    F21, Beaux-Arts

Bibliothèque administrative de la Ville de Paris
Bibliothèque de la Documentation française
    Problèmes généraux 1944 à 1952, Rélations diplomatiques, France–États-Unis
    Rélations culturelles
  Chambre de commerce et d'industrie de Paris
  Ministère des affaires étrangères
    États-Unis, Amérique 1944–52
    États-Unis, Amérique 1952–63
    Rélations culturelles 1945–59
Savigny-le-Temple
  Centre des archives économiques et financières

U.S. Periodicals

Advertising Age	Nation
America	National Geographic
ASTA Travel News	New Republic
Atlantic	Newsweek
Boston Globe	New Yorker
Business Week	New York Times
Chicago Daily Tribune	Parade
Christian Science Monitor	Reader's Digest
Commonweal	Saturday Evening Post
Congressional Record	Saturday Review
Ebony	This Week
Fortune	Time
Harper's	Travel
Holiday	Travel Europe
House and Garden	United Nations World
Life	U.S. News and World Report
Look	

French Periodicals

L'Aurore
Bulletin municipal officiel de la Ville de Paris, Débats des Assemblées
Cadres alimentation
Combat
Le Droit de vivre
L'Écho touristique
Les Échos
L'Express
Le Figaro
France-Soir
France-U.S.A.

George V: Bulletin du personnel de l'Hôtel George V
L'Hôtel-Café-Restaurant et le Travailleur des H.C.R.B. réunis de la région parisienne
L'Hôtellerie
L'Hôtellerie syndicaliste indépendante
Hôtels-Restaurants-Bars brasseries et limonadiers de France
L'Humanité
Journal officiel de la République française, Assemblée nationale, Débats
Journal officiel de la République française, Avis et rapports du Conseil économique et social
Journal officiel de la République française, Sénat, Débats parlementaires,
Libération
Le Matin
Le Monde
Notre métier: Bulletin du personnel des Hôtels George V—Plaza-Athénée
Paris Match
Paris-Presse
Le Populaire de Paris
Professions
Rapports France–États-Unis
Revue générale de l'hôtellerie, de la gastronomie, et du tourisme
Revue officielle de l'hôtellerie, de la restauration et du commerce des boissons
Le Trait d'union des hôtels-cafés-restaurants et cantines

Secondary Literature

Adler, Judith. "Youth on the Road: Reflections on the History of Tramping." *Annals of Tourism Research* 12 (1985): 335–54.

Adler, Selig. *The Isolationist Impulse: Its Twentieth Century Reaction*. New York: Free Press, 1957.

Anderson, Benedict. *Imagined Communities: Reflections on the Origins and Spread of Nationalism*. New York: Verso, 1983.

Andrieu, Pierre. *Histoire anecdotique des hôtels de France*. Paris: Editions mondiales, 1956.

Appadurai, Arjun. *Modernity at Large: Cultural Dimensions of Globalization*. Minneapolis: University of Minnesota Press, 1996.

Aron, Cindy S. *Working at Play: A History of Vacations in the United States*. New York: Oxford University Press, 1999.

Bachelier, Christian. "La Notion de patrimoine." *Bulletin de l'Institut d'histoire du temps présents* 43 (March 1991): 19–30.

Baranowski, Shelley, and Ellen Furlough, eds. *Being Elsewhere: Tourism, Consumer Culture, and Identity in Modern Europe and North America*. Ann Arbor: University of Michigan, 2001.

Barber, Benjamin R. *Jihad vs. McWorld*. New York: Times Books, 1995.

Baum, Warren C. "The Marshall Plan and French Foreign Trade." In *Modern France: Problems of the Third and Fourth Republics*, edited by Warren C. Baum, David S. Landes, and Edward Meade Earle, 382–402. New York: Russell & Russell, 1964.

Bederman, Gail. *Manliness and Civilization: A Cultural History of Gender and Race in the United States, 1890–1917*. Chicago: University of Chicago Press, 1995.

Belasco, Warren. *Americans on the Road: From Autocamp to Motel, 1910–1945*. Cambridge, Mass.: MIT Press, 1979.

Bender, Marilyn, and Selig Altschul. *The Chosen Instrument: Pan Am, Juan Trippe— the Rise and Fall of an American Entrepreneur*. New York: Simon and Schuster, 1982.

Bender, Thomas, ed. *Rethinking American History in a Global Age*. Berkeley: University of California Press, 2002.

Berg, A. Scott. *Lindbergh*. New York: G. P. Putnam's Sons, 1998.

Berghahn, Volker. *America and the Intellectual Cold Wars in Europe: Shepard Stone Between Philanthropy, Academy, and Democracy*. Princeton: Princeton University Press, 2001.

Berkowitz, Michael. "A 'New Deal' for Leisure: Making Mass Tourism during the Great Depression." In *Being Elsewhere: Tourism, Consumer Culture, and Identity in Modern Europe and North America*, edited by Shelley Baranowski and Ellen Furlough, 185–212. Ann Arbor: University of Michigan, 2001.

Bernstein, Irving. *Guns or Butter: The Presidency of Lyndon Johnson*. New York: Oxford University Press, 1996.

Bilstein, Roger E. *The Enterprise of Flight: The American Aviation and Aerospace Industry*. Washington: Smithsonian Institution Press, 2001.

Bloch-Lainé, François, and Jean Bouvier, *La France restaurée, 1944–1954, Dialogue sur les choix d'une modernisation*. Paris: Fayard, 1986.

Blume, Mary. *Côte d'Azur: Inventing the French Riviera*. N.p.: Thames and Hudson, 1992.

Boltanski, Luc. "America America . . . Le Plan Marshall et l'importation du 'management.'" *Actes de la recherche en sciences sociales* 28 (May 1981): 19–41.

Bossuat, Gérard. *La France, l'aide américaine et la construction européenne, 1944–54*. Paris: Comité pour l'histoire économique et financière de la France, 1992.

——. "Le Plan Marshall dans la modernisation de la France." In *L'Année 1947*, edited by Serge Berstein and Pierre Milza, 45–73. Paris: Presses de Sciences Po, 2000.

Bourseau, Marcel. *Traité pratique d'industrie hôtelière*. Paris: Flammarion, 1955.

Buell, Frederick. *National Culture and the New Global System*. Baltimore: Johns Hopkins University Press, 1994.

Buzard, James. *The Beaten Track: European Tourism, Literature, and the Ways to 'Culture,' 1800–1918*. Oxford: Clarendon Press, 1993.

Calder, Lendol. *Financing the American Dream: A Cultural History of Consumer Credit*. Princeton: Princeton University Press, 1999.

Cazes, Bernard, and Philippe Mioche, eds. *Modernisation ou décadence: Études, témoinages et documents sur la planification française*. Aix-en-Provence: Université de Provence, 1990.

Cazes, G. *Le Tourisme international: Mirage ou stratégie d'avenir?* Paris: Hatier, 1989.

Charensol, Georges, and Roger Regent. *50 ans de cinéma avec René Clair*. Paris: La Table ronde, 1979.

Cobble, Dorothy Sue. *Dishing It Out: Waitresses and their Unions in the Twentieth Century*. Urbana: University of Illinois Press, 1991.

Cohen, Lizabeth. *A Consumer's Republic: The Politics of Mass Consumption in Postwar America*. New York: Alfred A. Knopf, 2003.

Coleman, Peter. *The Liberal Conspiracy: The Congress for Cultural Freedom and the Struggle for the Mind of Postwar Europe*. New York: Free Press, 1989.

Collins, Robert M. "The Economic Crisis of 1968 and the Waning of the 'American Century.'" *American Historical Review* 101 (April 1996): 396–422.

Confino, Alon. *The Nation as a Local Metaphor: Württemberg, Imperial Germany, and National Memory, 1871–1918*. Chapel Hill: University of North Carolina Press, 1997.

Conn, Peter. *Pearl S. Buck: A Cultural Biography*. Cambridge: Cambridge University Press, 1996.

Connelly, Matthew, "Taking Off the Cold War Lens: Visions of North-South Conflict during the Algerian War for Independence." *American Historical Review* 105 (June 2000): 739–69.

Connors, Martin, and Jim Craddock, eds. *VideoHound's Golden Movie Retriever*. Detroit: Visible Ink, 1999.

Coombs, Philip H. *The Fourth Dimension of Foreign Policy: Educational and Cultural Affairs*. New York: Harper & Row, 1964.

Corbin, Alain. *Les Filles de noce: Misère sexuelle et prostitution aux 19e et 20e siècles*. Paris: Aubier Montaigne, 1978.

Costigliola, Frank. "Culture, Emotion and the Creation of the Atlantic Identity, 1948–1952." In *No End to Alliance: The United States and Western Europe: Past, Present and Future*, edited by Geir Lundestad, 21–36. New York: St. Martin's Press, 1998.

———. *France and the United States: The Cold Alliance since World War II*. New York: Twayne, 1992.

———. "The Nuclear Family: Tropes of Gender and Pathology in the Western Alliance." *Diplomatic History* 21 (Spring 1997): 163–83.

Crick, Malcolm. "Representations of International Tourism in the Social Sciences: Sun, Sex, Sights, Savings, and Servility." *Annual Review of Anthropology* 18 (1989): 307–44.

Cross, Gary. *An All-Consuming Century: Why Commercialism Won in Modern America*. New York: Columbia University Press, 2000.

Culler, Jonathan. *Framing the Sign: Criticism and its Institutions*. Oxford: Basil Blackwell, 1988.

Cuordileone, K. A. "'Politics in an Age of Anxiety': Cold War Political Culture and the Crisis in American Masculinity, 1949–1960." *Journal of American History* 87 (September 2000): 515–45.

Dean, Robert D. *Imperial Brotherhood: Gender and the Making of Cold War Foreign Policy*. Amherst: University of Massachusetts Press, 2001.

Dowty, Alan. *Closed Borders: The Contemporary Assault on Freedom of Movement*. New Haven: Yale University Press, 1987.

Dulles, Foster Rhea. *Americans Abroad: Two Centuries of American Travel*. Ann Arbor: University of Michigan Press, 1964.

Duroselle, Jean-Baptiste. *France and the United States: From the Beginnings to the Present*. Translated by Derek Coltman. Chicago: University of Chicago Press, 1978.

Endy, Christopher. "Travel and World Power: Americans in Europe, 1890–1917." *Diplomatic History* 22 (Fall 1998): 564–94.

Engerman, David. "A Research Agenda for the History of Tourism: Towards an International Social History." *American Studies International* 32 (October 1994): 3–31.

Enloe, Cynthia. *Bananas, Beaches, and Bases: Making Feminist Sense of International Politics*. Berkeley: University of California Press, 1989.

Esposito, Chiarella. *America's Feeble Weapon: Funding the Marshall Plan in France and Italy, 1948–1950*. Westport, Conn.: Greenwood Press, 1994.

Evanson, Norma. *Paris: A Century of Change, 1878–1978*. New Haven: Yale University Press, 1979.

Federici, Silvia. "The God that Never Failed: The Origins and Crises of Western Civilization." In *Enduring Western Civilization: The Construction of the Concept of Western Civilization and Its "Others,"* edited by Silvia Federici, 63–89. Westport, Conn.: Praeger, 1995.

Fichtenbaum, George L. *Passport to the World: The History of ASTA*. Alexandria, Va.: American Society of Travel Agents, 1990.

Filene, Peter. " 'Cold War Culture' Doesn't Say It All." In *Rethinking Cold War Culture*, edited by Peter J. Kuznick and James Gilbert, 156–74. Washington: Smithsonian Institution Press, 2001.

Fousek, John. *To Lead the Free World: American Nationalism and the Cultural Roots of the Cold War*. Chapel Hill: University of North Carolina Press, 2000.

Fox, Stephen. *The Mirror Makers: A History of American Advertising and Its Creators*. Urbana: University of Illinois Press, 1997.

Frangialli, Francesco. *La France dans le tourisme mondial*. Paris: Economica, 1991.

Frank, Dana. *Buy American: The Untold Story of Economic Nationalism*. Boston: Beacon Press, 1999.

Frank, Robert. *La Hantise du déclin: La France, 1920–1960: Finances, défence et identité nationale*. Paris: Belin, 1994.

Frank, Thomas. *The Conquest of Cool: Business Culture, Counter Culture, and the Rise of Hip Consumerism*. Chicago: University of Chicago Press, 1997.

Fried, Albert. *McCarthyism: The Great American Red Scare, A Documentary History*. New York: Oxford University Press, 1997.

Furlough, Ellen. "Making Mass Vacations: Tourism and Consumer Culture in France, 1930s to 1970s." *Comparative Studies in Society and History* 40 (April 1998): 247–86.

———. "Packaging Pleasures: Club Méditerranée and French Consumer Culture, 1950–1968." *French Historical Studies* 18 (Spring 1993): 65–81.

———. "Une leçon des choses: Tourism, Empire, and the Nation in Interwar France." *French Historical Studies* 25 (Summer 2002): 441–73.

Furlough, Ellen, and Rosemary Wakeman. "Composing a Landscape: Coastal Mass Tourism and Regional Development in the Languedoc, 1960s–1980s." *International Journal of Maritime History* 9 (June 1997): 187–211.

———. "La Grande Motte: Regional Development, Tourism, and the State." In *Being Elsewhere: Tourism, Consumer Culture, and Identity in Modern Europe and North America*, edited by Shelley Baranowski and Ellen Furlough, 348–72. Ann Arbor: University of Michigan, 2001.

Fussell, Paul. *Thank God for the Atom Bomb and Other Essays*. New York: Ballantine, 1988.

Gautier, Marcel. *L'Industrie hôtelière*. Paris: Presses universitaires de France, 1962.

——. *Métiers et main-d'oeuvre dans l'industrie hôtelière*. Paris: Éditions Eyrolles, 1955.

Gavin, Francis J. "Defending Europe and the Dollar: The Politics of the U.S. Balance of Payments, 1958–1968." Ph.D. diss., University of Pennsylvania, 1997.

——. "The Gold Battles within the Cold War: American Monetary Policy and the Defense of Europe, 1960–1963." *Diplomatic History* 26 (Winter 2002): 61–94.

——. "The Legends of Bretton Woods." *Orbis* 40 (Spring 1996): 183–98.

Geyer, Michael, and Charles Bright. "World History in a Global Age." *American Historical Review* 100 (October 1995): 1034–60.

Gienow-Hecht, Jessica C. E. "Art Is Democracy and Democracy Is Art: Culture, Propaganda, and the *Neue Zeitung* in Germany, 1944–1947." *Diplomatic History* 23 (Winter 1999): 21–43.

——. "Shame on US? Academics, Cultural Transfer, and the Cold War—A Critical Review." *Diplomatic History* 24 (Summer 2000): 465–94.

Ginier, Jean. *Les Touristes étrangers en France pendant l'été*. Paris: Éditions Génin, 1969.

Girard, Augustin, and Geneviève Gentil, eds. *Les Affaires culturelles au temps d'André Malraux, 1959–1969*. Paris: Documentation française, 1996.

Goldstone, Patricia. *Making the World Safe for Tourism*. New Haven: Yale University Press, 2001.

Gordon, Bertram M. "The Decline of a Cultural Icon: France in American Perspective." *French Historical Studies* 22 (Fall 1999): 625–51.

——. "*Ist Gott Französisch?* Germans, Tourism, and Occupied France, 1940–1944." *Modern and Contemporary France* (1996): 287–98.

Goujon, Paul. *Cent ans de tourisme en France*. Paris: Cherche-Midi, 1989.

Gould-Davies, Nigel. "The Logic of Soviet Cultural Diplomacy." *Diplomatic History* 27 (April 2003): 193–214.

Graebner, William. *The Age of Doubt: American Thought and Culture in the 1940s*. Boston: Twayne, 1990.

Green, Nancy L. "The Comparative Gaze: Travelers in France before the Era of Mass Tourism." *French Historical Studies* 25 (Summer 2002): 422–40.

——. *Ready-to-Wear and Ready-to-Work: A Century of Industry and Immigration in Paris and New York*. Durham: Duke University Press, 1997.

Griffith, Robert. "Dwight D. Eisenhower and the Corporate Commonwealth." *American Historical Review* 87 (February 1982): 87–122.

——. "The Selling of America: The Advertising Council and American Politics, 1942–1960." *Business History Review* 57 (Autumn 1983): 388–412.

Grosser, Alfred. *Affaires extérieures: La politique de la France, 1944–1989*. Paris: Flammarion, 1989.

Grossman, Peter Z. *American Express: The Unofficial History of the People Who Built the Great Financial Empire*. New York: Crown Publishers, 1987.

Haddow, Robert H. *Pavilions of Plenty: Exhibiting American Culture Abroad in the 1950s*. Washington: Smithsonian Institution Press, 1997.

Hall, Colin Michael. *Tourism and Politics: Policy, Power, and Place*. Chichester, England: John Wiley & Sons, 1994.

Hanna, Martha. "French Women and American Men: 'Foreign' Students at the University of Paris, 1915–1925." *French Historical Studies* 22 (Winter 1999): 87–112.

Harp, Stephen L. *Marketing Michelin: Advertising and Cultural Identity in Twentieth-Century France*. Baltimore: Johns Hopkins University Press, 2001.

Hazbun, Waleed. "Between Global Flows and Territorial Control: The State, Tourism Development, and the Politics of Reterritorialization in the Middle East." Ph.D. diss., Massachusetts Institute of Technology, 2002.

Hecht, Gabrielle. *The Radiance of France: Nuclear Power and National Identity after World War II*. Cambridge, Mass.: MIT Press, 1998.

Held, David, and Anthony McGrew, et al. *Global Transformations: Politics, Economics, and Culture*. Stanford: Stanford University Press, 1999.

Helleiner, Eric. *States and the Reemergence of Global Finance: From Bretton Woods to the 1990s*. Ithaca: Cornell University Press, 1994.

Heppenheimer, T. A. *Turbulent Skies: The History of Commercial Aviation*. New York: John Wiley & Sons, 1995.

Herman, Ellen. *The Romance of American Psychology: Political Culture in the Age of Experts*. Berkeley: University of California Press, 1995.

Hitchcock, William I. *France Restored: Cold War Diplomacy and the Quest for Leadership in Europe, 1944–1954*. Chapel Hill: University of North Carolina Press, 1998.

Hixson, Walter L. *Parting the Curtain: Propaganda, Culture, and the Cold War, 1945–1961*. New York: St. Martin's Press, 1997.

Hoffman, Elizabeth Cobbs. *All You Need Is Love: The Peace Corps and the Spirit of the 1960s*. Cambridge, Mass.: Harvard University Press, 1998.

Hoffmann, Stanley. *Le Mouvement poujade*. Paris: Armand Colin, 1956.

Hogan, Michael J. "Corporatism: A Positive Appraisal." *Diplomatic History* 10 (Fall 1986): 363–72.

——. *A Cross of Iron: Harry S Truman and the Origins of the National Security State, 1945–1954*. Cambridge: Cambridge University Press, 1998.

——. *The Marshall Plan: America, Britain, and the Reconstruction of Western Europe, 1947–1952*. Cambridge: Cambridge University Press, 1987.

Hoganson, Kristin. "Cosmopolitan Domesticity: Importing the American Dream." *American Historical Review* 107 (February 2002): 55–83.

Holsti, Ole R. *Public Opinion and American Foreign Policy*. Ann Arbor: University of Michigan, 1996.

Hudson, Kenneth, and Julian Pettifer. *Diamonds in the Sky: A Social History of Air Travel*. London: Bodley Head, 1979.

Hunt, Michael H. *Ideology and U.S. Foreign Policy*. New Haven: Yale University Press, 1987.

——. "The Long Crisis in U.S. Diplomatic History: Coming to Closure." *Diplomatic History* 16 (Winter 1991–92): 115–40.

Institut national de la statistique et des études économiques. *Annuaire statistique de la France*. Paris: Institut national de la statistique et des études économiques, 1953–98.

Iriye, Akira. "Culture and International History." In *Explaining the History of American Foreign Relations*, edited by Michael J. Hogan and Thomas G. Paterson, 214–25. Cambridge: Cambridge University Press, 1991.

———. *Global Community: The Role of International Organizations in the Making of the Contemporary World*. Berkeley: University of California Press, 2002.

Jackle, John A., Keith A. Sculle, and Jefferson S. Rodgers. *The Motel in America*. Baltimore: Johns Hopkins University Press, 1996.

Jarrett, Lucinda. *Stripping in Time: A History of Erotic Dancing*. New York: HarperCollins, 1997.

Jocard, Louis-Michel. *Tourisme et l'action de l'état*. Paris: Éditions Berger-Levault, 1965.

Johnson, Walter, and Francis J. Colligan. *The Fulbright Program: A History*. Chicago: University of Chicago Press, 1965.

Kaufman, Burton I. *Trade and Aid: Eisenhower's Foreign Economic Policy, 1953–1961*. Baltimore: Johns Hopkins University Press, 1982.

Kazin, Michael. *The Populist Persuasion: An American History*. New York: Basic Books, 1995.

Killick, John. *The United States and European Reconstruction, 1945–1960*. Edinburgh: Keele University Press, 1997.

Kipping, Matthias, and Ove Bjarnar. *The Americanisation of European Business: The Marshall Plan and the Transfer of U.S. Management Models*. New York: Routledge, 1998.

Klein, Christina. *Cold War Orientalism: Asia in the Middlebrow Imagination, 1945–1961*. Berkeley: University of California Press, 2003.

Koshar, Rudy. *German Travel Cultures*. New York: Berg, 2000.

———, ed. *Histories of Leisure*. New York: Berg, 2002.

Kramer, Lloyd S. *Threshold of a New World: Intellectuals and the Exile Experience in Paris, 1830–1848*. Ithaca: Cornell University Press, 1988.

Kuisel, Richard F. "American Historians in Search of France: Perceptions and Misperceptions." *French Historical Studies* 19 (Fall 1995): 307–19.

———. "Americanization for Historians." *Diplomatic History* 24 (Summer 2000): 509–15.

———. *Capitalism and the State in Modern France: Renovation and Economic Management in the Twentieth Century*. Cambridge: Cambridge University Press, 1981.

———. *Seducing the French: The Dilemma of Americanization*. Berkeley: University of California Press, 1993.

———. "Was de Gaulle Anti-American?" *La Revue Tocqueville/The Tocqueville Review* 13 (1992): 21–32.

Kunz, Diane B. *Butter and Guns: America's Cold War Economic Diplomacy*. New York: Free Press, 1997.

Kuznick, Peter J., and James Gilbert, eds. *Rethinking Cold War Culture*. Washington: Smithsonian Institution Press, 2001.

LaFeber, Walter. *The American Age: U.S. Foreign Policy at Home and Abroad*. 2nd ed., vol. 2. New York: Norton, 1994.

Lanfant, Marie-Françoise, John B. Allcock, and Edward M. Bruner, eds. *International Tourism: Identity and Change*. New York: SAGE, 1995.

Lanquar, Robert. *Le Tourisme international*. Paris: Presses universitaires de France, 1986.

Lavenir, Catherine Bertho. *La Roue et le stylo: Comment nous sommes devenus touristes*. Paris: Odile Jacob, 1999.

Lears, Jackson. *Fables of Abundance: A Cultural History of Advertising in America*. New York: Basic Books, 1994.

——. "A Matter of Taste: Corporate Cultural Hegemony in a Mass-Consumption Society." In *Culture and Politics in the Age of Cold War*, edited by Lary May, 38–57. Chicago: University of Chicago Press, 1989.

Lebovics, Herman. *Mona Lisa's Escort: André Malraux and the Reinvention of French Culture*. Ithaca: Cornell University Press, 1999.

——. *True France: The Wars over Cultural Identity, 1900–1945*. Ithaca: Cornell University Press, 1992.

Leff, Mark H. "The Politics of Sacrifice on the American Home Front in World War II." *Journal of American History* 77 (March 1991): 1296–1318.

Levenstein, Harvey. *Seductive Journey: American Tourists in France from Jefferson to the Jazz Age*. Chicago: University of Chicago Press, 1998.

Linderman, Gerald F. *The World within War: America's Combat Experience in World War II*. New York: Free Press, 1997.

Löfgren, Orvar. *On Holiday: A History of Vacationing*. Berkeley: University of California Press, 1999.

Lundestad, Geir. "Empire by Invitation? The United States and Western Europe, 1945–1952." *Journal of Peace Research* 23 (1986): 263–77.

Lynch, Frances M. B. *France and the International Economy: From Vichy to the Treaty of Rome*. London: Routledge, 1997.

MacCannell, Dean. *The Tourist: A New Theory of the Leisure Class*. New York: Schocken Books, 1989.

Maier, Charles S. "The Politics of Productivity: Foundations of American International Economic Policy after World War II." In *The Cold War in Europe*, edited by Charles S. Maier, 169–201. New York: Markus Wiener, 1991.

——. "Premises of the Recovery Program." In *Le Plan Marshall et le relèvement économique de l'Europe*, edited by René Girault and Maurice Lévy-Leboyer, 15–30. Paris: Comité pour l'histoire économique et financière de la France, 1993.

Marchand, Roland. *Advertising the American Dream: Making Way for Modernity, 1920–1940*. Berkeley: University of California Press, 1985.

——. "Visions of Classlessness, Quests for Dominion: American Popular Culture." In *Reshaping America: Society and Institutions, 1945–1960*, edited by Robert H. Bremner and Gary W. Reichard, 163–90. Columbus: Ohio State University Press, 1982.

Marès, Antoine, and Pierre Milza, eds. *Le Paris des étrangers depuis 1945*. Paris: Publications de la Sorbonne, 1994.

Margairaz, Michel. "Les Finances, le Plan Monnet et le Plan Marshall." In *Le Plan Marshall et le relèvement économique de l'Europe*, edited by René Girault and Maurice Lévy-Leboyer, 145–75. Paris: Comité pour l'histoire économique et financière de la France, 1993.

Martin, Richard. "Style from Paris, Reality from America: Fashion in *Life* Magazine, 1947–63." *Journal of American Culture* 19 (Winter 1996): 51–55.

Mathy, Jean-Philippe. *Extrême-Occident: French Intellectuals and America*. Chicago: University of Chicago Press, 1993.

May, Elaine Tyler. *Homeward Bound: American Families in the Cold War Era*. New York: Basic Books, 1988.

May, Henry F. *The End of American Innocence: A Study of the First Years of Our Own Time, 1912–1917*. New York: Alfred A. Knopf, 1959. Reprint, Chicago: Quadrangle, 1964.

May, Lary. "Making the American Consensus: The Narrative of Conversion and Subversion in World War II Films." In *The War in American Culture: Society and American Consciousness during World War II*, edited by Lewis A. Erenberg and Susan E. Hirsch, 71–102. Chicago: University of Chicago Press, 1996.

McClintock, Anne. " 'No Longer in a Future Heaven': Nationalism, Gender, and Race." In *Becoming National: A Reader*, edited by Geoff Eley and Ronald Grigor Suny, 260–84. New York: Oxford University Press, 1996.

McKenzie, Brian Angus. "Creating a Tourist's Paradise: The Marshall Plan and France, 1948 to 1952." *French Politics, Culture and Society* 21 (Spring 2003): 35–54.

——. "Deep Impact: The Cultural Policy of the United States in France, 1948 to 1952." Ph.D. diss., State University of New York, Stony Brook, 2000.

McQuaid, Kim. *Uneasy Partners: Big Business in American Politics, 1945–1990*. Baltimore: Johns Hopkins University Press, 1994.

Meigs, Mark. *Optimism at Armageddon: Voices of American Participants in the First World War*. New York: New York University Press, 1997.

Merrill, Dennis. "Negotiating Cold War Paradise: U.S. Tourism, Economic Planning, and Cultural Modernity in Twentieth-Century Puerto Rico." *Diplomatic History* 25 (Spring 2001): 179–214.

Meyerowitz, Joanne. "Beyond the Feminine Mystique: A Reassessment of Postwar Mass Culture, 1946–1958." In *Not June Cleaver: Women and Gender in Postwar America, 1945–1960*, edited by Joanne Meyerowitz, 229–62. Philadelphia: Temple University Press, 1994.

Miller, Karen. " 'Air Power is Peace Power:' The Aircraft Industry's Campaign for Public and Political Support, 1943–1949." *Business History Review* 70 (Autumn 1996): 297–327.

Mills, Sara. *Discourses of Difference: An Analysis of Women's Travel Writing and Colonialism*. New York: Routledge, 1991.

Milward, Alan S. *The European Rescue of the Nation-State*. With the assistance of George Brennan and Federico Romero. Berkeley: University of California Press, 1992.

——. *The Reconstruction of Western Europe, 1945–1951*. Berkeley: University of California Press, 1984.

Mosse, George L. *Nationalism and Sexuality: Middle-Class Morality and Sexual Norms in Modern Europe*. Madison: University of Wisconsin Press, 1985.

Muron, Louis. *Pompidou: Le Président oublié*. Paris: Flammarion, 1994.

Nielson, Georgia Panter. *From Sky Girl to Flight Attendant: Women and the Making of a Union*. Ithaca: ILR Press, 1982.

Ninkovich, Frank. *Modernity and Power: A History of the Domino Theory in the Twentieth Century*. Chicago: University of Chicago Press, 1994.

Nora, Pierre, ed. *Realms of Memory: Rethinking the French Past*. English edition edited by

Lawrence D. Kritzman. Translated by Arthur Goldhammer. New York: Columbia University Press, 1996–98.

Patterson, James T. *Mr. Republican: A Biography of Robert A. Taft.* Boston: Houghton Mifflin, 1972.

Peer, Shanny. *France on Display: Peasants, Provincials, and Folklore in the 1937 Paris World's Fair.* Albany, N.Y.: State University of New York Press, 1998.

Pells, Richard. *The Liberal Mind in a Conservative Age: American Intellectuals in the 1940s and 1950s.* New York: Harper & Row, 1985.

——. *Not Like Us: How Europeans Have Loved, Hated, and Transformed American Culture Since World War II.* New York: Basic Books, 1997.

——. "Who's Afraid of Steven Spielberg?" *Diplomatic History* 24 (Summer 2000): 495–502.

Pérez, Louis A., Jr. *On Becoming Cuban: Identity, Nationality, and Culture.* Chapel Hill: University of North Carolina Press, 1999.

——. "We Are the World: Internationalizing the National, Nationalizing the International." *Journal of American History* 89 (September 2002): 558–66.

Peterson, Theodore. *Magazines in the Twentieth Century.* Urbana: University of Illinois Press, 1956.

Picard, Michel, and Robert E. Wood, eds. *Tourism, Ethnicity, and the State in Asian and Pacific Societies.* Honolulu: University of Hawai'i Press, 1997.

Poirrier, Philippe. *L'État et la culture en France au XXe siècle.* Paris: Livre de Poche, 2000.

Portes, Jacques. *Une Fascination réticente: Les États-Unis dans l'opinion française.* Nancy: Presses universitaires de Nancy, 1990.

Poutet, Hervé. *Images touristiques de l'Espagne: De la propagande politique à la promotion touristique.* Paris: L'Harmattan, 1995.

Pratt, Mary Louise. *Imperial Eyes: Travel Writing and Transculturation.* New York: Routledge, 1992.

Price, Harry Bayard. *The Marshall Plan and Its Meaning.* Ithaca: Cornell University Press, 1955.

Rauch, André. *Vacances en France de 1830 à nos jours.* Paris: Hachette, 1996.

Rearick, Charles. *The French in Love and War: Popular Culture in the Era of the World Wars.* New Haven: Yale University Press, 1997.

Richter, Linda K. *The Politics of Tourism in Asia.* Honolulu: University of Hawai'i Press, 1989.

Rioux, Jean-Pierre. *The Fourth Republic, 1944–1958.* Translated by Godfrey Rogers. Cambridge: Cambridge University Press, 1987.

Roberts, Mary Louise. "Gender, Consumption, and Commodity Culture." *American Historical Review* 103 (June 1998): 817–44.

Robertson, Charles L. *The International Herald Tribune: The First Hundred Years.* New York: Columbia University Press, 1987.

Rodgers, Daniel T. *Atlantic Crossings: Social Politics in a Progressive Age.* Cambridge, Mass.: Belknap Press, 1998.

Romero, Federico. *The United States and the European Trade Movement, 1944–1951.* Translated by Harvey Fergusson II. Chapel Hill: University of North Carolina Press, 1992.

Rose, Lisle A. *The Cold War Comes to Main Street: America in 1950.* Lawrence: University of Kansas Press, 1999.

Rosenberg, Emily S. *Financial Missionaries to the World: The Politics and Culture of Dollar Diplomacy, 1900–1930.* Cambridge, Mass.: Harvard University Press, 1999.

——. *Spreading the American Dream: American Economic and Cultural Expansion, 1890–1945.* New York: Hill and Wang, 1982.

Ross, George. "Introduction: Janus and Marianne." In *Searching for the New France,* edited by James F. Hollifield and George Ross, 1–16. New York: Routledge, 1991.

Ross, Kristin. *Fast Cars, Clean Bodies: Decolonization and the Reordering of French Culture.* Cambridge, Mass: MIT Press, 1995.

Rousseau, Denys-Georges. *Le Facteur travail dans l'industrie du tourisme en France.* Thèse de doctorat, Université Paris-X Nanterre, 1973.

Rousso, Henry. *The Vichy Syndrome: History and Memory in France since 1944.* Translated by Arthur Goldhammer. Cambridge, Mass.: Harvard University Press, 1991.

Rupp, Leila J. *Worlds of Women: The Making of an International Women's Movement.* Princeton: Princeton University Press, 1997.

Sayre, Nora. *Running Time: Films of the Cold War.* New York: Dial Press, 1982.

Schneider, Andrea Kupfer. *Creating the Musée d'Orsay: The Politics of Culture in France.* University Park: Pennsylvania State University Press, 1998.

Schrijvers, Peter. *The Crash of Ruin: American Combat Soldiers in Europe during World War II.* New York: New York University Press, 1998.

Schulzinger, Robert D. *U.S. Diplomacy since 1900.* 4th ed. New York: Oxford University Press, 1998.

Schwartz, Rosalie. *Pleasure Island: Tourism and Temptation in Cuba.* Lincoln: University of Nebraska Press, 1997.

Schwartz, Thomas Alan. *Lyndon Johnson and Europe: In the Shadow of Vietnam.* Cambridge, Mass.: Harvard University Press, 2003.

Shaffer, Marguerite S. *See America First: Tourism and National Identity, 1880–1940.* Washington: Smithsonian Institution Press, 2001.

Sherry, Michael. *In the Shadow of War: The United States since the 1930s.* New Haven: Yale University Press, 1995.

Skwiot, Christine M. "Itineraries of Empire: The Uses of United States Tourism in Cuba and Hawai'i, 1898–1959." Ph.D. diss., Rutgers University, 2002.

Solberg, Carl. *Conquest of the Skies: A History of Commercial Aviation in America.* Boston: Little, Brown, 1979.

Spurr, David. *The Rhetoric of Empire: Colonial Discourse in Journalism, Travel Writing, and Imperial Administration.* Durham: Duke University Press, 1993.

Steel, Ronald. *Walter Lippmann and the American Century.* Boston: Little, Brown, 1980.

Stowe, William W. *Going Abroad: European Travel in Nineteenth-Century American Culture.* Princeton: Princeton University Press, 1994.

Stovall, Tyler. *Paris Noir: African Americans in the City of Lights.* Boston: Houghton Mifflin, 1996.

Strasser, Susan, Charles McGovern, and Matthias Judt, eds. *Getting and Spending: European and American Consumer Societies in the Twentieth Century.* Washington: German Historical Institute, Cambridge University Press, 1998.

Strauss, David. *Menace in the West: The Rise of French Anti-Americanism in Modern Times*. Westport, Conn.: Greenwood Press, 1978.

Strout, Cushing. *The American Image of the Old World*. New York: Harper & Row, 1963.

Sutton, Horace. *Travelers: The American Tourist from Stagecoach to Space Shuttle*. New York: William Morrow, 1980.

Thomson, Charles A., and Walter H. C. Laves. *Cultural Relations and U.S. Foreign Policy*. Bloomington: University of Indiana Press, 1963.

Torrent, Régine. "L'Image du soldat américain en France, de 1943 à 1945." In *Les Américains et la France, 1917–1947: Engagements et représentations*, edited by François Cochet et al., 230–43. Paris: Maisonneuve et Larose, 1999.

Towner, John. "Approaches to Tourism History." *Annals of Tourism Research* 15 (1988): 47–62.

Tuppen, John. "France: The Changing Character of a Key Industry." In *Tourism and Economic Development: Western European Experiences*, edited by Allen W. Williams and Gareth Shaw, 191–206. New York: Belhaven Press, 1991.

Tye, Larry. *The Father of Spin: Edward L. Bernays and the Birth of Public Relations*. New York: Crown Publishers, 1998.

Urbain, Jean-Didier. *L'Idiot du voyage: Histoires de touristes*. Paris: Plon, 1991.

Urfalino, Philippe. *L'Invention de la politique culturelle*. Paris: Comité d'histoire du Ministère de la culture, 1996.

Urry, John. *The Tourist Gaze: Leisure and Travel in Contemporary Societies*. New York: SAGE, 1990.

U.S. Bureau of the Census. *Historical Statistics of the United States, Colonial Times to 1970*. Washington: U.S. Government Printing Office, 1975.

U.S. Department of State. *Foreign Relations of the United States, 1964–1968*. Vol. 8, *International Monetary and Trade Policy*. Washington: U.S. Government Printing Office, 1998.

Von Eschen, Penny M. "Who's the Real Ambassador? Exploding Cold War Racial Ideology." In *Cold War Constructions: The Political Culture of United States Imperialism, 1945–1966*, edited by Christian G. Appy, 110–31. Amherst: University of Massachusetts Press, 2000.

Wagnleitner, Reinhold. *Coca-colonization and the Cold War: The Cultural Mission of the United States in Austria after the Second World War*. Translated by Diana M. Wolf. Chapel Hill: University of North Carolina Press, 1994.

———. "The Empire of Fun, or Talkin' Soviet Union Blues: The Sound of Freedom and U.S. Cultural Hegemony in Europe." *Diplomatic History* 23 (Summer 1999): 499–524.

Wall, Irwin M. *The United States and the Making of Postwar France, 1945–1954*. Cambridge: Cambridge University Press, 1991.

Watts, Stephen. *The Ritz of Paris*. New York: W. W. Norton, 1963.

Weiner, Susan. *Enfants Terribles: Youth and Femininity in the Mass Media in France, 1945–1968*. Baltimore: Johns Hopkins University Press, 2001.

Weiss, Linda. *The Myth of the Powerless State*. Ithaca: Cornell University Press, 1998.

Wharton, Annabel Jane. *Building the Cold War: Hilton International Hotels and Modern Architecture*. Chicago: University of Chicago Press, 2001.

Whitfield, Stephen J. *The Culture of the Cold War*. Baltimore: Johns Hopkins University Press, 1991.

——. "The Image: The Lost World of Daniel Boorstin." *Reviews in American History* 19 (1991): 302–12.

Wittner, Lawrence S. *Rebels against War: The American Peace Movement, 1933–1983*. Philadelphia: Temple University Press, 1984.

Wooley, Wesley T. *Alternatives to Anarchy: American Supranationalism since World War II*. Bloomington: Indiana University Press, 1988.

Young, Patrick. "*La Vieille France* as Object of Bourgeois Desire: The Touring Club de France and the French Regions, 1890–1918." In *Histories of Leisure*, edited by Rudy Koshar, 169–89. New York: Berg, 2002.

Young, Robert J. "In the Eye of the Beholder: The Cultural Representations of France and Germany by the New York Times, 1939–1940." In *The French Defeat of 1940: Reassessments*, edited by Joel Blatt, 245–68. Providence: Berghahn Books, 1998.

Zdatny, Steven M. *The Politics of Survival: Artisans in Twentieth-Century France*. New York: Oxford University Press, 1990.

Zeiler, Thomas W. "Just Do It! Globalization for Diplomatic Historians." *Diplomatic History* 25 (Fall 2001): 529–51.

Zunz, Olivier. *Why the American Century?* Chicago: University of Chicago Press, 1998.

INDEX

72, 173–74, 175; seen as national symbols, 1, 58, 64, 81–82, 90–91, 174, 176; support from French state, 4, 7, 8–9, 11, 58–59, 61, 67–69, 71–72, 81, 83, 93, 94, 99, 153–54, 168–69, 172, 174, 177, 181, 205; and Americanization, 6, 9, 81–99 passim, 173–75; Marshall Plan campaign to reform, 9, 46, 81–99, 135, 136, 151; artisanal hospitality standards, 10, 81–82, 86–87, 89–90, 91–92, 94, 99, 151, 167–69, 172–73, 174–77; American tourists in, 11, 17, 57, 83, 87, 90, 159, 178; foreign investment in, 11, 58, 173–75; size of industry, 17, 56–57, 84, 168, 170, 173, 250 (n. 71); rating systems, 57, 83, 86, 88, 173; bathrooms, 58, 72, 82, 83, 86, 87–88, 92, 94, 99, 133, 135, 136; racial segregation in, 90–91

House and Garden (magazine), 107
House Beautiful (magazine), 48, 82
House Un-American Activities Committee (HUAC), 144, 185
Hughes, Howard, 40, 50
L'Humanité (newspaper), 73–74, 166–67, 197

Immigrants: as tourists, 49, 104
Indianapolis Star, 33
Information (newspaper), 74
Ingrand, Henri, 27, 59, 83, 91–92, 125
International Air Transport Association (IATA), 50, 128
Intercontinental Hotel Corporation, 84, 173–74
Isolationism, American, 52, 112; American critics of, 18, 23, 39–40, 42, 48, 118, 180, 185; French attempts to change, 24–25, 63
Italy, 16, 27, 58, 83, 104, 105, 107, 108, 111, 162

James, Henry, 16
Javits, Jacob, 179, 188
Johnson, Lyndon B., 182; administration of, 10, 11, 179, 182–202, 204
Joseph, Richard, 192
Jules-Julien, Alfred, 55, 56

Kelly, Gene, 109
Kennan, George F., 113, 142
Kennedy, John F., 133; administration of, 10, 11, 127, 145, 148–49, 186–87, 192
Keynesian economics, 34
KLM (airline), 136
Knight, Frances, 140
Korean War, 104, 114, 115, 123, 137
Kraft, Joseph, 196
Krier, Robert, 65

Labor. *See* Hotels, French: labor
Ladies' Home Journal, 38, 107
Language: Americans speaking French, 15, 19, 45, 64, 134, 143, 170, 207; French speaking English, 64, 70, 71, 121, 131, 173
Last Time I Saw Paris, The (Elliot Paul), 17
Latin America, 7, 33, 131, 148, 188, 189
Laughlin, Clara, 134
Le Pen, Jean-Marie, 166
Levenstein, Harvey, 16
Life, 18, 23, 25, 100, 102, 110, 123, 138, 147, 180. *See also* Luce, Henry
Li'l Abner, 49, 109, 147
Lindbergh, Anne Morrow, 30, 31
Lindbergh, Charles, 128
Lippmann, Walter, 113
Loire Valley, 63, 104, 105, 110
Lourdes, 24, 109
Luce, Clare Boothe, 37
Luce, Henry, 18, 19, 22, 37, 42, 113, 142

Mademoiselle, 131
Mailer, Norman, 136
Maine Development Commission, 44, 52
Malraux, André, 153, 157
March of Time, The (weekly newsreel series), 109
Maritime Commission, 50
Marjolin, Robert, 66
Marshall Plan, 8, 28–31, 43, 66, 82–83, 116, 123; travel development program, 8, 33–34, 42–54, 59, 81–99, 115, 118–19, 123, 184; efforts to reform French hotels, 9, 46,

207–8; group tours, 26, 48, 131–32, 140–44; efforts by U.S. government to reduce costs for, 47–48, 49–52, 87, 95–96, 128; and working class, 47, 50–52, 142–43; role in French postwar recovery, 53–54, 225 (n. 99); views on U.S. Cold War policies, 101, 103, 111, 116, 122–23; seen by Americans as symbols of U.S. superiority over Soviets, 142, 143, 147, 149, 183, 192, 201

Tourists, French, 154, 162. *See also* Social Tourism, French

Transnationalism, 5–6, 38–41, 58, 76, 205, 208, 215 (n. 16). *See also* Nationalism

Transportation, transatlantic, 15, 35–36, 49–52, 125, 128–29; shortages after World War II, 13, 25. *See also* Air travel; Ocean liners

Trans World Airlines (TWA), 37, 40, 41, 50, 113, 131, 192

Travel (magazine), 1, 38

Travel Advisory Committee, 45, 51

Travel Agent (trade journal), 187

Travel agents, 4, 50, 82, 87, 120, 132, 182, 192. *See also* American Society of Travel Agents

Travel Branch, Office of International Trade, 45, 46, 92

Travel constituency: defined, 4; members of, 8, 11, 33, 38, 55–57, 65–66, 69, 80, 92, 103, 114–15, 123–24, 179, 183–84, 191, 203

Travel Development Section (TDS). *See* Marshall Plan: travel development program

Travel industry, American international, 34–43, 44, 45, 46; opposition from domestic travel interests, 34, 52, 59; ties to U.S. government, 34–38, 42–46, 49–51, 114, 120, 186, 191–93. *See also* Air travel; Ocean liners; Travel agents

Travel industry, French: size of, 56–57; price freezes, 172, 175. *See also* Hotels, French; Restaurants, French

Travel Policy Committee, 43

Travel writers, 1, 4, 17, 28–32, 104–8, 117–18, 130, 132–36, 138–39, 141–42, 177–78, 192–94, 236–37 (n. 19)

Treasury, U.S. Department of, 189

La Tribune économique (newspaper), 62

Trippe, Juan, 4, 37, 39, 40, 42, 48, 50, 84, 128, 137, 192

Trohan, Walter, 196–97

Truman, Harry: administration of, 28–29, 31, 36, 43–44, 52, 123, 144. *See also* Marshall Plan

Truman, Margaret, 38, 39

Turkey, 84

Ugly American, The (William J. Lederer and Eugene Burdick), 10, 140

United Nations, 35, 38

United Nations World (magazine), 39, 116

United States Lines, 36, 37, 50

United World Federalists, 38–39, 40

University of Vermont, 115–16

U.S.-French diplomatic relations, 3–5, 203; immediately after World War II, 1, 13–15, 23, 26, 31, 63; during the Marshall Plan, 8, 72–76, 81, 96–98, 101, 108, 109, 122–23; tensions in 1960s, 10, 152, 154, 160–62, 177–80, 184, 190–91, 207. *See also* Atlantic Community; De Gaulle, Charles; Foreign aid; Marshall Plan

U.S. Information Agency (USIA), 5, 121–22, 137, 145, 146

U.S. News and World Report, 47, 129, 201

USS *United States*, 36

U.S. Travel Service, 185, 186

Versailles, 110

Veterans, American: visiting France, 13–15, 16, 47, 117

Vichy, 63. *See also* France: occupation by Germany

Vietnam, U.S. war in, 11, 152, 182–83, 186, 195–97

Visas, 4, 26, 34, 35, 40, 42, 43, 185; French waiver of for Americans, 73, 74, 76, 91, 204–5. *See also* Passports

Walter, Frances, 185
Washington Post, 27, 100, 117, 194
Wilkinson, Herbert, 92
Willkie, Wendell, 39
Wilson, Charles Edward, 146–47
Wilson, Edmund, 30
Wise, William, 46
Women: as travelers, 15, 16, 20, 54, 94, 100, 104, 106–7, 116, 130, 131; as service employees, 150, 170–71
Working-class tourism. *See* Social tourism, French; Tourists, American: and working class
World War II, 45, 49; effects on travel

industry, 1, 13, 17, 25, 35, 36, 57; battlefield tours, 14; American views of France during, 17–20. *See also* France: occupation by Germany
Wylie, Laurence, 178

XXe siècle (newspaper), 25

Young, Stephen, 160
Youth: travel by American, 107, 131; manners of French, 165–66. *See also* Student travel

Zunz, Olivier, 48